TORT LAW AND HUMAN RIGHTS

This is a completely revised and expanded second edition, building on the first edition with two principal aims: to elucidate the role that domestic tort principles play in securing to citizens the human rights standards laid down in the European Convention on Human Rights, including the new 'remedy' under the Human Rights Act 1998; and to evaluate tort principles for compliance with those standards.

The first edition was written when the Human Rights Act 1998 was newly enacted and many questions existed as to its potential impact on tort law. Answers to many of the questions, which were raised at that time, are only now emerging. Therefore, the text has been updated to reflect these developments. Whether it is appropriate to attribute particular goals and functions to tort law is highly contested and the analysis begins by locating the discussion within these contemporary debates. The author goes on to examine the extent to which the action against public authorities under section 7 of the Act has impacted on the development of common law principles, as well as the issue of the horizontal effect of the Act between non-state actors. New chapters include: 'A Human Rights Based Approach to Tort Law' and 'Public Authority Liability and Privacy—From Misuse of Private Information to Autonomy'.

Volume 23 in the series Hart Studies in Private Law

Tort Law and Human Rights

Second edition

Jane Wright

·HART·
PUBLISHING
OXFORD AND PORTLAND, OREGON
2017

Hart Publishing
An imprint of Bloomsbury Publishing Plc

Hart Publishing Ltd   Bloomsbury Publishing Plc
Kemp House   50 Bedford Square
Chawley Park   London
Cumnor Hill   WC1B 3DP
Oxford OX2 9PH   UK
UK

www.hartpub.co.uk
www.bloomsbury.com

Published in North America (US and Canada) by
Hart Publishing
c/o International Specialized Book Services
920 NE 58th Avenue, Suite 300
Portland, OR 97213-3786
USA

www.isbs.com

HART PUBLISHING, the Hart/Stag logo, BLOOMSBURY and the
Diana logo are trademarks of Bloomsbury Publishing Plc

First published 2017

© Jane Wright 2017

Jane Wright has asserted her right under the Copyright, Designs and Patents
Act 1988 to be identified as Author of this work.

British Library Cataloguing-in-Publication Data
A catalogue record for this book is available from the British Library.

ISBN: HB: 978-1-84113-907-4
        ePDF: 978-1-50991-316-9
        ePub: 978-1-50991-317-6

Library of Congress Cataloging-in-Publication Data

Names: Wright, Jane, 1957– author.

Title: Tort law and human rights / Jane Wright.

Description: Second edition. | Portland, Oregon : Hart Publishing, 2017. | Series: Hart
studies in private law ; volume 23 | Includes bibliographical references and index.

Identifiers: LCCN 2016049547 (print) | LCCN 2016049864 (ebook) | ISBN 9781841139074
(hardback : alk. paper) | ISBN 9781509913176 (Epub)

Subjects: LCSH: Torts—Great Britain. | Negligence—Great Britain. |
Human rights—Great Britain. | Human rights—Europe.

Classification: LCC KD1949 .W75 2017 (print) | LCC KD1949 (ebook) | DDC 346.4103—dc23

LC record available at https://lccn.loc.gov/2016049547

Typeset by Compuscript Ltd, Shannon

Printed and bound in Great Britain by TJ International Ltd, Padstow, Cornwall

To find out more about our authors and books visit www.hartpublishing.co.uk. Here you will find extracts, author
information, details of forthcoming events and the option to sign up for our newsletters.

PREFACE TO SECOND EDITION

My personal interest in the relationship between tort law and human rights was initially sparked by a series of cases brought against public authorities in the last two decades of the twentieth century, in which, despite egregious failings on the part of the relevant bodies, English courts were of the firm view that no duty of care at common law was owed to the claimants. Furthermore, in the absence of a developed system of public law remedies, claimants were left with no legal right to compensation. Where the facts of such cases engaged the human rights obligations of the United Kingdom, claimants had no choice other than to exercise their right of individual petition to the European Commission and Court of Human Rights in Strasbourg. All that seemed set to change with the advent of the Human Rights Act 1998 (HRA) and the introduction of a cause of action against public authorities under section 7. Unlike actions at common law, however, there is no right to damages under the HRA; remedies are governed by section 8, according to which damages are at the discretion of the court.

As I write, we are at yet another constitutional juncture. The new Conservative Government under the leadership of Prime Minister Theresa May has reaffirmed the Government's intention to introduce a British Bill of Rights and to repeal the HRA. She has stated, however, that she will not be pursuing a withdrawal from the European Convention on Human Rights (ECHR) due to lack of parliamentary support. Furthermore, citizens of the United Kingdom have just voted to leave the European Union, although the terms of the postulated 'Brexit' have yet to be negotiated.

A large question posed when the HRA was enacted was what impact the HRA would have on the development of common law tort principles and two questions in particular arose: first, to what extent would the HRA impact on relations between non-state actors as a result of the designation of the court as a public authority under section 6 HRA, the so-called 'horizontal effect' question; and, second, what impact would the HRA have on the development of common law principles in cases brought against public authorities, given that a claim for the violation of ECHR rights could now be brought against a public authority under section 7 of the Act.

As I remarked in the Introduction to the first edition, it was possible that the Act might stultify common law development if the possibility of awarding damages against a public authority under the statute is regarded as preferable to the expansion of the common law, because in that way the boundaries of negligence might be contained. As we shall see, it would seem that the possibility of the HRA claim has in fact generally curtailed the willingness of the courts to expand common law claims against public authorities. This statement holds true across areas as diverse as negligence, false imprisonment, misfeasance in public office, private nuisance and privacy (in the wider sense, beyond the evolving tort of 'misuse of private information').

A critical question regarding any new British Bill of Rights will be the scope of its accompanying remedial framework. If the HRA goes, then section 7 also goes, and the nature of its replacement will be critical for the protection of human rights in the United Kingdom. The Law Commission abandoned its work on the reform of state liability because the key stakeholder, namely the Government, was firmly opposed to its recommendations. This means that without the HRA, there could be a significant remedial gap in the protection of human rights. It is therefore a timely and opportune moment to take stock and to reflect upon the state of tort law and human rights today.

I have endeavoured to ensure that the law is up to date as at 1 June 2016.

Jane Wright, Essex
June, 2016

CONTENTS

TABLE OF CASES

TABLE OF LEGISLATION

National Instruments

Austria

1

Tort Law and Human Rights

Introduction

Context

Over 15 years have passed since the Human Rights Act 1998 (HRA) came into force on 2 October 2000, shortly before the first edition of *Tort Law & Human Rights* was published. The preoccupations of lawyers at that time examined through today's lens seem narrowly focused and parochial in the light of the turmoil that unfolded post 2000. The challenges that the shocking events of 9/11 would pose for human rights were unanticipated; arguably, the so-called 'War on Terror' paved the way for the most significant challenges for the effective protection of human rights that came before the courts on both sides of the Atlantic. The extent to which the HRA, or the courts' interpretation and application of it, have fulfilled their promise to 'bring rights home' is a matter for debate and its effectiveness as a vehicle for securing human rights has been challenged on all sides of the political spectrum. The HRA was described as 'an unprecedented transfer of political power from the executive and legislature to the judiciary, and a fundamental re-structuring of our political constitution'.[1] Just over a decade later, Ewing, in a well-worn theme, railed against the English judiciary for their excessive deference to the Executive and Parliament.[2]

The HRA has been subject to significant and sustained criticism from politicians of all persuasions including government ministers, the press and journalists, as well as academics.[3] Successive Home Secretaries have been required by the effect of Convention case law to develop meaningful strategies to protect the human rights of people in receiving countries of those whose presence in the United Kingdom has not been considered conducive to the public good. Members of the press

---

[1] KD Ewing, 'The Human Rights Act and Parliamentary Democracy' (1999) 62 *Modern Law Review* 79.
[2] KD Ewing, *Bonfire of the Liberties: New Labour, Human Rights, and the Rule of Law*, (Oxford, Oxford University Press, 2010).
[3] *Ibid*. For a critique see, M Amos, 'Problems with the Human Rights Act 1998 and How to Remedy Them: Is a Bill of Rights the Answer' (2009) 72 *Modern Law Review* 883.

have criticised the development of a new tort of privacy by a small cadre of the judiciary.

At the time of writing, the future looks bleak for the HRA. Against this hostile background, the Conservative Government elected in May 2015 pledged in their manifesto to repeal the HRA and to replace it with a British Bill of Rights. However, despite a huge amount of political rhetoric during the election campaign, repeal of the HRA was not included in the first Queen's Speech to Parliament and, moreover, there was no mention of the HRA in the Prime Minister's speech to the Conservative Party Conference in October 2015. It is also nine years since the then Prime Minister David Cameron set up a panel to draw up a British Bill of Rights and none has yet appeared. Political discourse is currently dominated by 'Brexit', and the Queens's Speech in May 2016 included a pledge to bring forward 'proposals' for a British Bill of Rights.

At a recent Prime Minister's Questions, David Cameron stated that proposals for a British Bill of Rights would be brought forward shortly.[4] The Minister for Justice in the Cameron administration, Rt Hon Michael Gove MP, who was tasked with the development of a consultation paper, gave evidence to the European Union Justice Sub-Committee of the House of Commons which was conducting an Inquiry on the Potential Impact on EU law of repealing the HRA. In his evidence, he stated that any new British Bill of Rights would put a 'gloss' on European Convention on Human Rights (ECHR) rights, rather than involving radical change. He envisaged that all rights included in the ECHR would be included in any new Bill, but two areas would likely be modified: first, in relation to obligations arising from the military when on active service abroad and, second, regarding the balance to be struck between the rights to freedom of expression and privacy. As this book goes to press, Prime Minister Theresa May has yet to make any comment regarding the future of the HRA. However, she has indicated that she will not pursue withdrawal from the ECHR due to lack of parliamentary support.

While the HRA itself may not be with us for very much longer, it seems highly unlikely (especially in light of the newly incumbent Prime Minister's comments) that we shall not remain a party to the ECHR so that the ECHR rights will continue to bind us in international law. The substance of the ECHR rights themselves will also have a status in domestic law, enshrined in the British Bill of Rights. This means that the interpretation of the substantive rights developed by English courts since the HRA came into force will continue to inform the work of English courts. The guiding principle behind the HRA is that UK citizens should be able to enjoy and access their rights in the United Kingdom and be spared the delay and expense of seeking justice at Strasbourg. Furthermore, the effect of 'bringing rights home' effectively means that there is less inclination by the Strasbourg Court to 'micro-manage' individual situations or review domestic policy-making and 'less inclination to disturb the rulings of national courts if the national courts

---

[4] Prime Minister's Questions in the House of Commons 3rd February 2016, accessed on BBC 2.

are visibly operating domestic remedies with an eye to compliance with Convention standards and case-law'.[5]

Given the apparently limited scope of any likely change, the then Justice Minister, Rt Hon Michael Gove MP, was recently pressed in evidence to the European Union Select Committee of the House of Lords to give reasons for the need to repeal the HRA. He stated that,

> Human rights have become associated with unmeritorious individuals pursuing through the courts claims that do not command public support or sympathy … more troublingly, human rights are seen as something that are done to British courts and the British people as a result of foreign intervention …. a part of the purpose of a British Bill of Rights is to affirm that [human rights] are fundamental British rights.[6]

There is of course a great irony here, the ECHR was the product of a momentous initiative led by Winston Churchill who established a conference at The Hague in 1948 and the first draft of the Convention was co-authored by David Maxwell-Fyfe, first Earl of Kilmuir, the future Conservative Lord Chancellor.[7] So, the ECHR contains very British rights and polls indicate overwhelming support for the rights guaranteed, although there are concerns regarding their interpretation and application.[8]

It is timely to critique the impact of both the ECHR and the HRA on English tort law principles. This distinction is drawn because there are in fact two streams of English law that have been shaped by the ECHR: first, there is a strong body of common law authority which has developed in response to the demands of the ECHR and which has not been shaped by the application or interpretation of the HRA itself (for example remedies in nuisance, privacy, defamation and decisions in negligence informed by the European Court of Human Rights' (ECtHR) decision in *Osman v United Kingdom*); second, there is now a substantial body of case law that has been directly informed by the HRA itself as the courts have responded to the various media in the HRA through which ECHR rights have been brought home.

Whatever form a new British Bill of Rights takes, ECHR rights will remain obligations in international law; the rights set out in Schedule 1 to the HRA are British rights. As discussion in the chapters that follow will demonstrate, the ECHR rights have continued to impact on the development of the common law, alongside the case law that has developed directly under the HRA itself.[9] This is not an 'angels

---

[5] P Mahoney, 'The Relationship between the Strasbourg Court and the National Court' (2014) *Law Quarterly Review* 130, 568–86.

[6] *The UK, the EU and a British Bill of Rights*, HL paper 139 (9 May 2016) [36].

[7] A Donald, J Gordon and P Leach (Human Rights and Social Justice Research Institute, London Metropolitan University), Equality and Human Rights Commission Report no 83, *The United Kingdom and the European Court of Human Rights*, Spring 2012.

[8] *Ibid*.

[9] See the comments of Lord Hoffmann in *Re McKerr* [2004] UKHL 12, [2004] 1 WLR 807 [63]; Lord Bingham in *R (Al-Skeini) v Secretary of State for Defence* [2007] UKHL 26 [10]. See generally Chapter 8 *Privacy—From Misuse of Private Information to Autonomy*.

on pinheads' semantic remark; in the event/when the HRA is repealed it will be highly material for citizens to understand how the existence and scope of their 'rights' is affected by the change. To the extent that the common law has now developed to reflect ECHR rights (as opposed to the HRA and the rights set out in Schedule 1 of the Act), repeal of the HRA should make no difference. It is necessary to draw a distinction between the impact of the ECHR and the impact of the HRA since as we shall see some of the most significant developments in the common law have not been consequent upon the HRA itself; rather the development of the common law has been informed and shaped directly by the principles of the ECHR, without the precise interpretation and application of the HRA ever being conclusively determined. Indeed, one commentator has described the common law as remaining 'fairly static' following the coming into force of the HRA.[10] This is an overstatement as the analysis and critique in the following chapters will demonstrate; if attention is directed purely towards the interpretation and impact of the HRA itself, then it is certainly true that the Act has touched but lightly upon the common law.

If the HRA is repealed and replaced with a British Bill of Rights, quite apart from the nature of the rights themselves, a crucial issue will be: what remedy is to be afforded at the domestic level for breach of the recognised rights? As we shall see, the remedy against public authorities under section 7 HRA has enabled English courts to reject the argument that the contours of the common law (in particular, the tort of negligence) should be mapped to afford remedies for ECHR rights; if a new British Bill of Rights is not accompanied by an appropriate remedial structure, the pressure upon the common law would be great. The introduction of a remedy against public authorities under section 7 HRA has weakened the argument that the common law should afford redress in cases of omissions to act. However, English law has now become somewhat incoherent as far as public authority liability is concerned. Our highest courts are in expansionist mood as far as the development of positive obligations under the HRA is concerned, while the principle of such development in the common law that would extend remedies to embrace the same factual situations has been rejected. This fact undermines the typical use of grounds such as 'non-justiciability' to deny tort claims against the same public authorities.

For the community of lawyers in the United Kingdom the ECHR in 1998 was a relatively unknown beast. Therefore, the response of the Judicial Studies Board was to put in place a training programme regarding both the Act and the ECHR for all full- and part-time members of the judiciary. The 1998–99 Annual Report of the Board acknowledged that only a few judges could claim expertise in the field. To the untrained eye such an admission might have seemed surprising given that the ECHR obligations had bound the United Kingdom in international law for nearly 50 years. While it is true that the ECHR had only a limited impact on the development of the common law prior to the HRA, the protection of human

---

[10] Amos (n 3) 4.

rights and the implementation of international human rights standards in the United Kingdom did not begin with the HRA. The ECHR and other international obligations have infused English law through various interpretative mechanisms and the mediation of such rights into English law continues quite apart from through the technical structure of the HRA.

As any discussion of the HRA must take place against the background of the traditional approach of the common law to the reception of international obligations, the following discussion will set the scene and describe the impact of the ECHR in the light of our international obligations and our tradition as a dualist state. The (possible) repeal of the HRA could mean that these rules become increasingly significant. As a result of the HRA, it would seem that in many ways we have become more, rather than less, dualist.

Context—The ECHR and the Development of English Law Prior to the HRA—the Monist/Dualist Divide

The protection of human rights in English law did not begin with the enactment of the HRA; the Act was supposed to bring 'rights home', but that is not to imply that hitherto the United Kingdom failed to protect the human rights of its citizens. The struggle to secure the rights of the aristocracy was manifest in Magna Carta and the centuries that followed witnessed the gradual subjection of the monarch to the will of the people and the piecemeal development of constitutional guarantees such as the Bill of Rights 1688 and the Habeas Corpus Act 1679. However, despite the introduction of a number of Bills in Parliament,[11] the United Kingdom resisted for many years the introduction of a domestic bill of rights and incorporation of the Convention. The English approach to the protection of human rights was premised upon the basis that citizens are free to do that which is not prohibited: this is the Diceyian world of 'residual' liberties where individual freedom is not laid determined or laid down by a constitutional document but is the outcome of the ordinary law of the land enforced by the courts. For Dicey, the danger of constitutions and bills of rights was that that which has been 'given' can be taken away.[12] The apparent ease with which the Government can propose the repeal of the HRA seems to play to Dicey's argument. Although described as a 'constitutional statute', the HRA is not entrenched and could be repealed by an ordinary statute. However, the doctrine of implied repeal is excluded by section 3(2)(a)

---

[11] Sir Edward Gardner QC MP introduced a Private Members' Bill into the House of Commons in 1987 and Lord Lester of Herne Hill QC introduced two bills on incorporation into the House of Lords in 1994 and 1996.

[12] AV Dicey, *Introduction to the Study of the Law of the Constitution*, 8th edn (London, Macmillan, 1915).

which provides that section 3(1) applies to primary and subordinate legislation whenever enacted.[13]

The traditional English position was described by Megarry J in the famous case of *Malone v Metropolitan Police Commissioner* where he said that 'England is not a country where everything is forbidden except what is expressly permitted: it is a country where everything is permitted except what is expressly forbidden'.[14] In contrast, in *R v Somerset County Council, ex parte Fewings*, Laws LJ stated that the opposite principle applied to public bodies:

> for public bodies the rule is opposite, and so of another character altogether. It is that any action to be taken must be justified by positive law. A public body has no heritage of legal rights which it enjoys for its own sake; at every turn, all of its dealings constitute the fulfilment of duties which it owes to others; indeed, it exists for no other purpose.[15]

Furthermore, in *Three Rivers District Council v Governor of the Bank of England (No 3)*, Lord Steyn stated that the rationale for the tort of misfeasance in public office is that executive or administrative power should only be exercised for the public good.[16]

At the heart of Dicey's work is the so-called 'equality principle' according to which all people of whatever rank are equally subject to the ordinary law of the land administered by the ordinary courts. The general principles of the Constitution have been developed through decisions taken by the courts and are imbued within the common law. His account was both normative and descriptive of the situation in English law at the time it was written and it is an expression of an ideology whose day has passed.[17] Dicey's account, however, serves to explain how English law had developed in terms of human rights protection in a piecemeal fashion to reach the situation pertaining as the HRA came into force. The common law has recognised rights that are good against all the world and that protect many aspects of our lives that are secured by human rights obligations; the trespass torts have long protected bodily integrity and liberty, as well as property.

When the United Kingdom signed the ECHR, it entered into treaty obligations with the other Contracting States, whereby each state agreed to secure to all those within its jurisdiction the rights and freedoms set out. Those obligations take effect as part of international law. The status of treaty obligations within domestic law is a matter for each Contracting State, some are monist, some dualist. For the monist, international and domestic law are part of one normative sphere so that international law subsists alongside commercial law, constitutional law and so on. In a state with a dualist tradition, such as the United Kingdom, international and

---

[13] *Thoburn v Sunderland City Council* [2003] QB 151.
[14] [1979] 1 Ch 344.
[15] [1995] 1 All ER 513, 524 [f]–[g].
[16] [2003] 2 AC 1 [190].
[17] AV Dicey, *Introduction to the Study of the Law of the Constitution'*, 5th edn (London, Macmillan and Co Ltd, 1897) 194. For discussion, see T Cornford, *Towards a Public Law of Tort* (Aldershot, Ashgate Publising, 2008) 9.

domestic law occupy separate normative spheres and treaties do not take effect until they have been transformed into domestic law through implementing legislation.[18] The effect of the HRA seems to be that the United Kingdom has arguably become more rather than less dualist. We see this in *Moohan*,[19] which concerned, *inter alia*, the domestic effect of the International Covenant on Civil and Political Rights (ICCPR). This treaty is part of the International Bill of Rights of the United Nations. Unlike the ECHR, there is no right of petition to the Human Rights Committee, its quasi-judicial adjudicative body, because the UK has not signed up to the Optional Protocol. The question in *Moohan* therefore related to the domestic effect of the international obligation.

In *Moohan*, the petitioners were Scottish prisoners denied the right to vote in the Scottish Referendum. They challenged the ban on prisoner voting set out in section 3 of the Representation of the People Act 1982 on the grounds that section 3 is incompatible with Article 3 of Protocol 1 to the ECHR and Article 25 of the ICCPR. The claim under the ECHR failed on the ground that the right set out in Article 3, Protocol 1 does not extend to referenda; the Supreme Court confirmed the orthodox position that as the ICCPR had not been incorporated into domestic law, Article 25 could not affect the legislative competence of the Scottish Parliament.[20]

The HRA did not incorporate the ECHR into English law: it is an Act designed to give 'further effect' to the ECHR. According to the White Paper, the aim of the Act is to provide an effective alternative to the cost and delay of taking proceedings to Strasbourg. The White Paper also suggested that the corollary of bringing rights home is that the Strasbourg Court would become familiar with the laws and customs of England and the English legal tradition would 'influence' the development of case law by the Court. A moment's pause reveals the inconsistency of this position: bringing rights home effectively should mean that English courts become much more familiar with Strasbourg jurisprudence as they engage with their statutory obligation under section 2 HRA to 'take into account' Strasbourg jurisprudence. If this is done effectively, Strasbourg will encounter English law less frequently as a result of a hoped for diminution in the number of applications to the ECtHR. A review of *The UK and the European Court of Human Rights* commissioned by the Equality and Human Rights Commission in 2012[21] included an analysis of petitions to Strasbourg between 1999 and 2012 and revealed that there are no discernible trends over that period in relation to either the number

---

[18] See R Higgins, *Problems and Process: International Law and How We Use It* (Oxford, Clarendon Press, 1994) 205.

[19] *Moohan v Lord Advocate* [2014] UKSC 67, [2015] AC 901.

[20] Applying *JH Rayner (Mincing Lane) Ltd v Department of Trade and Industry* [1990] 2 AC 418 and *Whaley v Lord Advocate* 2008 (HL) 107. See P Laverack, 'International Human Rights Law in Judicial Review: *Moohan v Lord Advocate* and *R (on the application of JS) v Secretary of State for Work and Pensions* as Guidelines to the Present and Post-Human Rights Act Legal Landscape' (2016) *European Human Rights Law Review* 1, 73–81.'

[21] Donald, Gordon and Leach (n 7).

of applications lodged (or allocated for decision) or the number of applications declared admissible or inadmissible. Between 1999 and 2010 around three per cent of cases were declared admissible with around 1.8 per cent of cases leading to a finding of a violation. The authors caution that great care should be exercised in interpreting the data as the numbers may include 'clone' cases, that is cases that raise the same type of complaint, for example prisoner voting rights in the United Kingdom. Unfortunately, data on application numbers from 1966 (when the right of individual petition was granted) to 1999 is not available.

Although we are a nation with a dualist tradition and therefore it is a matter of 'constitutional orthodoxy'[22] that treaty obligations are not given direct effect unless incorporated into domestic law, international treaty obligations may have an impact on national law in a number of ways. It remains well settled that international treaty obligations may be used to resolve an ambiguity in legislation as there is a presumption that Parliament intends to legislate in a manner which does not breach international treaty obligations.[23] In *Assange v Swedish Prosecution Authority*, Lord Dyson stated that 'there is no doubt a "strong presumption" in favour of interpreting an English statute in a way which does not place the United Kingdom in breach of its international obligations'.[24]

It is well settled that unincorporated treaties may have a bearing upon the development of the common law. Lord Bingham remarked that developments of the common law should normally be in harmony with the United Kingdom's international obligations.[25] The court may rely upon an unincorporated treaty where the common law is 'unclear or uncertain'. In *Derbyshire County Council v Times Newspapers Ltd*,[26] the Court of Appeal was called upon for the first time to decide whether a local authority, which is a body corporate, can sue for libel. All members of the Court of Appeal agreed that where the common law was uncertain (as in this case)[27] or ambiguous then the Court should have regard to the Convention in order to decide the case. Balcome LJ and Butler-Sloss LJ observed also, on the authority of *R v Chief Metropolitan Stipendiary Magistrate, ex parte Choudhury*,[28] that the Court would have regard to the Convention even where the common law was certain. However, in *Director of Public Prosecutions v Jones (Margaret)*,[29] Lord Slynn and Lord Hope considered that reference to the ECHR was inappropriate in the absence of doubt about the content of the common law. Lord Kerr has recently inferred that where there is doubt about the content of the common law, consideration of an international convention or treaty such as the ECHR would

[22] *R (SG and others) v Secretary of State for Work and Pensions* [2015] UKSC 16.
[23] *Salomon v Commissioners of Customs and Excise* [1967] 2 QB at 143 E–G; *Garland v British Rail Engineering Ltd* [1983] 2 AC 751 at 771 (Lord Diplock).
[24] [2012] 2 AC 471 [122].
[25] *A v Secretary of State for the Home Department (No 2)* [2005] UKHL 71, [2006] 2 AC 221.
[26] [1992] 1 QB 770.
[27] There were two conflicting decisions on the point: *Manchester Corp v Williams* [1891] 1 QB 94 and Bognor *Regis UDC v Campion* [1972] 2 QB 169.
[28] [1991] 1 QB 429.
[29] [1999] 2 AC 240.

be appropriate to determine what the common law position is or should be.[30] He acknowledged, however, that the orthodox common law position that treaties should not be incorporated through the backdoor had been reasserted.[31] Thus, there are many acknowledgements in the common law that drawing upon unincorporated treaties to inform the development of the common law is permissible, but within limits. The net effect of these observations is arguably a hardening of the dualist tradition. At the same time, it would seem that the courts are evincing a less receptive attitude to customary international law.

Customary International Law

The Court of Appeal decision in *Trendtex v Central Bank of Nigeria*[32] was for many years considered to indicate a greater willingness on the part of the courts to treat customary international law as part of the common law.[33] In *Trendtex*, Lord Denning held that the rules of customary international law are incorporated into English law automatically unless they conflict with an Act of Parliament. This view must now be modified in light of recent authority. It is clear in light of *R v Jones (Margaret)* that only Parliament can recognise new crimes so that although the crime of aggression was established in customary international law, it was not a crime under English law. Lord Hoffmann left open the question of the extent to which customary international law is generally relevant in domestic civil law.[34]

Recently, in *Keyu*, Lord Mance stated that:

> the presumption when considering [whether to recognise a rule of customary international law] is that Customary International Law, once established, can and should shape the common law, whenever it can do so consistently with domestic constitutional principles, statutory law and common law rules which the courts can themselves sensibly adapt without it being, for example, necessary to invite Parliamentary intervention or consideration.[35]

In *Keyu*,[36] the claimants argued that killings at the hands of British serviceman in Malaya in 1948 should be the subject of an investigation in accordance with Article 2 ECHR and argued, *inter alia*, that such an obligation was recognised as an obligation in customary international law. The Supreme Court held that having regard to the express provision by Parliament for the statutory investigation into deaths

---

[30] *SG* (n 22) [242].
[31] Lord Kerr cited *A v Secretary of State for the Home Department (No 2)* [2004] EWCA Civ 1123, [2005] 1 WLR 414, Laws LJ [226]–[267], Neuberger LJ [434].
[32] [1977] QB 529.
[33] M Hunt, *Using Human Rights Law in English Courts* (Oxford, Hart Publishing, 1997) 17.
[34] *R v Jones (Margaret)* [2006] UKHL 16, [2007] 1 AC 136 [59].
[35] *R (Keyu) v Secretary of State for Foreign and Commonwealth Affairs* [2015] UKSC 69, [2015] 3 WLR 1665 [150].
[36] *Ibid.*

in, *inter alia*, the Coroners and Justice Act 2009 and the Inquiries Act 2005 in addition to incorporation of Article 2 by the HRA, it was inappropriate to impose any further duty at common law; even if customary international law required such an investigation, which the Supreme Court denied, it could not be implied into the common law. Thus, it would seem that where an issue touches upon a field in which Parliament has legislated, there will be very limited scope for arguing that customary international law can have domestic application.

Prior to the enactment of the HRA, arguments raising ECHR issues were made in a rather sporadic fashion before the English courts. On the one hand, Hunt, placing emphasis on *Derbyshire County Council v Times Newspapers Ltd*,[37] argued that 'the reality of what [had] been taking place ... is nothing short of the emergence of a common law human rights jurisdiction'.[38] In their work on the *Democratic Audit of the United Kingdom*,[39] Klug, Starmer and Weir conducted a research project in 1993 using the LEXIS facility, the purpose of which was to study all cases from 1972 to 1993 in which either the Convention or the ICCPR was cited. Their research revealed that the Convention was cited in only 173 cases (0.2 per cent), but the Convention impacted in only 27 of these, of which 18 concerned freedom of expression. They concluded that the Convention affected the outcome in only three cases, one of which was *Derbyshire*. Klug and Starmer found that half the references to the ECHR occurred in the period post-*Brind*,[40] but they cautioned against drawing conclusions regarding the impact of the Convention on the common law. Their research revealed that in only two cases could the ECHR be said to have actually influenced the outcome and both of these concerned freedom of expression.

The point is that though the ECHR may have been referred to and discussed; there was a tendency merely to assert that the common law was compatible with Article 10. For example, Lord Goff in *Attorney-General v Guardian Newspapers Ltd* stated, without examining any of the relevant jurisprudence, that the English law of breach of confidence is consistent with Article 10 and went on to say: 'this is scarcely surprising, since we may pride ourselves on the fact that freedom of speech has existed in this country as long, if not longer than, it has existed in any other country in the world'.[41]

The European Union

The European Union has played a significant role in the field of human rights protection across many fields, but largely outside the scope of this work.

---

[37] See n 26.
[38] Hunt (n 33) 205.
[39] F Klug, K Starmer and S Weir, *The Three Pillars of Liberty* (London, Routledge, 1996) 106.
[40] *Brind v Secretary of State for the Home Department* [1991] 1 All ER 735.
[41] [1990] 1 AC 109 at 283.

The Charter of Fundamental Rights was made binding by the Treaty of Lisbon 2007 and entered into force on 1 December 2009. It includes most of the rights set out in the ECHR, as well as economic and social rights derived from the European Social Charter. Much confusion regarding the legal status of the Charter in UK law became apparent following remarks made *obiter* by Mostyn J in *R (on the application of AB) v Secretary of State for the Home Department*[42] to the effect that he had been under the impression the United Kingdom had secured an opt-out from the Treaty through Protocol No 3. A debate in the House of Commons followed and an Inquiry by the House of Commons European Scrutiny Committee was established.[43] The Committee found that Protocol 30 was designed for comfort rather than protection and that Ministers had contributed to confusion about the status of the Charter. Rather than granting an opt-out, the Protocol affirms that the provisions of the Charter apply only when Member States act within the scope of European Union law. Thus, the Charter does not create new rights. Furthermore, economic and social rights are not justiciable unless they have been given effect in national legislation (Article 1(2) of Protocol 30).

If a legal challenge is possible under both the HRA and the Charter, the benefit of the Charter route to the claimant is that the court is obliged to disapply an Act of Parliament that is inconsistent with the Charter. The court is limited in such a case under the HRA to issuing a declaration of incompatibility under section 4. In *Rugby Football Union v Consolidated Information Services*,[44] the RFU sought an order under Norwich Pharmacal principles to identify those who were advertising tickets for matches in breach of contract. The Supreme Court accepted that making such an order would be regarded as implementing EU law, namely the Data Protection Act 1998, and therefore the Charter applied. On the facts no breach of Article 8 of the EU Charter was established.

The United Kingdom has now voted to leave the European Union and it remains to be seen precisely what the terms of that exit will be. It is unlikely that that in itself will impact on the substance of the following discussion. Of critical importance is the potential repeal and replacement of the HRA which will clearly have enormous significance for the areas of law that are the focus of this book. We can take heart that there is no withdrawal from the Council of Europe in prospect, so the commitments in the ECHR will continue to bind the United Kingdom in international law. It is to be hoped that the excellent work that has taken place in the United Kingdom to bring rights home will not be set at nought.

---

[42] [2013] EWHC 3453, [2014] 2 CMLR 22.
[43] House of Commons European Scrutiny Committee, *The Application of the European Union Charter of Fundamental Rights in the United Kingdom: A State of Confusion*, 43rd Report of Session 2013–14, HC 979, 2 April 2014.
[44] [2012] UKSC 55, [2012] 1 WLR 3333.

The Second Edition

The author's argument prior to the first edition that the common law liability of public authorities should be developed to accommodate ECHR standards in order to ensure the effective protection of citizens in national law, was driven by the lack of adequate remedies at national level, specifically in cases that were predicated on omissions to act to protect those in vulnerable situations. In leading tort cases in the 1990s, no argument was put to the courts to the effect that the tort of negligence could be developed to provide a remedy that would satisfy the demands of Article 13.[45] Until the advent of the HRA, a person who claimed that they had suffered harm as a result of tortious conduct by a public body would need to seek redress by bringing proceedings in the ordinary courts through the usual actions begun by writ such as negligence, misfeasance in public office, etc. The determination of a number of complaints against public authorities from the decade immediately preceding the HRA engaged ECHR obligations. The right to an effective remedy enshrined in Article 13 ECHR has been described by the Grand Chamber as requiring that states provide a means whereby individuals 'can obtain relief at national level for violations of their Convention rights before having to set in motion the international machinery of complaint before the Court'.[46] Article 13 provides that 'Everyone whose rights and freedoms as set forth in this Convention are violated shall have an effective remedy before a national authority notwithstanding that the violation has been committed by persons acting in an official capacity'.

The author argued that the question of whether abused children can sue a local authority in negligence where the authority failed to act effectively over a long period so that the children continued to suffer abuse and neglect should have been influenced by their rights under the ECHR. The question of whether victims of crime may sue the police force in negligence for failure in investigation and whether those held in custody for extended periods should have a cause of action in negligence against the Crown Prosecution Service were all decided without any account being taken of ECHR obligations. A myriad of policy arguments were put forward to deny the possibility of liability, but the most persistent of these was probably the fear that the imposition of liability would lead to a diversion of scarce public resources from the functions a public authority should fulfil and the fear that liability would lead public authorities to carry out their duties in an excessively defensive frame of mind.

---

[45] Following *X (Minors) v Bedfordshire County Council* [1995] 2 AC 633, the author argued that the principles of *Derbyshire County Council v Times Newspapers Ltd* (n 26) could have been applied in order for an uncertain area of negligence law to be developed in a way that was compatible with the ECHR: see J Wright, 'Local Authorities, the Duty of Care and the European Convention on Human Rights' (1998) 18 *Oxford Journal of Legal Studies* 1.

[46] *Kudla v Poland* (2002) 35 EHRR 198.

All of this seemed set to change with the advent of the HRA and the introduction of a new right of action against public authorities under section 7 HRA. In the
first edition, the author suggested that the new action against a public authority
under section 7 HRA could well lead to the courts confining claimants to their
remedy under the HRA, rather than extending the boundaries of the common
law.[47] This is exactly what has happened as the discussion in the following chapters will demonstrate. However, as we see in Chapter 3, while the courts have been
unwilling, under the influence of the ECHR, to extend the boundaries of the common law in claims against public authorities, they have demonstrated exactly the
opposite tendency in their interpretation and application of the HRA, including
the claim under section 7. Thus, the courts have been willing to extend the state's
substantive obligations under the Convention Articles beyond those situations
that have been recognised by the ECtHR[48] and, what is more, in relation to claims
that potentially engage exactly the kind of resource arguments that are anathema
to common law decision-making.[49]

At the same time, there has sometimes appeared an apparent judicial willingness
to limit the protection offered by some of our well-established common law rights.
Thus, the tort of false imprisonment may no longer be compensated by other
than nominal damages[50] and the tort itself has been circumscribed by Article 5
ECHR.[51] The ECHR provides a floor of rights; it is important that rights which
form the bedrock of the common law should not be chipped away by a misguided
belief that our rights are whatever the ECHR says they are. Dicey was right that
bills of rights can be taken away. The judicial mood though is changing, possibly
in light of threatened repeal of the HRA. Our senior judges are now calling upon
practitioners not to neglect the common law. Baroness Hale has talked of common
law rights being 'on the march'. It has been argued that we are seeing a renaissance of 'common law constitutionalism' and we can see this by the judiciary making it clear that common law rights should be considered before recourse to the
HRA.[52] However, there are limits to the protection of human rights through the

[47] J Wright, *Tort Law & Human Rights*, 1st edn (Oxford, Hart Publishing, 2001) 45, 57 and text
accompanying n 116 in Chapter 2 and *Note on the Text*.
[48] See for example *Rabone v Pennine Care NHS Foundation Trust* [2012] UKSC 2, [2012] 2 AC 72
and potentially *Smith v Ministry of Defence* [2013] UKSC 41, [2014] AC 52.
[49] For example, *DSD v Chief Commissioner of Police for the Metropolis* [2015] EWCA Civ 646, *Smith
v Ministry of Defence, ibid*.
[50] *R (Lumba) v Secretary of State for the Home Department* [2012] 1 AC 245.
[51] *Austin v Commissioner of Police of the Metropolis* [2009] 1 AC 564, see discussion in Chapter 4.
[52] Lady Hale, 'UK Constitutionalism on the March?' (Constitutional and Administrative Law Bar
Association Conference, 12 July 2014); P Bowen, 'Does the Renaissance of Common Law Rights Mean
that the Human Rights Act 1998 is Now Unnecessary' (2016) *European Human Rights Law Review*
361–77, citing *Osborn v Parole Board* [2013] UKSC 61, [2014] AC 1115 [54]–[62]; *Kennedy v Information Commissioner* [2015] 2 AC 455 [133]; *R (on the application of Sturnham) v Parole Board* [2013] 2
AC 254 [28]–[29]; *R (on the application of Guardian News and Media) v City of Westminster Magistrates'
Courts* [2013] QB 618 [88]–[89]; and see M Elliott, 'Beyond the European Convention: Human Rights
and the Common Law' (2015) 68 *Current Legal Problems* 85–117.

common law: the cleavage between acts and omissions is hard-wired in English tort law and as we see in Chapter 6 this particular fault line has become ever more entrenched as a result of the HRA. To this extent the argument that the ECHR and the English common law should march hand in hand has generally fallen on deaf ears.

The policy arguments that lead the courts to refuse to recognise a duty of care in negligence are exactly the same types of consideration that shape ECHR obligations. The challenge for coherence is obvious. Of course, the same set of facts may give rise to different claims (for example, concurrent claims in contract and tort), but denying claims in negligence on policy grounds that do not bar, but shape, claims under the HRA, threatens the coherence of English law. For example, the Fatal Accidents Act 1976 (FAA) which sets out a very precise class of claimants is potentially undermined by the much less precise concept of 'victim' under the ECHR, as well as the possibility of receiving just satisfaction in a much wider variety of situations than under the FAA.[53] Furthermore, the rule of law requires that a citizen should be able to understand and predict the legal consequences that flow from their conduct; standards of conduct should not be variable.[54]

Conclusion—Structure of the Second Edition

While the structure of the second edition largely mirrors the first, there are some significant changes. First, we begin our analysis by examining what I have described as a 'human rights based approach' to tort law. This is not a term of art. The years since the first edition of *Tort Law & Human Rights* was published have witnessed a growing body of academic literature dedicated to exposition of the theoretical foundations of tort law and re-consideration (and rejection) of the views of some leading scholars that particular 'functions' can appropriately be ascribed to tort law. It would be remiss not to consider that debate; this author, though, quite clearly comes down on the side of the 'functionalists', at least insofar as tort principles have for many years been the *de facto* mechanism though which human rights violations might be remedied; furthermore, tort actions frequently engage human rights and such actions need to be evaluated in the light of the state's obligations.

In place of a chapter dedicated to *The Duty of Care and Compatibility with Article 6 of the Convention*, there is now instead a chapter entitled *Public Authority Liability Part 1—The Impact of the ECHR on the Common Law*. It is noteworthy that this discussion is among the briefer, signalling the relatively limited impact that the HRA/ECHR have had on public authority liability at common law. The

---

[53] See generally, J Wright, 'The Operational Obligation under Article 2 of the European Convention on Human Rights and Challenges for Coherence' (2016) *Journal of Tort Law* 7(1) 58–81.
[54] As observed by Lord Mance in *Smith v Ministry of Defence* (n 48).

first edition was written in the 'uncertain' shadow[55] of *Osman v United Kingdom*.[56] Until that decision was effectively overruled by *Z v United Kingdom*,[57] it seemed that English courts were required in any application to strike out a claim in negligence on the basis that no duty of care was owed to evaluate a claim in the light of the Article 6 jurisprudence on legitimacy and proportionality. In other words, Article 6 seemed set to shape the substantive tort of negligence. This could in principle have applied to a wide range of claims, although in *Osman*, the case was stark, as the facts clearly engaged the Article 2 ECHR right to life. This prospect was eliminated by the Court's retreat from *Osman* in *Z v United Kingdom*.

The discussion of privacy in Chapter 8 has been expanded to include the considerable developments in the protection of autonomy and prevention of intrusion that have taken place in the common law over the last 15 years. There is no separate chapter on Nuisance and the relevant discussion has been subsumed as appropriate within Chapter 4 on *The European Convention on Human Rights* and Chapter 5 on *Public Authority Liability Part 1*.

The absence of a bill of rights in the United Kingdom led to the 'piecemeal' protection of human rights through the development of various fields of law. The HRA was drafted with the intention of subjecting all areas of law to scrutiny for compliance with the ECHR rights included in the Act. The various media through which the Act aims to achieve its purpose are examined in Chapter 3. When and if the HRA is repealed all the indications are that a British Bill of Rights will include the ECHR rights and ECHR rights will continue to bind the UK internationally; furthermore, citizens of the United Kingdom will continue to have the right of individual petition to the ECtHR. It seems highly unlikely, whatever remedial structure accompanies a new Bill, that English courts will not draw upon the enormous body of case law that has been built up over the last 16 years.

---

[55] T Hickman, 'The "Uncertain" Shadow: Throwing Light on the Right to a Court under Article 6(1) ECHR' (2004) *Public Law* 122–45.
[56] (1998) 29 EHRR 245.
[57] (2002) 34 EHRR 3.

2

A Human Rights Based
Approach to Tort Law

Introduction

The years since the first edition of *Tort Law & Human Rights* was published have witnessed a growing body of academic literature dedicated to exposition of the theoretical foundations of tort law and re-consideration of the views of some leading scholars that particular 'functions' can be ascribed to tort law. It would be remiss not to consider that debate; this author, though, quite clearly comes down on the side of the 'functionalists' at least insofar as many tort actions serve *de facto* to promote the protection of human rights. The notion of 'function' is used in two ways. First, tort law rules may function as vehicles to secure the protection of human rights and they may in fact be shaped to ensure that human rights obligations are accommodated. So, for example, in Chapter 5 we see how *D v East Berkshire Community NHS Trust*[1] was decided by the Court of Appeal in direct response to the Strasbourg Court's judgment in *Z v United Kingdom*.[2] Second, the function of international human rights law is to ensure that states secure human rights obligations at domestic level. Therefore all laws which do engage human rights obligations must comply with the demands of those standards as a matter of international law, and if there is domestic legislation such as the Human Rights Act 1998 (HRA), must comply at domestic level too. This does not mean that tort law is an empty vessel into which human rights obligations are poured, far from it. However, it is frequently tort law that, in the absence of a constitutional remedy, will provide the best fit in terms of a remedy.

---

[1] [2003] EWCA Civ 1151, [2003] 4 All ER 796.
[2] (2002) 34 EHRR 97.

Why Tort Law and Human Rights?

It has been suggested that the aims of tort law and, by implication, the aims of human rights law are different. In a well-known quote in *Greenfield*, Lord Bingham stated that the HRA is 'not a tort statute' and 'its objects are different and broader'.[3] In *Watkins*, he stated that 'the primary role of tort is to provide monetary compensation for those who have suffered material damage rather than to vindicate the rights of those who have not'.[4] On the other hand, it has been suggested that the HRA is 'possibly the most important tort statute ever created'.[5]

With respect to the late Lord Bingham, his view was false. To draw a distinction between tort and human rights on the basis that the purpose of tort is to provide compensation is a false dichotomy. The ancient trespass torts embody rights that we have good against all the world, including the state, and where they are breached, we are entitled to damages as of right. Where our human rights are violated we may be entitled to compensation and in the case of some violations we must be awarded compensation in order to ensure that the right is properly protected. Remedial frameworks are an essential part of human rights law; indeed, jurisprudence under the European Convention on Human Rights (ECHR) has held on many occasions (quite apart from the effective remedy under Article 13) that the substance of a right requires that a civil remedy is available and that judicial remedies, while not mandatory, provide the best means of securing the right.[6]

The aim of the Council of Europe is the achievement of greater unity between its Members and one of the methods by which that is promoted is though the maintenance and realisation of human rights and fundamental freedoms. Thus, the governments agreed to 'take the first steps for the collective enforcement of certain of the rights' proclaimed by the United Nations in the Universal Declaration of Human Rights. The golden thread that runs through ECHR jurisprudence is the principle of 'effectiveness' and it is necessary for remedies to be 'effective',[7] otherwise states can disregard human rights with impunity.

It may be argued that tort law and human rights law occupy completely different normative spheres. There are those who argue that tort law principles instantiate corrective justice and are premised purely upon bilateral relationships. Human rights on the other hand are obligations owed both by states *inter se* and between states and individuals and they are endowed upon human beings simply by virtue of being human. All states have an interest in the effective protection of human

---

[3] *R (Greenfield) v Secretary of State for the Home Department* [2006] 2 AC [19]. See generally J Steele, 'Damages in Tort and under the Human Rights Act: Remedial or Functional Separation?' (2008) *Cambridge Law Journal* 67(3), 606–34.

[4] *Watkins v Secretary of State for the Home Department* [2006] UKHL 17, [2006] 2 AC 395 [19].

[5] R Stevens, *Torts and Rights* (Oxford, Oxford University Press, 2007) 289.

[6] See *Z v United Kingdom* (n 2).

[7] *Chahal v United Kingdom* (1997) 23 EHRR 413; *Keenan v United Kingdom* (2001) 33 EHRR 913.

rights and individuals within states have an interest in the effective protection of human rights as such states manifest commitment to democracy and the rule of law.

While there is no logical necessity for remedies for human rights violations to be provided within the framework of tort law, adopting the military metaphor of Lord Bingham (somewhat ironically given his observations in *Greenfield* and *Watkins*), it has been the law of tort 'which [bore] the heat and burden of the battle [to protect rights prior to the HRA]'.[8] One of the most famous cases to address the limit of lawful executive action and often described as the first example of the common law stepping in to protect individual human rights as we would understand the term, is the famous decision of *Entick v Carrington*,[9] to the effect that government agencies must have clear legal authority if they are to interfere with citizens' rights; in the case of *Entick* itself, the search of premises was challenged on the ground of trespass. Our rights to liberty and bodily integrity are protected by the traditional trespass torts; they are actionable *per se* and impose liability irrespective of harm or damage, although, in the absence of harm or damage, damages may only be nominal.[10]

In her leading work on *Remedies in International Human Rights Law*, Shelton points out that most systems of state liability for violations of international human rights norms are built upon tort frameworks which everywhere address the same problems: 'the foundation of liability, causation, justifications or excuses, and remoteness of damage'.[11] It is to tort law that claimants who have felt let down by the state's failure to protect them have frequently turned for redress. Human rights obligations are geared towards securing not only the well-being of individual citizens, but also the greater good, the public interest that we all share in living in a stable society, secure in wind and limb from inappropriate conduct by the state, as well as our fellow citizens. According to Shelton, 'violations of human rights are wrongs committed against the individual victim *and* against the social order, and may be considered particularly serious wrongs because human rights are "maximally weighty moral claims"'.[12] Of the Irish courts, it has been remarked that 'the courts have said they regard tort law as the presumptive remedial instrument for vindicating constitutional rights'.[13]

---

[8] Lord Bingham of Cornhill, 'Tort and Human Rights' in P Cane and J Stapleton (eds), *The Law of Obligations, Essays in Celebration of John Fleming* (Oxford, Clarendon Press, 1998) 1 at 2, quoted in J Wright, *Tort Law & Human Rights* (Oxford, Hart Publishing, 2001) 13.

[9] (1765) 19 State Tr 1029.

[10] For a recent example of the award of nominal damages following false imprisonment which did not cause loss or damage, see *R (Lumba) v Secretary of State for the Home Department* [2011] UKSC 12, [2012] 1 AC 245. See Chapter 4.

[11] D Shelton, *Remedies in International Human Rights Law*, 2nd edn (Oxford, Oxford University Press, 2005) 22.

[12] *Ibid* 10, quoting L Lomasky, '*Compensation and the Bounds of Rights*' in J Chapman (ed), *Compensatory Justice* (New York, New York University Press, 1991).

[13] W Binchy, 'Meskell, the Constitution and Tort Law' (2011) *Dublin University Law Journal* 33, 339.

If we are to consider the relationship, if any, between tort law and human rights, we should examine what we mean by the concept of human rights.

What are 'Human' Rights?

The HRA was enacted to give 'further effect' to the rights set out in the ECHR, a treaty signed in 1950 and which entered into force in 1953. It is but one treaty among many that protect the human rights of citizens and which has been signed and ratified by the United Kingdom. Under the system of international human rights protection, a state agrees with other Contracting States to secure the rights set out in the treaty documents.

The human rights movement grew from the ashes of World War II, when the birth of the United Nations paved the way for multilateral recognition and protection of human rights. Beginning with the springboard proclamation of the rights and duties set out in the Universal Declaration of Human Rights in 1948, states have committed themselves to a raft of treaty obligations and other standards aimed at securing the protection of human rights for human beings within their states. It was the Member States that 'pledged themselves to achieve, in cooperation with the United Nations, the promotion of universal respect for and observance of human rights and fundamental freedoms'.[14] Following the non-binding Universal Declaration,[15] the United Nations promulgated treaties across the fields of civil and political and economic and social rights, as well as specific conventions such as the Genocide Convention and the Convention Against Torture. Further standards have been recognised across many areas and their meaning has been fleshed out by the various judicial and quasi-judicial bodies such as the European Court of Human Rights (ECtHR) of the Council of Europe and the Human Rights Committee of the United Nations. Furthermore, the range of rights recognised and protected by customary international law has grown. It is the participating states that have the obligation to secure the rights protected by treaty obligations; it is the participating states that must defend claims of violation of treaties or customary international law.

Unlike domestic principles of tort law, which are premised on obligations arising from bilateral relationships, international human rights law obligations on states are obligations that are owed *erga omnes*. In other words, the obligations are owed towards the international community as a whole. The point about these obligations is that every state has a 'legal interest in the protection of certain basic rights

---

[14] Universal Declaration of Human Rights, Preamble.
[15] Many of the rights set out in the Universal Declaration are now binding by virtue of incorporation into treaties, as well as through forming part of the rules of customary international law which are binding on all states.

and the fulfilment of certain essential obligations'.[16] In the *Barcelona Traction* case, the International Court of Justice included 'the outlawing of acts of aggression, and of genocide, as also … the principles and rules concerning the basic rights of the human person, including protection from slavery and racial discrimination'.[17] Furthermore, the International Law Commission's Articles on State Responsibility acknowledge the right of any state to claim from the responsible state 'cessation of the internationally wrongful act' and 'performance of the obligation of reparation in accordance with the preceding articles, in the interest of the injured State or of the beneficiaries of the obligation breached'.[18] Thus, a human rights violation is an injury to the international community as a whole; international human rights law forms part of the *ordre public* of the international community of states. The same principle applies in national legal systems to the norms of public law. Cornford has argued persuasively that citizens who suffer loss as a result of a public law wrong should receive reparation. He argues that the norms of public law have a dual function. They ensure that public bodies act for the purposes for which their powers are granted and that public law wrongs are wrongs to society. However, public law norms also ensure that public bodies act fairly towards individuals and where the norms intended to protect individuals are breached, compensation is appropriate.

The need to do justice beyond the parties is a feature of the Human Rights Committee's jurisprudence under the Optional Protocol (which affords the right of individual petition) to the International Covenant on Civil and Political Rights (ICCPR). In its General Comment No 31 on the Nature of the General Legal Obligation Imposed on States Parties to the Covenant, the Committee alluded to its frequent practice to include 'the need for measures, beyond a victim-specific remedy, to be taken to avoid recurrence of the type of violation in question'.[19]

One of the most contested and fiercely debated questions that accompanied the enactment of the HRA was the question of 'horizontality': what impact would ECHR rights have on non-state actors? These debates largely ignored the obvious *a priori* question of who is bound by international human rights obligations. The following section will draw out these themes.

Who is Bound by Human Rights Obligations?

The obligations arising from international human rights law are generally not defined with regard to a specific duty holder, but this should not surprise us.

---

[16] J Crawford, *The International Law Commission's Articles on State Responsibility Introduction, Text and Commentaries* (Cambridge, Cambridge University Press, 2002) 79.

[17] *Barcelona, Traction, Light and Power Company, Limited,* Second Phase, ICJ Reports 1970,32 [34].

[18] State Responsibility Article 48 2(a) and (b), quoted in Crawford (n 16) 276.

[19] CCPR/C/21/Rev.1/Add/13 [17].

The relevant obligations have been created through the will of states, either through the formation of treaties or through custom and practice, as developments in customary international law. The language of the major standard setting instruments is couched in terms of states undertaking to 'respect and ensure',[20] 'to secure',[21] to 'undertake to adopt legislative or other measures to give effect to',[22] and to 'undertake to respect ... and to ensure'[23] the rights set out in the various treaty instruments. The duty holder in international law is clearly therefore identified; in order for these rights to become real and effective so that they are enjoyed by members of state populations they then have to be mediated into domestic legal systems. This process is much more nuanced and is devolved to the legislature, the executive and the courts, the acts of each branch of government engaging state responsibility in international law.[24] Where a state fails to comply, it is the state that will be answerable before the treaty body supervisory organs; it is the state that is the duty holder under international law.

The extent to which human rights obligations deriving from international law should bind non state actors directly is contentious and it is beyond the scope of this discussion to explicate in detail the various arguments. In his thorough analysis of *Human Rights Obligations of Non-State Actors*,[25] Clapham has examined the various arguments put forward to justify limiting the range of actors that should be bound by human rights obligations. Two key arguments are identified: First, the 'policy/tactical' argument that treating insurgents and groups other than the state as the bearers of human rights obligations will let states off the hook themselves by allowing them to point to violations committed by armed opposition groups. The fear is that human rights protection will ultimately be weakened if the state is able to accuse other groups of violating human rights—if state agents are violating human rights, discredit can be dissipated. Second, similar fears are raised regarding the attribution of human rights norms to corporations. Clearly, there are corporations with massive global reach and resources that exceed those of the weakest states. Fears have been expressed that extending human rights norms to corporations will allow governments to prevent their own actions from coming under the spotlight. Clapham has cited the views of diplomats at the UN Human Rights Commission:

> attempts to craft norms of this nature dangerously shift the focus of accountability for human rights violations away from States and toward private actors, thus creating the

---

[20] Article 2(1) ICCPR.
[21] Article 1 ECHR.
[22] Article 1 African Charter on Human and Peoples' Rights 1981.
[23] Article 1 American Convention on Human Rights.
[24] Difference Relating to Immunity from Legal Process of a Special Rapporteur of the Commission on Human Rights: 'according to a well-established rule of international law, the conduct of any organ of a State must be regarded as an act of that State. This rule ... is of a customary character ....'. ICJ Reports 1999, 62 at 87 [22], referring to the Draft Articles on State Responsibility, Art 6, now Art 4, quoted in Crawford (n 16) 95.
[25] A Clapham, *Human Rights Obligations of Non-State Actors* (Oxford, Oxford University Press, 2006).

perception that States have less of a responsibility to end human rights abuses for which they are responsible.[26]

That non-state actors have the capacity to impact negatively on the enjoyment of human rights is not in doubt, but it is analytically incorrect to describe the relevant conduct as being 'in violation' of human rights standards; the obligation to 'secure' human rights belongs firmly to states. Weissbrodt has suggested that rather than speaking of a human rights 'violation' by a private actor, it is better to describe such acts as 'abuses' of human rights, or failures to 'respect' human rights.[27] However, a cautionary note should be made. First, there is the legal doctrine of abuse of right which imports its own unrelated characteristics. Second, it is not clear what obligation the notion of 'respect' could imply. Whether a failure by a non-state actor to 'respect' another's human rights amounts to the breach of a legal obligation will clearly depend upon the ordering of private law rights in the state. Although the term 'horizontal effect' is undoubtedly a term of art in relation to international human rights standards and constitutional rights, it fails to capture the fact that the obligations of state and non-state actors are of a different order: the state may violate human and constitutional rights; non-state actors may cause injury and fail to respect the interests protected by the right, but they do not violate the relevant human right—it was never their obligation to secure or ensure it.

To take an example from a well-known ECHR case, *Plattform 'Ärzte für das Leben' v Austria*,[28] which concerned the Article 11 right to freedom of assembly. An anti-abortion group held a march and a meeting which was disrupted by counter-demonstrators. The claimants argued that there had been a breach of Article 1 because the police had failed to provide protection and had failed to ensure *Plattform*'s freedom of assembly. The ECtHR stated that:

> Genuine, effective freedom of peaceful assembly cannot, therefore, be reduced to a mere duty on the part of the State not to interfere: a purely negative conception would not be compatible with the object and purpose of Article 11. Like Article 8, Article 11 sometimes requires positive measures to be taken even in the sphere of relations between individuals, if need be.[29]

Making the enjoyment of Article 11 real and effective on facts such as these is the duty of the state which has a power to take the coercive measures that are necessary to prevent counter-demonstrators disrupting the lawful exercise of human rights. A non-state actor cannot be required by the state to step in to try to prevent other non-state actors from obstructing others exercising their human rights. Thus, it can be seen that horizontal effect of human/constitutional rights will at most

---

[26] *Ibid*, 44.
[27] D Weissbrodt, 'Non-State Entities and Human Rights within the Context of the Nation-State in the 21st Century' in M Castermans, F van Hoof and J Smith (eds), *The Role of the Nation-State in the 21st Century* (Dordrecht, Kluwer, 1998) 175–95, 194.
[28] (1988)13 EHRR 204.
[29] *Ibid* [32].

be a partial translation of the obligation into the private sphere: an obligation to 'respect', but not to protect or fulfil the relevant standards. While legal relations are affected by constitutional rights, such rights impose constitutional duties to protect and secure rights only upon the organs of the state. It is unusual for a state to determine that constitutional duties fall directly on non-state actors. However, as Gardbaum has pointed out, 'the fact that private actors are not bound by constitutional rights in no way entails that such rights do not govern their legal relations with one another'.[30] Ireland is frequently quoted as an example of a state that has opted for 'direct' horizontal effect, in thatcitizens may assert a violation of a constitutional rights, in the absence of any other cause of action.[31] However, the writer is not aware of a successful action founded on a failure to secure a positive obligation.

Thus, the state is the duty holder under international law. However, that individuals, corporations and other groups have the capacity to act in ways that threaten the effective enjoyment and fulfilment of human rights is not in doubt. States must act to ensure that the human rights of individuals in their territory are respected by non-state actors, but the human rights obligation remains that of the state. If I am not prosecuted for murder because the police authorities accept a bribe from me in return for destroying evidence, it is the state that has failed in its obligation to ensure respect for the right to life. In addition to effective criminal laws, the state should also put in place civil laws to enable victims of murder to bring civil claims. I may also have a claim against the state for failing effectively to provide operational protection to protect my human rights under domestic law, if the constitutional arrangements give me such a right, as for example in English law under section 7 of the HRA.

Thus, the relationship between human rights law and private law can be viewed as a triangular relationship. The failure to give effective operational protection to human rights gives rise to a claim against the state for that failure; the claim arising from death gives rise to a tort claim against the perpetrator. The non-state perpetrator may have failed to respect my human rights; but it was not their obligation *to secure* them. The obligation to secure the right through operational protection and appropriate legal frameworks lies with the state. The danger of recognising that the obligation lies elsewhere is that the state may be enabled to shift responsibility from itself.

In conclusion, it can reasonably be stated that all persons, whether individuals, corporations or states, have the obligation to 'respect' the human rights of others; the obligation to 'secure' human rights belongs firmly to states. As we have remarked, for private lawyers, an issue that dominated discourse around the

---

[30] S Gardbaum, 'The 'Horizontal Effect' of Constitutional Rights' (2003) 102 *Michigan Law Review* 387 at 389.

[31] See for example *Lovett v Gogan* [1995] ILRM 12; *Parsons v Kavanagh* [1990] ILRM 560, quoted by M Hunt, 'The Effect on the Law of Obligations' in BS Markesinis (ed), *The Impact of the Human Rights Bill on English Law* (Oxford, Clarendon Press, 1998) 165.

enactment of the HRA was the extent to which the Act would have 'horizontal effect': what impact would the Act have on legal relations between non-state actors?[32] The issue of horizontal effect of the HRA is fully discussed in Chapter 3.

The Right to an Effective Remedy

All the major international human rights treaties require that effective remedies should be available as a matter of domestic law for violations of the treaty obligations.[33] Article 13 ECHR provides that: 'Everyone whose rights and freedoms as set forth in this Convention are violated shall have an effective remedy before a national authority notwithstanding that the violation has been committed by persons acting in an official capacity'. Thus, as well as securing the substantive rights, states must ensure a remedy at domestic level. This Article has been described as one of the 'most obscure' provisions of the Convention.[34] The question the Court in Strasbourg will ask is whether there exists at domestic level legal machinery that could have prevented the violation, or where a violation has occurred, is there a means by which appropriate redress could be achieved?[35]

Article 2(3) ICCPR requires the state party to make reparation for violation of Covenant Rights. According to the Human Rights Committee, 'reparation can involve restitution, rehabilitation, and measures of satisfaction, such as public apologies, public memorials, guarantees of non-repetition and changes in relevant laws and practices, as well as bringing to justice perpetrators of human rights violations'.[36] The ECtHR has power to award just satisfaction under Article 41 of the ECHR where it finds that there has been a violation and if the internal law of the relevant state only allows partial reparation to be made. There is no corresponding power in the Human Rights Committee in relation to claims submitted under the Optional Protocol to the ICCPR.

Awards made by the human rights bodies encompass both material losses (loss of earnings, medical expenses, pensions, etc) and non-material damage (pain and suffering, humiliation, loss of enjoyment of life and loss of companionship or consortium). In determining awards, the supervisory bodies have drawn upon the principles of general international law regarding reparation. It is not surprising, therefore, that in principle awards of punitive or exemplary damages are not available: such a category of damages would be antithetical to the principle of

---

[32] Gardbaum (n 30).

[33] Article 2(3)(a) ICCPR, Article 13 ECHR.

[34] Judges Matscher and Pinheiro Farinha, partly dissenting in *Malone v UK* 7 EHRR 14 PC, quoted by D J Harris, M O'Boyle, EP Bates and CM Buckley, *Harris O'Boyle & Warbrick: Law of the European Convention on Human Rights*, 2nd edn (Oxford, Oxford University Press, 2009) 557.

[35] Harris, O'Boyle, Bates and Buckley, *ibid* 558.

[36] See General Comment No 31 (n 19) [16].

sovereign equality of states.[37] That said, the ECtHR frequently takes account of the nature of state conduct, and whether it is of a particularly egregious nature, in fixing awards of just satisfaction.[38]

Pertinent to the present discussion is the fact that it is a matter for domestic law how states provide Article 13 relief: it is up to them and they are 'afforded a margin of appreciation in conforming with their obligations'.[39] Thus, there is no requirement under ECHR jurisprudence for a violation to attract redress by way of the development of common law principles by the judges, nor on the other hand that there should be a statutory framework of remedies for ECHR violations. It is a matter for states how redress is provided. It is correct to observe that 'the Convention does not contain a general requirement that every emanation of the state must do whatever it lawfully can in order to increase the likelihood that there will be fewer violations of Convention rights in the future'.[40]

Having said that, clearly 'more important rights attract more stringent remedies', and it would be highly questionable for example whether violations of the Article 3 right to be free from inhuman and degrading treatment would be adequately redressed through an ombudsman scheme. In *Z v United Kingdom*,[41] which concerned a violation of the positive obligation to protect children from inhuman and degrading treatment, the ECtHR held that in the case of breaches of Articles 2 and 3, compensation should in principle be available for non-pecuniary damage. However, the Court declined to make any finding as to whether on the facts only court proceedings could provide effective redress, 'though judicial remedies indeed furnish strong guarantees of independence, access for the victim and enforceability in compliance with the requirements of Article 13 [the right to an effective remedy] (see *Klass v Germany*)'.[42] Article 13 was not included in the Schedule of rights annexed to the HRA, the justification being that section 7 provides the domestic analogy for Article 13. There is therefore no requirement for those whose rights are violated to have a remedy in tort law, or indeed in any other particular sphere of domestic law. Where a set of facts engages ECHR rights, what is important is that there is a means by which redress can be sought and one which is considered 'effective' for the purposes of Article 13.

---

[37] In *Velasquez Rodriguez v Honduras (Compensation)* ILR 95 at 306, the Inter-American Court of Human Rights rejected the notion that punitive or exemplary damages were available under international law. For a discussion of reparation for injury in international law, see Crawford (n 16) 211 *et seq.*

[38] *Selmouni v France* (2000) 29 EHRR 403.

[39] Harris, O'Boyle, Bates and Buckley (n 34) 559, citing *Smith and Grady v UK* 1999-VI, 29 EHRR 493 [135] and *Kudla v Poland* 2000-XI, 35 EHRR 198 [154].

[40] R Bagshaw, 'Tort Design and Human Rights Thinking' in D Hoffmann (ed), *The Impact of the UK Human Rights Act on Private Law* (Cambridge, Cambridge University Press, 2011) 123.

[41] In *Z v United Kingdom* (n 2) [108]–[109], the UK Government accepted that the range of remedies then available (compensation from the Criminal Injuries Compensation Board, invocation of the complaints procedure under the Children Act 1989 and complaint to the Local Government Ombudsman) was insufficient to satisfy the demands of Article 13.

[42] *Z v United Kingdom* (n 2).

Section 7 HRA affords a right of action against public authorities (other than courts) that act incompatibly with Convention rights; however, the HRA has been held not to apply retrospectively,[43] and English courts have generally refused to extend common law principles to provide such a remedy where this would be required after 2 October 2000. While tort principles could be adapted to afford a remedy, English courts have generally been reluctant to manipulate tort principles to clothe any remedial gaps. A critical question that would attend repeal of the HRA is: what remedial structure is put in place of sections 7–8 HRA? Chapters 5 and 6 critique the distinct bifurcation that now exists between claims that engage ECHR rights and which are now channelled through the HRA and other claims which may be brought in negligence.

On the other hand, there are domestic legal principles that constitute causes of action (obvious examples are the torts that are actionable *per se* such as the trespass torts and defamation, although this should be read subject to the requirement to show 'serious harm' introduced by section 1 Defamation Act 2013), as opposed to sets of facts, which quite clearly engage ECHR rights and such principles, whether drawn from the field of tort or elsewhere, must be compliant with the ECHR and its jurisprudence. This will be the case even though no public authority, other than the court, is involved. Thus, damages awards in defamation proceedings which are quite clearly an interference with the right to freedom of expression set out in Article 10(1) ECHR must be evaluated for proportionality in the light of ECHR jurisprudence.[44]

Tort Law Theory and Human Rights Law

The central aim of this work is to explore the relationship between tort principles and human rights law and does not seek to propose an overarching descriptive or normative theory of tort law. However, in light of the contemporary debates regarding the legitimate scope and functions of tort law, the omission of discussion of some reflections upon this theme from a human rights based perspective would be a significant gap. A number of theories that avowedly seek to describe tort law as we can see it have been put forward. In this writer's view all are susceptible to the criticism that their explanatory powers are limited and rather like a badly made jigsaw, there are simply too many pieces that do not fit.[45]

There are theorists who insist that tort law should be understood only from an internal point of view; it is just tort law and, famously, like love, private law

---

[43] *R v Kansal* [2001] UKHL 62, [2001] 3 WLR 1562; *Re McKerr* [2004] UKHL 12, [2004] 1 WLR 807; *R v Lambert* [2001] UKHL 37, [2002] 2 AC 545.

[44] *Tolstoy Miloslavsky v UK* (1995) 20 EHRR 442, A 316, applied in *John v MGN* [1996] 2 All ER 35.

[45] For a critique see J Goudkamp and J Murphy, 'The Failure of Universal Theories of Tort Law' (2016) 2 *Legal Theory* (in press).

has no goals.[46] It has no purpose other than to be tort law. However, there is an external scrutineer that cannot be escaped. International human rights law, as implemented by national legal systems, effectively requires the scrutiny of all law from an external point of view. The Joint Committee on Human Rights was established in the 2000–01 Parliamentary session to consider human rights matters and all government bills are routinely examined for compliance with human rights; Joint Committee reports are often considered by the courts.[47] This does *not* mean that common law tort principles must be shaped in order to fulfil the state's obligations. However, where an existing cause of action engages international human rights standards, that cause of action must meet the requirements of those standards: a very good example is the tort of defamation which clearly engages freedom of expression and quite often conflicts with other rights recognised by international human rights standards, the most obvious being privacy.

Contemporary tort scholarship has been much influenced by Weinrib, according to whom tort law is the reflection of autonomous principles which are geared to achieve corrective justice. On a corrective justice model, it is argued, 'policy' considerations which pervade the language of both tort cases and primers are irrelevant. The role of the court is solely to 'correct' the injustice that has occurred. In a recent essay, Weinrib stated that corrective justice received its classic formulation in Aristotle's *Nichomachean Ethics*, Book V, and is the idea that 'liability rectifies the injustice inflicted by one person on another'.[48] Aristotle contrasted corrective justice with 'distributive' justice which deals with the 'distribution of whatever is divisible (Aristotle mentions honours and goods) among the participants in a political community'.[49]

According to Weinrib, from the perspective of corrective justice, the court's role is to rectify the injustice that has occurred by undoing it. Its role is not to treat the situation as a 'morally neutral given' and then to consider the best course. Rather, the court should exact the 'gain' from the defendant and return it to the claimant: the remedy is correlatively structured. This takes us to the observation that is most pertinent for contemporary scholars of tort law: normative factors that are extraneous to the relationship between the parties are irrelevant since they shatter the requirement of correlativity. As Weinrib states:

> in specifying the nature of the injustice, the only normative factors to be considered significant are those that apply equally to both parties. A factor that applies to only one of

---

[46] EJ Weinrib, *The Idea of Private Law* (Cambridge, Massachusetts, Harvard University Press, 2006) 3.

[47] See generally D Feldman, 'Parliamentary Scrutiny of Legislation and Human Rights' [2002] *Public Law* 323; D Feldman, 'Can and Should Parliament Protect Human Rights' (2004) *European Public Law* 635; F Klug and H Wildbore, 'Breaking New Ground: The Joint Committee on Human Rights and the Role of Parliament in Human Rights Compliance' [2007] *European Human Rights Law Review* 231; Joint Committee on Draft Defamation Bill Session 2010–12 HL Paper 203 HC 930-1, published 19 October 2011.

[48] E Weinrib, 'Corrective Justice in a Nutshell' (2002) 52 *University of Toronto Law Journal* 349, discussed in W Lucy, *Philosophy of Private Law* (Oxford, Clarendon Press, 2007) 293 *et seq.*

[49] Weinrib, *ibid.*

the parties—for example, the fact that the defendant has a deep pocket or is in a position to distribute losses broadly—is an inappropriate justification for determining liability because it is inconsistent with the correlative nature of liability.[50]

Furthermore, a relationship of correlativity is necessarily bipolar and can link only the two parties; distributive justice may link any number dependent upon the criteria governing amongst whom the relevant goods may be divided.

Thus Weinrib, drawing upon Aristotle, presents us with two spheres of justice that do not intersect and posits that corrective justice alone is the appropriate sphere for the law of torts. It follows from his analysis that not only are 'policy factors' extraneous to the parties irrelevant; the notion that tort law may perform functions serving public goals that are wider than the correction of the injustice between the parties is equally irrelevant. Thus, 'deterrence' and 'loss-spreading', two functions frequently cited in the leading texts, have no place in determining the existence of liability.

A strand of thinking has grown under the influence of Weinrib, which is known as 'rights' or 'rights-based' analysis. This approach focuses on the bilateral relationship between the parties and denies any role for the pursuit of community welfare goals. Thus, 'Rights analysis in tort law is strongly associated with anti-instrumentalism and the idea that the law of torts is and should be concerned primarily or exclusively with inter-personal justice'.[51] When rights theorists identify themselves as interpretivists they are not merely describing the law as it is. Instead, their aim is to 'provide the most plausible, coherent and appealing account of the law as it stands'.[52]

Cane is right: 'fundamentalist, reductionist accounts of private law oversimplify and misrepresent complex legal phenomena' and they are 'historically implausible'. Furthermore, while being avowedly descriptive, they are prescriptive.[53] Such accounts are susceptible to the criticism that they disregard the parts of the jigsaw that do not fit; the cases in the law reports are replete with judicial discussion of policy considerations that are extraneous to the relationship between the litigating parties but which have undoubtedly informed the structure of the law.

Furthermore, the argument that tort law is best explained in terms of corrective (as opposed to distributive) justice is adequate only if we treat court decisions as relevant only to the parties to a dispute. As soon as we recognise that court decisions guide the conduct of non-parties and decide other disputes, then, says Cane, we can see that the law of tort is concerned with distributive justice.[54] He cites *Donoghue v Stevenson*,[55] which changed forever the relationship between manufacturers and consumers by giving the latter a right of action they did not have before, thus changing the distribution of wealth in society in a

[50] *Ibid*, 2.
[51] D Nolan and A Robertson (eds), *Rights and Private Law* (Oxford, Hart Publishing, 2012) 2.
[52] *Ibid*, 6.
[53] P Cane, 'Rights in Private Law' in *ibid*, 40–41.
[54] P Cane, *The Anatomy of Tort Law* (Oxford, Hart Publishing) 18.
[55] [1932] AC 562.

significant way. Cane has also criticised the tendency of corrective justice theorists to dismiss the pieces of the tort jigsaw that do not fit their paradigm (such as liability for nonfeasance and strict liability) as mistakes.[56] While the economic theorists ignore the issue of correlativity, Weinrib focuses on this 'to the virtual exclusion of everything else'.[57] This writer sympathises with Cane's view that human beings have very large numbers of different goals that they pursue and some of these conflict. He says: 'Tort law is infected with the same tendency to pursue multifarious and potentially conflicting goals as are other forms of human purposive activity'.[58] The paradigmatic example that causes great problems is the principle of vicarious liability which just does not fit a corrective justice model of tort law.

Lucy has argued with force that while philosophical accounts of private law should not simply repeat our textbooks, they should not overlook 'very significant features of the institution'. Like Cane, Lucy highlights the tendency to say that strict liability cannot be accounted for in a coherent theory of private law. He describes the view that the philosopher may come to the argument with a preconceived view as a tendency to possess 'philosophical pre-commitments'.[59] Lucy has argued that particular conceptions of either corrective justice or distributive justice are not essential to appreciate private law, but he goes further and suggests that they may actually 'impede appreciation of important features of the institution'.[60] He draws a metaphor between tailoring and private law. If everyone had 'an ideal' human body all clothes produced could fit perfectly well. The tailor could always set about his work with confidence. But, the human body is not predictable in all its physicality; if the suit is to fit, the body must be carefully measured. Lucy argues that philosophical accounts of private law need to be made to measure, not off the peg, and should appreciate (and not deny) 'all its particularities and significant features'.[61]

The corollary of an intense focus on the bilateral relationship is that policy considerations have no role to play; from the perspective of the corrective justice theorist this is as it should be since application of legal principle will lead us to the proper determination of legal conflicts.[62] The debate between those academic experts who argue that judicial decision-making is and should be informed by relevant policy considerations[63] and those for whom such an approach has the potential to lead to an unacceptable 'politicisation of the law'[64] is rich and eloquent.

---

[56] Cane (n 54) 223–24.

[57] *Ibid.*

[58] *Ibid.*

[59] W Lucy, *Philosophy of Private Law* (Oxford, Clarendon Press, 2007) 426.

[60] *Ibid,* 430.

[61] *Ibid,* 431.

[62] A Beever, *Rediscovering the Law of Negligence* (Oxford, Hart Publishing, 2007).

[63] J Stapleton, 'Duty of Care Factors: A Selection from Judicial Menus' in P Cane and J Stapleton (eds), *The Law of Obligations: Essays in Celebration of John Fleming* (Oxford, Clarendon Press, 1998); C Witting, 'The House that Dr. Beever Built: Corrective Justice, Principle and the Law of Negligence' (2008) *Modern Law Review* 621.

[64] Beever (n 62) 6.

The formalist position is attractive because it seems less susceptible to uncertainty and perhaps on one view is more consistent with the rule of law.

It is beyond the scope of this work to engage in this debate other than to observe that the determination of which 'rights' receive protection in the law of obligations is ultimately a policy choice (*Donoghue v Stevenson* is an example of such a policy, many more could be given), either by the courts or by the legislature. In the absence of action by the legislature, and it is undeniable that in principle it is the legislature that has access to specialist advice and knowledge and the democratic mandate to make such decisions,[65] it is quite simply the role of the judiciary in courtrooms to make such decisions. The decisions that are made need to comply with international human rights obligations to the extent that the latter are engaged and applicable.

The rights theorists consider that corrective justice and distributive justice occupy different legal and philosophical spheres. Distributive justice, concerned as it is with the fair distribution of goods and entitlements in society, is considered by many to be a political matter and decisions regarding such allocations are the preserve of Parliament and government. It is for government to determine how goods should be allocated between society's members: which children should qualify for special needs teaching is a classic example of a distributive decision. Typically, threshold levels of need will be set in order to access additional teaching support, beginning with the statementing process. Similarly, the elderly sick can access care services in their home when their needs are determined to have met the threshold level.

Corrective justice may have a role to play when the child or the elderly sick person does not get the teaching or care to which they are entitled. Thus, corrective justice mechanisms may be used to enforce claims that are justified by distributive justice. Cornford has criticised the view that holds that allowing claims against public authorities for failing to provide benefits is to tread on the political sphere occupied by distributive justice, because at all times, the distributive decision is a governmental one.[66] According to Cornford, a claim brought in respect of an undelivered entitlement is a claim in corrective or restorative justice. This approach is beautiful in its simplicity, but it does not fit many of the claims that are brought under the HRA, nor does it necessarily fit a claim under the common law that is recognised in order to provide an effective remedy for a human rights violation. This is because human rights jurisprudence does not fit neatly within the corrective/distributive and courts/government approach suggested by Cornford. As we shall see, human rights obligations do cast courts in the role of determining how resources are allocated, even in the sphere of civil and political, as opposed to economic and social, rights.[67] Their decisions will frequently

---

[65] Stevens (n 5), Ch 14 on *Policy*.

[66] T Cornford, *Towards a Public Law of Tort* (Aldershot, Ashgate Publishing Limited, 2008) 228.

[67] For example, see *DSD v Commissioner of Police for the Metropolis* [2015] EWCA Civ 646. See discussion in Chapter 4.

require the allocation of resources from the public purse in order to make good the implementation of the right.

To take an example, under some circumstances, Article 2 of the ECHR imposes positive operational obligations upon the state to protect individuals from the violent acts of third parties. It is subject to a reasonableness test which takes account of resources. Necessarily, the court is required to decide whether resources should have been used for this particular claimant. Generally, the defendant's resources are irrelevant to the question of liability in tort (the exception being *Goldman v Hargrave*[68]). The claim under the HRA is a legal claim in corrective justice to enforce an entitlement that is determined by applying the principles of distributive justice.

An aspect of the debate regarding the nature of 'private law' is the question of whether it is appropriate to ascribe different functions to the law of torts: writers frequently ask what the aims of tort law are.[69] The corrective justice theorist would say that tort law has only one function and that is to be tort law. The corollary of the rights-based approach is that it is wrong to ascribe any 'function' to tort law, other than the enforcement of rights in bilateral relationships which does not take account of factors beyond that relationship.

Functionalism and the External Point of View

Tort law may be variously perceived as a system to deter harmful conduct, to effect loss spreading and to ensure compensation to those who suffer harm. This view has been challenged by the corrective justice theorists who argue that tort law should be understood only from within: 'private law looks neither to the litigants individually nor to the interests of the community as a whole, but to a bipolar relationship of liability'.[70] On one hand, are those unlike Weinrib who agree with Lord Bingham's view that 'the overall object of tort law is to define cases in which the law may justly hold one party liable to compensate the other'.[71] This is what Stevens has described as 'the loss model' conception of the law of torts.[72]

Stevens has proposed that the infringement of rights, not the infliction of loss, is the gist of the law of torts.[73] It is obvious, he would argue, that a system of civil law which focuses solely upon the bilateral relationship between the parties and the question of whether the defendant has infringed the claimant's primary right has no interest in the wider question of the impact that a successful claim may have on

---

[68] [1967] 1 AC 645.
[69] G Williams, 'The Aims of the Law of Tort' [1951] *Current Legal Problems* 137; Lord Bingham, 'The Uses of Tort' (2010) 1 *Journal of European Tort Law* 1.
[70] Weinrib (n 46) 1.
[71] *Fairchild v Glenhaven Funeral Services Ltd* [2003] 1 AC 32 at [9].
[72] Stevens (n 5) 2.
[73] Stevens (n 5).

society more generally, in other words that the determination of this question by definition cannot engage policy issues. There are no relevant ripples beyond the bilateral relationship. Thus, the corollary of his argument is that it is no part of the judge's role to evaluate the policy factors that might argue in favour or against liability. He acknowledges that much insight has come from the work of the legal realists but such approaches are 'antithetical to treating rights seriously'. For Stevens, judges lack the technical competence to assess 'all of the reasons which could, in theory, be taken into account in reaching a decision'.[74] Implicit in Stevens' analysis is the rejection that the law of torts serves any purpose other than to be a part of the body of private law—it has no externally driven 'function'.

However, the law as it is in the books does not reflect an ideal model based upon bilateral relationships. Recent decisions regarding the tort of negligence are replete with appeals to 'policy' ranging from the decision that expert witnesses should no longer enjoy immunity from suit[75] to determination that a mother may receive a conventional award in wrongful pregnancy cases.[76]

One of the major challenges for the rights theorist is to explain what rights we have and where they come from. For Stevens, our legal rights derive from our moral rights and the starting point is the negative formulation of 'the golden rule': do not do unto others what you would not want done to you.[77] Beever has argued that it is not necessary to identify which rights are protected or where those rights come from. In fact, he states that those rights that are recognised by human rights law will do as an indicative list. This view of a sort of hermetically sealed body of law that is impervious to any externally agreed set of standards is inappropriate today. International human rights law is a set of standards to which states have committed themselves and which need to be implemented by national legal systems in order to secure compliance. Human rights standards embody values that the states constitutive of the international community have agreed upon and which are pervasive. In order to give effect to these rights under the ECHR, English law has empowered the judiciary to develop rights through the various interpretative dimensions of the HRA.

Self-evidently, English law has a function that, if not driven by, must certainly be evaluated for compliance with an external standard, that is the complex of standards agreed to by the state in international human rights law; in other words there is an external point of view and tort law like every other aspect of English law must comply in ways that are appropriate and required with the demands of those standards. This is most emphatically not an argument for horizontality; it is merely the empirical observation that the rules of tort law cannot only be examined from an internal point of view; there is, like it or not, an external standard. In many ways, the Stevens thesis is an attractive one—the judiciary are not economists or social scientists and do lack the technical competence to assess

---

[74] Stevens (n 5) 30–39.
[75] *Jones v Kaney* [2011] 2 AC 398.
[76] *Rees v Darlington Memorial NHS Trust* [2003] UKHL 52, [2004] 1 AC 309.
[77] Stevens (n 5) 332.

decisions on the basis of empirical observation and experience. But, demonstrably, their decision-making cannot be isolated from one very important 'policy' concern at least, the need to ensure compatibility with human rights standards. Thus, where a cause of action (rather than a set of facts, with regard to which there may be many ways of ensuring that human rights standards are met) engages ECHR rights, the classic example would be defamation, the balance defamation strikes between the competing rights of freedom of speech and the interest in reputation needs to be examined through the human rights lens.

Chester v Afshar[78] is an example of a case where the English courts were anxious to ensure that the claimant's right to autonomy was appropriately protected, although the actual loss suffered could not be accommodated by normal tort principles. What is interesting for present purposes is Stevens' acknowledgement that it would have been preferable for the House of Lords to follow *Rees v Darlington Area Health Authority*,[79] and to award a sum to reflect the fact that the claimant was denied the possibility of making an informed choice. The right infringed was that of personal autonomy, and, arguably, bodily integrity. It will strike the reader immediately that autonomy *per se*, or in human rights terminology, the right to private life, is not explicitly protected by tort law. Stevens is effectively arguing that tort law should be expanded to protect human rights, an external policy driver. He might counter this by saying no, it is the need to pretend to prove loss that is objectionable.

Concluding Remarks

This chapter has argued that tort law, like every other area of English law, whether termed public or private law, must comply with the international human rights standards agreed to by the United Kingdom. This is not an argument for the horizontal effect of human rights; rather, it is an acknowledgement that where a cause of action is based upon a set of facts that engage human rights, courts will need to ensure compliance. In the chapters that follow, we will argue that where there are remedial gaps in human rights protection, it may be appropriate for tort law to be tailored to meet those gaps. A repeal of the HRA may well lead to increasing pressure for tort law to be shaped to meet any remedial demands of human rights law.

The HRA is still with us, however, and even if repealed the areas of contention that it has generated, especially the nature and scope of the law-making relationship between the United Kingdom and Strasbourg, will remain. This theme is further drawn out in the following chapter which provides an analysis of the HRA and its application and interpretation by the courts.

---

[78] [2004] UKHL 41, [2005] 1 AC 134.
[79] [2003] UKHL 52, [2004] 1 AC 309.

3

The Human Rights Act

Introduction

The Human Rights Act 1998 (HRA) came into force on 2nd October 2000. The political context within which the Act operates has changed in ways that could barely have been anticipated when the Act received Royal Assent in 1998. At the time of parliamentary debates a major preoccupation for the press was the likely impact of the HRA upon the balance between privacy and freedom of expression. Who then could have foreseen 9/11, the so-called 'War on Terror' and war in Afghanistan and Iraq?

The HRA seems unlikely to be with us for much longer, but we have been promised a British Bill of Rights and the interpretive issues regarding the scope and reach of the European Convention on Human Rights (ECHR) rights will be with us whatever form these rights are protected at national level. Thus, issues such as the status of ECHR jurisprudence in English law and its impact on the doctrine of precedent, as well as the extent of any horizontal effect will no doubt consume the attention of courts and commentators alike. As we have seen,[1] indications are that the balance between some rights will be struck differently in a new British Bill of Rights. However, attempts to forge a different priority or emphasis should be undertaken with caution and an awareness that claimants will still have the right to petition Strasbourg, subject to the requirement to exhaust domestic remedies.[2] The following discussion will examine the aims of the HRA, followed by an analysis of the architecture of the HRA, and the means through which ECHR rights now pervade English law. We shall also consider the important issue of the nature of the law-making relationship between English courts and Strasbourg. This discussion provides the context for Chapter 4, which seeks to elaborate the obligations created by the Convention rights set out in Schedule 1 to the Act.

---

[1] See Chapter 1, *Introduction*, text accompanying n 4.
[2] Article 35 ECHR.

Aims of the HRA

The HRA does not 'incorporate' the rights set out in the ECHR; rather, as
Ewing observed, a certain number of the Convention rights have acquired a
defined status in English law.[3] The Preamble to the HRA provides that the Act
is to give 'further effect to rights and freedoms guaranteed under the ECHR' and
section 1(1) enumerates the effected Articles which are set out in Schedule 1. There
is a difference between rights under the ECHR and the rights set out in Schedule 1
to the HRA. The former bind the United Kingdom in international law as a party
to the Treaty; the latter are enforceable as a matter of English law in the terms set
out in the HRA.

During parliamentary debates some extravagant claims were made regarding
the intended effects of the HRA: English courts would be able to develop human
rights throughout society and a culture of human rights would develop; our
'standing [would] rise internationally';[4] the Act would 'strengthen representative
and democratic government' and create 'a new and better relationship between the
Government and the people'. Lord Irvine described the Bill as giving the courts 'as
much space as possible to protect human rights, short of a power to set aside or
ignore Acts of Parliament'.[5] In terms of its interpretation by the courts, however,
most of these observations are of little significance. The duty of the court in carrying out its constitutional task of interpreting the HRA is to seek to identify the
intention of Parliament expressed in the language used.[6] While the decision in
Pepper v Hart can be seen as an exception to this general rule, it is of limited application: *Hansard* may be resorted to as an aid to interpretation in order to prevent
the Executive from placing a meaning on words used in legislation which is different from that which ministers attributed when promoting the relevant Act; or
where a statement made by a minister is relevant to a challenge by way of judicial
review.[7]

On the other hand, there are statements that indicate a rather more modest
ambition for the HRA. During parliamentary debates, the then Home Secretary,
acknowledged the importance of the Bill, but described its function as 'limited',
to bring rights home.[8] The White Paper, *Rights Brought Home*, makes surprising

---

[3] KD Ewing, 'The Human Rights Act and Parliamentary Democracy' (1999) 62 *Modern Law Review*
79, 84.

[4] *Hansard*, HC Deb 16 February 1998, vol 307, col 769, Secretary of State for the Home Department,
Mr Jack Straw.

[5] *Hansard*, HL Deb 3 November 1997, vol 582, col 1229, The Lord Chancellor, Lord Irvine of Lairg.

[6] *Wilson v First County Trust Ltd (No 2)* [2003] UKHL 40, [2004] 1 AC 816 [56] (Lord Nicholls).
See also Lord Radcliffe in *Attorney General (Canada) v Hallet & Carey Ltd* [1952] AC 427 PC (Can),
discussed by A Kavanagh, 'The Role of Parliamentary Intention in Adjudication under the Human
Rights Act 1998' (2006) 26 *Oxford Journal of Legal Studies* 179.

[7] *Wilson v First County Trust Ltd (No 2)*, ibid.

[8] *Hansard*, HC Deb 16 February 1998, vol 307, col 772, Secretary of State for the Home Department,
Mr Jack Straw.

reading in light of the more expansive claims made for the HRA. The aim of the Bill was described as straightforward, 'to make directly accessible the rights which the British people already enjoy under the Convention. In other words, to bring those rights home.'[9] The White Paper described the road to Strasbourg as 'long and hard', as well as expensive, and declared unsatisfactory the fact that a victim of a breach of the Convention standards would not be able to bring a claim in the UK courts, simply because British law did not recognise the right in the same terms as the ECHR itself.[10] There is no reference to the development of a culture of rights or the *de facto* creation of a Bill of Rights for the United Kingdom. The modest aim is reflected in the Preamble to the HRA: 'An Act to give further effect to rights and freedoms guaranteed under the ECHR'. Lord Bingham remarked that the purpose of the HRA,

> was not to enlarge the rights or remedies of those in the United Kingdom whose Convention rights have been violated but to enable those rights and remedies to be asserted and enforced by the domestic courts of this country and not only by recourse to Strasbourg.[11]

The structure of the HRA is a simple one and reflects the Government's intention to secure compliance with ECHR standards by the Legislature, Executive and the Judiciary, while preserving the sovereignty of Parliament. The HRA does not simply say that the provisions of the ECHR have the force of law. Rather, each of the three branches of government has an obligation, directly or indirectly, to ensure compatibility with the Convention rights set out in Schedule 1 to the HRA. Section 19 requires ministers to certify whether provisions of Bills are compatible with the Convention rights and these statements are scrutinised by the Parliamentary Joint Select Committee on Human Rights which questions ministers and takes evidence;[12] under section 3, legislation must, so far as it is possible to do so, be read and given effect in a way which is compatible with the Convention rights; and section 6 imposes obligations on public authorities, which includes the courts, not to act in a way that is incompatible with the Convention rights. As a result, there exist side by side two bodies of law: Strasbourg case law reflecting the international obligations of the United Kingdom and domestic decisions of English courts taken in response to the HRA. Obviously, following mediation into English law through the HRA, the principles of Strasbourg decisions undergo a metamorphosis through which they become a part of the body of English precedent. There then exist side by side two sets of rights: rights under the ECHR and

---

[9] *Rights Brought Home* (Cm 3782, 1997) 1.19.

[10] *Ibid*, 1.16.

[11] *R (on the application of Begum) v Denbigh High School Governors* [2006] UKHL 15, [2007] 1 AC 100 [29].

[12] A Lester and K Taylor, 'The Parliamentary Scrutiny of Human Rights' in A Lester and D Pannick (eds), *Human Rights Law and Practice*, 2nd edn (London, LexisNexis, 2004) Ch 8. For example, on the introduction of the Communications Bill, which eventually became the Communications Act 2003, the Secretary of State made a statement under s 19(1)(b) that the Government wished to proceed with the Bill despite being unsure whether the absolute ban on political advertising in the broadcast media was compatible with the ECHR. In *R (on the application of Animal Defenders) v Culture Secretary*

rights under the HRA. In the words of Lord Hoffmann: 'The Act did not trans-mute international law obligations into domestic ones. It created new domestic rights.'[13] Thus, contrary to views expressed by some commentators, the HRA does not 'incorporate' ECHR rights into English law.[14] The two sets of rights are differ-ent creatures and ECHR rights continue to be justiciable at Strasbourg, subject of course to the requirement to exhaust domestic remedies.

Thus, legislation is to be interpreted 'so far as it is possible to do so … in a way which is compatible with Convention rights' (section 3(1)); where the court is sat-isfied that a provision of primary legislation is incompatible with a Convention right, the court may make a declaration of that incompatibility (section 4(2)). Pub-lic authorities, including the courts, must not act in a way which is incompatible with Convention rights and if they do so, they act unlawfully. The Act creates a framework of remedies in sections 7 and 8, according to which a claim will lie against a public authority which has acted, or proposes to act, unlawfully. The court has power under section 8(1) to grant such relief, or remedy, or make such order, within its powers as it considers just and appropriate. Section 8(2) provides for the possibility of an award of damages by a court which has power to award damages.

The Act says nothing in terms of the relationship between the common law and the HRA. Courts as public authorities must not act in a way which is incompat-ible with Convention rights and we shall see below the extent to which this section has impacted on law-making by the courts. However, section 11(b) does provide that a person's reliance on a Convention right does not restrict his right to make any claim or bring any proceedings which he could make or bring apart from sections 7 to 9. Thus, in appropriate cases a claimant may on the same facts seek a remedy under sections 7 and 8 HRA, as well as through a cause of action recog-nised at common law. The issue of public authority liability in negligence, or rather the lack of public authority liability in negligence, has arguably been of diminished importance in cases that engage the ECHR since the HRA came into force.[15] Cases on facts such as *Z v United Kingdom*,[16] in which the Government conceded that the Article 3 right to be free from inhuman and degrading treatment had been violated, can now be redressed at least in relation to facts that post-date 2nd October 2000.[17]

[2008] UKHL 15, [2008] 1 AC 1312, the House of Lords held that the prohibition on political advertis-ing was justified as being necessary in a democratic society and compatible with the ECHR.

[13] *Re McKerr* [2004] UKHL 12; [2004] 1 WLR 807 [68] and see also Lord Nicholls [26]; *R v Lyons* [2002] UKHL 44, [2003] 1 AC 976 [27] (Lord Hoffmann); *R (on the application of Al-Skeini) v Secretary of State for Defence* [2007] UKHL 26, [2008] 1 AC 153 [10] (Lord Bingham); *Re P (Adoption: Unmar-ried Couple)* [2008] UKHL 38, [2009] 1 AC 173 [31] (Lord Hoffmann). See also Laws LJ in *Begum v Tower Hamlets LBC* [2002] EWCA Civ 239, [2002] 1 WLR 2491 [17] who stated that the rights under the HRA are 'municipal rights'.

[14] cf R Wintemute, 'The Human Rights Act's First Five Years: Too Strong, Too Weak or Just Right?' (2006) 17 *Kings College Law Journal* 209.

[15] Dame Mary Arden, 'Human Rights and Civil Wrongs: Tort Law under the Spotlight', Hailsham Lecture [2010] *Public Law* 140–59.

[16] (2002) 34 EHRR 97.

[17] See the discussion of non-retrospectivity in the context of historic sexual abuse.

Thus, ECHR rights now become 'domesticated' by way of statutory interpretation through section 3 and through the development of the common law. This chapter will examine the response of the courts to the interpretative obligation under section 3, the obligation of the courts under section 6 and, in both cases, the impact of the rights on non-state actors ('horizontality'). We shall also examine the action under section 7 HRA and associated remedies under section 8.

The interpretation of the HRA has taken place in a myriad of situations and the general principles that have emerged will apply in any case where ECHR rights are engaged. With the benefit of hindsight, and in light of subsequent academic preoccupations, one of the most crucial aspects of the HRA relevant to law-making received comparatively little attention during both Parliamentary debates and in *Rights Brought Home* and this relates to the nature of the law-making relationship between Strasbourg and the UK courts. Strasbourg is certainly the final arbiter of the content of ECHR rights as a matter of international law. Two key questions arise: what role does Strasbourg jurisprudence play in shaping English law?; and the connected issue, what impact does Strasbourg jurisprudence have on the doctrine of precedent? Thus, we shall begin our examination of the courts' approach to interpretation of the HRA, with analysis of the law-making relationship between Strasbourg and the English courts.[18]

Law-Making under Section 2 HRA

The HRA itself provides a pithy statement regarding the weight to be attached to the ECHR jurisprudence by English courts in section 2(1), according to which

> [a] court or tribunal determining a question which has arisen in connection with a Convention right must take into account any judgment of the European Court of Human Rights, any opinion of the Commission, any decision of the Commission in connection with Article 26 or 27(2) of the Convention, or any decision of the Committee of Ministers taken under Article 46 whenever made or given, so far as, in the opinion of the court or tribunal, it is relevant to the proceedings in which that question has arisen.

Thus, the obligation on the face of the statute is clear—English courts are not bound by Strasbourg, but must take Strasbourg jurisprudence into account.

During the progress of the Human Rights Bill through Parliament, Lord Kingsland sought an amendment to clause 2 of the Bill so that the phrase 'must take into account any' would have been replaced by 'shall be bound by'.[19] In reply,

---

[18] This discussion draws upon J Wright, 'Interpreting Section 2 of the Human Rights Act 1998: Towards an Indigenous Jurisprudence of Human Rights' [2009] *Public Law* 595–616.

[19] Lord Kingsland, House of Lords Committee Stage, *Hansard*, HL Deb 18 November 1997, vol 583, col 511 quoted in J Cooper and A Marshall Williams, *Legislating for Human Rights, The Parliamentary Debates on the Human Rights Bill* (Oxford, Hart Publishing, 2000) 36.

Lord Irvine pointed out that the doctrine of precedent is inapplicable at Strasbourg, where the ECHR itself is the ultimate source of law. In addition, judgments of the European Court of Human Rights (ECtHR) are binding only on the
states parties to a case,[20] and it 'would be strange to require courts in the United
Kingdom to be bound by such cases'.

It is not surprising that the Strasbourg system does not formally embrace a
doctrine of precedent: states parties generally come from the civilian law tradition
where it is axiomatic that legal rules emanate from a sovereign legislator, with the
task of the judge (at least at a formal level) being to apply, rather than to make
the law.[21] Moreover, it has been asserted on many occasions that the ECHR is
a living instrument, which must be interpreted in the light of present day conditions so that, far from a doctrine of precedent being applied, its meaning will
change over time.[22] However, care should be taken not to overstate the principle:
the Strasbourg organs will generally follow their clear and constant jurisprudence
on any issue. While the ECtHR is not formally bound to follow its previous judgments, it has recognised that it is in the interests of 'legal certainty, forseeability
and equality before the law' that it should not without good reason depart from
'precedents' laid down in previous cases.[23] That said, there is an inevitable tension
that runs through the Strasbourg jurisprudence between the desire for consistency
and certainty and the need for the substantive content of ECHR rights to change
to reflect changing social conditions.

The process of fleshing out ECHR rights and commensurate obligations on
states takes the form of a dialogue between the supervisory bodies and the Contracting States in which 'the Court must have regard to the changing conditions
within … Contracting States generally and respond … to any evolving convergence
as to the standards to be achieved'.[24] The recognition of evolving standards is amply
illustrated by Strasbourg's response to the needs of British transsexuals who fought
over a period of more than 20 years for their post-operative gender to be properly
recognised. Thus, although the jurisprudence is frequently described as 'dynamic

---

[20] Article 46(1) ECHR.

[21] See, for example, Article 5 of the Code Civil of France which expressly forbids the judiciary
from making pronouncements of a general normative nature in the cases before them. See generally
F Wieacker, *A History of Private Law in Europe* (Oxford, Clarendon Press, 1995) 393; B Markesinis, *The
German Law of Torts*, 3rd edn (Oxford, Clarendon Press, 1994) 7.

[22] See *Tyrer v United Kingdom* (1978) 2 EHRR 1 (birching was degrading treatment within Art 3).
An illustration of evolving standards is afforded by the jurisprudence relating to the recognition of
the status of post-reassignment transsexuals from *Rees v United Kingdom* (1986) 9 EHRR 46; *Cossey
v United Kingdom* (1990) 13 EHRR 622 through to *Goodwin v United Kingdom* (2002) 35 EHRR, which
was followed domestically by *Bellinger v Bellinger* [2003] UKHL 21, [2003] 2 AC 467 which paved the
way for the Gender Recognition Act 2004. The size of the minority opinion grew progressively in the
Strasbourg authorities until *Goodwin*, when a Grand Chamber found that partial recognition of transsexuals' post-operative identity did not satisfy the state's positive obligation under Article 8 ECHR.

[23] *Goodwin, ibid*; *Pretty v United Kingdom* (2002) 35 EHRR 1 [75]; *Chapman v United Kingdom*
(2001) 33 EHRR 18.

[24] *Goodwin, ibid.*

and evolutive', as the cases brought by transsexuals demonstrate, the shape of the jurisprudence generally proceeds by degrees, rather than by radical shifts.[25]

However, it is not unknown for Strasbourg to change its position fairly peremptorily. Indeed, Lord Browne-Wilkinson expressed concern lest English courts should be tied to a jurisprudence that is by definition 'a shifting one'.[26] The unstable nature of Strasbourg jurisprudence is well illustrated by the shift in thinking that marked the transition from finding a violation of Article 6 against the United Kingdom in *Osman v United Kingdom*,[27] which was then superseded by a perception that the real mischief in cases such as *Osman* lay in the failure to afford an effective remedy as required by Article 13 ECHR. The *Osman* decision had provoked a sharp response from Lord Hoffmann who, writing extra judicially, was moved to observe that the case reinforced the doubts he had held 'for a long time about the suitability, at least for this country, of having questions of human rights determined by an international tribunal made up of judges from many countries'.[28] More moderately, Lord Browne-Wilkinson confessed that he found the decision difficult to understand.[29] Finally, in *Z v United Kingdom* the ECtHR took the view that the determination of whether or not a civil right was in issue such as to engage Article 6, was a matter for determination by the domestic court, not Strasbourg.[30]

Moreover, the lack of a formal system of precedent may lead to conflict between Strasbourg authorities, which must then be resolved by the English courts. The development of ECHR case law in relation to the important question of 'jurisdiction' and the territorial extent of the United Kingdom's responsibility under the ECHR (and therefore the HRA) illustrates the challenge for English courts in 'bringing rights home'. The answer to this question has significant implications for public authority liability under the HRA. Thus, in *R (on the application of Al-Skeini) v Secretary of State for Defence*,[31] the House of Lords was required to determine, first, whether complaints relating to British army activities in Iraq fell within the scope of the ECHR because they fell within the jurisdiction of the United Kingdom under Article 1 of the ECHR and, second, whether those activities fell within the scope of the HRA. In *R (on the application of B) v Secretary of State for Foreign and Commonwealth Affairs*, the Court of Appeal held that the jurisdiction under the HRA is co-extensive with 'the somewhat wider jurisdiction of the United Kingdom that Strasbourg has held to govern the duties of the United Kingdom under the Convention'.[32]

---

[25] See text accompanying n 22.

[26] *Hansard*, HL Deb 19 January 1998, vol 584, col 1268, quoted in Cooper and Williams (n 19).

[27] *Osman v United Kingdom* (1998) 29 EHRR 245. See discussion in Chapter 4—*The European Convention on Human Rights: Its Application and Interpretation.*

[28] Rt Hon Lord Hoffmann, 'Human Rights and the House of Lords' (1999) 62 *Modern Law Review* 159, 164.

[29] *Barrett v Enfield LBC* [2001] 2 AC 550.

[30] (2002) 34 EHRR 3.

[31] [2007] UKHL 26, [2008] 1 AC 153.

[32] [2004] EWCA Civ 1344, [2005] QB 643 [78].

By a majority of 4:1, Lord Bingham dissenting, the House decided that the obligation on a public authority under section 6 extends to acts 'within the juris-diction' of the United Kingdom, as determined in light of ECHR jurisprudence under Article 1: in other words, jurisdiction under the ECHR and HRA are co-terminous. The case law under Article 1 did not speak with one voice, however, and the Law Lords in the majority were unanimous that national courts should give pre-eminence to the Grand Chamber decision in *Bankovic v Belgium*,[33] rather than the subsequent Chamber decision in *Issa v Turkey*.[34] Lord Rodger, with whom Baroness Hale and Lord Carswell agreed, placed weight upon the fact that it was a decision of the Grand Chamber, the decision was unanimous, the parties were represented by distinguished counsel and the judgment of the court is care-fully reasoned. He stated: 'Everything about it suggests that it is intended to be an authoritative exposition of the concept of "jurisdiction" under Article 1'.[35] In *Bankovic*, the Grand Chamber had emphasised the centrality of *territorial* juris-diction under the ECHR and held that there was no jurisdictional link between the victims and the respondent states. In a volte-face, subsequently in *Al-Skeini v United Kingdom*[36] the ECtHR departed from its views in *Bankovic* and endorsed the reasoning of the chamber judgment in *Issa*.

Observations by English Courts Regarding the Section 2(1) Obligation

A number of observations have been made regarding the approach of English courts towards Strasbourg jurisprudence: first, in the absence of 'some special cir-cumstances', English courts should follow any clear and constant jurisprudence of the ECtHR;[37] in *Anderson*, Lord Bingham held that the House of Lords 'will not without good reason depart from the principles laid down in a carefully consid-ered judgment of the court sitting as a Grand Chamber'.[38] In *Anderson*, the House of Lords laid stress on the fact that the ECtHR had displayed a clear understand-ing of the role of the Home Secretary in tariff-fixing in English law. Conversely, in *R v Spear*,[39] the House was not convinced that the ECtHR had a sound grasp of

---

[33] (2001) 11 BHRC 435.
[34] (2004) 41 EHRR 567.
[35] *Al-Skeini* (n 31) [68].
[36] (2011) 53 EHRR 589.
[37] *R (on the application of Alconbury Developments Ltd) v Secretary of State for the Environment, Transport and the Regions* [2001] UKHL 23, [2002] AC 295 [26] (Lord Slynn); *R (on the application of Ullah) v Special Adjudicator* [2004] UKHL 26, [2004] 2 AC 323 [20] (Lord Bingham).
[38] *R (on the application of Anderson) v Secretary of State for the Home Department* [2002] UKHL 46, [2003] 1 AC 837 [18].
[39] [2002] UKHL 31, [2003] 1 AC 734.

principles of English law regarding courts martial and declined to follow *Morris v United Kingdom*.[40] In *Morris*, a Chamber of the ECtHR had found that court martial proceedings violated the Article 6 right to a fair trial because there was insufficient protection for ordinary members of the court. Lord Rodger (with whom all their Lordships agreed) alluded to the very fact-specific nature of ECHR jurisprudence and rejected the argument that the House should necessarily follow recent ECHR case law, although such authority demanded 'careful attention'.[41] For whatever reason,

> the European Court was given rather less information than the House about the safeguards relating to the officers serving on courts-martial ... like the European Court, the House must have regard to all the relevant factual information presented to it when deciding whether the safeguards of the independence and impartiality of the members of the courts-martial were adequate.[42]

Subsequently, in *Cooper v United Kingdom*,[43] a Grand Chamber of the ECtHR resiled from *Morris*. The ECtHR itself has said that it must always be borne in mind that Convention obligations bind the state in international law and '[i]t is for the Respondent State, and the Respondent State alone to take the measures it considers appropriate to ensure that its domestic law is coherent and consistent'.[44] In *Alconbury*, Lord Hoffmann observed that Strasbourg jurisprudence should not compel the House of Lords to reach a conclusion 'fundamentally at odds with the distribution of powers under the British constitution'.[45] Thus, where Parliament has delegated power to determine where the public interest lies in the application of social and economic policy, it is for the appropriate body to make that decision subject to the requirement of legality as enforced through the principles of judicial review.

In a key development, *R (on the application of Ullah) v Special Adjudicator*,[46] Lord Bingham made the following widely cited observations with which all other members of the House agreed, and which have been subsequently approved:[47]

> In determining the present question, the House is required by s 2(1) of the Human Rights Act 1998 to take into account any relevant Strasbourg case law. While such case

---

[40] (2002) 34 EHRR 52.

[41] *Spear* (n 39) [29]. See also Arden LJ in *Ofulue v Bossert* [2008] EWCA Civ 7, [2009] Ch 1 when she stated that English courts might depart from Strasbourg if the Strasbourg Court had misunderstood the effect of domestic law.

[42] *Spear* (n 39) [66] (Lord Rodger).

[43] (2004) 39 EHRR 8.

[44] *Marckx v Belgium* (1979) 2 EHRR 330.

[45] *Alconbury* (n 37) [76] quoted by M Amos, *Human Rights Law*, 2nd edn (Oxford, Hart Publishing, 2014) 20.

[46] [2004] UKHL 26, [2004] 2 AC 323 at [20].

[47] *R (on the application of S) v Chief Constable of South Yorkshire Police* [2004] UKHL 39, [2004] 1 WLR 2196 [27] (Lord Steyn); *M v Secretary of State for Work and Pensions* [2006] UKHL 11, [2006] 2 AC 91 [129] (Lord Mance); *Whaley v Lord Advocate* [2007] UKHL 53, 2008 SC (HL) 107 [18] (Lord Hope); *R (on the application of Gentle) v Prime Minister* [2008] UKHL 20, [2008] 1 AC 1356 [56] (Baroness Hale); *Smith v Ministry of Defence* [2013] UKSC 41, [2013] 3 WLR 69 [43] (Lord Hope).

law is not strictly binding, it has been held that courts should, in the absence of some special circumstances, follow any clear and constant jurisprudence of the ECtHR: see *R (on the application of Alconbury Developments Ltd) v Secretary of State for the Environment, Transport and the Regions* [2001] UKHL 23 at [26], [2001] 2 All ER 929 at [26], [2003] 2 AC 295. This reflects the fact that the European Convention is an international instrument, the correct interpretation of which can be authoritatively expounded only by the ECtHR. From this it follows that a national court subject to a duty such as that imposed by s 2 should not without strong reason dilute or weaken the effect of the Strasbourg case law. It is indeed unlawful under s 6 of the 1998 Act for a public authority, including a court, to act in a way which is incompatible with a convention right. It is of course open to member states to provide for rights more generous than those guaranteed by the convention, but such provision should not be the product of interpretation of the convention by national courts, since the meaning of the convention should be uniform throughout the states party to it. The duty of national courts is to keep pace with the Strasbourg jurisprudence as it evolves over time: no more, but certainly no less.

This observation provoked criticism because it appeared to create a ceiling on the rights that can be recognised and enjoyed as a result of the HRA: echoing Masterman,[48] Lewis argued that the effect of Lord Bingham's *dictum* is that municipal rights must always match the content of rights as determined by the ECtHR such that treaty obligations are 'mirrored' in municipal law.[49] Further, he has argued that the 'mirror principle' originated in HRA section 2 and that the courts have effectively rewritten section 2 so that English courts are *bound* by Strasbourg jurisprudence, which is contrary to the 'intent and wording' of the HRA. He expressed concern that 'in most circumstances it is not realistically possible to provide more generous rights protection than by interpretation of the Convention' and that adopting a mirror principle is 'contrary to the modern relationship between the House of Lords and Strasbourg'. Further, he stated that: 'If domestic courts cannot fall behind Strasbourg jurisprudence and cannot overtake it, their only option is to stay in line with it. English human rights law finds itself to be nothing more than Strasbourg's shadow'.[50]

A number of points must be made. The concerns expressed regarding Lord Bingham's speech in *Ullah* failed to take account of the context in which the remarks were made. Amongst the most politically sensitive cases under the HRA are those based upon the *Soering*[51] line of authorities, relating to the extent of state jurisdiction under Article 1 of the ECHR, where the United Kingdom could potentially incur responsibility for ECHR violations as a result of sending/returning an individual to another state which is not a signatory to the ECHR. Thus, the United Kingdom could violate Article 3 of the ECHR if it were knowingly to hand over a person to a state where there are substantial grounds for believing that there is a

---

[48] R Masterman, 'Section 2(1)' [2004] *Public Law* 725.
[49] J Lewis, 'The European Ceiling on Human Rights' [2007] *Public Law* 720.
[50] *Ibid*, 730.
[51] *Soering v United Kingdom* (1989) 11 EHRR 439.

real risk of the person being subjected to torture or inhuman or degrading treatment or punishment. *Ullah* was about exactly this type of obligation: the question was what degree of risk of a violation should be shown, where the right engaged is other than Article 3, in the *Ullah* case Article 9 (freedom of religion), if a claimant is to avoid deportation. In *JJ*, Lord Brown pointed out that these remarks and indeed his own in *Al-Skeini*, related to the reach of Article 1 ECHR, 'an issue on which the ECtHR in *Bankovic* ... had made plain that the "living instrument" approach does not apply'.[52] In other words, the Strasbourg Court has taken what might be viewed as a conservative approach to 'jurisdiction' under Article 1. It goes without saying that the development of responsibility for extra-territorial acts and omissions[53] could lead to potential liability for the United Kingdom of significant proportions given the disparity in the levels of human rights protection throughout the world. It is hardly to be imagined that the English *courts* would in this context assume an obligation for the state over and above that which has been recognised by Strasbourg. This sentiment was endorsed by Baroness Hale in *R (on the application of Gentle) v Prime Minister*. A unanimous House denied that the procedural obligation inherent in Article 2 mandated an independent public inquiry into the lawfulness of the Iraq invasion, Baroness Hale observing that:

> Parliament is free to go further than Strasbourg if it wishes, but we are not free to foist upon Parliament or upon public authorities an interpretation of a Convention right which goes way beyond anything which we can reasonably foresee that Strasbourg might do.[54]

The criticism which has been levelled at the courts' approach to s 2 is also misplaced because it fails to take account of the explicit purpose of the HRA. It is not a freestanding domestic bill of rights; it is a statute, with potentially far reaching effects, but a statute and one that has a clear intention to secure for all those within the jurisdiction of the United Kingdom at least the level of protection that Strasbourg provides. While the HRA has been described as a constitutional statute,[55] its enactment was justified on the 'mundane' grounds set out in the White Paper which, as described above, focused on the practical expediency of being able to sue in the United Kingdom, as opposed to having to go to Strasbourg.[56]

---

[52] *Secretary of State for the Home Department v JJ* [2007] UKHL 45, [2008] 1 AC 385 [106].

[53] Raised in acute form in *N v Secretary of State for the Home Department* [2005] UKHL 31, [2005] 2 AC 296 where the claimant who had 'full blown AIDS' argued that returning her to Uganda would condemn her to a premature and painful death and entail a violation of the Article 3 right to be free from inhuman treatment by the UK. A unanimous House held that individuals could not claim an entitlement to remain in order to continue to benefit from medical assistance, save in exceptional circumstances, which did not apply here.

[54] *Gentle* (n 47) [56].

[55] *Brown v Stott* [2003] 1 AC 681, [2001] 2 WLR 817, 835 (Lord Bingham), quoted by R Clayton, 'Judicial Deference and "Democratic Dialogue": The Legitimacy of Judicial Intervention under the Human Rights Act 1998' [2004] *Public Law* 33.

[56] Clayton, *ibid*, 38.

The courts can of course go further than Strasbourg where such developments are consistent with the common law and where they are acting within the range of responses that Strasbourg would foreseeably make. It might be thought that this is a circular argument since the courts develop the common law; however, in a system of precedent they do not have a free rein and the House of Lords has confirmed that (subject to one very limited exception) the domestic principles of precedent apply so that English authority will prevail, even where there is conflicting Strasbourg authority directly on point that is subsequent to an English decision taken in response to the HRA.[57]

Rejection of the 'Mirror' Principle

Recent developments in our most senior courts have evinced an evolution towards rejection of the 'mirror' principle and have confirmed that rights under Schedule 1 of the HRA are different in kind from rights under the ECHR. For example in *Nicklinson*,[58] which concerned the compatibility of the criminalisation of assisted suicide under section 2(1) Suicide Act 1961 with Article 8 ECHR, Lord Neuberger confirmed Lord Hoffmann's view that rights under the HRA are domestic and not international. He went on to confirm the view previously expressed by their Lordships that where Strasbourg has declined to lay down an interpretation for all Member States as it does when it says that a matter is within the margin of appreciation, it is for national courts to decide the matter for themselves.[59]

There has been much debate as to whether English courts could go further in their development of rights under the HRA than the Strasbourg Court. In the most *Ullah* adherent authority, *Ambrose v Harris*,[60] the Supreme Court by a majority of 4:1, Lord Kerr dissenting, held that it was not for the Supreme Court to expand the scope of ECHR rights under the HRA further than the jurisprudence of the ECtHR justified. Previously, in *Cadder*,[61] the Supreme Court took account of *Salduz v Turkey*[62] and held that admissions obtained while being interviewed under detention without access to legal advice or a solicitor being present could not be admitted in evidence as this would be incompatible with Articles 6(1) and 6(3)(c). In *Ambrose*, the question was whether the right of access to a lawyer prior to police questioning as established in *Salduz* applied only to questioning when a person has actually been taken into custody. All the accused had been questioned and had given incriminating answers prior to being taken to a police station.

---

[57] *Kay v Lambeth LBC* [2006] UKHL 10, [2006] 2 AC 465.
[58] *R (Nicklinson) v Ministry of Justice* [2014] UKSC 38, [2015] AC 657.
[59] *In re G (Adoption: Unmarried Couple)* [2009] AC 173 [50] (Lord Hope), [116] to [120] (Baroness Hale), [130] (Lord Mance).
[60] [2011] UKSC 43, [2011] 1 WLR 2435.
[61] *Cadder v HM Advocate* [2010] UKSC 43, [2010] 1 WLR 2601.
[62] (2008) 49 EHRR 421.

All three accused had been charged at the time they were questioned as they were no longer merely witnesses but had become suspects. Self-incriminating answers would be admissible provided that they were truly voluntary. In the case of one of the accused, although he had not been taken into custody he was handcuffed so that the situation was sufficiently coercive for the incriminating answers to questions without legal advice not to be admissible. Since Strasbourg had not ruled that a suspect who was not yet in custody should have access to a lawyer in order to comply with Article 6, the Supreme Court refused to rule that any statements made were automatically incompatible with fair trial rights under Article 6. Rather, the fact that the suspect did not have access to legal advice should be taken into account in assessing the overall fairness of the proceedings.

However, in *Rabone v Pennine Care NHS Trust*,[63] in holding that the positive operational obligation under Article 2 extended to a voluntary patient who committed suicide while on a home leave visit, the Supreme Court went beyond the instances of protection so far recognised under Article 2 by the ECtHR; in so doing, Lord Dyson for a unanimous court, and in the absence of an all fours authority, drew upon general principles established by Strasbourg case law. In so doing, it must be observed that the careful scheme of the Fatal Accidents Act 1976 is potentially undermined in claims against public authorities under Article 6 for failure to act compatibly with the positive operational obligation under Article 2.[64] *Ambrose v Harris* was not cited or discussed in *Rabone*. Similarly, in *Smith v Ministry of Defence*,[65] the Supreme Court refused to strike out an Article 2 claim against the army based upon failure to provide adequate equipment even though what little Strasbourg authority there is arguably points against such claims. These authorities are discussed in detail in Chapter 4.

Given the lack of a doctrine of precedent at Strasbourg, the fact that whether cases are taken to Strasbourg is contingent upon the extent to which ECHR rights are protected at national level, as well as the nature of the margin of appreciation doctrine, a slavish adherence to Strasbourg case law is clearly inappropriate. The words of former Registrar to the Court, Paul Mahoney, are prescient:

> The national judge will rarely, if ever, find in the [Strasbourg] jurisprudence the concrete answer to the particular case being adjudicated on. Rather, to the extent that it elucidates the relevant criteria for setting and using the analytical 'weighing scales' necessary for effecting the balancing exercise in different kinds of situations, the [Strasbourg] jurisprudence provides the domestic courts … with authoritative guidance. The broad conclusion on the effect of the [Strasbourg] jurisprudence for national judges is that it is to be treated, not as a series of specific precedents for a limited number of applications of the [Convention] safeguards in particular, given contexts, but as a source of guidance as to the philosophy, values or considerations to be weighed in the balance by national courts

[63] [2012] UKSC 2, [2012] AC 72.
[64] J Wright, 'The Operational Obligation under Article 2 of the ECHR and Challenges for Coherence—Views from the English Supreme Court and Strasbourg' (2016) 7 *Journal of Tort Law* 58.
[65] [2013] UKSC 41, [2013] 3 WLR 69.

when applying their own domestic law. Principles not precedents … [The] interpretative jurisprudence does not furnish anything like a detailed blueprint calling for rigorous and uniform application throughout the [Convention] community of participating countries. As regards both the regulatory framework and, above all, the outcome in individual cases, the scope for different solutions deemed appropriate for each [Convention] country remains, provided that the relevant [Convention] values and considerations are in substance integrated into the national analysis.[66]

Section 2 and the Doctrine of Precedent

The interplay of section 2 HRA with the doctrine of precedent has presented challenges for English courts. Where our senior courts have adopted a position that is inconsistent with a subsequent ECtHR decision, there is the possibility for two conflicting bodies of rules. The answer in such a case is for the lower court to grant a leapfrog certificate for appeal to the Supreme Court.[67]

In the 1966 Practice Direction, the House of Lords stated that it would in appropriate circumstances feel free to depart from its previous decisions. The Supreme Court will depart from its own decisions when they are contradicted by subsequent decisions of the Strasbourg Court, subject to the observations made above regarding the weight that the Supreme Court attributes to the ECHR jurisprudence. It is unlikely that the Supreme Court would decline to follow the clear and constant jurisprudence of the Grand Chamber at Strasbourg, especially in a case where the Court has recognised limited or no margin of appreciation.

However, the doctrine of precedent continues to apply to lower courts so that they are bound to follow decisions of the House of Lords and Supreme Court notwithstanding subsequent contradictory Strasbourg decisions, unless exceptional circumstances exist. The 'extreme' circumstances established by Lord Bingham in *Kay v Lambeth Borough Council*[68] were:

(i)   the effect of the HRA was to undermine the policy considerations that underpinned the relevant House of Lords' authority;
(ii)   judgment was given before the HRA came into force;
(iii)   no reference was made to the ECHR in any of the opinions; and
(iv)   the very children who lost their claim in negligence before the House of Lords succeeded in establishing a breach of Article 3 and received substantial reparation.[69]

---

[66] P Mahoney (UK judge of the ECtHR and former Registrar of the Court), 'The Relationship between the Strasbourg Court and the National Courts' (2014) *Law Quarterly Review* 568–86, 579.

[67] See for example *Miller v Associated Newspapers Ltd* [2016] EWHC 397, discussed in Chapter 7, text accompanying (n 139).

[68] [2006] UKHL 20, [2006] 2 AC 465.

[69] *X (Minors) v Bedfordshire County Council* [1995] 2 AC 633, *Z v United Kingdom* (n 30).

The Excluded Rights

Two rights were excluded from Schedule 1 of the HRA: Article 1, according to which states agree to 'secure to everyone within the jurisdiction the rights and freedoms set out', and Article 13 which provides that 'everyone whose rights and freedoms are violated shall have an effective remedy before a national authority notwithstanding that the violation has been committed by persons acting in an official capacity'. The scope of Article 1 has assumed a significance that was not anticipated during the legislative process. We have now reached a position where a person (who may or may not be a UK citizen since Article 1 confers rights on 'everyone' within the jurisdiction) outside the territories of both the United Kingdom and the Council of Europe Member States may have standing before the English courts where he can claim to be a victim of an act that is unlawful under the HRA and which has occurred outside those territories. The following discussion will therefore set out the extent of jurisdiction under the HRA.

Article 1—Jurisdiction

The leading English case on jurisdiction under Article 1 is the Supreme Court decision in *Smith v Ministry of Defence*[70] which confirms that the correct interpretation of the Convention can only be expounded by the ECtHR and that the duty of English courts is to keep pace with the European Court so that the reach of Article 1 under English law is co-extensive with the scope of the obligations imposed upon the United Kingdom by the ECHR. Thus, in terms of interpretation, Article 1 is different from the rights set out in Schedule 1 to the HRA as to which our jurisprudence is still evolving and the 'living instrument' approach does not apply.[71]

In *Smith*, which consisted of three consolidated appeals, the claimants brought claims against the Ministry of Defence (MOD) in both negligence and for breach of Article 2 under the HRA, based upon the defendant's failure to provide suitably protective equipment (the so-called Snatch Land Rover cases) to soldiers on active service in Iraq. The MOD argued that the Article 2 claims were bound to fail because the deaths occurred outside the United Kingdom's jurisdiction. In deciding that the soldiers were within the jurisdiction for the purposes of the HRA, the Supreme Court drew upon the leading Strasbourg authority, *Al-Skeini v United Kingdom*,[72] which concerned claims arising from the deaths of Iraqi citizens at the hands of British forces in Basra. That case related to the deaths of six civilians in Basra in 2003 while the UK was an occupying power. Five claims were brought in

---

[70] *Smith* (n 65).
[71] *Smith* (n 65) [44] (Lord Hope).
[72] *Al-Skeini* (n 36). For discussion, see M Milanovic, '*Al-Skeini* and *Al-Jedda* in Strasbourg' (2012) *European Journal of International Law* 23(1) 121–39.

relation to deaths in the field; the sixth concerned the death of a civilian who had been arrested and taken to a British base where he had met an extremely violent death.

The Grand Chamber confirmed that jurisdiction is primarily territorial but 'acts of the Contracting States performed, or producing effects, outside their territories can constitute an exercise of jurisdiction in exceptional cases'.[73] The Grand Chamber confirmed that there are two distinct categories of exceptional case which are, first, state agent authority and control and, second, effective control of an area.

State Agent Authority and Control

This principle has three aspects. First, it will include the acts of diplomatic and consular agents, who are present on foreign territory in accordance with the provisions of international law. Second, the Court has also recognised the exercise of extra-territorial jurisdiction by a Contracting State when, through the consent, invitation or acquiescence of the government of that territory, it exercises some or all of the public powers which would normally be exercised by that government. Finally, the Court's case law demonstrates that in certain circumstances the use of force by a state's agents operating outside its territory may bring the individual under the control of the state's authorities into the state's Article 1 jurisdiction. It is important to note that what is decisive here is the exercise of physical power and control over the person in question.[74] This observation helps to explain why the ECtHR did not formally overrule *Bankovic v Belgium* in *Al-Skeini*.

The application in *Bankovic* was brought against the 17 NATO and Council of Europe Member States which were responsible for an air strike on the offices of Serbian national radio during the Kosovan war in 1999 by relatives of journalists killed. The applicants argued the victims had been within the 'effective control' of the respondent states because the military aircraft and their bombs were under the complete control of the respondents. In *Bankovic*, the European Court of Human Rights held that Article 1 essentially reflects a territorial notion of jurisdiction.[75]

In *Al-Skeini*, the fact of governmental control indicated the exercise of authority and control within Article 1. Following the removal from power of the previous regime on 1 May 2003, and until the transfer of authority to the Interim Government on 28 June 2004, the United Kingdom and the United States had been the occupying powers in Iraq and had assumed the exercise of some of the public powers normally exercised by a sovereign government. The United Kingdom

---

[73] *Al-Skeini* (n 36) [131].
[74] *Al-Skeini* (n 36) [136].
[75] *Bankovic v Belgium* (2007) 44 EHRR SE5.

in particular had assumed authority and responsibility for maintaining security and supporting the civil administration in the province in South-East Iraq. The ECtHR held that:

> In those exceptional circumstances the United Kingdom, through its soldiers engaged in security operations in that area during the relevant period, had exercised authority and control over individuals killed in the course of those security operations, so as to establish a jurisdictional link between the deceased and the United Kingdom for the purposes of Article 1. In particular, it was undisputed that the deaths of the relatives of the first, second and fourth to sixth applicants had been caused by the acts of British soldiers during the course of security operations. It followed that in all those cases there had existed a jurisdictional link between the United Kingdom and the deceased for the purposes of Article 1. The third applicant's wife had been killed during an exchange of fire between a patrol of British soldiers and unidentified gunmen and it was not known which side had fired the fatal bullet. However, since the death had occurred in the course of a UK security operation, during which British soldiers had taken part in the fatal exchange of fire, there had likewise existed a jurisdictional link between the United Kingdom and the wife of the third applicant.[76]

Further:

> It is clear that, whenever the State through its agents exercises control and authority over an individual, and thus jurisdiction, the State is under an obligation under Article 1 to secure to that individual the rights and freedoms under Section 1 of the Convention that are relevant to the situation of that individual. In this sense, the Convention rights can be divided and tailored.[77]

The ECtHR found that the United Kingdom exercised jurisdiction in relation to all six claimants through the authority and control that was exercised through its soldiers and the exercise of powers of government. In *Bankovic*, the ECtHR had suggested that for jurisdiction to follow, a state should be in a position to deliver the full package of rights set out in the ECHR—*Al-Skeini* makes it clear this is not the case. It is different where the state exercises control over territory—in that case the package of rights should not be divided and tailored because in principle there is no reason why all rights should not be secured to the population.

Effective Control over an Area

Where a Contracting State has established effective control over territory as a result of military action, whether lawful or unlawful, different consequences will

---

[76] *Al-Skeini* (n 36) [149] to [150].
[77] *Ibid.*

follow. The state will, in relation to the territory under its control, have responsibility to secure the entire range of rights set out in the ECHR.[78]

Smith v MOD—Application of Al-Skeini by the Supreme Court

Lord Hope's application of the *Al-Skeini* principles in *Smith* bears detailed discussion. Lord Hope, giving the leading judgment, noted that the United Kingdom has just as much authority and control over its armed forces when serving abroad as when in the United Kingdom. In terms of *Al-Skeini*, the relevant category of jurisdictional competence under Article 1 is state agent authority and control. There was no effective control over territory. The military presence in Iraq in 2005 and 2006 was to provide security and help with reconstruction and the local administration was in the hands of the Iraqi Government.[79]

The question that arises is whether the United Kingdom had jurisdiction over citizens of Iraq (*Smith* was a claim brought by *British* service personnel) *after* the hand-over of power to the Iraqi Government—the ECtHR had emphasised the element of public powers in *Al-Skeini*, such powers would seem to be lacking in *Smith*.

Application Beyond the Armed Forces?

In *Smith*, the claimants were members of the armed forces who sought redress for failures by the British Government to protect their right to life and they were held to be within the jurisdiction under the HRA. In *Al-Skeini*, claims had been brought by Iraqi nationals and jurisdiction was founded upon the exercise of powers of government. The obvious question is what would be the position in relation to a claim by a national of a state in which the United Kingdom is giving security assistance, but where there is no effective control of an area, no exercise of governmental power and where the military cause the death of a national arguably in violation of Article 2 but outside an army security base. There is no direct precedent but *Al-Skeini* and *Smith* certainly point in favour of jurisdiction under the HRA. At the time of writing, proposals for a British Bill of Rights are still awaited. The former Justice Minister indicated that such a Bill would put a gloss on the rights and responsibilities of the military when serving abroad, so it seems highly likely that an attempt will be made to clarify and limit the effect of *Al-Skeini*.[80]

We shall now move on to consider the mediation of ECHR rights into English law through the HRA, beginning with the section 3 obligation.

[78] *Al-Skeini* (n 36) [136].
[79] *Smith* (n 65) [31] (Lord Hope).
[80] For criticism of the application of *Al-Skeini* to the battlefield, see *Mohammed Serdar v MOD* [2015] EWCA Civ 843, [2016] 2 WLR 247.

The Section 3 Interpretative Obligation

Section 3(1) HRA provides that, 'So far as it is possible to do so, primary legislation and subordinate legislation must be read and given effect in a way which is compatible with the Convention rights'.[81] The doctrine of implied repeal is excluded by section 3(2) which states that section 3 does not affect the validity of any incompatible primary or subordinate legislation. Where a court determines that a provision in primary legislation is incompatible with a Convention right, it *may* make a declaration of that incompatibility (section 4). Section 4 gives the senior courts[82] a power to issue a declaration of incompatibility where they are satisfied a provision is incompatible with a Convention right. Thus, the court has a discretion whether to make a declaration of incompatibility.[83] Such a declaration does not affect the validity, continuing operation or enforcement of the provision in respect of which it is made and is not binding on the parties to the proceedings in which it is made.[84]

The declaration of incompatibility has been described as a measure of last resort.[85] According to the Seventh Report of the Joint Committee on Human Rights, there is a significant downward trend in declarations of incompatibility with only three being made during Parliament 2010–15, with a total of 29 in the period from 2 October 2000 to March 2015.[86]

It is clear that the Act imposes a strong interpretative obligation upon the courts, 'So far as it is possible ....'.[87] The White Paper acknowledged that the drafting goes far beyond the rule hitherto applied that the courts could resort to the Convention in order to resolve ambiguity in legislation. The section applies to all legislation, whether enacted before or after the Act, and makes no distinction between public and private bodies. The leading authority on the interpretation of legislation remains *Ghaidan v Godin-Mendoza*[88] where the Court held, pursuant to section 3 HRA, that it was possible to give effect to paragraph 2 of Schedule 2 to the Rent Act 1977 in a way that was compatible with the Convention rights by reading it as extending to persons living with the original tenant as if they were his or her wife or husband, with the result that the defendant's longstanding homosexual relationship with the original tenant allowed him to succeed to the tenancy. This

---

[81] The following discussion draws upon Wright (n 18).

[82] According to s 4(5) 'court' means the Supreme Court, the Judicial Committee of the Privy Council, the Courts-Martial Appeal Court, in Scotland the High Court of Judiciary sitting otherwise than as a trial court or the Court of Session and the High Court and the Court of Appeal in England and Northern Ireland.

[83] *Nicklinson* (n 58).

[84] Section 4(6) HRA.

[85] *R v A* [2001] UKHL 25, [2002] 1 AC 45 [44] (Lord Steyn).

[86] Human Rights Joint Committee Seventh Report, www.parliament.uk, 11 March 2015 [4.1].

[87] *R v Director of Public Prosecutions, ex p Kebilene* [1999] 3 WLR 972 (Lord Steyn and Lord Cooke).

[88] [2004] UKHL 30, [2004] 2 AC 557.

obviously was an action between non-state actors and the rule in section 3(1) was applied without any consideration of the fact that neither party before the Court was a public authority. It is instructive to review *Ghaidan* to tease out the limits to interpretation.

Lord Rodger described the broad sweep of section 3(1) as crucial to the workings of the 1998 Act and pointed out that it applies whenever legislation must be interpreted, so that whenever a public authority is considering its obligations under legislation, compliance with ECHR rights should be sought. Lord Nicholls stated that:

> Section 3 enables language to be interpreted restrictively or expansively. But section 3 goes further than this. It is also apt to require a court to read in words which change the meaning of the enacted legislation so as to make it Convention-compliant. In other words the intention of Parliament in enacting section 3 was that, to an extent bounded only by what is 'possible' a court can modify the meaning, and hence the effect, of primary and secondary legislation.[89]

Lord Steyn urged a purposive approach:

> The second factor may be an excessive concentration on linguistic features of the particular statute. Nowhere in our legal system is a literalistic approach more inappropriate than when considering whether a breach of a Convention right may be removed by interpretation under section 3. Section 3 requires a broad approach concentrating, amongst other things in a purposive way on the importance of the fundamental right involved.[90]

Lord Rodger stated that when the court spells out the words that are to be implied, it may look as if it is 'amending' the legislation, but that is not the case. If the court implies words that are consistent with the scheme of the legislation but necessary to make it compatible with Convention rights, it is simply performing the duty which Parliament has imposed on it and on others. It is reading the legislation in a way that draws out the full implications of its terms and of the Convention rights. By its very nature, an implication will go with the grain of the legislation. By contrast, using a Convention right to read in words that are inconsistent with the scheme of the legislation or with its essential principles as disclosed by its provisions does not involve any form of interpretation, by implication or otherwise. It falls on the wrong side of the boundary between interpretation and amendment of the statute.

Thus, the courts cannot in their section 3 role go against the grain of legislation as demonstrated by *R (Anderson) v Secretary of State for the Home Department*. The House of Lords was satisfied that section 29 Crime (Sentences) Act 1997 which gave power to the Home Secretary to recommend release on licence of life prisoners, was incompatible with ECHR rights. However, in the words of Lord Bingham, to preclude such participation by the Home Secretary would not be

---

[89] *Ibid* [32].
[90] *Ibid* [41].

'judicial interpretation but judicial vandalism'.[91] Lord Bingham had regard to the well-known words of Lord Nicholls of Birkenhead in *In re S (Minors) (Care Order: Implementation of Care Plan)*,[92] where the relevant distinction between interpreting and legislating is drawn:

> The Human Rights Act reserves the amendment of primary legislation to Parliament. By this means the Act seeks to preserve parliamentary sovereignty. The Act maintains the constitutional boundary. Interpretation of statutes is a matter for the courts; the enactment of statutes, and the amendment of statutes, are matters for Parliament.

The approach that English courts should take to statutory interpretation under section 3 HRA is not free from difficulty. The attitude English courts must take towards Strasbourg case law is constrained by the obligation in section 3: 'so far as it is possible to do so, primary and subordinate legislation must be read and given effect in a way which is compatible with the Convention rights'. It is implicit that not all legislation can be rendered compatible with the Convention rights. While section 3 is the prime remedial remedy, it is not clear what 'test is to be applied in separating the sheep from the goats'.[93]

The question arises whether English courts are free to go beyond the confines of Strasbourg case law in determining what the content of the rights is. Alluding to Baroness Hale, what are the 'Convention rights' for the purposes of the 1998 Act?[94] As we have seen, several of our most senior judges have emphasised that the rights in the HRA are domestic rights, and logically, therefore, it would seem that there should not be a ceiling on the rights enjoyed.[95] In *Re P (Adoption: Unmarried Couple)*, Baroness Hale held expressly that Parliament had intended that the courts should be able to develop a human rights jurisprudence beyond the level of protection afforded by Strasbourg.[96] In *Begum v Tower Hamlets LBC*, Laws LJ described the Court's task as not simply being,

> to add on the Strasbourg learning to the corpus of English law as if it were a compulsory adjunct from an alien source, but to develop a municipal law of human rights by the incremental method of the common law, taking account of Strasbourg jurisprudence.[97]

On the other hand, the HRA was drafted in order to preserve the sovereignty of Parliament and s 3 represents an incursion on that sovereignty to the extent that the original intent of Parliament may be thwarted. As Lord Nicholls cautioned in *Re S*, s 3 is concerned with 'interpretation' and the HRA preserves the constitutional boundary so that 'interpretation' is a matter for the courts; 'enactment' and 'amendment' are matters for Parliament.[98] Further, he stated that 'a meaning

---

[91] [2003] 1 AC 837, 883 [30].
[92] [2002] 2 AC 291.
[93] *Ghaidan* (n 88).
[94] *Re P* (n 13) [116] (Baroness Hale).
[95] *Re P* [33] (Lord Hoffmann), with whose speech Lord Hope and Lord Mance expressed agreement.
[96] *Re P* [119].
[97] *Begum* (n 11) [17].
[98] *Re S (Minors)* [2002] UKHL 10, [2002] 2 AC 291 [39], to the same effect Lord Hope [108].

which departs substantially from a fundamental feature of an Act of Parliament is likely to have crossed the boundary between interpretation and amendment' and 'when a court [interprets legislation under s 3] it is important the court should identify clearly the particular statutory provision ... whose interpretation leads to that result'.[99] In *Anderson*,[100] the House of Lords concluded that the power of the Home Secretary, rather than a judicial body, to order release on licence of convicted murderers, was incompatible with Article 6 ECHR. However, it was not possible to read section 29 of the Crime (Sentences) Act 1997 as precluding participation by the Home Secretary as this would amount to 'judicial vandalism', removing the 'very core and essence, the 'pith and substance' of the measure' and section 3 did not give the courts power to go that far.[101]

The judiciary has used the techniques of 'reading in' and 'reading down' in order to achieve Convention-compatibility under section 3.[102] It is difficult to predict when courts will use the power of interpretation under section 3, rather than issuing a declaration of incompatibility under section 4. The extent to which English courts will use their powers under section 3 to take legislation outside the ambit of the original parliamentary intention seems to depend upon a number of factors: first, whether the right in question is expressed in unqualified terms; second, whether the scope of the right has been determined by Strasbourg, in which case it is likely that English courts will follow that jurisprudence, particularly if the case law is clear and consistent;[103] where there is no case law on the issue in question, or it is a matter that Strasbourg has determined falls within the national margin of appreciation, then English courts will come to their own view. The Article 6 right to a fair trial, which is expressed in absolute terms (although the constituent elements embodied in Article 6(1) are not in themselves absolute), has generated a number of decisions where the courts have been prepared to revise (arguably to the point of emasculation in *R v A (No 2)*) the import of legislation in order to secure a fair trial,[104] through the application of general principles developed by Strasbourg, and in the absence of authority 'on all fours'[105] with the English decisions. The notion of a 'ceiling' on rights in these cases is completely without foundation.

---

[99] *Ibid* [40] and [41].

[100] *Anderson* (n 38).

[101] *Ghaidan* (n 88) [111] (Lord Hope).

[102] For example, *R v Lambert* [2001] UKHL 37, [2002] 2 AC 545; *R v A (No 2)* [2001] UKHL 25, [2002] 1 AC 45 discussed by A Kavanagh, 'Judging the Judges' [2009] Public Law 287, esp 298.

[103] Somewhat bizarrely, the lack of any authority under Article 5 ECHR on facts comparable to the control order litigation led Lord Carswell to observe that the House should be cautious before departing from the current Strasbourg case law, but without ever identifying precisely what that current case law is or how it could be applied: *JJ* (n 52) [83].

[104] *R v Lambert* (n 102); *R v A (No 2)* (n 102).

[105] *Secretary of State for the Home Department v MB and AF* [2007] UKHL 46, [2008] 1 AC 440 (Baroness Hale).

In *B v Secretary of State for the Home Department*,[106] the House of Lords considered whether immigration appellate authorities acting under section 65 of the Asylum and Immigration Act 1999 should take account of the impact of proposed removal from the United Kingdom on all those who share the applicant's family life, or its impact on the appellant only. In concluding that the expansive view is to be preferred, there is a brief discussion of Strasbourg case law, but no sense of obligation to achieve slavish adherence to another body of jurisprudence. Lord Brown, giving judgment for a unanimous court, cited with approval *Huang v Secretary of State for the Home Department*: 'The main importance of the [Strasbourg] case law is in illuminating the core value which Article 8 exists to protect'.[107] Similar observations can be made regarding *R (on the application of Laporte) v Chief Constable of Gloucestershire*, where the House of Lords found that the interception of coaches carrying demonstrators bound for Fairford air base and their subsequent forced return to London constituted a violation of the Article 11 right to freedom of assembly. Lord Bingham was highly critical of the police conduct and argued forcefully that if the police required more extensive powers to control demonstrations, they should be the product of legislative enactment, rather than judicial decision.[108]

An illustration of the difference that relevant Strasbourg authority may make is afforded by two House of Lords' decisions: *M v Secretary of State for Work and Pensions*[109] and *Re P*.[110] Where it is argued that legislation should be interpreted in a way that is clearly at odds with the 'original' intention of Parliament as manifested in the relevant legislation, courts have regarded their role with caution and have sought an interpretation within the limits of relevant ECHR jurisprudence. It could be argued that this approach is consistent with the need to resist assuming the mantle of a legislator. Parliament intended to preserve its own sovereignty and as a matter of statutory interpretation it might be thought that the courts cannot go beyond the scope of the rights as they have been interpreted by Strasbourg. This was the view of the majority in the House of Lords in *M v Secretary of State for Work and Pensions*. The House refused to recast the Child Support (Maintenance Assessments and Special Cases) Regulations 1992[111] so that gay couples were assessed for contributions in the same way as heterosexual couples. In that case, M, a non-resident mother, lived with a partner of the same sex and they owned a house with a mortgage for which they were both responsible. Under the Regulations, her partner's contribution to the mortgage was treated as reducing her deductible housing costs with the effect that her child support contribution

---

[106] *B* [2008] UKHL 39, [2009] 1 AC 315.
[107] *Huang v Secretary of State for the Home Department* [2007] UKHL 11, [2007] 2 AC 167 [186].
[108] *R (on the application of Laporte) v Chief Constable of Gloucestershire* [2006] UKHL55, [2007] 2 AC 105 [52].
[109] *M v Secretary of State for Work and Pensions* (n 47).
[110] *Re P* (n 13).
[111] SI 1992/1815.

was greater than it would have been if she had been in a heterosexual relationship. M appealed against the assessment of child support on the ground that her situation fell within the ambit of the protection given to the rights to respect for private and family life by Article 8 and that she had suffered discrimination contrary to Article 14.

By a majority (Baroness Hale dissenting), the Lords held that the right to private life was not engaged and that according to the present state of Strasbourg jurisprudence[112] homosexual relationships did not fall within the scope of the right to respect for family life protected by Article 8 and that the respect afforded to those relationships was within the scope of the margin of appreciation afforded to states. The Regulations had in fact been amended by the Civil Partnership Act 2004 and the House considered that they had represented accepted societal values at the time. Baroness Hale delivered a strongly worded dissent in which she commended the UK Government for passing the Civil Partnership Act 2004 and putting an end to the discriminatory treatment of same-sex couples. But, she went on to say, 'can this be an objective justification for not having recognised it sooner?' She did not see how it could be; however, the 'rightness' of state conduct is not the test by which legislation is evaluated: section 3 only tests for compatibility with the Convention rights and on these facts the House of Lords found that the United Kingdom was not wanting according to Strasbourg standards.

Lewis suggested[113] that the decision in *M* is difficult to reconcile with their Lordships' earlier decision in *Ghaidan v Godin-Mendoza*.[114] However, in *Ghaidan* it was accepted by all parties that the Article 8 right to respect for the home (rather than family life) was engaged, so as Lord Mance was at pains to point out in *M*, there is no inconsistency. In *M*, their Lordships found that Strasbourg had rejected the recognition of homosexual relationships as falling within the concept of family life in *Mata Estevez*[115] on the basis that, as there was still little common ground between the Contracting States, this is an area where states still enjoy a wide margin of appreciation. Thus, the ECtHR had had the opportunity to eliminate discrimination between heterosexual and homosexual couples and had declined to do so. There was therefore authority denying the claimant's claim and the House of Lords can be seen to defer to the judgment of Parliament.

In complete contrast with *M*, however, the view that Strasbourg jurisprudence is a straightjacket was firmly rejected in *Re P*.[116] The applicants were a man and woman living together in a stable relationship since before the birth of the woman's daughter. According to Article 14 of the Adoption (Northern Ireland) Order 1987,[117] joint applications to adopt a child could only be made by a married couple.

---

[112] *Mata Estevez v Spain* Reports of Judgments and Decisions 2001-VI, 311.
[113] Lewis (n 49).
[114] *Ghaidan* (n 88).
[115] *Mata Estevez* (n 112).
[116] *Re P* (n 13).
[117] SI 1987/2203.

The applicants sought a declaration that Article 14 of the Order was incompatible with their rights under Articles 8 and 14 of the ECHR and that their application to adopt should be considered; by a 4:1 majority (Lord Walker dissenting) the House of Lords agreed.

The decision is a determined negation of any 'mirror' principle and an assertion of the obligation on UK courts to give effect to the 'domestic rights' set out in the HRA. Their Lordships took the view that the rights set out in the HRA are domestic and not international (not the same as ECHR rights) and should be interpreted according to their proper meaning as in the case of any other statutory right.[118] There was (surprisingly) no Strasbourg authority directly on point regarding whether unmarried couples constitute a family for the purposes of Article 8, but taking account of recent developments regarding the rights of homosexuals not to suffer discrimination in the adoption process, in particular the effective overruling of *Fretté v France*[119] in *EB v France*,[120] the House considered it not at all unlikely that Strasbourg would hold that discrimination against an unmarried couple wishing to adopt would violate Article 14.[121] In *Fretté*, a Chamber of the ECtHR had held that it was within the margin of appreciation allowed to the state to discriminate against homosexual applicants as adoptive parents. The majority in the House also considered that even if the ECtHR were to revert to its position in *Fretté* that would mean the determination of who may adopt is within the state's margin of appreciation. Thus, given that the determination regarding who may adopt is within the state's margin of appreciation, English courts can come to their own view regarding the scope of Article 14. The effect of this decision is that English applicants will be able to claim rights under the HRA that have not been recognised explicitly by Strasbourg (because they fall within the margin of appreciation). Herring has suggested that the effect of *P* is that there are rights under the *ECHR* (emphasis added) that can be claimed in English law, which have not been recognised by the ECtHR.[122] Technically, this is not quite correct; they are 'Convention rights' under the HRA. The case does not resolve the larger question of the extent to which the court, rather than the legislature, should be able to take decisions that fall within the margin of appreciation accorded to the state.

There is an obvious conflict between the reasoning in *M* and *Re P*. Given that in *M* there was authority stating that whether or not a same sex couple constitutes a 'family' is within a state's margin of appreciation, the House of Lords could, if they had taken the same approach as in *Re P*, have found for the claimant. In *M*, it seems to have been material that the law had in fact been changed by the Civil Partnership Act 2004, so that the discrimination would no longer exist, and the House took the view that the law as previously stated was considered to have

[118] *Re P* (n 13) [27] (Lord Hoffmann).
[119] (2002) 38 EHRR 438.
[120] (2008) 47 EHRR 21.
[121] *Re P* (n 13) [27] (Lord Hoffmann).
[122] J Herring, 'Who Decides?' (2009) 125 *Law Quarterly Review* 1, 4.

been within the state's margin of appreciation at the relevant time. The House was perceptibly concerned not to step into the legislator's role. In a similar vein, *Bellinger*[123] can be seen as an authority for the proposition that where legislation to remedy incompatibility is perceived to be forthcoming, the court is less likely to act under section 3. In that case, the Government had announced its intention to bring forward primary legislation to allow transsexual people to marry in their new gender. The decision in *Re P* can be seen as an example of English courts adopting an evolutive approach to interpretation of the HRA rights, a technique frequently employed by the ECtHR.

In conclusion, we can see that over the period of the HRA, our senior courts have proceeded with caution, initially anxious to 'mirror' Strasbourg, lest they should assume the mantle of legislator. This caution has given way to a willingness to treat the ECHR as a floor of rights and to extend the ambit of rights under the HRA. As we observed in the *Introduction*, the opposite tendency is discernible in relation to the issue of judicial extension of liability of public authorities under the common law, which manifests a rather less 'activist' judiciary, despite the growing clamour from the judiciary not to neglect common law rights.

The extent to which the rights set out in Schedule 1 HRA would bind non-state actors provoked much debate before the Act came into force. The following section will address this important question, beginning with the impact of section 3.

Horizontality—The Impact of the HRA on Non-State Actors

An interesting feature of the academic debates that surrounded the legislative journey of the HRA was a preoccupation with the extent to which the HRA would have horizontal effect and thereby impact on legal relationships between non-state actors as a result of the court's obligation in section 6(1) HRA not to act in a way which is incompatible with the Convention rights. With the benefit of hindsight, the intense focus on the common law and the court's obligation under section 6 now seems disproportionate; arguably, the real power of the HRA to transform legal relations between non-state actors lies in the interpretative obligation enshrined in section 3.

The structure of the HRA allows for the possibility for the rights in Schedule 1 HRA to be mediated into the relationships between non-state actors in three ways: first, the interpretative obligation in section 3 applies to all primary and subordinate legislation; second, section 6(1) provides that 'it is unlawful for a public authority to act in a way which is incompatible with a Convention right'; and, finally, section 12(4) obliges the court to have particular regard to the importance

---

[123] *Bellinger v Bellinger* (n 22).

of the Convention right to freedom of expression if it is considering whether to grant any relief which, if granted, might affect the exercise of the Convention right to freedom of expression. The following section will discuss each of these issues in turn.

As we have seen, initially, there was a tendency to treat Strasbourg case law as a 'ceiling' when determining the content of Convention rights, especially in cases concerning legislation.[124] The discussion above demonstrates that English courts have recognised that the Convention rights effected by the HRA are domestic rights and therefore legitimately to be fleshed out as domestic rights, informed by, but unfettered, by Strasbourg case law. The question arises as to whether it makes any difference to section 3 interpretation that the parties before the courts are private actors. There is nothing on the face of the HRA itself to suggest that this should be so and our most senior courts have confirmed that the section 3 obligation applies to all legislation. Whether ECHR rights impact on private actors will depend upon, first, whether Convention rights are applicable.[125] The relevant questions are, first, whether the relevant facts engage Convention rights and second whether the Convention imposes an obligation on the state to secure the rights as between private persons.

In *X v Y*,[126] the claimant argued that his dismissal was unfair and in violation of his rights under the Employment Rights Act 1998 and the HRA. The claimant who was employed as a development officer with the probation service in a position of responsibility and trust accepted a caution for a sex offence in a public lavatory. Having confirmed that the Employment Rights Act 1998 and all other legislation is subject to the section 3 obligation, a unanimous Court of Appeal held that the Article 8 right to respect for private life was not engaged on the facts; the claimant had no reasonable expectation of privacy and the facts found did not therefore fall within the ambit of Article 8. The Court held that,

> in many cases it would be difficult to draw, let alone justify, a distinction between public authority and private employers. In the case of such a basic employment right there would normally be no sensible grounds for treating public and private employers differently in respect of unfair dismissal, especially in these times of widespread contracting-out by public authorities to private contractors.[127]

Mummery LJ was clear that in the case of a private employer, section 3 HRA is more relevant than section 6 as section 3 draws no distinction between legislation governing public authorities and legislation governing private individuals. The effect of the section 6 obligation on the court is to reinforce the extremely

---

[124] Jan Van Zyl Smit, 'Statute Law: Interpretation and Declarations of Incompatibility' in D Hoffmann (ed), *The Impact of the UK Human Rights Act on Private Law* (Cambridge, Cambridge University Press, 2011).

[125] G Phillipson, 'Clarity Postponed: Horizontal Effect after *Campbell*' in H Fenwick, R Masterman and G Phillipson (eds), *Judicial Reasoning under the UK Human Rights Act* (Cambridge, Cambridge University Press, 2007) 150, discussed by Smit, *ibid*, 69.

[126] [2004] EWCA Civ 662, [2004] ICR 1634.

[127] *Ibid* (Mummery LJ).

strong interpretative obligation imposed on the employment tribunal by section 3.[128]

An issue that has generated much uncertainty and litigation is the role that ECHR rights play in relation to property/right to respect for the home disputes where a landlord who may be public or private seeks possession of a property after the termination of a tenancy. It is beyond the scope of this work to address in detail the full panoply of case law and readers' attention is drawn to the voluminous literature on the subject.[129] Clearly, the application of human rights in the context of property and housing rights has the potential to disturb established distributions of property interest. Howell was moved to remark that, in the context of land law, 'the introduction of human rights values is a wild card which is wholly unpredictable in effect'.[130] For the sake of the present discussion what is important to try to discover is the extent to which the ECHR has been horizontally applicable; to the extent that general principles can be drawn out, they can of course be susceptible of wider application in factual situations outside the context of Article 8 rights. The role of the court under section 6 is critical to the horizontal effect debate, a fact which Mummery LJ will have been only too aware in *X v Y*, when he limited section 6 to being confirmatory of the obligation under section 3 HRA. So what does the jurisprudence regarding section 3, section 6 and Article 8 tell us?

First, in as we have seen in *Ghaidan v Godin-Mendoza*, the House of Lords applied section 3 to oblige a landlord to grant a statutory tenancy to a surviving same-sex partner under the provision of the Rent Act 1977 which referred to a person 'living with the original tenant as his or her wife or husband'.[131]

In *Manchester City Council v Pinnock*,[132] a tenant who had been 'demoted' under section 82A of the Housing Act as a result of the repeated anti-social and criminal conduct of members of his family challenged an order for possession issued pursuant to section 143D of the Housing Act 1996. A unanimous nine member panel of the Supreme Court, Lord Neuberger giving judgment, decided that in light of a consistent series of decisions by the ECtHR, it was time to depart from their previous decisions in *Harrow London Borough Council v Qazi*,[133] *Kay v Lambeth London Borough Council*[134] and *Doherty v Birmingham City Council*.[135] In this trilogy of cases, majorities in the House had determined that public authority tenants whose tenancies had come to an end could not challenge the proportionality under Article 8 ECHR of the decision by the local authority to seek possession.

---

[128] *Ibid*, [58].
[129] See generally A Goymour, 'Property and Housing' in Hoffman (n 124) 249, A Goymour, 'Proprietary Claims and Human Rights—A Reservoir of Entitlement' (2006) *Cambridge Law Journal* 63, 696.
[130] J Howell, 'The Human Rights Act 1998: Land, Private Citizen, and the Common Law' (2007) 123 *Law Quarterly Review* 618 at 643, quoted by R Walsh, 'Stability and Predictability in English Property Law—The Impact of Article 8 of the ECHR Reassessed' (2015) *Law Quarterly Review* 131, 585–609.
[131] Rent Act 1977 Schedule 1, para 2(2).
[132] [2010] UKSC 45, [2011] 2 AC 104.
[133] [2003] UKHL 43, [2004] 1 AC 983.
[134] *Kay* (n 57).
[135] [2008] UKHL 57, [2009] 1 AC 367.

In *Pinnock*, the Supreme Court held that a domestic court must have power to measure the proportionality of making an order for possession in favour of a public authority. Lord Neuberger was emphatic that nothing in the judgment 'is intended to bear on cases where the person seeking the order for possession is a private Landlord'.[136]

In terms of the mechanism through which the proportionality test came to be applied in *Pinnock*, the Court applied section 3 HRA and held that the relevant section of the Housing Act 1996, section 143D(2), should be read as allowing the court to exercise its powers necessary to consider and give effect to Article 8 and in claims for possession before the county court section 7(1)(b) confers the necessary jurisdiction. Section 7(1)(b) provides that

> A person who claims that a public authority has acted (or proposes to act) in a way which is made unlawful by section 6(1) may ....(b) rely on the Convention right or rights concerned in any legal proceedings, but only if he is (or would be) a victim of the unlawful act.

Importantly, the Court also held that it must be 'open to the court to consider whether the procedure has been lawfully followed, having regard to the defendant's Article 8 Convention rights and section 6 of the 1998 Act'.[137] Lord Neuberger also stated that this approach is borne out by section 7(1)(b).

While Lord Neuberger stressed that the Supreme Court was concerned only with the challenge to a possession order by the tenant of a local authority, the relevant principles of statutory interpretation apply to all legislation, and reliance upon the role of the court under section 6(1) cannot be confined to cases against public authorities. Section 6(1) states that it is unlawful for [an English court] 'to act in a way which is incompatible with a Convention right'. The task of the English court is to ensure that their decisions are compatible with ECHR rights by 'taking account of Strasbourg jurisprudence' (section 2(1)). Applying *Pinnock*, the approach the Supreme Court takes to section 2 is that:

> Where, however, there is a clear and constant line of decisions whose effect is not inconsistent with some fundamental substantive or procedural aspect of our law, and whose reasoning does not appear to overlook or misunderstand some argument or point of principle, we consider that it would be wrong for this court not to follow that line.[138]

In *Pinnock*, the ECHR jurisprudence is therefore brought to bear on the case in hand through three media: section 3 HRA, section 6 HRA and section 7(1)(b). There has been very little discussion by the courts of the court's role under section 6, but the acknowledgement of the court's role in *Pinnock* would have as much application in an action between private parties (assuming that is what the Strasbourg jurisprudence requires) as between public authority landlords and their tenants.

---

[136] *Pinnock* (n 132) [50].
[137] *Pinnock* (n 132) [77].
[138] *Pinnock* (n 132) [29].

In *X v Y*, Mummery LJ was careful in his linkage of section 3 and section 6 and to limit section 6 to a confirmatory role.

Much rented property is now in the private sector and the question arises whether an application for possession by a private landlord should be subject to proportionality considerations under Article 8. According to the latest estimates produced by the Government in England, *Dwelling Stock Estimates 2013: England*, the following breakdown is given: 23.2 million dwellings of which 14.7 million (63 per cent) were owner-occupied; 1.7 million (7.3 per cent) were let by local authorities; 2.33 million (10 per cent) were let by social rented sector landlords; and 4.2 million (18 per cent) were let by private landlords.[139] Clearly, Loveland is right that the question of whether possession proceedings by private landlords are caught by section 6 is important. However, Lord Neuberger was very careful to confine his remarks to actions for possession by public authority landlords.

It has been argued that:

> The Convention ought to be widely applicable in property disputes–whether the disputes are vertical or horizontal, whether they arise in the Strasbourg court or the domestic courts, and whether they concern legislation or the common law. Adopting this strategy avoids having to draw unprincipled distinctions: at all levels property law should be open to scrutiny. This means that attention will rightly shift to the compatibility issue to determine the impact of the Convention on property law.[140]

This is a very sweeping statement which jars with a number of the basic premises of international human rights law, which is that human rights obligations are owed by states, rather than private individuals.

As we have argued, *respecting* (rather than *securing*) others' human rights is an obligation that individual citizens owe *inter se*; what individuals do not owe is positive obligations to secure the rights of others, for example, the right to a home. The right to a home is an economic and social right and a right owed to everyone by the state. Introducing proportionality arguments into private property law disputes is arguably to apply considerations of distributive justice between non-state actors and to tread the path of government by interfering with democratically agreed distributions of property interest. Furthermore, the ECtHR has frequently asserted the large margin of appreciation afforded to the state in socio-economic matters; the margin of appreciation doctrine has no direct application at state level, but the recognition of a wide margin makes it difficult for a claimant to establish that action/inaction is 'incompatible' with ECHR rights.

For example, in *Blecic v Croatia*,[141] the first section of the ECtHR held that there had been no violation of the applicant's Article 8 rights in circumstances where

---

[139] Department for Communities and Local Government (2014), *Dwelling Stock Estimates 2013: England*, www.gov.uk/government/uploads/system/uploads/attachment_data/file/285001/Dwelling_Stock_Estimates_2013_England.pdf, quoted by I Loveland, 'Horizontality of Article 8 in the Context of Possession Proceedings' (2015) *European Human Rights Law Review* 2, 138–48.
[140] (Goymour in Hoffman n 129) 273.
[141] (2004) 41 EHRR 185.

the protected tenancy of her home had been terminated by the Croatian Court on the ground that she had ceased to occupy it for 10 months during 1991–1992. Her case was that it had been her home since 1953, and that her absence had been attributable to armed conflict in Dalmatia, but it was held that it had been her 'personal decision ... to leave'. The European Court said, at para 65:

> State intervention in socio-economic matters such as housing is often necessary in securing social justice and public benefit. In this area, the margin of appreciation available to the state in implementing social and economic policies is necessarily a wide one. The domestic authorities' judgment as to what is necessary to achieve the objectives of those policies should be respected unless that judgment is manifestly without reasonable foundation.

The question of the applicability of Article 8 in the realm of rented property in the private sector has come before the Court of Appeal recently in *McDonald v McDonald*.[142] Ms McDonald was a woman with mental health problems. Her parents bought a house with the assistance of a mortgage and then, in breach of the mortgage, agreed to let the house to their daughter on an assured shorthold tenancy. The parents defaulted and the mortgagee then brought possession proceedings against Ms McDonald in the parents' name, as the terms of the mortgage entitled the mortgagee so to do. The Court held that the clear mandatory terms of section 21(4)[143] of the Housing Act 1988 meant that the Court could not apply the proportionality test implied into Article 8.2 of the Convention unless there were clear and constant jurisprudence of the ECtHR that the test applied where possession was sought by a private landlord.

Arden LJ considered the few Strasbourg cases that concern the application of Article 8 to those dispossessed of their home at suit of a private party and concluded that,

> In none of these cases was there any decision that the proportionality test applied to a case involving a private landlord or co-owner. It was simply assumed to be the case that the proportionality test applied as if the landlord (or co-owner) was in the public sector. In my judgment, that is not enough to make it a clear and constant line of decisions if there are other indications that there is a countervailing principle.[144]

There was no recognition that the 'mirror' principle has not been applied consistently, and in a number of cases has been positively rejected.

---

[142] [2014] EWCA Civ 1049, [2015] 2 WLR 567.

[143] Section 21(4) provides (as amended by section 98(3) of the Housing Act 1996): 'a court shall make an order for possession of a dwelling-house let on an assured shorthold tenancy which is a periodic tenancy if the court is satisfied—(a) that the landlord or, in the case of joint landlords, at least one of them has given to the tenant a notice in writing stating that, after a date specified in the notice, being the last day of a period of the tenancy and not earlier than two months after the date the notice was given, possession of the dwelling-house is required by virtue of this section; and (b) that the date specified in the notice under paragraph (a) above is not earlier than the earliest day on which, apart from section 5(1) above, the tenancy could be brought to an end by a notice to quit given by the landlord on the same date as the notice under paragraph (a) above.'

[144] *McDonald* (n 142) [33].

The decision has come in for a hefty amount of criticism, but for different reasons. Lees has argued[145] that the mandatory wording of section 21 meant that the Court could not apply section 3 to achieve a Convention compatible interpretation. It has to be said that this flies in the face of *Pinnock*, where the Supreme Court was equally confronted with the mandatory wording of section 143D(2) but nonetheless held that section 143D(2) should be read as not excluding the power to consider proportionality under Article 8. Lees criticises the Court for failing to distinguish direct horizontality where the obligation to consider proportionality falls upon the landlord and indirect horizontality by way of statute. A legitimate response is that there is no need to draw the distinction: it is so obvious that it was simply assumed by the Court.

Loveland has criticised the Court's failure to take up the mantle thrown down by the ECtHR in relation to Article 8. Having noted the Strasbourg tendency to draw out Article 8 principles from disparate 'privacy' claims, he has argued that, 'This collapsing of cases concerned with different aspects of Article 8 of the ECHR into a common principle rather suggests that there is no good basis for recognising horizontal effect in privacy cases, but not in possession proceedings'.

It is perfectly true that general principles concerning the protection of personal integrity and well-being can be drawn from the Strasbourg case law under the Article 8 right to respect for private life. However, the 'right to respect', is essentially negative in nature in the sense that it requires non-state actors to refrain from interfering with the well-being of other non-state actors. Thus, publication of private information by one non-state actor (a positive act) may be restrained by another non-state actor; similarly, unwanted intrusive behaviour that violates the respect for private life can be restrained. This writer is not aware of any case law the thrust of which is that one non-state actor should provide resources for the benefit of another non-state actor which would be the case where property rights are adjusted between private parties through interpretation of housing and property legislation in the way advocated by Goymour and other commentators.

It is presumably the recognition of the fundamental distinction between civil and political rights and economic and social rights that lies behind Arden LJ's extensive focus on the opinion of Gaetano J in *Buckland v United Kingdom*.[146] He stated that,

> In my view while it is perfectly reasonable to require that an eviction or repossession notice issued by the Government or by a local authority—*both of which are normally under a public law obligation to provide accommodation for people within their jurisdiction—or possibly even by a private entity in receipt of public funds*, should be capable of being challenged on the grounds of proportionality, when the landlord is a private individual the tenant's right should in principle be limited to challenging whether the

---

[145] E Lees, 'Horizontal Effect and Article 8: *McDonald v McDonald*' (2015) *Law Quarterly Review* 131 (Jan) 34–39.
[146] (2013) 56 EHRR 16.

occupation—tenancy, lease, to litigation between non-state encroachment concession, etc—has in fact come to an end according to law.

At bottom, Gaetano's concern is that the Article 8 right is a right to 'respect' for one's home, it is not a right to a home.

The Section 6 Obligation and the Courts

Section 6 HRA is the provision which most excited early academic debate amongst common lawyers as it is the section which appears to be the critical medium through which Strasbourg jurisprudence would have power under the HRA to inform the development of the common law.[147] Predictions regarding the extent to which human rights obligations would reach non-state actors consumed academics and practitioners alike. However, faced with the reality of 'bringing rights home', those predictions have caused much less excitement among the judiciary. Looking back over the last 15 years, it is apparent that, in the case of both public authorities and non-state actors, it is the jurisprudence under the ECHR itself which has wrought significant change in the common law, without the precise meaning of section 6 ever being determined or the section being applied in any formal sense. Reviewing those early academic debates, it is striking also that reflection upon the twin questions of first, why, and, second, the extent to which a non-state actor should be called to deliver on human rights obligations is largely absent.

A close reading of commentary at that time reveals a range of views. If we view horizontality as a spectrum, the strongest argument in favour of horizontal effect was made by Wade who suggested that the provisions of the HRA '[since they are unqualified in their terms] apply as much in claims against private parties as they do in claims against public authorities'.[148] This conclusion, he argued, is the obvious consequence of including the courts within the definition of 'public authority' in section 6(3). A court would be 'unable to give a lawful judgment, if a Convention rights point arises, except in accordance with that right'. At the other end of the spectrum, Lord Justice Buxton argued that since the Convention rights have only been assertable against organs of state, the same must follow in relation to a 'Convention right' under the HRA.[149] Hunt argued that the inclusion of courts and tribunals in the definition of public authorities must mean that 'all law, other than unavoidably incompatible legislation is to be subjected to Convention rights'.[150] In his early writing on horizontality, Phillipson viewed the issue as

---

[147] This section draws upon J Wright, 'A Damp Squib? The Impact of Section 6 HRA on the Common Law: Horizontal Effect and Beyond' [2014] *Public Law* 289.

[148] HWR Wade, 'Horizons of Horizontality' (2000) *Law Quarterly Review* 116 (Apr) 217–24.

[149] Lord Justice Buxton, 'The Human Rights Act and Private Law' (2000) 116 *Law Quarterly Review* 48.

[150] M Hunt, 'The "Horizontal Effect" of the Human Rights Act' [1998] *Public Law* 423.

perhaps the most 'problematic aspect' of the HRA and 'an issue of potentially great importance'.[151] He concluded that

> [Claimants] seeking to invoke Convention rights in private common law cases will not be able to rely solely on the right in question but will have to anchor their claim in an existing common law cause of action; They may then invoke the relevant Convention rights in support of their claim.[152]

Much analysis of section 6(3) of the HRA has focused on the extent to which Convention rights may impact on legal relations between private parties from a theoretical perspective focussing on models of horizontality,[153] rather than beginning with an approach based upon interpretation of the statutory text itself, allied to analysis of the relevant Strasbourg jurisprudence. Early debates suggested that the appropriate model of horizontal effect was a matter of judicial choice and tended to neglect the structure, wording and aim of the HRA itself, as well as the detail of Strasbourg case law.[154] Hunt in his early analysis of the potential reach of the ECHR neglected any detailed engagement with Strasbourg jurisprudence, merely noting that 'Convention case law will be important'.[155] The tendency by academics to focus on abstract considerations of models of horizontality has obscured the debate; an examination of case law reveals a pragmatic approach rooted in the interpretation of the Act and Strasbourg case law. After noting the high level of abstraction in academic debate, Mummery LJ was moved to remark with some prescience that 'the facts of particular cases and the legal contexts in which they fall to be decided tend to put very general propositions into a more limited and manageable perspective'.[156]

This writer is not aware of any English case that would amount to the imposition of a human rights obligation on a non-state actor, other than an obligation to behave in a way that respects the right: in other words, there may be a duty not to conduct oneself in such a way that one interferes with a ECHR right to the extent that such is recognised by the state. Adopting the taxonomy of the United Nations, as a private citizen I have an obligation to respect your private law rights, but I do not have an obligation to protect or fulfil such rights as are recognised in domestic law. Furthermore, I have no obligation to secure your rights from invasion by others. For example, unlike the state, I have no obligation to ensure within reasonable limits that you are able to exercise your right to freedom of expression

---

[151] G Phillipson, 'The Human Rights Act, "Horizontal Effect" and the Common Law: A Bang or a Whimper?' (1999) 62 *Modern Law Review* 824.

[152] *Ibid*, 847.

[153] See for example, AL Young, 'Mapping Horizontal Effect' in Hoffmann (n 124) 16–47.

[154] See for example, BS Markesinis (ed), 'Introduction' to *The Impact of the Human Rights Bill on English Law* (Oxford, Clarendon Press, 1999) 7, 'What form our horizontality will take will really be up to our judges to determine, though, again, the debates which have taken place in Germany on this issue could be put to good use'.

[155] M Hunt, 'The Effect on the Law of Obligations' in Markesinis, *ibid*, 175.

[156] *X v Y* (n 126) [45].

in accordance with Article 10 ECHR. The difference between 'respecting' rights and securing them is absolutely key. It is noteworthy that in one of his articles, Wade states that

> [since the oppressive governments such as Nazi Germany] a new culture of human rights has developed in the Western world, and the citizen can legitimately expect his human rights will be respected by his neighbours as well as by his government. This must be the spirit of the Act.[157]

The language is that of 'respect': by focusing on the notion of respect, the issue of 'horizontal effect' seems so much less controversial.

Turning to the HRA, clearly section 6 is the key provision through which the ECHR may permeate private common law. Section 6(i) provides that: 'It is unlawful for a public authority to act in a way which is incompatible with a Convention right'; according to section 6(3)(a): 'In this section public authority includes a court or tribunal'. The following discussion will examine the section 6 obligation in respect to a range of academic perspectives regarding the appropriate interpretation of section 6 in light of the emergent views of the English courts, before turning to examine the HRA and Strasbourg jurisprudence in more detail. Where it is claimed that a court has acted incompatibly with a Convention right, proceedings under section 7(1)(a) may only be brought by exercising a right of appeal.[158] So, how can a court act incompatibly with a Convention right? It is helpful to separate these elements of the discussion as much of the academic debate has taken place in the absence of a deep engagement with the Strasbourg jurisprudence.

Interpreting the Section 6 Obligation: 'Compatibility' and 'Convention Rights'

Surprisingly, given its centrality to the HRA, there seems to have been very little discussion judicially or otherwise of precisely what we mean by the concept of 'incompatibility'. It is of interest to note that Parliamentary draftsmen did not borrow wholesale from the language of the ECtHR; if they had they would more than likely have spoken of a duty not to *violate* ECHR rights. However, the difference in language can be explained by the fact that the ECHR rights are obligations of the United Kingdom as a state in international law. The aim of the HRA is to give further effect to those rights in English law. If any branch of government acts in such a way as to put the United Kingdom in breach of its obligations, the ECHR is violated. The difficulty for a court is to determine how those rights should be mapped onto domestic law. As Clayton and Tomlinson suggest, 'incompatible' means 'inconsistent' with a Convention right and an act will be 'inconsistent' with

---

a Convention right if it constitutes a violation of that right, but not otherwise.[159] The question then is: how can a court act incompatibly with ECHR rights, other than in the application of its own processes and procedures?

Public authorities, other than courts, clearly have the capacity to act or omit to act in such a way that the rights of individuals are violated and if not redressed appropriately before the English courts, the possibility of recourse to Strasbourg remains. If police authorities tap telephones without lawful authority or detain citizens without lawful excuse, they act incompatibly with the safeguards laid down in the ECHR and a claim will be brought against the relevant public authority under section 7 HRA. The development of substantive law is more problematic. If English courts are to act incompatibly with ECHR rights in the development of common law rules, this must be because the rules created are in some way incompatible with the substantive content of ECHR rights; in other words the rules themselves violate ECHR rights.

Given that we have seen that human rights obligations bind states in international law and that those obligations may require states to control the acts of non-state actors so that they in turn respect the rights of others, the nature of the 'positive obligation' to control the non-state actor is critical to the horizontal effect debate. As Williams and Phillipson have stated, there are two aspects to this enquiry which require the court to first consider whether the Convention right in question has any relevance to the particular dispute before it so the court needs to 'enquire whether Strasbourg has found that right to bear the content argued for by the claimant and, [secondly] to require positive state intervention between private parties'.[160]

In their work on horizontal effect, Williams and Phillipson have argued that the courts may exceptionally be obliged to create new causes of action 'provided that this is the end point of a process of incremental development'.[161] They do not provide a substantive justification for their argument. Presumably, they would view the common law developments in the protection of the Article 8 right to respect for private life as such an example. However, there was no obligation on *the courts*, as opposed to Parliament, to take steps to further protect the right. Indeed, it could be argued (as have sections of the press) that the recognition of a privacy right was akin to a 'legislative' act which needed to be accompanied by parliamentary and public debate to assess the wider repercussions of recognising the right, for example, the conditions governing injunctive relief such as the 'super-injunction'.[162] Arguably, such developments are exactly the sort of social

---

[159] R Clayton and H Tomlinson, *The Law of Human Rights*, 2nd edn (Oxford, Oxford University Press, 2009) 5.14.
[160] G Phillipson and A Williams, 'Horizontal Effect and Constitutional Constraint' (2011) 74(6) *Modern Law Review* 879, 886.
[161] *Ibid*, 885.
[162] In respect of which Lord Neuberger issued *Practice Guidance (Interim Non-Disclosure Orders)* [2012] 1 WLR 1003.

and policy developments that should only be shaped by Parliament.[163] It is axiomatic that complaints relating to intrusions into privacy by the media engage positive obligations under the ECHR and the Court has stressed that appropriate steps are firmly within the state's margin of appreciation.[164]

In view of Strasbourg's continuing reluctance to engage with the issue of *how* the state should comply with its positive obligations, it is difficult to see why the courts should be *required* to ensure compatibility of the common law with ECHR rights (as opposed to Parliament being required to legislate) except where there is an extant cause of action that engages the Convention rights of the parties. The observations by the High Court in the recent *Nicklinson* decision[165] underscore the point. Tony Nicklinson suffered from 'locked in syndrome' following a stroke and argued that his catastrophic physical disabilities should allow him to choose to end his life by voluntary euthanasia. He sought a declaration that 'it would not be unlawful, on the grounds of necessity, for Mr Nicklinson's GP, or another doctor, to terminate or to assist the termination of his life'.[166] There is no Strasbourg authority to support the argument that a blanket ban on voluntary euthanasia is incompatible with Article 8 and in *Haas v Switzerland*[167] the Court held that states have a wide margin of appreciation in this area. Where a matter is within the margin of appreciation left to states, it is up to the state to decide which organ of government should decide which legal regime to adopt.[168] The High Court concluded that it was not the right *locus* to make 'major changes involving matters of controversial social policy' which are for Parliament to determine.[169] The Court also highlighted the often overlooked fact that common law rules develop in the context of bilateral dispute resolution and may therefore be ill-suited to development for application in wider contexts. Thus, there will be many instances where it is not only difficult to see why the courts 'must' develop the common law; there are also situations which by their very nature require legal evaluation within a framework which will consider the wider ramifications of legislation. Why then should the courts, as opposed to the legislature, be required to act?

In order to make good the Phillipson and Williams argument on this, we need to establish that there is an obligation on the court to shape the legal relations between non-state actors. Positive obligations are not apparent on the face of the ECHR but have been developed through case law.[170] When we examine

---

[163] See *Bellinger v Bellinger* (n 22) for the same sort of arguments in relation to s 3 HRA and Lord Phillips in *Smith v Chief Constable of Sussex Police* [2008] UKHL 50, [2009] 1 AC 225 [102] regarding his preference that Parliament should legislate regarding public authority liability for negligent conduct rather than courts recognising new duty situations.

[164] *Mosley v United Kingdom* (2011) EHRR 30 [108]–[111].

[165] *R on the application of Nicklinson v Ministry of Justice* [2012] EWHC 2381.

[166] *Ibid* at [18].

[167] (31322/07) (2011) 53 EHRR 33.

[168] *Nicklinson* (n 58) [119].

[169] *Nicklinson* (n 58) [79]. For similar observation by the Supreme Court, see *R (on the application of Nicklinson) v Ministry of Justice* [2014] UKSC 38, [2015] AC 657.

[170] See generally, A Mowbray, *The Development of Positive Obligations under the ECHR*, (Oxford, Hart Publishing, 2004).

Strasbourg case law, we find plenty of examples of an obligation being recognised upon the *state* to regulate such conduct. The justification for recognising positive obligations to regulate the behaviour of non-state actors lies in Article 1 of the ECHR, according to which states are obliged to 'secure' to individuals within the jurisdiction the rights set out in the ECHR. The first case that recognised this obligation was *X and Y v The Netherlands*,[171] where the state had failed to secure the right to respect for private life of a mentally disabled young woman who had been sexually assaulted; as she lacked capacity no criminal prosecution could be brought against her assailant. This gap in the criminal law amounted to a violation of the state's positive obligation under Article 8 to secure her right to respect for private life. In *Costello-Roberts v UK*,[172] corporal punishment at a private school fell within the ambit of the right to education which is protected by the First Protocol to the ECHR. The ECtHR held that 'the state cannot absolve itself from responsibility' to secure a Convention right by 'delegating its obligations to private bodies or individuals'.[173]

The difficulty with the Phillipson and Williams argument is that it is very unusual for Strasbourg to indicate which branch of government should secure a right. So, returning to the example of privacy from media intrusion in the UK, while English law was deficient in failing to secure the right to respect for private life, any violation of Article 8 was a violation by the United Kingdom. The Strasbourg jurisprudence on positive obligations under Article 8 requires that states take steps to protect ECHR rights as between non-state actors, but it generally does not indicate which branch of government should secure the right. Indeed, as is clear from *X and Y*, 'the choice of the means calculated to secure compliance with Article 8 in the sphere of the relations of individuals between themselves is in principle a matter that falls within the Contracting States' margin of appreciation.'[174] In *X and Y*, the Court did find that the availability of civil remedies was insufficient in the case of the wrongdoing inflicted upon Miss Y. On the facts, the availability of civil law remedies did not discharge the Article 8 obligation, but the Court made the following important observation:

> … the Court, which on this point agrees in substance with the opinion of the Commission, observes that the choice of the means calculated to secure compliance with Article 8 in the sphere of the relations between themselves is in principle a matter that falls within the Contracting States' margin of appreciation. In this connection, there are different ways of ensuring 'respect for private life', and the nature of the State's obligation will depend on the particular aspect of private life that is at issue. Recourse to the criminal law is not necessarily the answer.[175]

---

[171] (1985) 8 EHRR 235.
[172] (1993) 19 EHRR 112.
[173] *Ibid* [27].
[174] *X and Y* (n 171) [24].
[175] *Ibid.*

In the case of media intrusion and privacy, it could be argued that a failure to develop the action for breach of confidence would demonstrate that *English law* was not compatible with the ECHR, not that English courts had failed to act compatibly with the ECHR since there is nothing in the jurisprudence to require English courts to act to protect the right. Rather, it could be argued equally that Parliament had acted incompatibly with the ECHR in failing to enact a privacy law.

Lord Hoffmann indicated a preference for such a restrictive view when he equated the notion of 'acting incompatibly' with ECHR rights with 'violating' the ECHR. So, in *Wainwright v Home Office*[176] he concluded that, in the event that the ECtHR should find that Article 8 had been violated (which it did, inevitably),[177] that would merely show that there was a gap in English remedies that had now been filled by sections 6 and 7 HRA. Furthermore, in a different context, when the House of Lords was asked to rule upon the question whether English courts should override the immunity of Saudi Arabia in order to allow a compensation claim for torture to proceed before the English courts on the basis that the *ius cogens* norm forbids torture is a superior norm to the principle of sovereign immunity, Lord Hoffmann declared that:

> The *jus cogens* is a prohibition on torture. But the United Kingdom, in according state immunity to the Kingdom, is not proposing to torture anyone. Nor is the Kingdom, in claiming immunity, justifying the use of torture. It is objecting in limine to the jurisdiction of the English court to decide whether it used torture or not.[178]

This writer would argue that the corollary of the observations made above is that in order for the English court to be *required* to recognise a new cause of action, Strasbourg would need to have held that the English common law itself should be developed accordingly. Such a course is highly unlikely, particularly given the fact that the common law tradition of recognising new private law rights is peculiar to the United Kingdom and Ireland (within Europe). Subsidiarity is a principle that runs throughout Strasbourg jurisprudence; Strasbourg organs constantly reiterate that how the ECHR is implemented in domestic law is a matter for the Contracting States. In an early discussion of the Article 13 right to an effective remedy, the Court stated that 'neither Article 13 nor the Convention in general lays down for the Contracting states any given manner for ensuring within their internal law the effective implementation of any of the provisions of the Convention'.[179] This does not mean to say that extant rules which do offend the ECHR should not be susceptible to judicial development—this takes us back to the distinction between acts and omissions. Existing common law rules that violate the ECHR should be altered by the courts to reflect ECHR norms; where there are gaps in domestic

---

[176] [2003] UKHL 53, [2004] 2 AC 406.
[177] *Wainwright v United Kingdom* (2007) 44 EHRR 40.
[178] *Jones v Saudi Arabia* [2006] UKHL 26 [44].
[179] *Swedish Engine Drivers' Union v Sweden* (1976) 1 EHRR 617 [50], see also *Silver v United Kingdom* (1983) 5 EHRR 347 [113].

law, it may well be more appropriate for Parliament to respond rather than for the courts to undertake rule development.

While attractively simple compared with a number of analyses that have been put forward regarding the extent to which the Convention rights have horizontal effect, the Phillipson and Williams thesis is not directly supported by any authority, neither English common law nor Strasbourg jurisprudence. While *Campbell v MGN Ltd* may be seen as the final step in the recognition of a new tort of misuse of private information,[180] it could not plausibly be argued that this was *required* by the HRA or indeed the ECHR. The United Kingdom needed to take steps to protect privacy, but it did not necessarily fall to the courts to do this.

Notwithstanding the apparent lack of explicit judicial concern regarding the impact of section 6(3) of the HRA on doctrine, Phillipson and Williams have asserted that the judges have made 'significant and creative use of the Convention in private common law [but] they have proceeded step by step, without creating brand new Convention-based causes of action or instantaneously fashioning existing ones into compatibility'.[181] This somewhat overstates what the courts have done. With the exception of the development of privacy of information and (to a lesser extent) defamation,[182] the HRA itself (as opposed to the ECHR) has had remarkably little influence on the development of private common law. The authors describe their analysis as predicated on the distinction between 'incremental' and 'legislative' style common law development. Given that English courts have always engaged in incremental development (and sometimes legislative development), and sometimes in light of Strasbourg jurisprudence, it is very hard to see that the Phillipson and Williams argument adds anything to our understanding about common law reasoning, either with or without the HRA. Even in the case of the wrongful disclosure of private information, it is arguable that the changes that have occurred in the structure of the action for breach of confidence were foreshadowed long before the HRA came into force, the impetus to free up the action from the well-established requirements of the equitable action[183] lying in the well-known dictum of Lord Goff in *Spycatcher*[184] which was taken up by Laws LJ in *Hellewell v Chief Constable of Derbyshire*,[185] paving the way for *Douglas v Hello! Ltd*[186] and the final determinative step in *Campbell v MGN Ltd*.[187]

A close reading of *Douglas v Hello! Ltd* reveals that it was arguably the English case law together with the Strasbourg decision of *Spencer (Earl) v UK*[188] that was determinative of the recognition of the new tort of misuse of private information

---

[180] [2004] 2 WLR 1232 [14] (Lord Nicholls).
[181] Phillipson and Williams (n 160) 879.
[182] For a similar view, see K Oliphant, 'Defamation' in Hoffmann (n 124) 204.
[183] See Megarry J in *Coco v AN Clark (Engineers) Ltd* [1969] RPC 41 [49].
[184] See the speech of Lord Goff in *A-G v Guardian Newspapers Ltd (No 2)* [1990] 1 AC 109, 281.
[185] [1995] 1 WLR 804 at 807.
[186] [2001] 2 All ER 289.
[187] *Campbell* (n 180).
[188] 25 EHRR CD 105.

through the action for breach of confidence rather than the HRA itself. As soon as we move outside the areas of privacy of information and defamation (and it should be recalled that defamation itself had long felt the influence of the ECHR),[189] the HRA has had little 'direct' impact on private common law. Arguably, there are areas of the common law that have been influenced by an increasing culture of rights,[190] but these developments have not been shaped by the HRA itself.

In terms of the impact of section 6 HRA on the common law, a distinction needs to be drawn between causes of action that engage ECHR rights and sets of facts that may engage ECHR rights. If a cause of action engages ECHR rights, then clearly the court must act compatibly with those rights;[191] a classic example would be defamation which by its very nature engages the freedom of expression of the speaker and the reputation of the defamed, both protected rights under the ECHR. It will be argued that if a cause of action does not exist, there can be no *requirement* to develop the common law, for the simple reason that ECHR rights are exigible against the state and ECHR jurisprudence consistently refrains from directing states regarding which arm of the state is required to provide the remedy. The classic distinction between acts and omissions in the common law provides an analogy here. Thus, it would be impossible to say that *the courts are acting* incompatibly with ECHR rights. A refusal by the courts to develop the common law may mean that English law violates ECHR rights, but this in itself does not mean that the court is acting incompatibly with an ECHR where no relevant cause of action exists. The fact that the United Kingdom may be in violation of ECHR rights does not in itself justify the creation of new causes of action by the courts. The distinction between rights and remedies is fundamental here.

Article 13 of the ECHR was not incorporated into English law; thus unless a substantive right incorporates a remedial element which is judicial in nature (see below), it would be difficult to argue that English courts are acting incompatibly with ECHR rights when they refuse to open up the constraints of the common law.[192] Even where there is a remedial element within a substantive right under the ECHR (which may be the case, for example under Article 2, which requires that there should be criminal and civil remedies available in cases of murder where the state is at fault),[193] the fact that section 7 HRA provides a remedy for a breach of the ECHR right obviates the need to recognise a cause of action at common law. This view is supported by case law.

[189] An excellent example is *Reynolds v Times Newspapers Ltd* [1999] 3 WLR 1010, which effectively revolutionised the rules on qualified privilege but, importantly, prior to the HRA.
[190] See for example the recognition of the conventional sum for injury to autonomy in wrongful birth cases as recognised in *Rees v Darlington Memorial Hospital NHS Trust* [2004] 1 AC 309 (cf *McFarlane v Tayside Health Board* [2000] 2 AC 59) and the pragmatic approach to causation in *Chester v Afshar* [2005] 1 AC 134 in order to protect the autonomy of the claimant.
[191] See Baroness Hale in *Campbell* (n 180) at [132].
[192] See *Wainwright v Home Office* [2003] 3 WLR 1137.
[193] *Mastromatteo v Italy* 2002 –VIII GC.

In *Venables v News Group Newspapers Ltd*,[194] Butler-Sloss LJ held that the duty of the court is to act compatibly with Convention rights 'in adjudicating upon existing common law causes of action and does not encompass the creation of a freestanding cause of action based directly upon the Articles of the Convention'. Baroness Hale in *Campbell* discussed the injunction upon the courts in the HRA: 'the 1998 Act does not create any new cause of action between private persons. But if there is a relevant cause of action applicable, the court as public authority must act compatibly with both parties Convention rights'.[195] Further, she said that the courts would

> not invent a new cause of action to cover types of activity which were not previously covered: see *Wainwright v Home Office* [2003] 3 WLR 1137 ... [Having described the treatment of Mrs Wainwright and her son as a "gross invasion of their privacy", Baroness Hale continued] That case indicates that our law cannot, even if it wanted to, develop a general tort of invasion of privacy. But where existing remedies are available, the court not only can but must balance the competing Convention rights of the parties.[196]

There is another reason for English courts to exercise restraint in their role as common law 'legislators' and this lies in the doctrine of precedent. In *Kay v Lambeth LBC*,[197] the House of Lords reiterated the importance of adherence to this doctrine. Lord Bingham referred to this 'cornerstone' of our legal tradition and quoted Lord Hailsham who said, 'in legal matters, some degree of certainty is at least as valuable a part of justice as perfection'.[198] For present purposes, there is a more pertinent factor that impinges on the extent to which English courts should innovate in the light of ECHR jurisprudence and this lies in the margin of appreciation doctrine. Lord Bingham in *Kay* described the margin of appreciation as the 'fundamental reason' for adhering to the doctrine of precedent since it accords

> a margin ... often generous to the decisions of national authorities and attaches much importance to the peculiar facts of the case. Thus it is for the national authorities, including national courts particularly, to decide in the first instance how the principles expounded by Strasbourg should be applied.[199]

Furthermore, the Supreme Court has recently reaffirmed the importance of adherence to the doctrine of precedent so that lower courts must follow cases decided in superior courts, notwithstanding intervening conflicting ECHR jurisprudence. In *Manchester City Council v Pinnock*,[200] a nine judge panel stated that the Supreme Court is not bound to follow every decision of the ECtHR; the obligation in section 2 HRA is to take account of Strasbourg jurisprudence, but the Supreme

---

[194] [2001] 1 All ER 908.
[195] *Campbell* (n 180) [132].
[196] *Campbell* (n 180) [133].
[197] *Kay* (n 57).
[198] *Cassell v Broome Ltd* [1972] AC 1027.
[199] *Kay* (n 57) [44].
[200] [2010] 3 WLR 1441.

Court is not bound to follow. However, the expectation that Strasbourg will be followed arises

> where there is a clear and constant line of decisions whose effect is not inconsistent with some fundamental substantive or procedural aspect of our law, and whose reasoning does not appear to overlook or misunderstand some argument or point of principle ....[201]

In *Flood v Times Newspapers Ltd*, Lord Phillips reduced the statutory obligation in s 6 and s 2 HRA to an obligation, in developing the common law, 'to have regard to the requirements of the Convention'.[202]

Section 6—Remedies against Public Authorities

In the first edition, we suggested that the advent of section 7 of the HRA could lead English courts to restrict common law development in the form of new causes of action/extension of existing causes of action against public authorities on the basis that where facts occurring post-HRA engage ECHR rights, a victim would henceforth be able to bring a claim against a public authority under section 7 HRA.[203] Argument and discussion of section 6(3) in this context has been scant, but the resounding response from English courts regarding arguments that the principles underpinning common law actions against public authorities should be developed in the light of the HRA has been negative. Lord Bingham alone amongst senior judiciary urged that the law of tort should develop incrementally and by analogy and should not leave important questions to be addressed by the Convention— rather he supported evolution.[204] The following discussion will examine the (lack of) impact of section 6 on claims for redress against public authorities.

As far as public authority liability is concerned, those who have argued for the convergence of the common law and ECHR rights have been disappointed. The introduction of a cause of action for breach of ECHR rights under section 7 HRA has meant that the courts generally have been unreceptive to arguments that it is necessary to develop the common law to develop analogous remedies against public authorities. Instead, English courts have regarded the HRA as the appropriate vehicle for seeking redress against public authorities which has meant that the analysis of the common law in light of ECHR jurisprudence has been relatively

---

[201] *Ibid* [48].

[202] *Flood v Times Newspapers Ltd* [2012] UKSC 11 [46]. In a similar vein, in *Jameel v Dow Jones & Co Inc*, Lord Phillips described the Court's obligation in s 6 HRA as an obligation 'to administer the law in a manner which is compatible with Convention rights, in so far as it is possible to do so' [2005] EWCA Civ 75, [2005] QB 946 [40], see discussion in Chapter 7, text accompanying n 57.

[203] J Wright, *Tort Law & Human Rights* (Oxford, Hart Publishing, 2001) Chapter 2 and Note on the Text.

[204] *JD v East Berkshire Community Health NHS Trust* [2005] 2 AC 373 [50].

slight. It is not an exaggeration to say that, apart from privacy from media intrusion and to a lesser extent defamation, the courts have not been persuaded by their status under section 6 HRA as public authorities of the necessity to absorb Strasbourg principles into private law to any significant extent.

One of the few cases to address explicitly the impact of section 6(3) in claims against public authorities is *Lawrence v Pembrokeshire County Council,*[205] a case based upon post-HRA facts. The claimants argued that the Court should recognise a duty of care on a local authority owed to parents regarding the exercise of child protection responsibilities by social workers. This was an attempt to persuade the Court of Appeal to reject the clear authority of the House of Lords in *JD v East Berkshire Community Health NHS Trust,*[206] denying a duty of care to parents, the distinguishing feature being that the claim in *JD* was based upon pre-HRA facts. Counsel argued that by virtue of sections 6, 2 and 11 HRA, Parliament clearly contemplated a parallel remedy at common law to reflect ECHR provision. Auld LJ, giving judgment for the Court, repeated the assertion of Richards LJ during the hearing that neither Strasbourg jurisprudence nor responsiveness of the common law to the needs of the time requires the Court to secure harmonisation of the two systems.

In *Wainwright v Home Office*[207] the House of Lords held that there was no common law tort of invasion of privacy where a mother and son had been searched in a manner that constituted a violation of the prison's internal rules and was not protected by statutory authority. Lord Hoffmann gave the leading speech, with all other Law Lords expressing full agreement. He took the view that the coming into force of the HRA

> [weakened] the argument for saying that a general tort of invasion of privacy is needed to fill gaps in existing remedies. Sections 6 and 7 of the Act are in themselves substantial gap fillers; if it is indeed the case that a person's rights under Article 8 have been infringed by a public authority, he will have a statutory remedy.[208]

Buxton LJ alone in the Court of Appeal referred to s 6(3) HRA and remarked that there are many difficulties with the argument that the recognition of the Court as a public authority could be used to create private law rights in broadly the same terms as ECHR rights:[209] the question could not be resolved without much fuller argument.

In *Watkins v Secretary of State for the Home Department,*[210] the House of Lords was required to reconsider the principles of the tort of misfeasance in public office, namely whether special damage is required in order to found a claim. No argument was put to the Court either in relation to section 6 HRA or any relevant

---

[205] [2007] 1 WLR 2991.
[206] *JD* (n 204).
[207] *Wainwright* (n 176).
[208] *Wainwright* (n 176) [34].
[209] *Wainwright* (n 176) [92].
[210] [2006] 2 AC 395.

ECHR rights: it was accepted that the Article 6 right of access to a court is clearly engaged on the facts. Mr Watkins' correspondence with his legal advisers had been opened in breach of the Prison Rules on three separate occasions, two of which occurred before 2 October 2000, the day on which the HRA came fully into force, one after. It was uncontested that the prison officers had deliberately and in bad faith broken the prison rules by opening and reading Mr Watkins' correspondence. The House of Lords allowed the Home Secretary's appeal, holding that proof of special damage is an essential ingredient of the tort. Lord Bingham acknowledged that there is an 'obvious public interest in bringing public servants guilty of outrageous conduct to book. Those who act in such a way should not be free to do so with impunity'.[211] However, there were a number of reasons why the common law should not be adapted to accommodate the claim including the fact that it was 'undesirable to introduce by judicial decision, without consultation, a solution which the consultation and research conducted by the Law Commission may show to be an unsatisfactory part of what is in truth a small part of a wider problem'.[212] Furthermore, he stated that:

> I have myself questioned, albeit in a lone dissent, whether development of the law of tort should be stunted, leaving very important problems to be swept up by the European Convention (*D v East Berkshire Community NHS Trust* [2005] 2 AC 373, para 50), but the observation was made in a case where, in my opinion, the application of familiar principles supported recognition of a remedy in tort, not a case like the present where the application of settled principle points strongly against one. A fourth reason for not adopting the rule for which the respondent contends is to be found in enactment of the 1998 Act: it may reasonably be inferred that Parliament intended infringements of the core human (and constitutional) rights protected by the Act to be remedied under it and not by development of parallel remedies.[213]

Lord Bingham's fourth reason has surfaced in a number of judicial pronouncements and it is by no means unusual for English courts to justify restrictions on the availability of remedies at common law where there are alternative means of redress.[214] Although this argument may be an old argument, it is, contrary to views recently expressed, very much alive and kicking.[215] In *Smith v Chief Constable of Sussex Police*,[216] where the claimant was seriously assaulted by his former lover

---

[211] *Ibid* at [8].

[212] *Ibid* at [26].

[213] *Ibid* and to similar effect see also Lord Rodger at [64] and Lord Walker at [173].

[214] See the well-known speech of Lord Browne-Wilkinson in *X (Minors)* (n 69) where he said that 'If there were no other remedy for maladministration of the statutory system for the protection of children, it would provide substantial argument for imposing a duty of care. But the statutory complaints procedures contained in section 76 of the [Children Act 1980] and the much fuller procedures now available under the 1989 Act provide a means to have grievances investigated, though not to recover compensation'. See generally, J Bell, *Policy Arguments in Judicial Decisions* (Oxford, Clarendon Press, 1983).

[215] See the discussion by Donal Nolan in 'Negligence and Human Rights Law' (2013) *Modern Law Review* 7692 at 316.

[216] *Smith* (n 163).

after reporting escalating threats including death threats to the police, the Law Lords again took the view, *inter alia,* that it was not necessary to extend the tort of negligence now that a claim could be brought against the police under section 7 HRA where a breach of ECHR rights is alleged.

> To the extent that Articles 2 and 3 of the Convention and sections 7 and 8 HRA already provide for claims to be brought in these cases, it is quite simply unnecessary now to develop the common law to provide a parallel cause of action—although it might have been otherwise had the *Osman* line of authority become established before the HRA came into force.[217]

In a similar vein *Jain v Trent SHA,*[218] where the local authority obtained an *ex parte* order requiring the claimants to discontinue their business of running a care home, the local authority had been negligent in their use of statutory powers and the claimants were financially ruined. One of the reasons given by the Court of Appeal for denying a duty of care at common law was the fact that on post HRA facts a claim would lie against the public authority under section 7 HRA and Article 1 of Protocol 1 of the ECHR.

There is an assumption underlying these remarks that there is an equivalence between tort based actions such as negligence, misfeasance in public office, privacy and the like and claims brought under section 7 HRA. Furthermore, there has been an increasing tendency to conceptualise tort actions as vehicles for the 'vindication' of 'rights'.[219] It is doubtful that the concept of 'vindication' has anything to add to our understanding of how and why rights are protected and how their violation is remedied.[220] Furthermore, the Supreme Court has rejected the argument that 'vindicatory' damages are available in tort.[221]

While the same set of facts may give rise to a claim under section 7 HRA and the common law, for example under the tort of negligence, the two actions are conceptually distinct. Rules on limitation, heads of damage, breach and causation and (obviously) the range of claimants are different.[222] Indeed, Lord Bingham took the view that the HRA is not a 'tort statute' and its objects are different and broader.[223] If we are to avoid incoherence, we must remember that rights good against all

---

[217] Smith (n 163) [136] (Lord Carswell).

[218] [2009] UKHL 4, [2009] 1 AC 853.

[219] See the discussion by J Steele, 'Damages in Tort and under the Human Rights Act: Remedial or Functional Separation' [2008] *Cambridge Law Journal* 67(3), 606–34.

[220] See K Barker, 'The Mixed Concept of Vindication' in SGA Pitel, JW Neyers and E Chamberlain, *Tort Law: Challenging Orthodoxy* (Oxford, Hart Publishing, 2013) 59.

[221] *R (Lumba) v Secretary of State for the Home Department* [2012] AC 245.

[222] For a thorough treatment of these themes, see Nolan (n 215) and see also, J Varuhas, 'A Tort-Based Approach to Damages under the Human Rights Act 1998' (2009) 72 *Modern Law Review* 750–82.

[223] *R (Greenfield) v Secretary of State for the Home Department* [2005] 1 WLR 673, [2005] 2 All ER 240 at [18]–[19]. *Cf* Steele (n 219) who suggests that at first blush Lord Bingham's perspective might be taken to imply that the HRA objects are in fact narrower than the law of torts, but then clarifies that his comments related to the role of damages under the Act, which Lord Bingham took to be narrower than under the common law.

legal persons and human rights occupy different legal and conceptual spaces.[224] It could be argued that the urge for convergence in common law rules and the HRA rules harks back to the practical reality that in the pre-HRA era, as Lord Bingham remarked, it was the law of tort which bore 'the heat and burden of the battle' to protect human rights.[225] In terms of implementation of the ECHR into English law in the pre-HRA era, a claimant had no alternative but to rely on the common law to try to vindicate human rights.

In cases such as *Lawrence* and *Watkins* there is an assumption that where ECHR rights have been violated by a public authority the claimant will be able to bring an action under section 7 HRA. There is a glaring example of a class of claimants who may not be able to do this. The HRA is not retrospective so claims based upon pre-2nd October 2000 facts will not ground an action under section 7. Victims of historic sexual abuse which occurred many years before the HRA still need to rely on the common law. They were neglected, in some cases allegedly deliberately overlooked, by public authorities which were on notice of the abuse and failed to act. In such cases, ECHR rights have been violated and redress should be provided at domestic level. This issue is further explored in Chapter 6.

In recent dicta, our senior judges have urged litigants to focus on common law rights first, where a right is protected under both the common law and the HRA.[226] This is sensible where such rights are clearly recognised by the common law; the continuing refusal to accommodate positive obligations in negligence on the part of public authorities remains a significant obstacle to the litigant who seeks justice by way of the common law.

The present discussion would not be complete without acknowledging the indirect effect of the HRA on a limited subset of negligence claims against public authorities, which are discussed in the next section.

Indirect Effect of the HRA in Actions against Public Authorities

The introduction of a cause of action under section 7 HRA has had an indirect, limited impact on the development of common law redress against public authorities. In *D v East Berkshire and Community NHS Trust*,[227] the Court of Appeal held that the policy considerations set out in *X (Minors) v Bedfordshire County Council*[228]

---

[224] See Nolan (n 215).

[225] Lord Bingham of Cornhill, 'Tort Law and Human Rights' in P Cane and J Stapleton (eds), *The Law of Obligations, Essays in Celebration of John Fleming* (Oxford, Clarendon Press, 1998) 1 at 2.

[226] For discussion see P Bowen, 'Does the Renaissance of Common Law Rights Mean the Human Rights Act 1998 is Now Unnecessary?' (2016) 4 *European Human Rights Law Review* 361–77.

[227] [2004] QB 558.

[228] *X (Minors)* (n 69).

which led to the denial of a duty of care owed to children regarding the exercise of statutory child protection obligations, were undermined by the possibility of claims being brought against a public authority under the HRA. In future, local authorities could be subject to claims under the HRA so that the policy arguments regarding the negative impact of the prospect of litigation on local authorities were no longer sustainable. The Court of Appeal therefore held that the local authorities did owe a duty of care to the children (but not the parents). Clearly, this reasoning could apply equally to other claims where facts engage ECHR rights such that a claim may be brought against a public authority under section 7. This reality did not assist the parents in *JD* whose claims in negligence were rejected on the basis that it would not be fair, just and reasonable to recognise a duty of care to parents owing to the inherent conflict of interest between a parent and child in child protection investigations, a view confirmed by the House of Lords.[229]

It has been suggested that the Court of Appeal decision in *JD* is inconsistent with *Gorringe v Calderdale MBC*,[230] in that contrary to *Gorringe* a public authority can as a result of the reasoning in *JD* be rendered liable for failing to confer a benefit on the claimant.[231] To the extent that *JD* recognises the possibility of a duty of care at common law in parallel with the positive obligation arising under Article 3 ECHR, this is correct. However, it must be borne in mind that in the case of *JD* itself, the claims were based upon acts of commission (wrongful removal of children from parents) and not omission (in contrast to *X v Bedfordshire County Council*, where the local authority had failed to take the children into its care) and therefore *Gorringe* is distinguishable on the facts. If the decision in *JD* is extended to include cases of omission as exemplified by the facts in *X (Minors)*, then there would be a conflict with *Gorringe*. However, it is certainly true that the Court of Appeal took the view that it was departing from *X (Minors)*. The reason the litigation played out in this way was probably attributable to a general tendency at that time not to distinguish properly between cases of omission and commission respectively.

Concluding Remarks on Section 6 HRA

Given the furore among private lawyers that greeted the advent of the HRA, it might appear remarkable that so few cases have raised explicit argument regarding the interpretation of section 6 HRA and its application, whether horizontally or vertically. However, close examination of Strasbourg case law, which did not always accompany those early debates, reveals that Strasbourg treads warily in

---

[229] *JD* (n 204).
[230] [2004] 1 WLR 1057.
[231] Nolan (n 215) 304.

the field of the positive obligation to control private parties in their relationships *inter se*. We should not therefore be surprised that in the absence generally of any strong steer, English courts have not found it necessary to express concluded views on the scope of section 6 HRA. Perhaps this is how it should be. Arguably, the significance and weight of 'human' rights obligations become weakened if every bilateral dispute is examined through the lens of the HRA and human rights. The indications are that after an initial flurry of excitement, ECHR obligations are perceived as concerning primarily the relationship between the state and the individual.

Some common lawyers were apt to believe that where the HRA led, so the common law would follow in the creation of new forms of common law redress against public authorities. Indeed, section 11 HRA preserves the right to rely on ECHR rights in proceedings apart from sections 7–9 HRA. Instead, the reverse has been true. In the case of public authority defendants, as we have seen the introduction of the HRA has taken the pressure off the need to expand the common law. We now see a rather more sharp division between public and private law spheres. The problematic issue of omissions in the common law, does not trouble the ECtHR, which, on the right facts, will recognise positive obligations. The jurisprudence on positive obligations under Articles 2 and 3 ECHR has grown enormously over the last 18 years and is fully discussed in Chapters 4 and 6. This reality has meant that the tensions in the common law have weakened as section 7 HRA provides an opportunity for those harmed by the action/inaction of public authorities to receive redress, at least where ECHR rights are engaged.

Remedies under the Act—Sections 7 and 8 HRA

The HRA was drafted in such a way that the same set of facts could give rise to claims being brought against a public authority under section 7 HRA and by way of common law causes of action. Section 11(b) preserves the right to 'make or bring any claim or bring any proceedings which he could make or bring apart from sections 7 to 9'. In the first edition, we suggested that the court's obligation under section 6(3) might lead to the extension of common law obligations on the part of public authorities; this has not happened. For the reasons given earlier in this chapter, such developments are clearly no longer plausible. The following discussion will therefore be restricted to examining the remedial structure of the HRA in the light of recent English and Strasbourg case law.

Section 7(1) HRA provides that a person who claims that a public authority has acted (or proposes to act) in a way which is made unlawful by section 6(1) may: (a) bring proceedings against the authority under the HRA in the appropriate court or tribunal; or (b) rely on the Convention right or rights in any legal proceedings, but only if he is (or would be) a victim of the unlawful act.

Victim Status

Under the HRA, the right to bring an action against a public authority which has acted in a way which is incompatible with a Convention right is available only to a 'victim' of the unlawful act (s 7(1) HRA). Section 7(7) provides that a person is only a 'victim' if s/he would be a victim for the purposes of Article 34 ECHR. Article 34 provides that the Court 'may receive applications from any person, non-governmental organisation or group of individuals claiming to be the victim of a violation … '. In order to bring a claim, the claimant must be able to show that he or she has been directly affected in question by the violation. However, indirect victims may be within section 7 if they can show that they have suffered as a result of the violation. This possibility has been important in relation to claims under Article 2 where the direct victim has died.

Thus, in *Rabone v Pennine Care NHS Foundation Trust*,[232] Mr and Mrs Rabone were able to bring a successful claim under the substantive (as opposed to procedural) element of the Article 2 right to life following the death of their daughter who committed suicide while on home leave from the care of the local health authority. The reason that next of kin may claim to be victims was discussed by Lord Dyson in *Rabone* and this lies in the principle of 'effectiveness'. *Yasa v Turkey*[233] concerned a claim brought by a nephew in relation to his uncle's death allegedly at the hands of the security forces. The ECtHR held in *Yasa* that, in the light of established principles, the deceased's nephew could claim to be a victim of an act as tragic as the murder of his uncle. The 'established principles' to which the Court refers are those set out in *Loizidou v Turkey (Preliminary Objections)*. The Court stated that

> [the] object and purpose of the Convention, a treaty for the collective enforcement of human rights and fundamental freedoms, requires that its provisions be interpreted and applied in the light of its special character and so as to make its safeguards practical and effective.[234]

The principle of effectiveness is frequently relied upon by the Strasbourg organs in order to justify the expansion of the state's obligations beyond those that might ordinarily be contemplated within domestic jurisdictions.

It has long been said that (unlike actions in judicial review) Article 34 does not allow complaints *in abstracto*: there is no possibility of an *actio populalis* so that complaints should be brought by those directly affected by a violation. However, in *Centre for Legal Resources on behalf of Valentin Câmpeanu v Romania*,[235] exceptionally, the ECtHR permitted an application by an non-governmental organisation (NGO) for a violation of Article 2 where a highly vulnerable adult person,

---

[232] *Rabone* (n 63).
[233] (1998) 28 EHRR 408.
[234] *Loizidou v Turkey (Preliminary Objections)* (1995) 20 EHRR 99 [42].
[235] ECtHR [GC] 17 July 2014, no 47848/08.

HIV positive with serious learning difficulties, no next of kin and who had grown up in the care of the state, died following appalling neglect in a state run institution and in violation of Article 2. The ECtHR was at pains to stress the exceptional nature of the case, the fact that at domestic level no objection had been taken to the Centre for Legal Resources and the fact that otherwise there would be no possibility of examining a very serious allegation at international level; without jurisdiction a state might escape accountability as a result of its own failure to appoint a representative for the deceased. This represents though a considerable extension of the Court's jurisdiction through the application of the 'effectiveness' principle and will undoubtedly inform the litigation strategies of human rights NGOs.

However, it is clear under the HRA that interest groups may only bring claims under the Act in relation to an unlawful act if they would be a victim of the unlawful act. Section 7(3) provides that where proceedings are brought on an application for judicial review, the applicant must satisfy the victim test in order to demonstrate sufficiently in relation to the unlawful act. Exceptionally the Equality and Human Rights Commission may bring proceedings under the HRA without being a victim.[236]

The approach of the ECtHR to attribution of 'victim' status under Article 3 ECHR (prohibition of torture, inhuman or degrading treatment or punishment) is quite different. In determining whether a family member can claim a violation, the Court will look for special factors over and above the closeness of the emotional or family tie with the deceased. Such factors are analogous to the proximity factors that English courts look for in relation to claims for psychiatric harm suffered by secondary victims of negligence.[237] Thus in *Cakici v Turkey*,[238] the Court held that: Whether a family member is such a victim will depend on the existence of special factors which gives the suffering of the applicant a dimension and character distinct from the emotional distress which may be regarded as inevitably caused to relatives of a victim of a serious human rights violation. Relevant elements will include the proximity of the family tie—in that context, a certain weight will attach to the parent-child bond—the particular circumstances of the relationship, the extent to which the family member witnessed the events in question, the involvement of the family member in the attempts to obtain information about the disappeared person and the way in which the authorities responded to those enquiries. The Court would further emphasise that the essence of such a violation does not so much lie in the fact of the 'disappearance' of the family member but rather concerns the authorities' reactions and attitudes to the situation when it is brought to their attention. It is especially in respect of the latter that a relative may claim directly to be a victim of the authorities' conduct.[239]

---

[236] See s 30(1) Equality Act 2006. See generally, M Amos (n 45) 32.

[237] *Alcock v Chief Constable of South Yorkshire Police* [1992] 1 AC 310.

[238] (2001) 31 EHRR 5 [98].

[239] For an analogous claim brought under the common law where the House of Lords held that there was no duty of care owed by the police in their treatment of a witness to the racially motivated murder of Stephen Lawrence, see *Brooks v Commissioner of Police for the Metropolis* [2005] 1 WLR 1495.

It will be apparent that the effect of applying the 'victim' test to determine standing is that the list of those who may claim damages in their own right is extended considerably beyond the class of claimants recognised by the Fatal Accidents Act 1976 (FAA). Furthermore, awards by the ECtHR have in some cases been much greater than those contemplated by the FAA. There is a significant variability in awards, with sums ranging from 15,000 euros for siblings to 65,000 euros for a father and son jointly. While in principle a parent may recover damages in respect of a deceased adult child, the claimant victim must demonstrate a breach of the relevant right in Schedule 1 HRA. It seems unlikely that the parents in *Hicks v Chief Constable of South Yorkshire Police*,[240] whose daughters were so tragically killed as a result of negligence at the Hillsborough football stadium, would now have a better claim under the HRA as 'mere' professional negligence seems unlikely to constitute a breach of Article 2.[241]

Limitation

Claimants must bring proceedings within one year of the date on which the act complained of took place (s 7(5)(a)), but the court has jurisdiction to extend this as it 'considers equitable having regard to all the circumstances' (s 7(5)(b)).[242] It is clear that the HRA does not have retrospective effect, save for the one instance set out in section 22(4) which provides that:

> Section 7(1)(b) applies to proceedings brought by or at the instigation of a public authority whenever the act in question took place; but otherwise that subsection does not apply to an act taking place before the coming into force of that section.

The courts have held that the HRA does not apply to the acts of courts, tribunals or public authorities which took place before 2 October 2000.[243] This is of more than academic interest. In Chapter 4 we examine the issue of historic sexual abuse of children; it is likely that claims against public authorities (both the police and social services) will surface for many years to come. According to the current state of the common law, no claim will lie against a public authority that is premised upon an omission to act. Section 6 HRA will not avail in such cases. Although the Court of Appeal departed from *X (Minors)*[244] in *JD v East Berkshire Community NHS Trust*,[245] it is possible that the decision could be confined to acts of commission. This though seems unlikely given that the galvanising force was the ECtHR

---

[240] [1992] All ER 65.
[241] See J Wright, 'The Operational Obligation under Article 2 of the European Convention on Human Rights and Challenges for Coherence—Views from the English Supreme Court and Strasbourg' (2016) *Journal of European Tort Law* 7(1), 51–81.
[242] See for example *Rabone* (n 63).
[243] *R v Lambert* (n 102), *R v Kansal* [2001] UKHL 62, [2001] 3 WLR 751.
[244] *X (Minors)* (n 69).
[245] *JD* (n 204).

decision in *Z v United Kingdom* where a serious violation of Article 3 (the right not to suffer inhuman and degrading treatment) was found.

Remedies

Section 8 governs remedies in relation to the HRA cause of action and provides as follows:

1. In relation to any act (or proposed act) of a public authority which the court finds is (or would be unlawful), it may grant such relief or remedy, or make such order, within its powers as it considers just and appropriate.
2. But damages may be awarded only by a court which has power to award damages, or to order payment of compensation, in civil proceedings.
3. No award of damages is to be made unless, taking account of all the circumstances of the case, including –
   (a) any other relief or remedy granted, or order made, in relation to the act in question (by that or any other court), and
   (b) the consequences of any decision (of that or any other court) in respect of that act
   the court is satisfied that the award is necessary to award just satisfaction to the person in whose favour the award is made.
4. In determining –
   (a) whether to award damages, or
   (b) the amount of an award
   the court must take into account the principles applied by the ECtHR in relation to the award of compensation under Article 41 of the Convention.

Thus, English courts are required to take into account the principles applied by the ECtHR in making awards of just satisfaction and that goes to *quantum* as well as determining whether an award should be made.

The House of Lords held that the HRA is not a tort statute and English courts should not apply domestic scales of damages.[246] In *Anufrijeva v London Borough of Southwark*, the Court of Appeal had identified the ending of a violation as the primary aim of human rights cases and stated that 'In considering whether to award compensation and, if so, how much, there is a balance to be drawn between the interests of the victim and those of the public as a whole'.[247] However, the Court of Appeal had also suggested that where damages would be an appropriate remedy, levels of tort awards as reflected in the guidelines issued by the Judicial Studies Board may provide some rough guidance. The House of Lords' disapproval of this view could not have been more explicit in *R (on the application of Greenfield)*

---

[246] *Greenfield* (n 223).
[247] *Anufrijeva v London Borough of Southwark* [2004] 2 QB 1124. For discussion, see Law Commission, *Remedies against Public Bodies: A Scoping Report*, 10 October 2006 at pp 4–5.

v Secretary of State for the Home Department.[248] In the context of a breach of
the Article 6 right to a fair hearing, Lord Bingham gave the leading speech for a
unanimous House and stated that 'the focus of the convention is on the protection
of human rights and not the award of compensation'.[249]

Although *Greenfield* concerned a violation of the procedural rights enshrined in
Article 6, Lord Bingham's observations on the role of the new HRA remedy have
general application to awards of damages under the HRA and bear repeating here:

> the 1998 Act is not a tort statute. Its objects are different and broader. Even in a case
> where a finding of a violation is not judged to afford the applicant just satisfaction, such
> a finding will be an important part of his remedy and an important vindication of the
> right he has asserted. Damages need not ordinarily be awarded to encourage high stand-
> ards of compliance by member states, since they are already bound in international law
> to perform their duties under the convention in good faith … the purpose of incorporat-
> ing the convention in domestic law through the 1998 Act was not to give victims better
> remedies at home than they could recover in Strasbourg but to give them the same rem-
> edies without the delay and expense of Strasbourg … s 8(4) requires a domestic court
> to take into account the principles applied by the European Court … . There could be
> no clearer indication that courts in this country should look to Strasbourg and not to
> domestic precedents.[250]

Lord Bingham's observations have rightly been criticised as being based upon the
erroneous view that tort law is about compensation for loss.[251] Tort law protects
rights and has been an effective mechanism for protecting what are now conceived
as 'human' rights long before the international community addressed its collective
will to agreeing international human rights standards. On the other hand, civil
rights of action against the state and the payment of compensation are frequently
required in order for the enjoyment of human rights to be real and effective. It
is not only Article 13 that requires the payment of compensation in appropriate
cases.[252] Lord Bingham set up a false dichotomy between the objects of tort and
the objects of the HRA in *Greenfield*. Lord Scott in *Ashley* observed that, 'the principal aim of an award of compensatory damages is to compensate the claimant for
loss suffered, [but] there is no reason in principle why an award of compensatory
damages should not also fulfil a vindicatory purpose'.[253]

Booth and Squires writing in 2006 remarked that, in cases brought under the
HRA, the common law approach to damages seems generally to have been adopted

---

[248] *Greenfield* (n 223).
[249] *Greenfield* (n 223) [9]. See also his observations in *Watkins* (n 210) regarding levels of awards by
Strasbourg which tend to be ungenerous.
[250] *Greenfield* (n 223).
[251] R Stevens, *Torts and Rights* (Oxford, Oxford University Press, 2007) 288–89; Varuhas (n 222) 74;
Steele (n 219) 634.
[252] For example, see discussion of the legal 'frameworks' required by the positive obligations under
Arts 2 and 4, text accompanying n 58, Chapter 4.
[253] *Ashley v Chief Constable of Sussex Police* [2008] 1 AC 962 [22] quoted by Varuhas (n 222) 74.

by the courts.[254] This is no longer the case. *Greenfield* has been endorsed at the highest level in *Faulkner*, where the Supreme Court confirmed that any award of damages should be guided by the clear and consistent practice of the ECtHR and *quantum* should broadly reflect the level of awards made by the European Court in favour of applicants from states with a similar cost of living.[255] *Faulkner* concerned an indeterminate sentence prisoner whose case for release was not considered by the Parole Board within a reasonable time after the end of the tariff period. It was held that damages should ordinarily be awarded where it has been established on the balance of probabilities that the prisoner has been detained beyond the date when he would ordinarily have been released. Even where it is not established that an earlier release would have occurred, there is a strong but not irrebuttable presumption that delay in violation of Article 5(4) will cause a prisoner to suffer feelings of frustration and anxiety and in such cases an award of damages on a modest scale should ordinarily be awarded.

In his comprehensive study, Varuhas has argued strongly that damages awarded for the violation of human rights should be modelled on the torts that are actionable *per se* since they serve to vindicate rights. He has argued that there is nothing in the HRA which requires a slavish mirroring of the approach of the ECtHR under Article 41 ECHR. The result has been to 'preclude development of a domestic jurisprudence of human rights damages which is sensitive to English legal tradition and economic conditions, as well as deeper thinking as to the theoretical underpinnings of the remedy'.[256] There is much to be said for the argument, but while the HRA does not bind English courts to the Article 41 jurisprudence, section 8(4) clearly requires English courts to take account of both principles and levels of award. Furthermore, the HRA was intended to afford in English courts the justice that applicants would receive in Strasbourg, 'bringing the rights home'. Lord Bingham in *Greenfield* stated that the aim of incorporating the Convention 'was not to give victims better remedies at home than they could recover in Strasbourg but to give them the same remedies without the delay and expense of resort to Strasbourg'.[257]

In his study, Varuhas has criticised the tendency of the courts to treat damages as of 'secondary, if any, importance, and a remedy of last resort'.[258] There are exceptions, but these are largely under the umbrella of Articles 2 and 3. It is important in this connection to recall that Article 13 requires the payment of compensation where the most important Convention rights (Articles 2 and 3) have been violated.[259] Varuhas has criticised the tendency of English courts to

---

[254] C Booth QC and D Squires, *The Negligence Liability of Public Authorities* (Oxford, Oxford University Press, 2006) 7.118.
[255] *R (Faulkner) v Secretary of State for Justice* [2013] UKSC 23, [2013] 2 AC 254.
[256] Varuhas, *Damages and Human Rights* (Oxford, Hart Publishing, 2016) 5.
[257] *Greenfield* (n 223) [19].
[258] Varuhas (n 256) 92.
[259] *Z v United Kingdom* (n 30) [109]; *E v UK* (2003) 36 EHRR 31 [110].

ignore Article 13, especially when the ECtHR has signalled a more aggressive approach to enforcement of Article 13 so that the subsidiary aim of the ECHR can be realised.[260]

One thing about which commentators agree is that it is a challenge to identify the principles applied by Strasbourg in making awards of just satisfaction.[261] Frequently, the Court will limit itself to stating that the award is made on an 'equitable basis'. Attempts have been made to achieve greater consistency at Strasbourg with the setting up of an Article 41 unit with the Registry of the Court to advise the Chambers on the appropriate levels of award. In *Rabone*,[262] Lord Dyson stated that in the absence of guideline cases in which the range of compensation is specified and relevant considerations articulated, it is necessary for the domestic courts to do their best in the light of such guidance as can be gleaned from Strasbourg.

In *Faulkner*, the Supreme Court set out guidance for the future regarding submissions on the case law of the ECtHR regarding Article 41. Exhibiting some frustration, Lord Reed remarked that the Court had been faced with a 'blizzard' of authorities from which extracting principles required painstaking effort. In future an agreed Scott schedule should be placed before the Court which would provide the following information: 1. The name and citation of the case, and its location in the bound volumes of authorities; 2. The violations of the Convention which were established, with references to the paragraphs in the judgment where the findings were made; 3. The damages awarded, if any. It is helpful if their sterling equivalent at present values can be agreed; 4. A brief summary of the appellant's contentions in relation to the case, with references to the key paragraphs in the judgment; 5. A brief summary of the respondent's contentions in relation to the case, again with references to the key paragraphs.

Lord Reed suggested that as the practice of the European Court is increasingly absorbed by our own courts, the remedy under the HRA will become 'naturalised' so that the first point of reference in determining awards will be our own case law, rather than the international court.[263]

It is frequently asserted that punitive/exemplary damages are not in principle awarded by the ECtHR. However, this received opinion,[264] as it has been described by Fairgrieve, is not supported by the jurisprudence. The conduct of the defendant state and the seriousness of the violation are frequently referred to as aggravating factors that influence the level of an award. Thus, in *Tas v Turkey*,[265] where

---

[260] Varuhas (n 256) 330.

[261] D Fairgrieve, 'The HRA 1998, Damages and English Tort Law' in D Fairgrieve, M Andenas and J Bell, *Tort Liability of Public Authorities in Comparative Perspective* (British Institute of International and Comparative Law, 2002); A Burrows, 'Damages and Rights' in D Nolan and A Robertson (eds), *Rights and Private Law* (Oxford, Hart Publishing, 2012).

[262] *Rabone* (n 63).

[263] *Faulkner* (n 255) [29]. For discussion see M Andenas, E Bjorge and D Fairgrieve, 'A Fair Price for Violations of Human Rights' (2014) *Law Quarterly Review* 130 (Jan) 48–52.

[264] Fairgrieve (n 261) 92.

[265] (2001) 33 EHRR 325.

the applicant's son died in the custody of the security forces and in unexplained circumstances, the Court in making its award referred to the 'indifference and callousness of the authorities to the applicant's concerns' and the 'acute anguish and uncertainty which the court assumed the applicant suffered'. Other examples can be given where it would seem that the particularly serious nature of the violation(s) is reflected in the levels of compensation awarded by the ECtHR.[266]

In *Anufrijeva* and *Watkins*, English courts held that punitive damages are not available under section 8(3) HRA. In *D v Commissioner of Police for the Metropolis*,[267] claims for damages under the HRA were brought by two victims of the serial black cab rapist, John Worboys. Each claimant had received payments to settle civil actions; the claims here related to the breach of the requirement to conduct an effective investigation which is inherent within Article 3. In one case Green J found that the assault would have been avoided if Article 3 had not been breached; this causal element was lacking in the earlier case. Green J awarded damages to both victims citing the 'profound failure' to protect the public. The damages in the civil action had been exclusively for harm caused by Worboys' tortious acts. Damages for harm caused by the police failings had not been pleaded. Settlement of that action had specifically made clear that it was at an undervalue, and left open the possibility of claims against others to make up the shortfall. A category of harm attributable to the Article 3 violation could be identified, for which no compensation had already been paid, but otherwise there was an overlap between the civil claims and the instant claim. The Court had therefore to consider the civil claim, but was not hidebound by the damages awarded because its jurisdiction was based on equity, not on tort.[268]

It has been argued by a number of commentators that levels of award in respect of non-pecuniary loss under the HRA should be determined by applying the scales of quantum for tort compensation by analogy. This argument has been forcefully made by Burrows, notwithstanding his view that the HRA cause of action is not a tort. This writer would take the opposite view: the HRA cause of action is a tort and there are sound reasons why tort scales would be inappropriate guides. The HRA has created a category of civil wrong in respect of which the court has a power to award damages. Stevens has described the HRA as the most important 'tort statute' ever enacted.[269] For some commentators and judges the fact that damages are at the discretion of the court means that the cause of action is not a tort. However, all definitions of tort begin by saying that a tort is a civil wrong. Furthermore, there are other examples of causes of action created by statute which

---

[266] *Aksoy v Turkey* (1997) 23 EHRR 553; *Assenov v Bulgaria* (1998) 28 EHRR 652; *Selmouni v France* (1999) 29 EHRR 403. See F Bydlinski, 'Methodological Approaches to the Tort Law of the ECHR' in A Fenyes, E Karner, H Koziol, E Steiner (eds), *Tort Law in the Jurisprudence of the European Court of Human Rights* (Berlin/Boston, Walter de Gruyter GmbH & Co KG, 2011) who discusses the Court's response to 'particularly bare-faced' intentional breaches of law at 2/23.

[267] [2014] EWHC 2493, [2015] 1 WLR 1833.

[268] *Ibid* [47], [56]–[63].

[269] Stevens (n 251), 289.

no one would seriously doubt are torts, but for which an award of damages is discretionary. Section 3 of the Protection from Harassment Act 1997 creates a new tort and section 3(2) provides that damages are discretionary. Furthermore, as in the case of torts generally, an employer may be vicariously liable for harassment under the Act.[270] We have previously suggested that

> It has always been the case ... that a right of action and remedies are different creatures and it does seem appropriate to speak of the HRA remedy as a tort, if attention is focused on the nature of the wrong rather than the remedy.[271]

The Law Commission in its report *Damages under the Human Rights Act 1998* argued that the HRA creates a new form of action for breach of statutory duty.[272] Clerk & Lindsell have described the action as a 'constitutional tort'.[273] Varuhas has remarked that 'private law', 'tort' and 'public law' have no settled meaning so that classifying the claim as a tort or private law claim would not lead us to any one remedial approach.[274] It is, however, important for the purposes of exposition how we classify a cause of action. A student of tort law would be extremely misled by any tort law text that did not provide an account of the rights and obligations that arise under the HRA.

On the other hand, as we have seen, Lord Bingham took the view that the HRA is 'not a tort statute' but, as Stevens has argued, this is because he took the view that the law of torts 'is solely concerned with compensation for loss'. Lord Browne in *Van Colle*[275] and, more recently, Laws LJ in *D v Commissioner of Police for the Metropolis*,[276] have fallen into the same trap, convinced that the law of tort is about compensation for loss. Laws LJ illustrated his argument by saying that in the negligence claim the focus is on the defendant's loss; indeed, damage is the gist of the claim but that does not apply to other torts. Damages awarded in common law claims are by no means always compensatory: thus, we have nominal, contemptuous damages and exemplary damages.[277] That this is not the case is demonstrated most powerfully by the torts that are actionable *per se* and which can be seen as effective vehicles to vindicate rights of personal integrity, rights that long predated the HRA and which have always been essential bulwarks against unlawful state action. The 'staggering march'[278] of the negligence action which is premised upon the need to demonstrate loss/damage has arguably clouded all our thinking.

---

[270] *Majrowski v Guy's and St Thomas's NHS Trust* [2006] UKHL 34.

[271] K Stanton, M Harris, P Skidmore and J Wright, *Statutory Torts* (London, Sweet & Maxwell, 2003) 144.

[272] Law Commission and Scottish Law Commission, *Damages under the Human Rights Act 1998* (Law Com No 266, 2000; Scottish Law Com No 180, 2000) discussed by D Fairgrieve (n 261) 83.

[273] *Clerk & Lindsell on Torts*, 21st edn (London, Sweet & Maxwell, 2014), 14–68, electronic resource.

[274] Varuhas (n 256) 4.

[275] *Van Colle v Chief Constable of Hertfordshire Police* [2008] UKHL 50, [2009] 1 AC 225 [138].

[276] *DSD v Commissioner of Police for the Metropolis* [2015] EWCA Civ 646, [2016] QB 429161 [30] and [65]–[67].

[277] Fairgrieve (n 261) 91.

[278] T Weir, 'The Staggering March of Negligence' in P Cane and J Stapleton, *The Law of Obligations: Essays in Celebration of John Fleming* (Oxford, Oxford University Press, 1998).

Insofar as it is possible to identify the 'principles' which inform the award of 'just satisfaction' by the ECtHR, the following represents a summary of the approach that has been consistent:

i.   If the nature of the reach allows of *restitutio in integrum* it is for the respondent state to effect it.

ii.   In principle, the Court awards both pecuniary and non-pecuniary damage, in either case the applicant must establish a causal link between the violation complained of and the alleged pecuniary damage. The Court has held on a number of occasions that where the violation consists of a failure to accord the victim due process, for example access to a court under Article 6(1), it will not speculate as to the outcome of the proceedings had the violation not occurred. However, the Court seems to be resiling from this position so that the Court will award damages for 'lost opportunities'. In *Weeks v UK*, the applicant was awarded compensation for the lost opportunity he suffered as a result of being unable to challenge the lawfulness of his detention in violation of Article 5(4).[279]

iii. The Court will take into account any conduct by the applicant that may have contributed to the violation, thus a principle akin to contributory negligence is applied by the Court.

iv.   The Court awards damages for various types of pecuniary loss, including reduction in the value of property,[280] loss of past and future earnings[281] and medical expenses.

v.   The range of categories of harm included under the umbrella of 'non-pecuniary damage' is very wide when compared with allowable heads of damage in tort. Thus, the following, which do not need to be consequent upon any personal injury or other harm are included: 'trauma, anxiety, and feeling of injustice',[282] 'feeling of helplessness and frustration',[283] 'inconvenience ... substantial anxiety and distress', 'distress and anxiety (through witnessing a continuing violation and the deterioration in another's health),[284] 'harassment ... humiliation .... stress'.

vi.   The conduct of the victim of a violation will be relevant to the award of damages and in this sense it is true to say that the Court makes moral judgments about the applicant before it.[285] Thus, in *McCann Farrell and Savage v UK*,[286] no award of compensation was made having regard to the fact that three terrorists were intending to plant a bomb in Gibraltar.

---

[279] *Weeks v UK* (1988) 10 EHRR 293.
[280] *Pine Valley Developments v Ireland* (1993) 16 EHRR 379.
[281] *Young, James and Webster v UK* (1982) 4 EHRR 38.
[282] *McMichael v United Kingdom* (1995) 20 EHRR 205.
[283] *Papamichaelopoulos v Greece* (1996) 21 EHRR 439.
[284] *Lopes Ostra v Spain* (1994) 20 EHRR 277.
[285] A Mowbray, 'The European Court of Human Rights Approach to Just Satisfaction' [1997] Public Law 647.
[286] (1995) 21 EHRR 97.

Concluding Remarks

In this chapter, we have sought to describe the architecture or framework of the HRA and how ECHR principles developed at Strasbourg are mediated into English law and become part of English law. Under section 6, the Act has created a new public authority tort that consists of acting in a way which is incompatible with a Convention right. The HRA provides the framework by which the tort is established. The substantive content of the tort is fed by the obligations that have been undertaken by the United Kingdom in entering into the ECHR and which have been elaborated by the ECtHR. The following chapter will therefore examine ECHR jurisprudence relating to the rights set out in Schedule 1 HRA and which English courts are required to take into account under section 2.

4

The European Convention on Human Rights

Part 1—General Principles of Interpretation

Introduction

This chapter is divided into two parts. Part 1 conveys in broad terms the key general principles that guide Strasbourg in the interpretation of the European Convention of Human Rights (ECHR). Part 2 examines the Strasbourg jurisprudence relating to the Protected Rights under the Human Rights Act 1998 (HRA), as well as key cases that have been decided by the English courts. Section 7 HRA has introduced a statutory cause of action against public authorities that act incompatibly with the rights set out in Schedule 1 to the Act. English courts must take account of Strasbourg jurisprudence under section 2 HRA; the scope of the cause of action is therefore informed by reference to the case law in relation to specific rights and, arguably, the general principles of interpretation developed by Strasbourg since the ECHR came into force on 3 September 1953.

The United Nations Vienna Declaration and Programme of Action, adopted by the World Conference on 25 June 1993, called upon states to treat human rights 'globally in a fair and equal manner, on the same footing, and with the same emphasis'. However, a reading of the major human rights instruments reveals that human rights standards do not all require the same degree of protection at all times, and this comment applies with equal force to the Convention and its jurisprudence and indeed to English case law under the HRA. The 'foreign cases' discussed below are perhaps the clearest examples of the nuanced approach the courts take to the protection of human rights; where an individual faces the prospect of torture or ill-treatment on return to another state, the bar to prevent return is not set so high as in a case where he might face a violation of the right to freedom of expression. It is possible therefore to conceive of the Convention as a hierarchy of rights. For example, states are permitted, 'in time of war or other public emergency threatening the life of the nation', to take measures derogating from certain of their obligations under the Convention (Article 15), provided that certain conditions are satisfied. However, states cannot derogate from Article 2 (the right to life), except in respect of deaths resulting from lawful acts of war, nor Article 3 (the right not to be tortured or suffer inhuman and degrading treatment or punishment), Article 4(1) (prohibition of slavery or servitude) and Article 7 (no punishment without law). These rights therefore represent the irreducible core rights that must be protected under any circumstances. War, civil insurrection and other public emergency will not operate to reduce the obligation of the state.[1]

At the lower end of the 'hierarchy' are the 'personal freedom' Articles set out in Articles 8 to 11: Article 8 (the right to respect for private and family life, home and correspondence), Article 9 (freedom of thought, conscience and religion), Article 10 (freedom of expression) and Article 11 (freedom of association). These rights may be the subject of derogation under Article 15 and they may also be subject to limitations and restrictions imposed by the state. The common structure of these Articles is that paragraph 1 sets out the right and paragraph 2 sets out the grounds upon which the right may be limited or restricted. Although initially conceived in relation to derogations under Article 15, it is regarding permitted limitations that Strasbourg has developed its extensive 'margin of appreciation doctrine', discussed below. For the moment, suffice to say that this doctrine operates to create a sphere of deference on the part of Strasbourg to the Contracting States. It is a mechanism that has operated so that, in the first analysis, it is left to the state to determine whether the need to restrict or limit the right arises. This does not mean that Strasbourg does not retain supervisory jurisdiction, rather that in certain circumstances the initial assessment of the exigencies of a situation fall to be determined by the state. How great the margin is, will depend upon the interest at stake and the aim of the restriction: where national security and morals are sought to be protected a wide margin is accorded, while restricting freedom of expression under Article 10(2) in order to 'maintain the authority and impartiality of the judiciary' calls for a narrower margin. The narrower margin is dictated because it is possible to achieve 'an objective understanding of the content of the interest sought to be protected'.[2] The margin of appreciation is not a 'hands off' doctrine; rather, it envisages that the state will weigh up the various elements of the ECHR in order to determine the content of the right and to evaluate the reasons for interfering with the right.[3] In *Hirst v UK (No 2)* (which concerned the total ban on prisoner voting), the Court noted that neither the UK Parliament nor the UK courts had carried out any exercise to balance the prisoners' right to vote and the public interest. The Grand Chamber concluded that: 'a general, automatic and indiscriminate restriction on a vitally important Convention right must be seen as falling outside any acceptable margin of appreciation, however wide that margin might be ...'[4]

---

[1] Subject to the operation of a margin of appreciation under Article 15, discussed below.

[2] See the discussion of *Sunday Times v UK* 2 EHRR 245 [59] discussed by DJ Harris, M O'Boyle, EP Bates and CM Buckley, *Harris O'Boyle & Warbrick: Law of the European Convention on Human Rights*, 2nd edn (Oxford, Oxford University Press, 2009) 355.

[3] Harris, O'Boyle and Warbrick, *ibid* 350.

[4] *Hirst v UK (No 2)* (2006) 42 EHRR 849.

The Convention, together with its Protocols, sets out the rights that states are obliged by Article 1 to 'secure to everyone' within the jurisdiction. There is no need for a person to be a citizen or to have any residence rights within a state in order for the obligation to arise and indeed much domestic case law has arisen in relation to challenges regarding deportation and extradition of foreign nationals.[5] As we have seen in Chapter 3, the Supreme Court has held that jurisdiction under the HRA may extend to operations and activities on foreign territory.[6]

There has been considerable development of the concept of jurisdiction and therefore state responsibility under Article 1 ECHR through the cases arising from the conflicts in Iraq and Afghanistan. However, those cases set out the extent of extraterritorial jurisdiction of the United Kingdom under the HRA for acts and omissions in areas of the globe where there has been effective state control over territory or persons by the United Kingdom. There is another type of case where the responsibility of the United Kingdom may be engaged by a decision to remove a person to another state because that person will be exposed to the risk of an event which would be a violation of the Convention upon being returned to a non-member of the Council of Europe. The classic authority is *Soering v United Kingdom*,[7] where the European Court of Human Rights (ECtHR) held that extradition of the applicant to the USA would expose him to a real risk of treatment going beyond the threshold set by Article 3 (in this case the so-called 'death row phenomenon') and the decision to extradite, if implemented would therefore give rise to a breach of Article 3. The Contracting State is thus liable for the decision to expel or remove rather than the treatment meted out in the third state. The threshold for engagement of the right under the HRA is variable according to which right is in play.

The threshold under both the ECHR and HRA in relation to Article 3 is that an individual needs to show that there are substantial grounds for believing that an individual would face a real risk of being subjected to treatment contrary to Article 3 if removed to another state.[8] So far as other Articles are concerned, the House of Lords held in *R (on the application of Ullah) v Special Adjudicator*[9] that it must be shown that there would be a flagrant denial or gross violation of the right whereby the right would be completely denied or nullified in the destination country.

The story of the Convention is that of a search for shared European values, a search for consensus between the Contracting States—the development of the jurisprudence can be seen as an exercise in comparative law on a grand scale. In Chapter 3 we examined the interpretation of section 2 HRA and the impact of Strasbourg jurisprudence on English law, including the doctrine of precedent. When English courts seek to flesh out the bare bones of the Convention text in

---

[5] See generally M Amos, *Human Rights Law*, 2nd edn (Oxford, Hart Publishing, 2014).

[6] *Smith v Ministry of Defence* [2013] UKSC 41, [2014] AC 52.

[7] (1989) 11 EHRR 439.

[8] *Ibid*; *N v Secretary of State for the Home Department* [2005] UKHL 31, [2005] 2 AC 296.

[9] [2004] UKHL 26, [2004] 2 AC 323 [20].

new areas under the HRA, the domestic rules of the Member States of the Council of Europe may be relevant to determine whether there is consensus on an issue such that a European standard can be found. As we have seen in the previous chapter there has been a growing willingness on the part of English courts to develop a distinctive body of English human rights law so that the fact that Strasbourg has not yet pronounced may not be a barrier to further development of a right.

General Principles of Interpretation Applied by Strasbourg

The Convention is a treaty and is therefore to be interpreted according to the rules of international law on the interpretation of treaties.[10] The basic rule is contained in Article 31 of the Vienna Convention on the Law of Treaties 1969 which provides that a treaty is to be interpreted in good faith and in accordance with the ordinary meaning to be given to the terms of the treaty in their context and in the light of its object and purpose. Context comprises in addition to the text, including its preamble and annexes, any agreements relating to the treaty made between all parties in connection with the treaty. The Strasbourg organs have adopted a teleological approach to interpretation, with the emphasis on purposive construction in the light of 'the object and purpose' of the Convention. Summarising its approach, the Strasbourg Court has said that:

> Under the Vienna Convention on the Law of Treaties, the Court is required to ascertain the ordinary meaning to be given to the words in their context and in the light of the object and purpose of the provision from which they are drawn … The Court must have regard to the fact that the context of the provision is a treaty for the effective protection of individual human rights and that the Convention must be read as a whole, and interpreted in such a way as to promote internal consistency and harmony between its various provisions … The Court must take into account any relevant rules and principles of international law applicable in relations between the Contracting Parties … Recourse may also be had to supplementary means of interpretation, including the preparatory works to the Convention, either to confirm a meaning determined in accordance with the above steps, or to establish the meaning where it would otherwise be ambiguous, obscure or manifestly absurd or unreasonable …[11]

It is rare for Strasbourg to consider the *travaux preparatoires*, since the golden thread that runs through the jurisprudence is the constant refrain that the Convention is a 'living instrument' which must be interpreted in the light of present-day conditions.[12] This approach has been applied in a number of areas where the

---

[10] *Golder v UK* (1975) 1 EHRR 524 [29].
[11] *Saadi v United Kingdom* (2008) 47 EHRR 427 [62].
[12] *Tyrer v United Kingdom* (1978) 2 EHRR 1 [31].

Court has considered that domestic legal rules are out of step with wider European standards. So, for example, laws which treated illegitimate children less favourably than the legitimate were found to be in violation of the Convention, as was the former criminal law in Northern Ireland which completely criminalised homosexual sex. A good illustration of the 'living instrument' is provided by the cases regarding the requirement for states to give formal recognition to the new gender of post-operative transsexuals. In *Sheffield and Horsham*,[13] the applicants challenged the refusal of the UK to allow amendment of a birth certificate following gender reassignment surgery in order to reflect the post-operative identity. They alleged a violation of the Article 8 right to respect for private life. The Court found that there was still medical uncertainty in this field and that there was no uniformity of approach among states. However, the UK was advised that the matter should be kept under review in the light of advances in science and changing social attitudes. Finally, in *Goodwin*, the Court recognised that although there was not yet a clear common European approach, the international trend was in favour of not only the social acceptance of transsexuals, but also legal recognition of the new gender of post-operative transsexuals.[14] The House of Lords has also held that: 'As an important constitutional instrument the convention is to be seen as a "living tree capable of growth and expansion within its natural limits"'.[15]

There are limits to the living instrument approach and it is noticeable that references to the evolving interpretation of ECHR rights are relatively sparse in the reasoning of the English Supreme Court.[16] In *Moohan*, Lord Kerr, considering the disenfranchisement of Scottish prisoners from voting in the Scottish Referendum, argued that it was imperative to interpret the Convention as a 'living instrument' and furthermore that the Convention should be interpreted in light of its object and purpose—the relevant purpose here being the guarantee of an 'effective political democracy'.[17] There are of course constraints upon the ECtHR in that the development of its case law must be in harmony with other principles of international law; Strasbourg case law does not develop in a vacuum.[18]

Apart from determining the reach of particular rights in petitions taken by applicants, Strasbourg has developed what might be described as broad principles of 'interpretation', which may now be applied by English courts by virtue of s 2 HRA. These principles may be of particular importance where English courts are determining claims under the HRA and there is no previous case that seems directly relevant. So, for example, it is customary for Strasbourg to examine state

---

[13] *Sheffield and Horsham v United Kingdom* (1999) 27 EHRR 163.

[14] *Goodwin v United Kingdom* (2002) 35 EHRR 447.

[15] *Brown v Stott* [2003] 1 AC 681.

[16] But see *Rabone v Pennine Care NHS Trust* [2012] UKSC 2, [2012] 2 AC 72 and *Smith* (n 6).

[17] *Moohan v Lord Advocate* [2014] UKSC 67, [2015] AC 901. In the Preamble to the ECHR, the Contracting States '[reaffirmed] their profound belief in those Fundamental Freedoms which are the foundation of justice and peace in the world and are best maintained ... by an effective political democracy ... and by a common understanding and observance of the Human Rights on which they depend'.

[18] *Neulinger and Shuruck v Switzerland* [2011] 1 FLR 122.

practice in order to determine whether there is state consensus upon an issue. An illustrative example is the determination that a taking of property in violation of Article 1 of Protocol No 1 required payment of compensation: this conclusion was gleaned from the practice of the States parties.[19] It is clearly legitimate for English courts, in the absence of a definitive ruling from Strasbourg, to seek solutions to novel questions by looking for the consensus among other Council of Europe states and by examining the evolving standards of other Council of Europe members.

Conversely, where there is no consensus, the ECtHR has tended to apply 'a lowest common denominator' approach or to accommodate variations in state practice through the 'margin of appreciation doctrine'.[20] In *R (on the application of Animal Defenders) v Culture Secretary*,[21] the House of Lords, clearly rejecting any sense of being bound by Strasbourg, held that the absolute prohibition of political advertising in the broadcast media was compatible with Article 10 ECHR, despite the authority of the European Court in *VgT Verien gegen Tierfabriken v Switzerland*.[22] Lord Bingham alluded to a lack of consensus among the Member States and the consequent wider margin of appreciation and held that, in the absence of a 'settled practice ... it may be that each state is best fitted to judge the checks and balances necessary to safeguard, consistently with Article 10, the integrity of its own democracy'.[23]

Section 2 HRA does not make any reference to case law other than that of Strasbourg, so it might be thought that English courts are free to take into account other comparative material in determining any question relating to the Convention rights; there is nothing on the face of section 2 to suggest that English courts may not seek solutions from foreign jurisdictions. The Preamble to the ECHR recites the Universal Declaration of Human Rights, which clearly inspired the drafting of the ECHR, as well as the International Bill of Rights. It has been suggested that English courts should be able to use comparative jurisprudence where 'there is little or no steer from the Strasbourg organs'[24] and that case law from other (non-Council of Europe) jurisdictions is often referred to in interpreting the HRA and Convention rights.[25] It is submitted that the latter is an overstatement. There are examples of English courts straying beyond the confines of the Council of Europe to determine the scope of an ECHR right such as *R (on the application*

---

[19] *James v United Kingdom* (1986) 8 EHRR 123 (54), discussed in this context by Harris, O'Boyle and Warbrick (n 2) 8.

[20] Harris, O'Boyle and Warbrick (n 2) 9.

[21] [2008] UKHL 15, [2008] 1 AC 1313.

[22] (2001) 34 EHRR 159.

[23] *Animal Defenders* (n 21) [35], Baroness Hale, Lord Carswell and Lord Neuberger concurring.

[24] F Klug, 'The Human Rights Act 1998, *Pepper v Hart* and All That' [1999] *Public Law* 246, 251, quoted by J Lewis, 'The European Ceiling' [2007] *Public Law* 720, 732.

[25] Amos (n 5) 27.

of Pretty) v Director of Public Prosecutions,[26] but more recently the courts have seemed less inclined to do so. Indeed, some scepticism has been expressed regarding whether English courts should look beyond Strasbourg case law.[27] Lord Hope observed in *N v Secretary of State for the Home Department* that:

> ... [I]t is not for [the House of Lords] to search for a solution to her problem which is not to be found in the Strasbourg case law. It is for the Strasbourg court, not us, to decide whether its case law is out of touch with modern conditions and to determine what further extensions, if any, are needed to the rights guaranteed by the Convention.[28]

As with *Ullah*,[29] though, this observation is in the context of whether Convention rights should be extended which would have very significant financial consequences for the United Kingdom (the provision of medical care to AIDS sufferers). Unusually, in *Re P*, one of their Lordships did rely upon authority from the South African Constitutional Court in emphasising that the paramountcy of the best interests of the child is the explicit goal of the relevant legislation.[30]

A search of the database containing all the case law under the ECHR reveals very limited reference by the Strasbourg Court to comparative material beyond the Council of Europe zone. Applicants frequently make arguments by reference to other non-Council of Europe national systems but the Court very rarely justifies its reasoning in this way. It is customary for the Court to recite international materials on any question and the Court has stressed that its decisions should be consistent with other international law obligations[31] but the reasoning of the Court is generally premised upon European authorities. The emphasis is always upon the search for consensus amongst Council of Europe states.[32] The Court occasionally refers to other treaties and monitoring bodies, but references to national jurisdictions are sparse indeed. So, while section 2 is apparently silent as to the use of comparative material, the signal from Strasbourg is clear. As a matter of impression, it would seem that the appetite of English courts for comparative law at least *in the*

---

[26] [2001] UKHL 61, [2002] 1 AC 800. Lord Bingham paid particular attention to *Rodriguez v Attorney General (Canada)* [1994] 2 LRC 136, but in the absence of any ECHR authority was not prepared to hold that the refusal of the Director of Public Prosecutions to give an undertaking not to prosecute Mrs Pretty's husband violated any Convention rights. Lord Hope did suggest that a strained reading of Article 8 ECHR might have been appropriate 'if there was evidence of international opinion in favour of assisted suicide'. There was none [101].

[27] *Dyer v Watson* [2002] UKPC D 1, [2004] 1 AC 379 (Lord Hope).

[28] *N v Secretary of State for the Home Department* [2005] UKHL 30, 2 AC 296 [25]. See also Lord Bingham and Lord Rodger in *Sheldrake v DPP* [2004] UKHL 43, [2005] 1 AC 262 [33] and [58], quoted by Lewis (n 24).

[29] *R (on the application of Ullah) v Special Adjudicator* (n 9) and see Chapter 3.

[30] *Re P (A Child) (Adoption: Unmarried Couples)* [2008] UKHL 38, [2009] 1 AC 173 [17]. See Lord Hoffmann's discussion of *Du Toit v Minister for Welfare and Population Development* (2002) 13 BHRC 187 Con Ct (SA).

[31] *Golder* (n 10); *Al-Adsani v United Kingdom* (2002) 34 EHRR 11; *Neulinger v Switzerland* [2011] FLR 122.

[32] See for example *Stjerna v Finland* (1997) 24 EHRR 195; *Vo v France* (2005) 40 EHRR 12; *Evans v United Kingdom* (2008) 46 EHRR 34.

context of the HRA is now squarely focused on the Council of Europe, rather than other common law jurisdictions.[33]

However, in determining difficult contemporary moral questions the Court may on occasion examine other domestic jurisdictions: recent examples include the Chamber's examination of *Rodriguez v Att Gen (Canada)*[34] in *Pretty v United Kingdom*[35] and the use of US and Israeli authorities in *Evans v United Kingdom*.[36] However, arguably, the foreign authorities made no difference to the outcome in the decisions.

According to Article 1 of the Convention, each state agrees 'to secure to everyone within [its] jurisdiction the rights and freedoms defined in Section 1 of the Convention'. The Convention does not specify *how* the rights and freedoms are to be protected: the obligation on the state is to secure the substance of the right and Article 13 provides that everyone whose rights and freedoms are violated 'shall have an effective remedy before a national authority notwithstanding that the violation has been committed by persons acting in an official capacity'. Thus, the means by which the right is secured is a domestic issue. For example, in *Guerra v Italy*,[37] the applicants complained that the local authority had failed to take appropriate steps to reduce the risk of pollution from a factory. They sought an order from the ECtHR which would have required the state to decontaminate an industrial site and to conduct inquiries to identify serious effects on residents who it was believed had been exposed to carcinogenic substances. The Court observed that it had no power under the Convention to accede to this request and stated that:

> it is for the State to choose the means to be used in its domestic legal system in order to comply with the provisions of the Convention or to redress the situation that has given rise to the violation of the Convention.[38]

Article 13 was not included within the rights that are listed in Schedule 1 to the HRA, because the action under section 7 and the remedy in Section 8 is intended to be the vehicle through which an individual seeks a remedy in the English courts. Although it is generally true to say that the means by which rights are protected is a domestic matter, the European Court has on occasion indicated the nature of the remedy that should be provided. Thus, in *Z v United Kingdom*, the Court highlighted the principle of subsidiarity: it is for states to enforce Convention rights in

---

[33] See, for example, *Reynolds v Times Newspapers Ltd* [2001] 2 AC 127, where even before the HRA came into force Lord Nicholls stated, 'our inclination ought to be towards the approach that prevails under the jurisprudence on the Convention' and Lord Cooke rejected the argument for a generic privilege category for political speech as this would divert the court from 'the European path'. The decision in *Jameel v Wall Street Journal SPRL* [2006] UKHL 44, [2007] 1 AC 359 revealed not a single reference to any other common law jurisdiction in their Lordships' speeches. Cf *R (Nicklinson) v Ministry of Justice* [2014] UKSC 38, [2015] AC 657 which presents a rather more nuanced picture.
[34] (1990) BMLR 1 Sup Ct (Can).
[35] (2002) 35 EHRR 1.
[36] *Evans* (n 32).
[37] (1998) 26 EHRR 357.
[38] *Ibid* [74].

'whatever form they happen to be secured in the domestic legal order'.[39] However, the Court confirmed that there is a limit to the discretion afforded to the state and the scope of the obligation will vary depending upon the nature of any violation. The Court held that where an allegation is made that there has been a failure to protect someone from the abusive acts of others, there should be a mechanism for establishing liability and in the case of breaches of Articles 2 and 3 compensation should in principle be available for non-pecuniary damage. However, the Court declined to make any finding as to whether on these facts only court proceedings could provide effective redress but gave a strong steer saying that, 'judicial remedies indeed furnish strong guarantees of independence, access for the victim and enforceability in compliance with the requirements of Article 13'.

The Margin of Appreciation Doctrine

The primary responsibility for the protection of human rights lies with the States parties to the ECHR and the role of the Convention and Court are subsidiary to national systems; the Court is responsible for reviewing the implementation of ECHR standards by the states. Strasbourg has developed the margin of appreciation doctrine in recognition that

> an area of discretionary choice of action as to both initial policy and then implementation in individual cases is available to the national authorities in certain contexts when they are regulating the exercise of a Convention right. The result of this principle of interpretation, whenever it enters into play, is that the Strasbourg Court will exercise a degree of judicial self-restraint when reviewing decisions taken by national authorities, in particular rulings by national courts, the degree of restraint varying according to the context.[40]

Simply put, the margin acts as a sphere of deference to states when they take measures which impact on the enjoyment of the Convention rights. Although originally applied in the context of derogations under Article 15 (in particular in relation to the state's assessment of whether there is a state of emergency that threatens the life of the nation[41]), it is in the context especially of the rights set out in Articles 8–11 that Strasbourg has developed a substantial 'margin of appreciation' doctrine.

The scope of the margin allowed to a state is variable depending upon the nature of the interest at stake and the grounds for interfering with that interest. The doctrine can make it difficult to predict outcomes. An example of a case with

[39] [2001] 2 FLR 612, (2001) 34 EHRR 97 [108].
[40] P Mahoney, 'The Relationship between the Strasbourg Court and the National Courts' (2014) *Law Quarterly Review* 130, 568–86.
[41] Following the declaration of incompatibility in *A v Secretary of State for the Home Department* [2004] UKHL 56, [2005] 2 AC 68 regarding the detention provisions in the Anti-Terrorism Crime and Security Act 2001, the United Kingdom withdrew its derogation under Article 15.

two forces pulling in opposite directions is *Smith and Grady v United Kingdom*,[42] where the applicants challenged the policy of excluding homosexuals from the armed forces. On the one hand is the well-established principle that a state is accorded a wide margin of appreciation in matters of national security; on the other, the application concerned a most intimate aspect of private life and, therefore, particularly serious reasons are required in order to justify any interference. The Court was clearly influenced by other states' policies and concluded that although the interference with the Article 8 right was 'in accordance with the law' and accepted that it was in the interests of national security, the exclusion of the applicants was not necessary in a democratic society. This decision and others shows that the Court will require states to substantiate the risks that are alleged to justify interference.

The following discussion will take the reader through the steps taken in order to assess whether a limitation on a right is consistent with Convention obligations. In order for a state to establish that a limitation is permitted under the Convention, three things must be established:

(i)   the limitation is 'in accordance with' (Article 8) or 'prescribed by' (Articles 9, 10 and 11) law;
(ii)   the limitation pursues a legitimate aim; and
(iii)   the limitation is 'necessary in a democratic society'.

With regard to (i), although there is a difference in drafting between Article 8 and the other personal freedom Articles, in *Malone v United Kingdom*, the Court stated that both formulations should be given the same interpretation. For an interference to be 'in accordance with the law', it is necessary that there should be legal provision, which may be contained in either written or unwritten law.[43] In the *Sunday Times*, the Court held that 'prescribed by law' means that:

> First, the law must be adequately accessible: the citizen must be able to have an indication that is adequate in the circumstances of the legal rules applicable to a given case. Secondly, a norm cannot be regarded as 'law' unless it is formulated with sufficient precision to enable the citizen to regulate his conduct: he must be able—if need be with appropriate advice—to foresee to a degree that is reasonable in the circumstances, the consequences which a given action may entail. Those consequences need not be foreseeable with absolute certainty: experience shows this to be unattainable. Again, whilst certainty is highly desirable, it may bring in its train excessive rigidity and the law must be able to keep pace with changing circumstances. Accordingly, many laws are inevitably couched in terms which, to a greater or lesser extent, are vague and whose interpretation and application are questions of practice.[44]

In the *Sunday Times* case, the Court found that the common law offence of contempt of court was formulated with sufficient precision to enable the applicants

---

[42] (1999) 29 EHRR 493.
[43] *Malone* (1985) 7 EHRR 14; *Sunday Times v United Kingdom* (1979) 2 EHRR 245 [297].
[44] *Sunday Times, ibid* [49].

to make an assessment of the consequences that publication in violation of an injunction would entail. However, the injunction to prevent the *Sunday Times* from publishing an article concerning the research, testing and marketing of the drug Thalidomide by Distillers was found to violate the Article 10 right to freedom of expression because it was disproportionate to the aim pursued. In *Malone v United Kingdom*,[45] the Court addressed the quality of domestic law, stating that the law should be compatible with the rule of law which implies that there should be a measure of protection against arbitrary interferences by public authorities with the rights safeguarded by Article 8(1).

Secondly, the state must demonstrate that any limitation on a right pursues one of the aims laid down in the second paragraphs of Articles 8–11. In this regard, the test applied by Strasbourg appears to be subjective: did the relevant authority at the date of interference intend to pursue a particular aim? Unless there is anything to suggest that another purpose was pursued, the Government's explanation will be accepted. Whether in fact the aim is supportable is in any event implicitly assessed at the third stage of the Court's enquiry: whether the action taken was 'necessary in a democratic society'.

In order for the state to demonstrate the necessity requirement, it must satisfy two conditions: first, the interference complained of must correspond to a 'pressing social need' and, second, the interference must be proportionate to the aim pursued.[46] It is in relation to the first requirement that Strasbourg has developed its margin of appreciation doctrine, and the degree of margin will depend upon the aim. Two examples will illustrate the point.

In *Handyside v United Kingdom*, the applicant was a publisher and distributor of the Little Red Schoolbook, which contained advice aimed at teenaged schoolchildren, including advice on sexual and drug-related matters. The book had been prepared with the help of children and schoolteachers and had been widely distributed in Western Europe, having first been published in Denmark. Upon publication in England, the applicant was convicted of violating the Obscene Publications Act 1959, as amended, and he then petitioned the European Commission on Human Rights, alleging a violation of his Article 10 right to freedom of expression. The UK Government argued that the interference was justified for the 'protection of morals'. The Court noted that the machinery of protection established by the Convention is subsidiary to national systems safeguarding human rights, and, moreover, there is no uniform conception of morals, stating that:

> The Convention leaves to each Contracting State, in the first place, the task of securing the rights and freedoms it enshrines ... In particular, it is not possible to find in the domestic law of the various Contracting States a uniform conception of morals. The view taken by their respective laws of the requirements of morals varies from time to time and from place to place, especially in our era which is characterised by a rapid and far-reaching evolution of opinions on the subject. By reason of their direct and continuous

---

[45] *Malone* (n 43).
[46] *Olsson v Sweden* (1989) 11 EHHR 259.

contact with the vital forces of their countries, State authorities are in principle in a better position than the international judge to give an opinion on the exact content of these requirements as well as on the 'necessity' of a 'restriction or penalty' intended to meet them ... 'necessary' is not synonymous with 'indispensable', neither has it the flexibility of such expressions as 'admissible', 'ordinary', 'useful', 'reasonable' or 'desirable' ... it is for the national authorities to make the initial assessment of the reality of the pressing social need implied by the notion of 'necessity' in this context. Consequently, Article 10(2) leaves to the Contracting States a margin of appreciation.[47]

The Court, however, went on to say that such a margin is not unlimited; if it were, any protection afforded by the Convention would be illusory. The final determination whether a restriction or penalty is reconcilable with ECHR rights is made by Strasbourg. In *Handyside*, having regard to the state's margin of appreciation, the fact that the book had circulated freely within other Contracting States did not mean that the criminal conviction was a violation of Article 10. Each state had fashioned their approach in the light of differing prevailing views about the demands of the protection of morals. In *Handyside* we see that a wide margin of appreciation was given to the state when making its assessment of the need to protect morals and the state was acting within that margin when it seized the offending book.

A different conclusion was reached in the *Sunday Times* case, when the Government sought to justify the imposition of an injunction to prevent publication of an article about the drug Thalidomide at a time when the House of Lords held that the litigation was not dormant. The Government argued that the aim of the injunction was 'maintaining the authority and impartiality of the judiciary'. The Court examined the House of Lords' decision which aimed to prevent pre-judging of the issues and 'trial by newspaper' and concluded that the aim of the injunction was legitimate. However, this case was distinguishable from *Handyside* in relation to the margin of appreciation, because unlike the issue of morals, the domestic practice of states revealed much common ground. Accordingly, it is clear that more extensive European supervision corresponded to less discretionary power of appreciation. The Court found the injunction was disproportionate to the aim pursued. Thus, where there is consensus between states, the margin of appreciation allowed for state judgment will be restricted.

The Margin of Appreciation in English Law—Deference

Before the HRA came into force, there was much discussion regarding the role that the margin of appreciation would play at domestic level.[48] It was generally

---

[47] *Handyside v United Kingdom* (1979–80) 1 EHRR 737 [43].

[48] Amos (n 5) 96; R Singh, M Hunt and M Demetriou, 'Current Topic: Is there a Role for the "Margin of Appreciation" in National Law after the Human Rights Act?' [1999] *European Human Rights Law Review* 15; D Pannick, 'Principles of Interpretation of Convention Rights under the Human Rights Act and the Discretionary Area of Judgment' [1998] *Public Law* 545.

accepted that margin doctrine itself could have no direct application in a domestic court. However, it was quickly accepted that an analogous doctrine of 'deference' to an appropriate primary decision-maker should be accorded. Initially, deference was accorded on the basis of the democratic credentials of the primary decision-maker (whether the Executive, Legislature or another public authority).[49] However in *Huang v Secretary of State for the Home Department*,[50] the House of Lords moved away from democratic credentials to *expertise* as the basis for deference, especially if the relevant decision-maker has already used that expertise to evaluate the proportionality of an interference with Convention rights. However, according weight to the primary decision-maker and the fact that a primary decision-maker has specialist expertise and access to appropriate advice will not relieve the court from determining whether an interference with rights is proportionate. It is important that the decision-maker itself considers whether any interference with rights is proportionate.[51]

It should be noted that the ECtHR is apt to defer to the domestic courts where due consideration has been given to relevant rights, including considerations of proportionality. For example, in cases concerning personal privacy and the need to consider competing claims under Article 8 and Article 10, where the balancing exercise has been conducted by national authorities which have applied ECHR principles, the Court has said that would require strong reasons to substitute its views for those of domestic courts.[52]

Positive Obligations

There is an extensive jurisprudence regarding positive obligations upon the state; these obligations are the basis for state engagement in relationships between non-state actors. Thus, an ECHR right may require the state to take steps to regulate relationships between non-state actors. As we have seen in Chapter 2, the human rights obligation is that of the state; the state is then required as a matter of domestic law to take steps to ensure the full enjoyment of the 'human' right. In a line of cases, particularly under Article 8, Strasbourg has held that states have an obligation to make real and effective the enjoyment of the rights set out in the ECHR, to the extent of regulating the conduct of non-state actors. A right to privacy that is exigible against a private actor derives from this positive obligation on the state. However, Strasbourg has held that in relation to certain positive obligations

---

[49] See *R v Director of Public Prosecutions, ex p Kebilene* [1999] 3 WLR 972 (Lord Hope).

[50] [2007] UKHL 11, [2007] 2 WLR 581.

[51] *R (Begum) v Headteacher and Governors of Denbigh High School* [2006] UKHL 15. See generally D Mead, 'Outcomes Aren't All: Defending Process-Based Review of Public Authority Decisions under the Human Rights Act' [2012] *Public Law* 61.

[52] *Von Hannover v Germany (No 2)* (2012) 55 EHRR 15; *Axel Springer AG v Germany* (2012) EHRR 6. See generally Chapter 8 *Privacy—From Misuse of Private Information to Autonomy*.

(including those under the Article 8 right to respect for private life), states enjoy a wide margin of appreciation in determining compliance.

Part 2—The ECHR Protected Rights

The following section will draw out key principles of the rights set out in Schedule 1 to the HRA, as developed by Strasbourg and interpreted by English courts. The reader's attention is drawn to the discussion in Chapter 3 of the obligation under section 2(1) HRA 'to take account' of Strasbourg case law. In early authorities there seemed to be a slavish adherence to the so-called 'mirror' principle whereby English courts effectively considered themselves *bound* by ECHR jurisprudence; more recent developments indicate a desire to apply properly the wording of section 2 and to 'take account' of the Strasbourg jurisprudence. Furthermore, our senior judiciary is increasingly reminding litigants to rely upon the common law. For example, in *Kennedy v Information Commissioner*, Lord Mance has reminded us that the Convention rights represent a 'threshold' level of protection and that the development of the common law did not come to an end with the passing of the HRA.[53]

Article 2—The Right to Life

The right to life, while the most fundamental of all rights, is not expressed in the ECHR in absolute terms. The death penalty is preserved by Article 2(1), and Article 2(2) permits the use of force which is no more than absolutely necessary in three instances. However, it should be noted that section 1(1)(c) HRA gives further effect to Articles 1 and 2 of Protocol No 6 to the Convention which provides for the abolition of the death penalty except in respect of acts committed in time of war or of imminent threat of war.

The obligation under Article 2 can be broken down into three elements: (i) the state is enjoined to refrain from the intentional and unlawful taking of life; (ii) the state may have a positive duty to safeguard life provided that certain conditions are met; and (iii) there is a procedural duty to investigate deaths where the substantive obligations are engaged. Proceedings concerning the intentional deprivation of life are rare.[54] In *Smith v Ministry of Defence*, the Supreme Court confirmed that there is no intentional deprivation of life within Article 2(1) when servicemen and women are deployed on active service 'overseas as part of an organised military

---

[53] *Kennedy v Information Commissioner* [2014] UKSC 20, [2015] AC 455. See generally discussion in Introduction.
[54] See generally Amos (n 5) 186 *et seq.*

force which is properly equipped and capable of defending itself, even though the risk of their being killed is inherent in what they are being asked to do'.[55]

The Positive Obligation to Protect Life

For English tort lawyers, the key aspect of Article 2 is undoubtedly the positive obligation to take appropriate steps to safeguard life that has been recognised by Strasbourg as implicit within the Convention. This obligation was recognised for the first time in *LCB v United Kingdom*.[56] Although the applicant could not establish that her father's service in the Royal Air Force during the Christmas Island nuclear tests in 1957–58 was a cause of her leukaemia, nor that had she been provided with more information about the tests and possible consequences she might have obtained earlier medical intervention and mitigated the effects of her illness, the case is important for the statement of principle made. There the Court stated that if there had been reason to believe the applicant was in danger of contracting a life-threatening disease the authorities would have been under a duty to make that known to her, whether or not they considered that the information would have helped her. Thus, the violation is in the failure to inform and causation is irrelevant.[57]

Framework Obligation

The obligation under Article 2 requires states to put in place appropriate criminal law sanctions to deter the commission of offences and to put in place law enforcement machinery in order to properly enforce the criminal law. The ECtHR found against Turkey in a number of cases where complaints were made that a journalist working for a Kurdish newspaper[58] and a doctor who had treated members of the Kurdish terrorist organisation, the PKK, were murdered by members of the state security forces.[59] These claims could not be proved but the Court found that the authorities were aware that journalists, doctors and others associated with the PKK and Turkish separatism had been subject to a campaign of attacks and threats, possibly with the active involvement or acquiescence of the state security forces. At the time a number of emergency measures were in place, including the transfer of jurisdiction away from courts to councils of civil servants and there had been a series of failures to investigate alleged human rights violations by the state security forces. The Court found that these defects undermined the effectiveness

---

[55] *Smith* (n 6).
[56] (1998) 27 EHRR 212.
[57] *Ibid* [40].
[58] *Kilic v Turkey* (2001) 33 EHRR 1357.
[59] *Mahmut Kaya v Turkey* ECHR 2000-III.

of the protection afforded by the criminal law in the south-east region during the period relevant to this case. It considered that this permitted or fostered a lack of accountability of members of the security forces for their actions which, as the Commission stated in its report, was not compatible with the rule of law in a democratic society respecting the fundamental rights and freedoms guaranteed under the Convention. Thus there was a violation of Article 2.

Where the taking of life is unintentional, for example in cases of medical negligence, a civil remedy may be sufficient. In *Calvelli and Ciglio v Italy*,[60] a baby died shortly after birth, allegedly as a result of medical negligence. Owing to delays in investigation, criminal proceedings were time-barred. The Court found it unnecessary to consider whether these delays gave rise to a breach of Article 2 because the applicants could pursue a civil claim which could then be followed by disciplinary proceedings. The Court stated that the positive obligation to protect life applied to the sphere of public health and required

> an effective independent judicial system to be set up so that the cause of death of patients in the care of the medical profession, whether in the public or the private sector, can be determined and those responsible made accountable.

A very important question (especially in light of a possible repeal of the HRA) is whether the positive obligation under Article 2 deriving from *Osman v United Kingdom*, discussed below, requires that a victim should have a civil remedy *against the state*. In *Osman*, this question was left open because it was considered more appropriate under Articles 6 and 13. In *Mastromatteo v Italy*,[61] where the applicant's son had been murdered by released prisoners, the Court held that Article 2 does require a civil remedy against the state where a murder has occurred for which the state has been at fault. *Mastromatteo* tells us that in a post-HRA world if there is no remedy akin to section 7, English courts would be under significant pressure to resile from the common law principle of no-liability for omissions in cases against public authorities on such facts that engage ECHR rights.

The Positive Operational Obligation under Article 2

As is now well-known, in an important development the ECtHR has recognised that there may be an obligation upon states to take active steps to protect the life of a person at risk. In the first edition we identified the source of the relevant risk as the criminal acts of a third party; importantly, the jurisprudence has now moved beyond the criminal sphere to encompass other sources of threat to life.

In *Osman v United Kingdom*,[62] the applicant and his family had become the target of a dangerous stalker who eventually killed the father of the family,

---

[60] [2002]-Application No 32967/96 I (ECtHR Grand Chamber) [49], [51], discussed by Harris, O'Boyle and Warbrick (n 2) 41.

[61] Reports of Judgments and Decisions 2002-VIII, 151 (GC).

[62] (1998) 29 EHRR 245.

Mr Osman and wounded his son Ali Osman. The applicants complained of violations of Articles 2 and 6 (the right to a fair trial, discussed below). The ECtHR held that state responsibility under Article 2 was not engaged because the applicants had not established a decisive point at which it could be said that the police knew or ought to have known of the existence of a real and immediate risk to the lives of the Osman family. In view of the important statements of principle made by the ECtHR which have become the foundation of the positive operational obligation, the scope of the duty as described is set out in full by the Court:

> In the opinion of the Court where there is an allegation that the authorities have violated their positive obligation to protect the right to life in the context of their above-mentioned duty to prevent and suppress offences against the person (see paragraph 115 above), it must be established to its satisfaction that the authorities *knew or ought to have known at the time of the existence of a real and immediate risk to the life of an identified individual or individuals from the criminal acts of a third party and that they failed to take measures within the scope of their powers which, judged reasonably, might have been expected to avoid that risk.* The Court does not accept the Government's view that the failure to perceive the risk to life in the circumstances known at the time or to take preventive measures to avoid that risk must be tantamount to gross negligence or wilful disregard of the duty to protect life (see paragraph 107 above). Such a rigid standard must be considered to be incompatible with the requirements of Article 1 of the Convention and the obligations of Contracting States under that Article to secure the practical and effective protection of the rights and freedoms laid down therein, including Article 2 .... For the Court, and having regard to the nature of the right protected by Article 2, a right fundamental in the scheme of the Convention, it is sufficient for an applicant to show that the authorities did not do all that could be reasonably expected of them to avoid a real and immediate risk to life of which they have or ought to have knowledge. This is a question which can only be answered in the light of all the circumstances of any particular case.[63]

The Court held that there was no decisive stage in the series of events when the police knew or ought to have known, that there was a real and immediate risk to the Osman family such as to engage the positive obligation under Article 2.

In an important qualification, the Court noted that the positive obligation could not be open-ended or unrealistic and stated that:

> Bearing in mind the difficulties involved in policing modern societies, the unpredictability of human conduct and the operational choices that need to be made in terms of priorities and resources, such an obligation must be interpreted in a way which does not impose an impossible or disproportionate burden on the authorities. Accordingly, not every claimed risk to life can entail for the authorities a Convention requirement to take operational measures to prevent that risk from materialising.

Thus, the standard applied in relation to positive obligations under Article 2 (and indeed Article 3) appears broadly to mirror the negligence standard established

---

[63] *Ibid* at [116].

in the *Bolam* test,[64] at least insofar as a reasonable standard is applied. The ECtHR emphatically rejected the Government's argument that the bar under Article 2 should be set as high as wilful disregard of duty or gross negligence. In *NHS Trust A v M*, Butler-Sloss P held that the *Osman* test 'bears a close resemblance to the standard adopted in the domestic law of negligence and approximates to the obligation recognised by the English courts in the *Bolam* test …'.[65] However, the test differs from *Bolam* in that the defendant's resources are a factor to be taken into account under Article 2. While the cost of taking precautions is relevant to the standard of care in negligence,[66] the exception in *Goldman v Hargrave*[67] aside, the defendant's resources are not generally relevant to the standard of care in negligence.

While the *Osman* duty is couched in terms of risk from the criminal acts of a third party, it has matured in the 15 years since the first edition and a number of violations of the operational obligation have been found in relation to threats from individuals and as well as from other dangerous activities for which the state was responsible. In *Opuz v Turkey*,[68] the applicant complained that the authorities had failed to protect her and her mother from domestic violence which resulted in the death of her mother. The applicant and her mother suffered repeated violence from the applicant's partner, which they reported to the police. He was charged with offences including attempted murder and threatening to kill, but he was released on bail. While awaiting trial he murdered the applicant's mother. He was released from prison pending an appeal and the applicant complained she was given inadequate protection. The Turkish authorities were found to have violated their positive obligation to protect the right to life of the applicant's mother within Article 2 and violations of Article 3 and gender-based discrimination in violation of Article 14 read in conjunction with Articles 2 and 3 were found. The Court found that domestic violence was effectively tolerated by the authorities.

Some commentators suggested that the advent of the HRA might mean that the decision of the Court of Appeal in *R v Cambridgeshire District Health Authority, ex parte B* would be overturned. In *B*, a child's father challenged the health authority's refusal to fund further expensive treatment for his daughter who was terminally ill with an aggressive form of cancer.[69] In fact, there appears to have been relatively limited reliance upon the HRA in relation to drug-rationing decisions and this is probably due to the relative weakness (from a potential applicant's viewpoint) of the Strasbourg jurisprudence in this area. Thus, in *Hristozov v Bulgaria*,[70] the

---

[64] *Bolam v Freiern Hospital Management Committee* [1957] 1 WLR 582, [1957] 2 All ER 118.

[65] *NHS Trust A v M* [2001] Fam 348 at [35].

[66] *Latimer v AEC Ltd* [1953] AC 643.

[67] [1967] 1 AC 645.

[68] (2009) 50 EHRR 695, cited in *Michael v Chief Constable of South Wales* [2015] UKSC 2, [2015] AC 1732.

[69] *R v Cambridgeshire District Health Authority, ex parte B* [1995] 1 WLR 898, discussed by P Havers QC and N Sheldon, 'The Impact of the Convention on Medical Law' in R English, and P Havers QC (eds), *An Introduction to Human Rights and the Common Law* (Oxford, Hart Publishing, 2000) 24.

[70] App 47039/11 and 358/12, 13 November 2012.

applicants argued that the authorities' refusal to authorise an experimental anti-cancer drug was in breach of their right to life. The drug company had offered to make the drug available free of charge in return for data on the effect on patients. The Bulgarian authorities refused to permit this. The ECtHR found no violation of Article 2: Article 2 requires states to put a legal framework in place requiring hospitals to adopt appropriate measures to protect patients' lives. However, this obligation did not require states to regulate access to unauthorised medical products in a particular way. The ECtHR has generally been slow to interfere with resource allocation decisions within public services.

It is trite to observe that there is no neat dividing line between civil and political rights (of which the Convention is broadly composed) on the one hand, and economic, social and cultural rights on the other: their substantive content may overlap and what is more both sets of rights carry financial obligations for states. The difference between the two lies in their justiciability: economic, social and cultural rights generally occupy a weaker normative area, with recourse to judicial supervision by way of court proceedings confined to the civil and political category. This does not mean to say that such rights, or elements of them, cannot be justiciable, but it remains the fact that many states are reluctant to see areas of justiciability expand: governments fear a demand that resources cannot possibly meet and courts are wary of overstepping the bounds of their role as the third branch of government.

As we have seen in *Osman*, the relevant test is that 'reasonable' measures should be taken: provided that a health authority has asked itself the right questions and arrived at a defensible conclusion, it is highly unlikely that Strasbourg would seek to interfere with that decision. The same principles apply in relation to claims that engage the right to respect for private life under Article 8. Thus in the recent decision, *McDonald v UK*,[71] regarding a withdrawal of night-time care by a local authority, the Court stressed the wide margin of appreciation to the state in issues of general policy, including social, economic and health care policies. The Court stated that the margin is particularly wide when it involves assessment of priorities in the context of the allocation of limited state resources. However, in those cases that have been brought post-HRA in the medical field regarding rationing decisions, the application of the HRA has meant that there has been a shift from *Wednesbury* unreasonableness to proportionality as the standard for review.[72] The significance of this shift is that it becomes easier to challenge decisions by public authorities as they are now required to give reasons for their decisions. With *Wednesbury*, a claimant has to show irrationality on the part of the public body; in the case of proportionality the burden is on the public authority, which has to

[71] (2015) 60 EHRR 1.
[72] *R (on the application of Condliff) v North Staffordshire Primary Care Trust* [2011] EWCA Civ 910.

demonstrate how it has arrived at a conclusion after taking account of relevant interests.[73]

The Article 2 obligation now encompasses dangerous situations and activities that have been initiated or tolerated by the state. Thus, in *Öneryildiz v Turkey*,[74] the applicant and his family had lived near to a tip used by local councils. The relevant regulatory law had not been complied with and experts had warned about the dangers of a methane explosion which eventually happened causing a landslide that engulfed the settlement resulting in several deaths. The public authority had set up and authorised the operation of the site and had known or ought to have known of the serious and immediate risk to life. The shanty town that was destroyed had been built illegally, but the municipal authorities had tolerated the development and provided connections to services and the residents paid local taxes. The positive obligation to protect life had been breached.

Can Professional Negligence be a Breach of the Operational Obligation under Article 2?[75]

In the first edition, we raised the question as to whether instances of medical negligence on facts such as *Bolitho v City & Hackney Health Authority*[76] might engage the operational obligation under Article 2. It will be recalled that in *Bolitho*, the failure of a doctor to attend a two-year-old with respiratory difficulties (the child suffered a cardiac arrest and brain damage) was conceded by the defendants to be a breach of the common law duty of care. The parents brought proceedings in negligence, but the problem issue was causation: the defendants argued that even if the doctors had attended she would not have intubated the child and that, applying the *Bolam* standard,[77] non-intubation would have been a reasonable response and the injury, therefore, could not have been avoided. Evidence was given by two groups of expert witnesses, one would have intubated, and the other would not. The House of Lords considered that both views were defensible and negligence could not therefore be established.

---

[73] K Syrett, *Law, Legitimacy and the Rationing of Healthcare* (Cambridge, Cambridge University Press, 2007) 166–67, discussed in E Jackson, *Medical Law* (Oxford, Oxford University Press, 2013) 90. The Supreme Court has however declined to decide that proportionality should be substituted for *Wednesbury* unreasonableness in order to assess the lawfulness of interference with common law fundamental rights: *R (on the application of Keyu) v Foreign and Commonwealth Office* [2015] 3 WLR 1665 [133] (Lord Neuberger), discussed by P Bowen, 'Does the Renaissance of Common Law Rights Mean that the Human Rights Act 1998 is Now Unnecessary?' (2016) *European Human Rights Law Review* 4, 361–77.
[74] (2004) 41 EHRR 325.
[75] This discussion draws on J Wright, 'The Operational Obligation under Article 2 of the European Convention on Human Rights and Challenges for Coherence—Views from the English Supreme Court and Strasbourg' (2016) 1 *Journal of European Tort Law* 58.
[76] [1998] AC 232.
[77] *Bolam* (n 64).

On the question of whether acts of medical negligence may constitute a breach of Article 2, the ECtHR has decided *Powell v United Kingdom*. In *Powell*, parents of a young child complained that the death of their son through negligence engaged the responsibility of the state under Article 2. The claim concerning a child who had died from undiagnosed Addisons' disease was held inadmissible by a Chamber of the Court which declared that:

> The court accepts that it cannot be excluded that the acts and omissions of the authorities in the field of health care policy may in certain circumstances engage their responsibility under the positive limb of Article 2. However, where a contracting state had made adequate provision for securing high professional standards among health professionals and the protection of the lives of patients, it cannot accept that matters such as error of judgment on the part of a health professional or negligent coordination among health professionals in the treatment of a particular patient are sufficient of themselves to call a contracting state to account from the standpoint of its positive obligations under Article 2 of the Convention to protect life.[78]

In a similar vein, in *Stoyanovi v Bulgaria*, concerning an application by the parent of a soldier who had died during a parachute training exercise, the Court held that damage would only be a violation of the state's positive obligations under Article 2 if caused by insufficient regulations or insufficient control, 'but not if the damage was caused through the negligent conduct of an individual or the concatenation of unfortunate events'.[79]

In *Oneryildiz*, the ECtHR did not in terms refer to *Powell* but drew on that language saying,

> Where it is established that the negligence attributable to State officials or bodies … goes beyond an error of judgment or carelessness in that the authorities *fully realising the likely consequences and disregarding the powers vested in them*, failed to take measures that were necessary and sufficient to avert the risks, the fact that those responsible have not been charged with a criminal offence or prosecuted may amount to a violation of Article 2.[80]

There is an implication here that errors of judgment or what might be termed 'ordinary' professional negligence are not violations of the operational obligation. Failure to provide remedies for such negligent conduct at state level would be a breach of the primary framework duty incumbent on a state under Article 2, but that should not be confused with the substantive operational obligation. This distinction is important for any state, such as the United Kingdom, which has different remedies depending upon the classification of the right infringed—whether common law or statutory under the HRA.

In *Savage v South Essex Partnership NHS Foundation Trust*,[81] the House of Lords held that the positive obligation arose in the case of a psychiatric patient detained

---

[78] *Powell v United Kingdom* (2000) 30 EHRR CD 362 at 364.
[79] Application No 42980/04 (unreported) given 9 November 2010.
[80] *Öneryildiz* (n 74).
[81] [2009] AC 681.

in hospital under the Mental Health Act 1983. In so doing, the House was not following Strasbourg as there was no decision concerning a detained patient, as opposed to mentally ill prisoners or detainees. The Supreme Court has now gone a step further in *Rabone v Pennine Care NHS Trust*,[82] holding that a *voluntary* psychiatric patient who committed suicide while on home leave was entitled to the protection of the operational obligation under Article 2. An obvious question that arises is why did Melanie Rabone's case which concerned an error of professional medical judgment fall within the sphere of the operational duty under Article 2 rather than under *Powell*? It is important to remember that we are addressing the liability of the state under Article 2 rather than the liability of the medical practitioner in negligence at common law.

The judge at first instance and the Court of Appeal had determined that *Rabone* fell within the *Powell* line of authority. Lord Dyson, giving the leading judgment, set out to discover the essential features of those cases where the operational duty had already been recognised by Strasbourg and built upon cases recognising the duty to protect prisoners from other inmates[83] and from suicide.[84] He held that the existence of a 'real and immediate risk' is a necessary but not a sufficient condition. The decisive issues were the assumption of responsibility by the state for the individual's welfare and safety (including by the exercise of control) and the particular vulnerability of the victim. Lord Dyson noted that in circumstances of 'sufficient vulnerability' the ECtHR has been prepared to find a breach of the operational duty even where there has been no assumption of responsibility such as the failure of a local authority to exercise its powers to protect children at risk of abuse. In a sense, this is entirely the point of the operational obligation under Article 2, to make sure that the state does protect those in need where it is reasonable to expect this.

In *Watts v United Kingdom*, the ECtHR even went so far as to accept that the badly managed transfer of elderly residents from their nursing home could impact on their life expectancy and therefore Article 2 was engaged. The Court cited *Oneryildiz* and stated that, 'obligations under Article 2 are engaged in the context of any activity, whether public or not in which the right to life may be at stake'.[85]

In Chapter 5 we discuss in detail the development of the operational obligation in English law from *Van Colle v Chief Constable of Hertfordshire Police*[86] to the most recent decision in *Michael v Chief Constable of South Wales*.[87] At the time of writing, English courts have said that there is no need to 'gold plate' the remedy that is now available under section 7 HRA by recognising a duty of care at common law in

---

[82] *Rabone* (n 16).
[83] *Edwards v United Kingdom* (2002) 35 EHRR 487.
[84] *Keenan v United Kingdom* (2001) 33 EHRR 913.
[85] *Watts v United Kingdom* (2010) 51 EHRR SE 66 [82], discussed by Baroness Hale in *Rabone* (n 16) [96]–[100].
[86] [2008] UKHL 50, [2009] 1 AC 225.
[87] *Michael* (n 68).

relation to obligations arising under Articles 2 and 3 ECHR.[88] If the HRA is repealed and replaced by a Bill of Rights, there will no longer be any remedy under section 7 and, assuming that the United Kingdom remains a party to the ECHR, we will still be required by Article 13 to provide an effective remedy for violations of Articles 2 and 3. Furthermore, *Mastromatteo* requires such a remedy against the state. The (prospective) Bill of Rights may include such a remedy; if it does not, English courts will be faced squarely with the need to consider whether the onus is upon them to shape the common law to accommodate such claims. If a Bill of Rights includes a provision requiring the courts to develop the common law in such a way as to promote the objects of the ECHR or Bill of Rights, there would be ample scope, indeed arguably an obligation, to reflect positive obligations in the law of torts.[89]

In the absence of an effective remedy that complies with Article 13 ECHR, it would be possible to argue that customary international law requires a remedy at domestic level and that recognition of such a remedy is not inconsistent with Parliamentary intention.[90] As Shelton has observed,[91] in most countries, state liability has been built within the framework of tort law. Furthermore, this state practice arguably constitutes customary international law. The Namibian Supreme Court has held that [in view of the wide acceptance that there is a right to a remedy for governmental misconduct] 'it is arguable that the right to an effective remedy forms part of customary international law'.[92] The *dictum* of Chief Justice Holt in *Ashby v White*, 'If the plaintiff has a right, he must of necessity have a means to vindicate and maintain it' is frequently cited;[93] whether it supports a claimant's case depends upon the existence of the 'right' claimed. Clearly, it cannot be used to claim a 'right' where such is not recognised.

Generally, as we have seen, Strasbourg does not indicate which arm of the state is responsible for developing remedies. In a common law jurisdiction, however, it is not unreasonable for both claimants and supervising bodies to look to the courts to fulfil this aspect of the United Kingdom's obligations. Since the litigation that gave rise to *X (Minors) v Bedfordshire County Council*[94] and *Osman v Ferguson*,[95] ECHR jurisprudence has developed so that there is a significant body of case law demonstrating when positive obligations arise. In the absence of a statutory framework that provides a remedy at domestic level for such breaches of

---

[88] *Michael* (n 68) [125] (Lord Toulson).

[89] For an example of such law-making, see the decision of the South African Constitutional Court in *Carmichele v Minister of Safety and Security* (2001) 12 BHRC 12.

[90] See the remarks of Lord Mance in *R (Keyu)* (n 73); *Introduction*; text accompanying n 31 and *Kennedy v Information Commissioner* (n 53).

[91] D Shelton, *Remedies in International Human Rights Law* (Oxford, Oxford University Press, 2005 online).

[92] *Mwandingi v Minister of Defence* [1991] 1 SA 851 (Namib), quoted by Shelton, *ibid*. See also *People's Union for Democratic Rights v The State of Bihar* AIR (SC) 355 (1978). See S Bandes, 'Reinventing *Bivens*: The Self-Executing Constitution' (1995) 68 *California Law Review* 289.

[93] 92 Eng Rep 126 (KB 1703), cited by Shelton, *ibid*.

[94] [1995] 2 AC 633.

[95] [1993] 4 All ER 344.

human rights obligations, the rules of customary international law could arguably be invoked as the basis for such a development at national level.

The Procedural Obligation to Investigate

The duty to investigate originates in Strasbourg case law and is premised upon the need to ensure that the substantive right is effective in practice.[96] The obligation arises not only in cases where individuals have been killed as a result of lethal force used by state agents, but in relation to deaths which occur and which engage the responsibility of the state. The obligation to investigate is 'parasitic upon the existence of the substantive right'.[97] In *Smith*, the Supreme Court held that the duty arises where there are grounds for suspecting that a death may engage the substantive obligations under Article 2.[98] In *Smith* a soldier had died from heat stroke while serving in Iraq. The Court held that the death of a serviceman on active service did not automatically trigger the procedural obligation; however, in this case evidence suggested that there had been a failure to protect soldiers from extreme temperatures. This failure could indicate 'operational or system failure on the part of the state' so that it was arguable a breach of the substantive obligation in Article 2 had occurred.[99]

Thus, where the operational obligation is engaged, the duty to investigate will arise. The duty is a mechanism through which public bodies can be held accountable for deaths for which they are arguably responsible. In *R (Takoushis) v HM Coroner for Inner North London*,[100] a voluntary patient in the care of Chase Farm hospital committed suicide and the family requested that the coroner's inquest should be held with a jury. The Court of Appeal held that where a person has arguably died as a result of medical negligence, the state must have a system for the investigation of the facts and the determination of civil liability. The Court held that the possibility of civil redress and the traditional inquest satisfied the Article 2 obligation.

In *R (Humberstone) v Legal Services Commission*,[101] the time taken for an ambulance to arrive triggered the Article 2 obligation to undertake an enhanced investigation. In *R (Medihani) v HM Coroner for Inner South District of Greater London*,[102] the Administrative Court found that the substantive obligation to protect a young girl who had been murdered had arguably been breached. Therefore, on an application for judicial review, the decision not to resume an inquest was unlawful.

---

[96]   *R (Gentle) v The Prime Minister* [2008] UKHL 20, [2008] 1 AC 1356 [5] (Lord Bingham). See generally Amos (n 5) 204.

[97]   Amos (n 5) 206.

[98]   *R (Smith) v Secretary of State for Defence* [2010] UKSC 29, [2011] 1 AC 1.

[99]   Amos (n 5).

[100]   [2005] EWCA Civ 1440, [2006] 1 WLR 461.

[101]   [2010] EWCA Civ 1479, [2011] 1 WLR 1460.

[102]   [2012] EWHC 1104 (Admin).

Article 3: Freedom from Torture or Inhuman or Degrading Treatment or Punishment

The Article 3 prohibition on torture, inhuman or degrading treatment or punishment enshrines an absolute obligation from which no derogation under Article 15 is permitted even in time of war or public emergency.[103] Not only that, unlike most other Articles, it is expressed in unqualified terms. The difference between torture and other forms of ill-treatment is often one of degree, but an essential feature of torture is the deliberate nature of the ill-treatment. Thus, according to the United Nations Convention Against Torture and Other Cruel, Inhuman or Degrading Treatment or Punishment,

'torture' means any act by which severe pain or suffering ... is intentionally inflicted for such purposes as obtaining from him a confession, punishing him for an act he or a third person has committed or is suspected of having committed ...[104]

In *Ireland v UK*, the Court defined torture as 'deliberate inhuman treatment causing very serious and cruel suffering'. In this case, the Court disagreed with the Commission's view that the so-called 'five techniques' (wall-standing, hooding, subjection to noise, deprivation of sleep and deprivation of food and drink) used in the interrogation of IRA internees amounted to torture. Although the five techniques undoubtedly amounted to inhuman and degrading treatment, 'they did not occasion suffering of the particular intensity and cruelty implied by the word torture so understood'.[105] It was also held by the Commission and the Court in *Ireland v UK* that ill-treatment must attain a minimum level of severity if it is to fall within the scope of Article 3 and that such an assessment of the minimum is relative, depending upon all the circumstances of the case, 'the duration of the treatment, its physical or mental effects and, in some cases, the sex, age and state of health of the victim'.[106]

As the Strasbourg organs have always stressed, the ECHR is a living instrument and its interpretation has changed over time to reflect contemporary views. Although a majority in the Court in 1978 found that the five techniques did not constitute 'torture', it is almost certain in light of recent authorities that if the same facts came before the Court now there would be a finding of torture.[107]

The period of the so-called 'War on Terror' led to pressure from states to dilute this obligation where cases have concerned threats from alleged terrorists. In the United Kingdom, the foreign cases have proved especially challenging

---

[103] See generally Harris, O'Boyle and Warbrick (n 2) 69 *et seq.*

[104] United Nations Convention Against Torture and other Cruel, Inhuman or Degrading, Treatment or Punishment 1984, Art 1.

[105] *Ireland v UK* (1979–80) 2 EHRR [167].

[106] *Ibid* [162].

[107] See *Selmouni v France* (2000) 29 EHRR 403; B Rainey, E Wicks and C Ovey, *Jacobs, White & Ovey: The European Convention on Human Rights* (Oxford, Oxford University Press, 2014) 174.

for Home Secretaries seeking to deport individuals to states where it is alleged a person will face a risk of treatment contrary to Article 3. In the *Chahal* case, the United Kingdom wanted to deport Chahal, a Sikh separatist, to India because it was argued that he had been involved in terrorist activities and posed a threat to national security in the United Kingdom. The Court found that were he to be returned, there was a very real risk that he would be a victim of ill-treatment by the police and stated that:

> Article 3 enshrines one of the most fundamental values of democratic society. The Court is well aware of the immense difficulties faced by States in modern times in protecting their communities from terrorist violence. However, even in these circumstances, the Convention prohibits in absolute terms torture or inhuman or degrading treatment or punishment, irrespective of the victim's conduct.[108]

Positive Obligations

As in the case of Article 2, positive obligations which are not apparent from the text of the ECHR inhere in Article 3. There are two dimensions: first, there is an obligation to protect individuals from treatment by third parties that reaches the threshold set out in the jurisprudence and, second, there is a procedural duty to carry out an effective investigation into such ill-treatment. Furthermore, as in the case of Article 2, Article 1 read together with Article 3 'requires States to take measures designed to ensure that individuals within their jurisdiction are not subjected to ill-treatment, including ill-treatment administered by private individuals …'[109]

In *DSD v Commissioner of Police for the Metropolis*, discussed below, counsel argued that the fact that Article 1 has not been included in the schedule to the HRA must mean that the positive obligations derived from Article 3 do not apply in English law. This argument was given short shrift by Laws LJ for a unanimous Court of Appeal.[110] He held that the omission of Article 1 can be readily explained as that is the Article by which the States parties agree to be bound by ECHR rights; at domestic level the appropriate analogy is with section 6(1) HRA.

Ill-Treatment by Third Parties

Strasbourg jurisprudence has established that the state has a positive obligation to protect individuals from treatment by private individuals that meets the Article 3 threshold. This obligation derives from the cases of *Costello-Roberts v United Kingdom*[111] and *A v United Kingdom*.[112] In *A*, the applicant was beaten with a

---

[108] *Chahal v United Kingdom* (1997) 23 EHRR 413 [79].
[109] *Moldovan and others v Romania* (2007) EHRR 302 [98].
[110] [2015] EWCA Civ 646, permission to appeal to the Supreme Court granted 26 February 2016.
[111] (1994) 19 EHRR 112.
[112] (1999) 27 EHRR 611.

garden cane by his stepfather. The stepfather was prosecuted for assault occasioning actual bodily harm. The trial judge directed the jury that the prosecution was required to prove that the beating was not a reasonable punishment and the jury brought in a verdict of not guilty. At Strasbourg, the Commission unanimously found a violation of Article 3 and this was accepted by the British Government before the Court. The Court derived the positive obligation from the Article 1 obligation to secure the rights and freedoms in the ECHR together with the substantive right in Article 3. The Court stated that

> children and other vulnerable individuals, in particular, are entitled to State protection, in the form of effective deterrence, against such breaches of personal integrity ... it is a defence to a charge of assault on a child the that the treatment in question amounted to 'reasonable chastisement' ... In the Court's view, the law did not provide adequate protection to the applicant against treatment or punishment contrary to Article 3.[113]

In *A*, at issue was the lack of protection for children through the scope of English criminal law. The Court further developed the scope of the positive obligation in the well-known case of *Z v United Kingdom*.[114] This was the Strasbourg litigation that followed upon *X (Minors) v Bedfordshire County Council*.[115] Four of the five siblings who had been denied any common law remedy in negligence by the House of Lords took their complaint to Strasbourg alleging a breach of Article 3 by the UK Government in relation to the inhuman and degrading treatment they had suffered. The Commission found unanimously that the Government was in breach of its positive obligation to take positive steps to protect the children from ill-treatment prescribed by the Article. Before the Court, the UK Government conceded that Article 3 and Article 13 (the right to an effective remedy) had been breached. The Grand Chamber was unanimous in finding a violation and in an important finding indicated that Article 3 may in appropriate circumstances require the state to do more than have in place effective criminal law sanctions against such conduct by third parties. The Court stated that:

> [measures to ensure that individuals are not subject to treatment contrary to Article 3] should provide effective protection, in particular of children and other vulnerable persons and include reasonable steps to prevent ill-treatment of which authorities had or ought to have had knowledge (mutatis mutandis, the *Osman v United Kingdom* judgment of 28th October 1998).

> 74. There is no dispute in the present case that the neglect and abuse suffered by the four applicant children reached the threshold of inhuman and degrading treatment ... This treatment was brought to the local authority's attention, at the earliest in October 1987. It was under a statutory duty to protect the children and had a range of powers available to them, including the removal of the children from their home. These were, however, only taken into emergency care, at the insistence of the mother, on 30 April 1992. Over

---

[113] *Ibid* [22]–[24].
[114] *Z* (n 39).
[115] *X (Minors)* (n 94).

the intervening period of four and a half years, they had been subjected in their home to what the consultant child psychiatrist who examined them referred as horrific experiences ... The Criminal Injuries Compensation Board had also found that the children had been subject to appalling neglect over an extended period and suffered physical and psychological injury directly attributable to a crime of violence ... The Court acknowledges the difficult and sensitive decisions facing social services and the important countervailing principle of respecting and preserving family life. The present case, however, leaves no doubt as to the failure of the system to protect these applicant children from serious, long-term neglect and abuse.

In *E v United Kingdom*,[116] the authorities had failed to monitor the situation after a stepfather had been convicted of sexual abuse, and so it was held that they should have found out that he was abusing the children and done something to protect them. On the question of causation the Court held that it was not necessary for the applicants to show that 'but for' the failing of the public authority the ill-treatment would not have happened. The Court stated:

> The test under Article 3 however does not require it to be shown that 'but for' the failing or omission of the public authority ill-treatment would not have happened. A failure to take reasonably available measures which could have had a real prospect of altering the outcome or mitigating the harm is sufficient to engage the responsibility of the state.[117]

The positive obligation under Article 3 was considered by the Supreme Court in *re E*,[118] which concerned the policing of a loyalist 'protest' in Belfast targeted at catholic children and their parents as they walked to primary school. The applicant applied by way of judicial review for a declaration that the failure of the RUC to protect the applicant and her daughter was a breach of Article 3. The behaviour was extreme; Baroness Hale spoke of the consternation and amazement of the public as, day after day, little girls walking to school with their parents were subject to a barrage of clamour, insults, abuse and offensive missiles. The police decided not to permit the children's normal route on foot because the situation was too dangerous. So for several weeks parents and children had to use an alternative and longer route to school. When school resumed after the summer break the protest resumed but was increasingly violent. The mob shouted threats, abuse and obscenities and an explosive device was used. The police created a 'corridor' so children and parents could walk through the loyalist area. The applicant complained on behalf of her daughter that failures in policing exposed her daughter to inhuman and degrading treatment contrary to Article 3.

It was conceded that the treatment reached the level of severity demanded by Article 3. 'Reasonableness' had to be assessed in the light of the evidence and applying a test of proportionality. The police were uniquely placed through their expertise and intelligence sources to make a judgment on the wisest course to take and had available information about what would be likely to happen if they

---

[116] (2002) 36 EHRR 519.
[117] *Ibid* [99].
[118] [2008] UKHL 66, [2009] 1 AC 536.

took a certain course of action. They had formed the view that the best course was to seek a community negotiated solution rather than making arrests and actively disrupting the activities of the so-called 'protestors'. This approach had been challenged by the Northern Ireland Human Rights Commission as intervener. Giving the leading judgment, Lord Carswell stated that acceptance of the validity of the course which they adopted is a matter of what Lord Bingham of Cornhill described in *Huang* as,

> performance of the ordinary judicial task of weighing up the competing considerations on each side and according appropriate weight to the judgment of a person with responsibility for a given subject matter and access to special sources of knowledge and advice.[119]

The police had such responsibility and were uniquely placed through their experience and intelligence to make a judgment on the wisest course to take in all the circumstances. The Supreme Court here applied 'deference' in the context of Article 3. It is doubtful that deploying a proportionality test in the context of positive obligations is appropriate and there is no Strasbourg authority to suggest that positive obligations under Articles 2 and 3 are to be examined through the lens of proportionality. The Court itself should make a judgment as to whether the public authority has discharged its positive obligation by applying the test set out in *Osman*. Where a public authority interferes with a right (under Articles 8–11) then it must show that it pursued a legitimate aim and that the interference was proportionate to the pursuit of that aim. The burden is on the public authority to demonstrate proportionality. In the case of failures to act, the burden is on the applicant to show that the authorities 'did not do all that could reasonably be expected of them'.[120]

Duty to Investigate

The second dimension to the positive obligation under Article 3 is the requirement for an effective investigation capable of leading to prosecution of well-founded allegations of such ill-treatment, whether by state agents or private individuals. Such an investigation should, in principle, be capable of leading to the establishment of the facts and to the identification and punishment of those responsible.[121]

The scope of the duty to investigate has been considered recently by the Court of Appeal in *DSD v Commissioner of Police of the Metropolis*,[122] the case of the notorious black-cab rapist John Worboys who raped and sexually assaulted 105 women over a six-year period before he was arrested and charged. The claim

---

[119] *Huang* (n 50) [16].
[120] TR Hickman, 'The Reasonableness Principle: Reassessing its Place in the Public Sphere' (2004) 63(1) *Cambridge Law Journal* 166–98, 189.
[121] *O'Keeffe v Ireland* (2014) 59 EHRR 15.
[122] *DSD* (n 110).

was brought under section 7 HRA alleging a failure to conduct an effective investigation as required by Article 3. The quality of the investigation carried out was so defective that Laws LJ for a unanimous Court of Appeal found it 'inescapable' that Green J found a violation of Article 3. Green J found a series of 'systemic failings' in five different areas: (i) failure properly to provide training; (ii) failure properly to supervise and manage; (iii) failure properly to use available intelligence sources; (iv) failure to have in place proper systems to ensure victim confidence; and (v) failure to allocate adequate resources.

One of the most significant elements was the failure to allocate appropriate resources—this policy decision by the Metropolitan Police was driven by the impact of targets; a deliberate policy decision was taken not to focus on sexual assaults as opposed to other less complex offences that would be easier to clear up. *DSD* is an excellent illustration of how human rights standards can ensure accountability of public authorities and require them to ask themselves the right questions when they allocate resources. How public authorities allocate resources is perhaps the best example of an area of activity that is likely to be considered 'non-justiciable' at common law.

In *Rowling v Takaro Properties Ltd*, Lord Keith gave a prime example of the sort of decision that is not suitable for judicial resolution: 'discretionary decisions on the allocation of scarce resources or the distribution of risks'.[123] This is exactly the sort of decision that is considered amenable to judicial evaluation in the sphere of human rights protection. *DSD* also emphasises that the obligations under the ECHR are obligations of means and not results. Thus, as we have seen in *E v United Kingdom*, unlike the tort of negligence, satisfaction of the 'but for' test is not necessary in order to establish a violation of the ECHR. As Laws LJ stated,

> Because the focus of the human rights claim is not on loss to the individual, but on the maintenance of a proper standard of protection, the court is in principle concerned with the State's overall approach to the relevant ECHR obligation. This emphasis is in my judgment behind much of the language used in the cases cited to us (the emphasis in what follows is mine): the investigation 'should in principle be capable of leading to the establishment of the facts of the case and to the identification and punishment of those responsible'. This is not an obligation of result, but one of means... Lord Bingham's reference in *Greenfield* to 'minimum standards in the protection of the human rights' is of a piece with these formulations.[124]

---

[123] [1988] AC 473, 501. See also *Home Office v Dorset Yacht Co Ltd* [1970] AC 1004, 1065 (Lord Diplock); Lord Slynn in *Barrett v London Borough of Enfield* [2001] 2 AC 550 at [97], 'the truest test for liability is whether the particular issue is justiciable ... the two tests (discretion and policy/ operational) ... are guides .... The greater the element of policy,...the more likely it is that the matter is not justiciable ...'. See also *Lonrho Plc v Tebbit* [1982] AC 173. For criticism of 'justiciability' as a touchstone for liability, see S Bailey, 'Public Authority Liability in Negligence: The Continuing Search for Coherence' (2006) 26 LS 155–84. See also D Fairgrieve, *State Liability in Tort* (Oxford, Oxford University Press, 2003).
[124] *DSD* (n 110) [68]–[69].

It is worth highlighting that both Laws LJ in *DSD* and Lord Bingham in *Greenfield* press home the need to focus on standards of protection; that is why the 'but for' test is irrelevant. The primary aim of human rights standards is first and foremost to protect individuals by ensuring that states take effective steps to implement human rights; an effective remedy is what a claimant is entitled to seek when there has been a failure to implement human rights standards effectively and a part of that remedy will be the payment of compensation in appropriate cases. It is unnecessary for a victim to show that harm would have been averted if appropriate standards had been observed.

Article 4—Protection from Slavery and Forced Labour

Article 4(1), a non-derogable freedom, prohibits slavery or servitude. Article 4(2) prohibits forced or compulsory labour and is intended to protect individuals who are at liberty. This Article has assumed increasing importance in the light of the growing phenomenon of people trafficking.

Slavery connotes being wholly in the ownership of another person, while servitude suggests a lesser form of control by another. In *Siliadin v France*,[125] the applicant had been brought from Togo to France to work as a domestic maid for her father's relative. She worked long hours, had no papers and was frightened to contact the authorities because of her immigration status. The Strasbourg Court held that although the applicant was not 'owned' by the couple, the working conditions were such that she had been held in servitude.

As with Articles 2 and 3, the Convention may require a state to take operational measures to protect victims or potential victims from treatment in breach of Article 4. The threshold for engagement mirrors the *Osman* 'real and immediate risk' test. The standard of care requires the authorities to take appropriate measures within the scope of their powers to remove the applicant from the situation of risk.[126]

Article 4 also entails a procedural obligation to investigate where there is a credible suspicion that an individual's rights under the Article have been violated. Such an investigation must be independent from those implicated in the events and capable of leading to the identification and punishment of individuals responsible, an obligation not of result but of means. A requirement of promptness and reasonable expedition is implicit in all cases but where the possibility of removing the individual from the harmful situation is available, the investigation must be undertaken as a matter of urgency. The victim or the next-of-kin must be involved

[125] (2006) 43 EHRR 287.
[126] *Rantsev v Cyprus and Russia* (2010) 51 EHRR 1.

in the procedure to the extent necessary to safeguard their legitimate interests. In instances of trafficking, cross border cooperation between states is also required.[127]

In *CN v United Kingdom*,[128] the Strasbourg Court held that the absence of a criminal offence of domestic servitude meant that the state had failed in its positive obligation to protect the applicant. In *CN* the Court summarised the state's obligations under Article 4, the need to criminalise behaviour and the need to investigate.

The Modern Slavery Act 2015 consolidates and clarifies the existing offences of slavery and human trafficking. Section 1(1) provides for an offence of slavery, servitude and forced or compulsory labour. Section 1(2) requires that subsection 1 be interpreted in accordance with Article 4 ECHR; this formulation is slightly different from section 2 HRA which requires the court to 'take account of' ECHR jurisprudence. The Modern Slavery Act does not create a tort, but section 8(1) enables the court where a person is found guilty of a slavery or trafficking offence under section 1 (which includes servitude and forced labour) to make reparation to the victim. Victims of trafficking can bring claims for breach of contract, protection from harassment and false imprisonment in the high court or county court. The tort of false imprisonment requires the claimant to suffer a deprivation of liberty which will not be the case with servitude; while an individual's autonomy is necessarily curtailed when a person is held in servitude, they will not be deprived of liberty sufficient to make out the tort.

Article 5: Right to Liberty and Security

The protection of liberty of the individual is at the core of any democratic society and its importance is demonstrated by the fact that many of its protections are absolute and it is narrowly construed. The protection of liberty and freedom from arbitrary arrest and detention is pre-eminent amongst the human rights protected by international instruments and domestic constitutions. Long before the law of human rights had been refined and developed to protect rights as diverse as the right to education and the right to privacy, Magna Carta declared that: 'no freeman shall be taken or imprisoned … but …. by the law of the land'. According to Blackstone, the right to liberty is an 'absolute right inherent in every Englishman'.[129] The ancient prerogative writ of habeas corpus has been described as 'the most important writ known to the constitutional law of England,' affording as it does a swift and imperative remedy in all cases of illegal restraint or confinement'.[130] Quite apart from the writ of habeas corpus and the tort of false imprisonment, the right to liberty is now further protected under English law by Article 5 of the ECHR.

---

[127] *Ibid.*
[128] Application No 4239/08 13 November 2012 [80].
[129] R Kerr (ed), *Blackstones Commentaries on the Laws of England*, 4th edn (John Murray, 1876) 100, 105.
[130] *Home Secretary v O'Brien* [1923] AC 603, 609.

Article 5 aims to ensure that any deprivation of liberty shall be 'properly imposed', its lawfulness 'open to challenge so that a person unlawfully detained may be set free', and that the place of detention 'conforms to the purpose for which it is imposed'.[131] Article 5, along with Article 6, has attracted almost all state derogations under Article 15.[132]

All legal systems apply a principle of necessity in times of war or public emergency; Article 15 ensures that measures adopted are subject to scrutiny under the ECHR. The first requirement to satisfy Article 15 is that there should be a 'public emergency threatening the life of the nation'. In the well-known case of *A and others v United Kingdom*,[133] the Court was required to consider whether the UK derogation under Article 5(1) permitting detention without trial of foreign nationals suspected of involvement with terrorist activities was based upon a public emergency within Article 15. The UK Government argued that the public emergency flowed from the terrorist attacks in New York, Washington DC and Pennsylvania on 11 September 2001. No other party to the ECHR had derogated from the ECHR rights in response to the attacks and at the time there had been no terrorist attacks linked to 9/11 in the UK. In fact, such attacks materialised in the London bombings of July 2005.

By a majority of 8:1, the House of Lords was satisfied that there was a public emergency that threatened the life of the nation and that imprisonment without trial was a proportionate response, but the limitation to foreign nationals was discriminatory and the UK had not derogated from Article 14 (non-discrimination). The Grand Chamber agreed that there was a public emergency within Article 15 and indicated that it would only interfere with the national court's assessment if it had misinterpreted or misapplied Article 15 or come to a manifestly unreasonable conclusion. However, the Strasbourg Court upheld the House of Lords' judgment that the deprivation of liberty was disproportionate and not 'strictly required' by Article 15 because it targeted only foreign nationals and there were also threats from UK nationals associated with Al-Qaeda and other groups.

Not only must any deprivation of liberty conform with the substantive and procedural rules of national law, but equally must be in keeping with the purpose of Article 5, namely the protection of the individual from arbitrary detention. Article 5 sets out a general right to liberty and security and then lists cases in paragraphs (a) to (f) where there may be a deprivation of liberty in accordance with a procedure prescribed by law. Grounds include detention after conviction by a competent court, detention following arrest for the purposes of trial, detention of persons of unsound mind.

---

[131] *R (on the application of Munjaz) v Mersey Care NHS Trust* [2003] EWCA Civ 1036, [2004] QB 395 [70], quoted by Amos (n 5) 269.

[132] Jacobs, White & Ovey (n 107) 113.

[133] (2009) 49 EHRR 29.

The Gateway to Article 5—'Deprivation of Liberty'

Article 5 prohibits a 'deprivation of liberty' save in the cases set out. In many cases, it will be obvious whether there has been a deprivation of liberty. Imprisonment following conviction of a criminal offence and detention in a secure hospital are obvious examples. But, in some cases it may be more difficult to determine whether the facts fall within Article 5. The Strasbourg Court will consider factors such as the type, duration, effects and manner of implementation of the control imposed on the applicant. The *Guzzardi* case is often cited as a classic example of a borderline case.[134] In *Guzzardi*, the applicant was suspected of being a member of the Mafia and was ordered to remain on a small island near Sardinia for several months. He was required to remain within an area comprising two and a half square kilometres which included a village inhabited by other men who were subject to the same residence order. His family was allowed to live with him and he was allowed to work, although due to the scarcity of employment he could not find a job. He was subject to a curfew and required to report to the police twice a day. He was not allowed to make a telephone call or see a visitor without the permission of the police. The Strasbourg Court likened the applicant's situation to that of an open prison and held that there had been a deprivation of liberty.

Once it has been shown that there has been a deprivation of liberty, a state must establish that it was in accordance with a procedure prescribed by law for one of the purposes set out in Article 5(1)(a) to (f). The police tactic of 'kettling' protestors was challenged under Article 5 in *Austin v Commissioner of Police for the Metropolis*.[135] This is an important case because it highlights the dangers for the effective protection of human rights when a domestic court seeks to modify by way of interpretation the wording of the Convention text. It is also an example of a failure to distinguish sufficiently the common law rules from the requirements of the ECHR. We have noted the tendency of litigators to neglect common law rights. In *Austin*, counsel for the claimants conceded that if Article 5 was not engaged the tort of false imprisonment had not occurred. This is quite simply wrong. Each action has its own rules and to subsume false imprisonment into an alien framework in this way threatens the existence of common law rules that have been recognised for centuries; so much for common law fundamental rights.

Austin v Commissioner of Police

The proceedings were brought by claimants, Austin and Saxby, who were detained within a police cordon for over seven hours at Oxford Circus during the anti-globalisation demonstration on 1 May 2001. Austin had come to London with

---

[134] *Guzzardi v Italy* (1981) 3 EHRR 333 discussed by Jacobs, White and Ovey (n 107) 215.
[135] [2009] 1 AC 564.

her partner to demonstrate; Saxby was a bystander who became caught up in the throng. Neither claimant was violent or disorderly. Austin requested permission to leave the crowd at around 3.45 pm in order to collect her child from a crèche; she was refused permission and according to her witness statement became frantic with worry until she managed to contact a friend by mobile phone and arrange for her daughter to be collected. There was no dispute that the great majority of people demonstrating, including Austin, were committed to peaceful demonstration and 'that those threatening or causing the violence were a minority, and included many who were not demonstrating at all, but just using the demonstration as a cover for crime'.[136] Conditions within the police cordon became progressively more unpleasant: it was a wet and chilly afternoon and the prolonged detention meant that people were forced to urinate in the street. Tugendhat J described the situation as a 'serious interference with human dignity'.[137]

The claimants brought proceedings in private law for false imprisonment, as well as clams under section 7 of the HRA 1998 for breach of the right to liberty guaranteed by Article 5 ECHR. Both claims failed: the action for false imprisonment was litigated as far as the Court of Appeal and foundered on the ground that the imprisonment was justified on the ground of necessity in order to avoid a breach of the peace; the claim under Article 5 was rejected by the House of Lords on the basis that there had been no deprivation of liberty and thus Article 5 had not been engaged on the facts.

The claimants' litigation strategy was ill considered. In the House of Lords it was accepted on both sides that, if the appellant's (Austin's) detention was an unlawful deprivation of liberty contrary to Article 5(1) of the ECHR, then the tort of false imprisonment had also occurred because steps taken to prevent a breach of the peace could not be justified. Conversely, and more importantly, if there had not been a deprivation of liberty within Article 5, the exercise of powers by the police to prevent a breach of the peace was lawful. As Fenwick has discussed,[138] the entire legal argument focused on whether there was a deprivation of liberty within Article 5 and the lawfulness of the extensive exercise of powers to curb a breach of the peace was not subject to critical examination. This seems a misconceived approach. There is no necessary equivalence between the common law tort of false imprisonment and the HRA; it has been said on many occasions that the HRA is a floor of rights and section 11 HRA preserves all common law rights. At the time the Human Rights Bill was proceeding through Parliament, the Lord Chancellor stated that the purpose of section 11 HRA is to clarify that the Convention rights are a 'floor of rights'. If there are other different or superior rights under UK law,

[136] *Ibid* [184].
[137] The first instance decision is reported at *Austin v Metropolitan Police Commissioner* [2005] EWHC 480, [2005] HRLR 20 [10].
[138] H Fenwick, 'Marginalising Human Rights: Breach of the Peace, 'Kettling', the HRA and Public Protest' [2009] *Public Law* 737–65.

the Human Rights Bill does not take them away.[139] To the same effect, recently, in *Kennedy v Information Commissioner*, Lord Toulson deprecated the 'baleful and unnecessary tendency' to overlook the common law; it was not the purpose of the HRA that the common law should become an ossuary.[140] In *Austin*, the House of Lords determined that the police action did not constitute a deprivation of liberty within Article 5 and there was therefore no enquiry as there would have been in a claim for false imprisonment regarding the necessity for the police action in relation to the individual claimants; thus, the claimants had failed to get through the Article 5 gateway.

On any ordinary understanding of 'liberty', being restrained in the cold for a period of seven hours within a cordon, particularly after a peaceful request to leave the cordoned off group of protestors, suggests that one has been deprived of that fundamental right. The House of Lords was in a bind. Any deprivation of liberty would require justification under parameters of Article 5. The judge at first instance held that there had been a deprivation of liberty, but that the detention fell within Article 5(1)(c) as it was imposed with the conditional purpose of arresting those who might lawfully be arrested to prevent such persons committing crimes of violence. The Court of Appeal disagreed; rightly so, it was an exercise in crowd control, not detention for the purpose of arrest.

The response of the House of Lords was effectively to re-write Article 5 of the ECHR by declaring that only an 'arbitrary' deprivation of liberty will fall within Article 5; the word 'arbitrary' does not appear in Article 5. The House examined the motives for the police authority's action and held that it was possible to say that Article 5 was not even engaged on the facts because any deprivation of liberty was not 'arbitrary'. Lord Hope recognised the practical difficulties of interpreting the ECHR in this context while at the same time pointing to the immanent finding:

> The right which is guaranteed by Article 5(i) is an absolute right. But it must first be held to be applicable. To what extent, if at all, is it permissible in the determination of that issue to balance the interests of the individual against the demands of the general interest of the community.[141]

The correct answer, taking account of ECHR jurisprudence as required by section 2(1) HRA, is that it is not permissible to invoke a general public interest defence in order to oust the operation of Article 5. So, how did the House of Lords justify its conclusion?

In the leading speech, Lord Hope began by observing that ECHR jurisprudence shows that whether there is a deprivation of liberty, as opposed to restriction

---

[139] *Hansard*, HL Deb 18 November 1997, vol 583, col 510, discussed by F Klug, 'The Human Rights Act, *Pepper v Hart* and all that' [1999] *Public Law* 246–73.

[140] *Kennedy* (n 53) [133]. See also the trenchant views of Lord Mance at [46] who urged that the starting point in any case should be the common law.

[141] *Austin* (n 135) [2].

of movement, is a matter of degree and intensity.[142] The fundamental question for the House, though, was whether it is relevant in determining the ambit of Article 5(i) to 'have regard to the purpose for which a person's freedom of movement has been restricted?' Lord Hope acknowledged that there is nothing in the wording of the ECHR to support this, but,

> there are sufficient indications elsewhere in the court's case law that the question of balance is inherent in the concepts that are enshrined in the Convention and that they have a part to play when consideration is being given to the scope of the first rank of fundamental rights that protect the physical security of the person.[143]

Without overstatement, this is a dangerous gloss to put on the ECHR jurisprudence, and one for which there is no foundation. There is no authority for including the question of balance as an aid to interpret the scope of absolute rights relating to liberty and security of the person. The criteria for engagement of Article 3 (torture) and Article 5 are the manner of treatment of the individual (in the case of Article 5 'degree and intensity'); the purpose or motive behind the treatment is clearly irrelevant and importing general fair balance concepts from other areas of the jurisprudence ultimately leads to the familiar 'ticking bomb' justification for torture—clearly unlawful under ECHR and other international human rights standards. So how did Lord Hope justify his approach? The answer lies in a misinterpretation of *Saadi v United Kingdom*.[144]

In *Saadi*, the ECtHR examined the detention of the claimant at Oakington, while his asylum claim was determined, for compatibility with Article 5. The Court held that any deprivation of liberty should be in keeping with protecting the individual from arbitrariness. In other words, where there is a deprivation of liberty, it should not be arbitrary. In *Austin*, Lord Hope collapsed the two so that lack of arbitrariness means there can be no deprivation of liberty: thus, 'benign' intentions on the part of the state can mean that there has been no deprivation of liberty. The potentially dangerous consequences of taking this approach were subsequently manifested in the context of mental health in *Cheshire West v P*[145] The Court of Appeal, aided by *Austin*, was able to hold that there had been no 'deprivation of liberty' where a person's life was completely under the control of his carers at a care home which meant that review by the Court, otherwise required by Article 5(4), was not required. As the Court of Appeal observed in *P and Q v Surrey County Council*,[146] the right in paragraph 4 of Article 5 is a 'valuable' right which pursuant to statutory guidance gives the right to review on an annual basis whether the claimant's needs are met, and imposes a duty on the Court periodically to review the necessity for arrangements that deprive a person of their liberty.

---

[142] *Guzzardi* (n 134) [92].
[143] *Austin* (n 135) [27].
[144] (2007) 44 EHRR 50.
[145] [2011] EWCA Civ 1257, [2012] 1 FLR 693, discussed below, subsequently overruled by the Supreme Court in *Surrey County Council v P and Cheshire West v P* [2014] UKSC 19, [2014] AC 896.
[146] [2011] EWCA Civ 190, [2011] HRLR 19.

Austin at the ECtHR

On 15 March 2012, judgment was handed down in *Austin v United Kingdom*,[147] the Court finding by a majority that the kettling of protestors on May Day 2001 did not amount to a deprivation of liberty and therefore Article 5 was not engaged on the facts. However, the reasoning is much narrower than that of Lord Hope; indeed, the Court has followed the approach of Lord Walker in affirming that the general purpose behind a measure has not been taken into account by the ECtHR. The Court declared that:

> Indeed it is clear … that an underlying public interest motive, for example to protect the community against a perceived threat emanating from an individual, has no bearing on the question whether that person has been deprived of his liberty, although it might be relevant to the subsequent inquiry whether the deprivation of liberty was justified under one of the paragraphs of Article 5(i) (see *A v United Kingdom*, *Enhorn v Sweden* and *M v Germany*).

While this observation might appear to be a welcome brake on the potential for restriction in the scope of Article 5 signalled by the House of Lords in *Austin*, the Strasbourg Court went on to hold that the requirement to take account of the 'type' and 'manner of implementation'[148] of the measure in question enabled it to have regard to the specific context and circumstances surrounding types of restriction other than the paradigm example of confinement in a cell.[149] The Court reaffirmed the exhaustive nature of the permissible grounds of restriction in paragraphs (a) to (f) of Article 5 and signalled that *Austin* is probably at the outer limits of what would be permissible under Article 5, observing that it cannot be excluded that the use of control and containment techniques may give rise to an unjustified deprivation of liberty under Article 5(i). The Court found that the police acted to

> isolate and contain a large crowd, in volatile and dangerous conditions. As the Government pointed out …, the police decided to make use of a measure of containment to control the crowd, rather than having to resort to more robust methods, which might have given rise to a greater risk of injury to people within the crowd.[150]

Subsequently, the Court has reiterated that Article 5 should be narrowly construed. The Court held that the holding of Chechen refugees for several hours by the Georgian police was a violation of Article 5. The Court held that,

> Article 5(1) does not permit a balance to be struck between the individual's right to liberty and the State's interest in addressing security threats … If detention does not fit

---

[147] (2012) 55 EHRR 14.
[148] *Guzzardi* (n 134) and *Engel v Netherlands* (1979–80) 1 EHRR 647.
[149] *Austin v UK* (n 147) [59].
[150] *Ibid*, [66].

within the confines of the paragraphs as interpreted by the Court, it cannot be made to fit by an appeal to the need to balance the interests of the State against those of the detainee.[151]

Thus, it is clear: the pursuit of state interest in general terms cannot be used to justify detention.

Austin in the Court of Protection

It is obvious that Article 5 provides important protection for those who lack capacity to make decisions for themselves. It is not inherently unlawful for an individual to be deprived of their liberty; the effect of being deprived of one's liberty is that Article 5 becomes engaged and as a result the public authority must justify the deprivation. The potential danger of interpreting Article 5 in such a way that benign intent of purpose means a restraint on liberty is not caught by Article 5 is illustrated by the litigation that culminated in the (welcome) Supreme Court decision in *Surrey County Council v P* and *Cheshire West v P*.[152]

In the first case, *Surrey County Council v P*, two sisters had learning disabilities and did not have capacity to consent to the arrangements made by the local authority for their care. They had been removed from their abusive home environment into the care of the local authority. P was placed in foster care, attended a further education unit, went on trips and holidays and was happy in her new environment. She manifested no wish to leave, but had she attempted to do so, she would have been restrained by her foster mother. Her sister Q's behaviour was more challenging and she was generally less compliant. Q was placed in a small residential home for adolescents and attended the same further education unit as P. Q's needs required continuous supervision and control and had she tried to go out on her own she would have been prevented. In best interest proceedings in the Court of Protection, the judge held that the living arrangements for P and Q did not amount to a deprivation of their liberty within Article 5. The Court of Appeal dismissed their appeal, holding that the living arrangements were no more intrusive than necessary for their own protection and therefore neither P nor Q was deprived of her liberty within Article 5. The logical fallacy here is obvious; benign intent coupled with proportionality would take restrictions/deprivations of liberty out of Article 5 and remove such cases from the supervision of the courts.

The question before the Court in *Cheshire* was whether the living circumstances of a 38–year-old man born with cerebral palsy and Down's syndrome and with significant physical and learning disabilities amount to a deprivation of liberty. He lived in a care setting where Baker J found that the local authority and those

---

[151] *Baisuev and Anzorov v Georgia* (App 39804/04) 18 December 2012.
[152] *Surrey County Council v P and Cheshire West v P* (n 145).

working at the house had taken very great care to ensure that his life was as normal as possible. The type of accommodation was uncharacteristic of compulsory detention, P had regular contact with his family and enjoyed a social life with other residents and the community. However, Baker J decided that, overall, the steps needed to care for P led to the 'clear conclusion' that he was being deprived of his liberty. He said:

> On the other hand, his life is completely under the control of members of staff at Z house. He cannot go anywhere or do anything without their support and assistance. More specifically, his occasionally aggressive behaviour, and his worrying habit of touching and eating his continence pads, require a range of measures, including at times physical restraint, and, when necessary, the intrusive procedure of inserting fingers into his mouth whilst he is being restrained.[153]

The Court of Appeal did not agree; the judge should have taken account of the benevolent purpose of the restrictions imposed on P and should also have compared P's circumstances with others in a similar situation.

The Supreme Court held that the difference between a restriction on liberty and a deprivation of liberty is one of fact and degree and depends upon the actual situation of the person concerned. Applying *HL v United Kingdom*,[154] where people have been placed in hospitals or care homes, the relevant question is whether the person is under continuous supervision and control and whether they are free to leave. A majority in the Supreme Court held that the same test applies when a person is confined for a benevolent purpose in a non-institutional setting of normality to which they do not object. As a matter of policy, persons of extreme vulnerability need to be subject to periodic checks to make sure that the constraints on their lives were justified. In the case of P and Q, a majority agreed that there had been a deprivation of liberty. In the *Cheshire* case, the Supreme Court was unanimous that there had been deprivation of liberty; his life was under the complete control of his carers (Lord Neuberger, Baroness Hale, Lord Kerr and Lord Sumption) or the Court of Appeal should not have interfered with the judge's findings to that effect (Lord Clarke, Lord Carnwath and Lord Hodge).

Article 6—Right to a Fair Trial

The right in Article 6 to a fair trial applies to both civil and criminal matters. Article 6 applies to the 'determination of civil rights' and, in relation to these, accords a

---

[153] [2011] EWHC 1330 (Fam) [59].

[154] (2005) 40 EHRR 761. The English proceedings were *R v Bournewood Community and Mental Health NHS Trust* [1998] 3 WLR 107, which gave rise to the so-called 'Bournewood Gap' because the House of Lords had held that there was no deprivation of liberty where the Trust had admitted that if the informally admitted patient had tried to leave he would have been detained. If there is no deprivation of liberty there is no obligation on the state to ensure court review and supervision. The ECtHR found that this was a deprivation of liberty within Article 5.

right to a 'fair and public hearing within a reasonable time by an independent and impartial tribunal established by law'. The right includes the right of access to the court, in the words of the Strasbourg Court's *Golder* judgment:

> Article 6(1) secures to everyone the right to have any claim relating to his civil rights and obligations brought before a court or tribunal. In this way the Article embodies the 'right to a court', of which the right of access, that is the right to institute proceedings before courts in civil matters, constitutes one aspect only.[155]

However, as the Court has reiterated on numerous occasions, Article 6 does not guarantee any particular content for civil rights and obligations and extends only to claims which can be said 'at least on arguable grounds, to be recognised under domestic law'.[156] The Court has repeatedly stated that it cannot create by way of interpretation of Article 6 a substantive right which has no legal basis in the State concerned.[157] However, Article 6 will apply to disputes of a 'genuine and serious nature' concerning the actual existence of the right, as well as to the scope or manner in which it is exercised.[158] Where Article 6 is engaged, the procedural guarantees set out apply.

The first edition was written shortly after the ECtHR decided that the Court of Appeal's decision in *Osman v Ferguson*[159] (that the police owed no duty of care in negligence to Ahmet Osman) had violated the Article 6 right of access to a court. In *Osman*, Ahmet Osman was stalked by a dangerous obsessive school teacher, Paget-Lewis. The facts are well-known, but in summary after an escalating campaign of stalking, harassment and violence towards both Ahmet Osman and his family, Paget-Lewis shot and killed Ahmet's father, Ali, and then drove to the deputy headmaster's house and shot and injured the deputy headmaster and killed his son. The period of escalation took place over several months and the police were contacted by the Osman family on repeated occasions as they became progressively more terrified.

The Osman family instituted proceedings against the police force in negligence. On appeal, by the Metropolitan Police Commissioner, the Court of Appeal struck out the claim as disclosing no reasonable cause of action. Although a majority (McCowan and Simon Brown LJJ) considered that the claimants had an arguable case that 'there existed a very close degree of proximity amounting to a special relationship', the action was struck out unanimously on the grounds of policy which had been elaborated by Lord Keith in *Hill v Chief Constable of West Yorkshire*: the imposition of liability could lead to the exercise of the police function of investigation and suppression of crime being carried on in a detrimentally defensive frame of mind, it would be inappropriate to investigate how resources had been allocated

---

[155] *Golder* (n 10).
[156] *H v Belgium* Series A no 127-B (1987) [40]; *James* (n 19).
[157] *Roche v United Kingdom* (2006) 42 EHRR 599.
[158] *Z v United Kingdom* (n 39) [87]; *Markovic v Italy* at Reports of Judgments and Decisions 2006-XIV at [98].
[159] *Osman* (n 95).

to different lines of enquiry and how such enquiries had been prioritised and there could be a significant diversion of manpower and financial resources in defending such actions, all of which would distract attention from the important function of suppressing crime.[160] The Osman family then petitioned Strasbourg alleging violations of Articles 2, 6 and 8 of the Convention.

As we have seen,[161] the ECtHR found that there was no decisive stage in the series of events when the police knew, or ought to have known, that there was a real and immediate risk to the Osman family such as to engage the positive obligation under Article 2. However, in a finding that was to make a significant impact on the development of English law, the Court did find a violation of the Article 6 right of access to a court. The Court recalled that Article 6 embodies the 'right to a court' but that right is not absolute and may be subject to limitations, described in the following frequently used formula:

> these are permitted by implication since the right of access by its very nature calls for regulation by the State ... [the] Court must be satisfied that the limitations applied do not restrict or reduce the access left to the individual in such a way or to such an extent that the very essence of the right is impaired. Furthermore, a limitation will not be compatible with Art 6(1) if it does not pursue a legitimate aim and if there is not a reasonable relationship of proportionality between the means employed and the aim sought to be achieved.

The ECtHR found that Article 6 was applicable, because it accepted the Government's argument that the principle of *Hill* did not automatically doom to failure a civil action against the police for negligent conduct in the investigation or suppression of crime. Therefore, the applicants must be taken to have had a right, derived from the law of negligence, to seek adjudication on the admissibility and merits of an arguable claim that the duty of care criteria laid down in *Caparo* were satisfied.[162] This should have led the Court to then ensure that the procedural requirements of Article 6 had been met. The Court, however, blurred the distinction between substantive and procedural rights by subjecting the Court of Appeal's reasoning to an independent lawfulness test deriving from Article 6 jurisprudence which has been applied to 'limitations' on the Article 6 right. While the Court considered that the striking out of the claimant's negligence action was a restriction on the right of access to a court, the real reason for the strike out was the lack of a substantive right in the English tort of negligence.

The ECtHR found that the strike out procedure pursued a legitimate aim, namely 'that the interests of the community as a whole are best served by a police service whose efficiency and effectiveness ... are not jeopardised by the constant risk of exposure to tortious liability'.[163] However, the restriction was not proportionate; the Court of Appeal had proceeded on the basis that the exclusionary

---

[160] [1989] AC 53, 63.
[161] See discussion of the operational obligation under Article 2.
[162] *Osman* (n 62) [139].
[163] *Osman* (n 62) [149]–[150].

rule in *Hill* provided a watertight defence to the police and that the conferment of immunity, without inquiry into public policy arguments which pull in the other direction, amounted to an unjustifiable restriction on the applicant's right to have a determination on the merits of his or her claim in deserving cases. The requirement of proportionality meant that the Court should examine the scope of the rule as applied in the specific factual context. The Court considered that the fact that the applicants were claiming: an alleged failure to protect the life of a child, that the failure was the result of a catalogue of acts and omissions which amounted to grave negligence as opposed to minor acts of incompetence, that the police had assumed responsibility for their safety and that the harm sustained was most serious, meant that there must be a hearing on the merits.[164] If such competing policy concerns are not considered, 'there will be no distinction made between degrees of negligence or of harm suffered or any consideration of the justice of a particular case'.

The decision in *Osman* seemed to require English courts to shape the duty of care criteria to take account of the policy arguments highlighted by the ECtHR and these issues such as the seriousness of the harm and the seriousness of the negligence do not feature in any formal sense in the duty of care enquiry. Thus, *Osman v United Kingdom* blurred the distinction between substance and procedure. In a long line of jurisprudence, the Court has otherwise repeatedly stated that it cannot, through interpretation, create civil rights in Member States. The line of jurisprudence that influenced the Court in *Osman* is illustrated by the decisions in *Ashingdane v United Kingdom*,[165] *Fayed v United Kingdom*[166] and *Tinnelly & Sons Ltd and McElduff v United Kingdom*[167] where the Court has subjected restrictions on the right of access to a court to the proportionality test set out above.

In *Osman*, the Court stated that it must be satisfied that the limitations applied do not restrict or reduce the access left to the individual in such a way or to such an extent that the very essence of the right is impaired. Furthermore, a limitation will not be compatible with Article 6(1) if it does not pursue a legitimate aim and if there is not a reasonable relationship of proportionality between the means employed and the aim sought to be achieved.[168]

In *Osman* the ECtHR confused substance (not policed under Article 6) with procedure. The Court cited *Tinnelly* in support of its approach, but *Tinnelly* is a very different sort of case. Here, it was the action of the executive, rather than the courts, which had the effect of erecting a complete bar on access to the courts. The applicants, who had been led to believe that they would be awarded certain construction contracts, complained that they were victims of discrimination on the grounds of religious belief and/or political opinion which was declared unlawful

---

[164] *Osman* (n 62) [152]–[153].
[165] (1985) 7 EHRR 528.
[166] (1994) 18 EHRR 393.
[167] (1998) 27 EHRR 29.
[168] *Ibid.*

by the Fair Employment (Northern Ireland) Act 1976. In both cases, the Secretary of State for Northern Ireland had issued certificates pursuant to section 42(2) of the 1976 Act to the effect that the various actions of which the applicants complained were done for the purposes of safeguarding national security. The effect of the certificates was to prevent a tribunal from determining the complaints.

The Strasbourg Court acknowledged the importance of security considerations and of the need 'to display the utmost vigilance in the award of contracts for work involving access to vital power supplies or public buildings', but said that having regard to the principles developed by the Court, the issuing of certificates must be scrutinised to check the proportionality of this response to concerns for national security. The Court concluded that the certificates were a disproportionate restriction on the right of access to a court: the right guaranteed 'cannot be displaced by the *ipse dixit* of the executive'.[169] The Court noted that in other contexts the means had been found to protect national security while according procedural justice to the individual.[170]

There is a difference between *Tinnelly* and *Osman*; *Tinnelly* concerned the erection of a procedural bar to the assertion of a civil right, while *Osman* concerned the content of the tort of negligence. Examined through this lens, the decision in *Osman* is hard to defend. However, it must be recalled that *Osman v United Kingdom* was a case with stark facts concerning the right to life that pre-dated the HRA and at that time the tort of negligence was the only effective vehicle through which accountability of the police could be sought. Not only that, as Hickman has pointed out, the ECtHR had not at that point developed its jurisprudence regarding the state's obligation to investigate [putative] violations of the right to life; that procedural obligation through which failings on the part of the police authority will be investigated is now embedded in Article 2 jurisprudence, thus removing the need to stretch Article 6 inappropriately through the creation of a civil right where none had existed before.[171]

Thus, according to English law, in the absence of an action in the tort of negligence there was no effective mechanism through which the claimants could seek to make the public service charged with their care accountable. Although the ECtHR found no violation of Article 2 on the facts, the claim was a serious one and there needed to be the possibility of an effective remedy (as required by Article 13 ECHR).

While *Osman* was criticised by courts and commentators alike, its impact on the development of negligence has been substantial and is discussed in Chapter 5. It was not, however, to retain its authority in terms of Article 6 for long as the ECtHR beat a relatively hasty retreat in *Z v United Kingdom*.[172]

---

[169] *Ibid* [77].

[170] For example, in *Johnston v Chief Constable of RUC* [1986] ECR 1633, following the preliminary ruling of the European Court of Justice, the industrial tribunal took evidence in camera.

[171] T Hickman, 'The 'Uncertain Shadow': Throwing Light on the Right to a Court under Article 6(1) ECHR' [2004] *Public Law* 122–45.

[172] *Z* (n 39).

The Backlash against *Osman*—*Z v United Kingdom*

It will be recalled that *Z* is the Strasbourg claim brought by four of the five siblings who suffered appalling neglect and abuse at the hands of their parents, but whose negligence claim against the local authority was struck out on the ground that recognition of a duty of care would not be 'fair, just and reasonable'. The UK Government conceded that there had been a violation of the positive obligation to protect the children from inhuman and degrading treatment under Article 3 and the right to an effective remedy under Article 13. However, the Government contested the claim that the strike out of the negligence action amounted to a violation of the Article 6 right of access to a court. The Commission had seen no reason to distinguish *Z* from *Osman* and concluded that the applicants had been deprived of their right of access to a court by the strike out decision in *X (Minors)*. The next step therefore was to examine whether the decision of the House of Lords satisfied the requirements of legitimacy and proportionality laid down in *Ashingdane*[173] and *Lithgow v United Kingdom*.[174] In other words, did the restriction pursue a legitimate aim and was there a reasonable relationship of proportionality between the means employed (the strike out on the basis that no duty of care was owed) and the aim sought to be achieved. The aim of preserving the efficiency of the public service was found to be legitimate, but the restriction was a disproportionate interference with the Article 6 right, because there was no consideration of the seriousness of the damage or of the degree of negligence or the fundamental rights of the applicants which were involved.[175]

On the Article 6 claim in *Z*, the ECtHR disagreed with the Commission and departed from its reasoning in *Osman*, which it said had been based upon a misunderstanding of English law. In summary, the Court decided that when English courts determine the scope of the duty of care in negligence that is a substantive issue upon which the *Ashingdane* criteria (legitimacy and proportionality) cannot bite. Thus, when English courts refuse to recognise a duty of care in relation to a class of actors and or class of harm under the third head of *Caparo*[176] and thereupon strike out a claim that is not to create an immunity or an exclusionary rule that should then be evaluated for compliance with Article 6 jurisprudence regarding proportionality and legitimacy. Instead, what English courts are doing is to deny that (henceforth) there is an arguable claim, the existence of which would engage Article 6 obligations. The Court stated that its decision in *Osman* was based on an understanding of the law of negligence that now had to be

> reviewed in the light of the clarifications subsequently made by the domestic courts and notably the House of Lords. The Court is satisfied that the law of negligence as developed

---

[173] *Ashingdane* (n 165).
[174] (1986) EHRR 329.
[175] *Z v United Kingdom* (1999) EHRR CD 65 [114].
[176] *Caparo Industries Plc v Dickman* [1990] 2 AC 605.

in the domestic courts since the case of *Caparo* and as recently analysed in the case of *Barrett v Enfield LBC* includes the fair, just and reasonable criterion as an intrinsic element of the duty of care and that the ruling of law concerning that element in this case does not disclose the operation of an immunity. In the present case, the Court is led to the conclusion that the inability of the applicants to sue the local authority flowed not from an immunity but from the applicable principles governing the substantive right of action in domestic law. There was no restriction on access to court of the kind contemplated in the *Ashingdane* judgment.[177]

There is something of a perversity about this reasoning. The decision not to uphold the strike out in *Barrett* was clearly influenced by *Osman* and it was *Barrett* that reassured the ECtHR that application of the fair, just and reasonable requirement in *X (Minors)* does not disclose the operation of an immunity. Nevertheless, the Court was right to observe that the development of substantive law through the application of the *Caparo* principles, including the denial of a duty of care, is not in any way analogous to the issue of non-actionability in *Ashingdane*. Mr Ashingdane wished to challenge his detention in Broadmoor after the Home Secretary certified that he no longer posed the threat of violence and should be transferred to a local hospital. The move was resisted by staff at the most suitable hospital who argued that they did not have the resources to care for such an offender patient. Proceedings were stayed because the acts complained of were found to fall within the immunity created by the Mental Health Act 1959 which precluded legal challenge unless an act was done in bad faith or without reasonable care.

The 'misunderstanding of English law' adverted to by the Strasbourg Court in *Z* might have been avoided had Lord Keith not referred to police 'immunity' when he held that no duty of care was owed by the police in *Hill v Chief Constable of West Yorkshire*.[178] As Lord Browne-Wilkinson observed pertinently in *Barrett v London Borough of Enfield* regarding the use of the word 'immunity':

> Although the word 'immunity' is sometimes incorrectly used, a holding that it is not fair, just and reasonable to hold liable a particular class of defendants whether generally or in relation to a particular type of activity is not to give immunity from a liability to which the rest of the world is subject. It is a prerequisite to there being any liability in negligence at all that as a matter of policy it is fair, just and reasonable in those circumstances to impose liability in negligence.[179]

As Lord Steyn stated in *Brooks v Commissioner of Police of the Metropolis*, following the European Court's analysis in *Z*, it would be better for the principle in *Hill*'s case to be reformulated in terms of the absence of a duty of care rather than a blanket immunity.[180]

---

[177] *Z* (n 39) [101].
[178] *Hill* (n 160).
[179] [2001] 2 AC 550.
[180] [2005] UKHL 24, [2005] 1 WLR 1495 at [27].

There is, however, another perspective. For those who argue that an immunity can only arise where there is an exemption from liability to which others are subject, there is another way of looking at these cases. In Chapter 6 the issue of omissions/non-feasance is discussed in detail and how English courts have conceptualised recent cases on *Hill* and *Osman* type facts as omissions cases, for example *Smith*.[181] This has reinforced the view that such cases are not about immunity from suit for members of the police force because there is no general duty at common law for any person to go to another's aid. However, we could approach the question of liability of the police force in terms of recognition of their professional obligation to members of the public whom they serve. Other professionals such as doctors, nurses, teachers and social workers (at least in relation to children, if not their parents) owe duties of care to those individuals whose interests they serve. This is what Lord Kerr was getting at recently in *Michael v The Chief Constable of South Wales Police*[182] where he observed that, 'The common law has historically required professional persons carrying out a skill to do so with reasonable care and skill' and then went on to quote Tindal CJ in *Lanphier v Phipos* ((1838) 8 C & P 475, 479):

> Every person who enters into a learned profession undertakes to bring to the exercise of it a reasonable degree of care and skill. He does not undertake, if he is an attorney, that at all events you shall gain your case, nor does a surgeon undertake that he will perform a cure, nor does he undertake to use the highest possible degree of care and skill.[183]

When patients present themselves to hospitals or GP surgeries, the courts do not embark upon a long excursus to determine whether there has been an assumption of responsibility, the mechanism through which a duty of care on the part of the police may be established. Why should we treat members of the police force any differently?

Any doubts that Article 6 ECHR and its jurisprudence should impact upon the reasoning and determinations of English courts regarding the recognition of duties of care in negligence were finally laid to rest by the Court of Appeal's decision in *D v East Berkshire Community Health NHS Trust*.[184] *D* concerned a claim brought by a child and her father in relation to the father being denied access to his daughter after unfounded allegations that he might have sexually abused his daughter. In *D*, counsel sought to 'resurrect' *Osman* on the basis of observations made by Lord Walker in *Matthews v Ministry of Defence*.[185]

Lord Walker had referred to the important case of *Fayed v United Kingdom*[186] in which the Fayed brothers had argued that the defence of qualified privilege which

---

[181] *Smith v Chief Constable of Sussex Police* [2009] 1 AC 225.
[182] *Michael* (n 68).
[183] *Michael* (n 68) [178].
[184] [2004] QB 558.
[185] [2003] UKHL 4, [2003] 1 AC 1163.
[186] *Fayed* (n 166).

prevented their effective challenge of a report by inspectors under section 432 Companies Act 1985 was a violation of Article 6. The Court there observed that:

> Whether a person has an actionable claim may depend not only on the substantive content, properly speaking, of the relevant civil right as defined in national law but also on the existence of procedural bars preventing or limiting the possibilities of bringing potential claims to court. In the latter kind of case Article 6(1) may have a degree of applicability. Certainly the Convention enforcement bodies may not create by way of interpretation of Article 6(1) a substantive civil right which has no legal basis in the State concerned. However, it would not be consistent with the rule of law in a democratic society or with the basic principle underlying Article 6(1)—namely that civil claims must be capable of being submitted to a judge for adjudication—if, for example, a State could, without restraint or control by the Convention enforcement bodies, remove from the jurisdiction of the courts a whole range of civil claims or confer immunities from civil liability on large groups or categories of persons.

In an important observation, the Court added that

> It is not always an easy matter to trace the dividing line between procedural and substantive limitations of a given entitlement under domestic law. It may sometimes be no more than a question of legislative technique whether the limitation is expressed in terms of the right or its remedy.

In *Fayed*, the ECtHR did not consider it necessary to rule on whether the defence of qualifier privilege is, as the Government had argued, a matter relating to the content of a right, rather than a procedural issue, because the same issues of legitimate aim and proportionality would be raised if the complaint was treated as raising a substantive claim under Article 8. The defence was found to pursue a legitimate aim, namely the furtherance of the public interest in the proper conduct of the affairs of public companies and the remedy of judicial review was available to challenge the appointment of inspectors making the report, its contents or publication if there had been unfairness or breach of the rules of natural justice.

In *D*, the Court of Appeal did not consider that the shadow of *Osman* obscured the position in *D* as it was not an area where it was difficult to draw the line between procedural and substantive rules of law. Determination of what is fair, just and reasonable is to determine a principle of law in accordance with the doctrine of precedent.[187]

Thus, the distinction between substance and procedure is key to determining whether the Article 6 jurisprudence bites. But, as the Strasbourg Court remarked in an oft-cited *dictum* in *Fayed*, the distinction between substance and procedure is not always clear. In particular, state immunity has been classified as a procedural restriction on the right of access to a court so that the Article 6 jurisprudence will apply. The logical fallacy in this has been challenged by members of our most senior courts who have nevertheless followed the Strasbourg line.

---

[187] *D* (n 184) [22].

Article 6 and State Immunity

In *Fogarty v United Kingdom*,[188] the applicant had brought a successful claim in sex discrimination following her dismissal from employment by the US Embassy in London. She then applied unsuccessfully for other positions and the US pleaded state immunity in answer to her claim. The ECtHR applied the *Ashingdane* legitimacy criteria and held that the restriction on the right of access to a court was not disproportionate within Article 6.

The House of Lords and the Court of Appeal have found the Strasbourg reasoning regarding the reach of Article 6 to state immunity unconvincing. In *Holland v Lampen-Wolfe*,[189] the House of Lords held that Article 6 is not engaged by the rules on state immunity. Lord Millett (with whom Lords Cooke and Hobhouse agreed) stated that the Article does not confer on Contracting States powers they do not possess. The rule on state immunity he said is not a self-imposed restriction coming from within the state. It is a limitation imposed from without on the sovereignty of the state itself. In other words, the state does not at the outset have the jurisdiction contended for so there is no erection of an immunity barrier by the forum state. In *Osman* terms, there is no right contended for. The immunity claimed in that case was the immunity of the USA which had not been waived.

While Lord Bingham in *Jones v Saudi Arabia*[190] supported Lord Millett's reasoning in *Holland*, the House felt compelled to follow the Strasbourg Court's decision in *Al-Adsani v United Kingdom*[191] in which all the judges agreed that Article 6 was engaged in cases relating to state immunity. The claim in *Al-Adsani* was a claim based upon torture allegedly committed by Saudi Arabian officials.

In *Jones v United Kingdom*, the applicants challenged the House of Lords' decision that the principle of state immunity meant that they could not bring legal proceedings in the United Kingdom regarding allegations of torture suffered in Saudi Arabia. State immunity was applied to bar proceedings against both the state and the individual officials alleged to have committed the tort.[192] The ECtHR followed its previous jurisprudence in *Fogarty* and *Al-Adsani* and examined the 'restriction' for compliance with Article 6. The Court referred to what has been described by Hickman as the 'constitutional safeguard'[193] deriving from *Golder v United Kingdom*, and stated that:

> It would not, therefore, be consistent with the rule of law in a democratic society or with the basic principle underlying Article 6 § 1—namely that civil claims must be capable of being submitted to a judge for adjudication—if a State could, without restraint

---

[188] (2002) 34 EHRR 12.
[189] [2000] 1 WLR 1573.
[190] [2006] UKHL 26, [2007] 1 AC 270. For critique see J Wright, 'Retribution but No Recompense: A Critique of the Torturer's Immunity from Civil Suit' (2010) 30 *Oxford Journal of Legal Studies* 143–78.
[191] (2001) 34 EHRR 273.
[192] (2014) 59 EHRR 1.
[193] Hickman (n 171).

or control by the Convention enforcement bodies, remove from the jurisdiction of the courts a whole range of civil claims or confer immunities from civil liability on categories of persons. In cases where the application of the principle of State immunity from jurisdiction restricts the exercise of the right of access to a court, the Court is accordingly required to ascertain whether the circumstances of the case justified such restriction.

The Court found that sovereign immunity pursues the legitimate aim of promoting comity and good relations between states and measures which reflect generally recognised principles of international law cannot be regarded as disproportionate.[194]

In *Benkharbouche v Embassy of Sudan*,[195] the claimants were domestic staff employed in embassies whose employment claims (unfair dismissal, failure to pay the minimum wage and breach of the Working Time Regulations) were barred by the operation of the State Immunity Act 1978 (SIA)—as members of the mission within section 16(1)(a) of SIA they were excluded from the application of section 4. Giving judgment for the Court of Appeal, Lord Dyson acknowledged the conflict between the House of Lords in *Holland v Lampen-Wolfe* (Article 6 not engaged) and the *Al-Adsani* line of authority in the ECtHR. The Court found the reasoning of Lord Millett compelling but considered that the Article 6 jurisprudence should be followed and evaluated the restriction in section 16(1)(a) for legitimacy and proportionality. The rules on state immunity pursued the legitimate aim of promoting comity and respect for the sovereign equality of states; however section 16(1)(a) was not required by international law and was not within the range of tenable views of what was required. After an extensive consideration of relevant authorities, the Court of Appeal decided that it was impossible to conclude that there was any rule of international law requiring the grant of immunity in respect of employment claims by service staff in the absence of some special feature. As it was impossible to read down the relevant provisions under section 3 HRA so as to remove the immunity in a way that would be consistent with fundamental features of the legislative scheme, the Court granted a declaration under section 4(2) HRA that section 16(1)(a) in its application to the claimants breached Article 6.

The cases on sovereign immunity can be contrasted with the line of authority regarding the operation of section 10 Crown Proceedings Act 1947. In *Matthews v Ministry of Defence*,[196] the House of Lords was required to consider the effect of section 10 which provided that the Crown was not liable in tort when the Secretary of State certified that a member of the armed forces was entitled to a pension by reason of suffering attributable to service in the armed forces. The effect of section 10 is to substitute a system of no-fault compensation for claims for damages by service personnel based upon harm in service. In *Matthews*, following service in the Royal Navy between 1955 and 1968, the claimant was diagnosed with an asbestos-related disease. He claimed damages in negligence or breach of statutory

---

[194] *Jones* (n 192) [159].
[195] [2015] EWCA Civ 32.
[196] *Matthews* (n 185).

duty and the claim was rejected on the basis of section 10 with a certificate being issued by the Secretary under section 10(1)(b). The claimant argued that section 10 was incompatible with Article 6.

The question for the House of Lords was whether the effect of section 10(1) (b) and 2(b) is to impose a procedural bar on the appellant's right to claim damages rendering Article 6 applicable, or whether it qualifies the section 2 right from the outset as a matter of substantive law; if the latter, there would be no 'right' on which Article 6 could bite. A unanimous House of Lords held that the effect of section 10 was to impose a limitation which operated as a matter of substantive law. Lord Bingham traced the history of the Crown Proceedings Act and observed that the right which Mr Matthews sought to achieve (an action in tort against the Crown) had never existed in English law. In a similar vein, Lord Walker emphasised that the sections as a whole have the 'effect of removing to a large extent but not to an unlimited extent, a general pre-existing immunity expressed in the maxim that "the king can do no wrong"'. Lord Walker gave a number of examples of what would clearly be procedural bars on the right of access to a court: security for costs order, limitation periods, and the requirement to seek leave to institute or continue proceedings in the case of a vexatious litigant.

When the same issue came before the ECtHR in *Roche v United Kingdom*,[197] the Strasbourg Court upheld the House of Lords' reasoning by the slimmest of majorities (9:8). The Court laid stress on the history of the legislation and the fact that the right created in section 2 was always subject to section 10 which preserved the preclusion from claiming damages in the case of servicemen. The Court confirmed that Article 6(1) secured the procedural right to have a claim relating to civil rights and obligations brought before a court, but did not guarantee any substantive content for those rights. Although the distinction might be a fine one, it would always be determinative. The importance of the careful evaluation by the House of Lords as to whether the legislation set out the scope of the substantive law was noted, the Court remarking that the starting point in assessing whether any restriction was substantive or procedural was the relevant domestic law, and the Court would need strong reasons to disagree with the findings of a superior national court in this regard.

The House was unanimous in finding that *Tinnelly* was a very different sort of case. Lord Hoffman observed that if section 10 had been directed towards enabling 'the Secretary of State to swoop down and prevent people with claims against the Crown bringing them before the courts' then that type of restriction would be subject to Article 6 supervision.

Whatever the merits or otherwise of *Osman*, English courts subsequently displayed a reluctance to strike out claims in negligence on the basis of assumed facts.[198] In the immediate aftermath, the House of Lords' decisions in

---

[197] (2006) 42 EHRR 30.
[198] See discussion in Chapter 5.

Barrett v London Borough of Enfield[199] and *L (A Child) v Reading Borough Council*[200] were cases where the House refused to strike out the claims. More recently, in litigation brought by Kenyan nationals in respect of alleged torture and mistreatment under the colonial administration in the 1950s, McCombe J declared that where the law is not clear, it is undesirable to strike out claims on the basis of a lack of a duty of care on disputed facts.[201]

Article 7—Non-Retroactivity

This Article embodies the well-established principle of non-retroactivity: a person cannot be convicted of a criminal offence save in accordance with a law extant at the time the offence was committed. The importance of this right is demonstrated by the fact that no derogation under Article 15 is permitted. It is a little used provision and while some torts may constitute criminal offences,[202] it is likely to be of little relevance in the field of tort generally.

Article 8—The Right to Respect for Private and Family Life, Home and Correspondence

Article 8 encompasses a broad and growing range of issues, including privacy, secret surveillance, paternity and identity rights, reproductive rights, child and family law, immigration law, prisoners' rights, mental health rights, death and dying, environmental protection, inheritance, access to health care and medicine and tenant's rights.[203]

'Private life' includes 'a person's physical and psychological integrity: the guarantee afforded by Article 8 is intended to ensure the development, without outside interference, of the personality of each individual in his relations with other human beings'.[204] This observation relates to the content of the core concept of

---

[199] *Barrett* (n 123).

[200] [2001] 1 WLR 1575.

[201] *Mutua v Foreign and Commonwealth Office* [2011] EWHC 1913 [138]; *Smith v Ministry of Defence* (n 6); and see D Fairgrieve, 'Suing the Military: The Justiciability of Damages Claims against the Armed Forces' (2014) *Cambridge Law Journal* 73(1) 18–21.

[202] See for example the crime of harassment under the Protection from Harassment Act 1997. The first edition gave the example of the rarely used tort of criminal libel; the offences have now been abolished, seditious, defamatory and obscene libel by the Coroners and Justice Act 2009, s 73 and blasphemous libel by the Criminal Justice and Immigration Act 2008, s 79.

[203] For a comprehensive discussion, see Amos (n 5) 409–526; *Harris O'Boyle & Warbrick* (n 2) 321–424; Jacobs, White and Ovey (n 107) 361–409.

[204] *Botta v Italy* (1998) 26 EHRR 241 [32].

private life and this, coupled with the fact that the state may have positive obligations to protect an individual's physical and psychological integrity, means that a wide range of activities may be protected and a number of positive steps may be required by states. A state must put in place laws to protect people from the criminal acts of others. In the widely cited case of *X and Y v The Netherlands*,[205] the state was in violation of Article 8 where owing to a *lacuna* in the criminal law, a rapist could not be prosecuted because the victim was a minor and mentally disabled. Where it is argued that domestic law gives inadequate protection to the physical well-being of the individual, it is likely that a claim will be pleaded as both a violation of Article 3 (inhuman and degrading treatment), as well as Article 8, even where the actual ill-treatment is inflicted by private non-state actors.[206]

Strasbourg has become increasingly vigilant to guard the physical well-being of vulnerable members of society, by finding violations of Article 3, rather than Article 8, and by finding that Article 2 is engaged in an increasingly broad range of circumstances. Article 3 is a non-derogable right and therefore deserving of the highest level of protection. In *X and Y*, decided in 1985, the Court preferred to approach the case under Article 8 and having found a violation stated that it did not need to examine the case under Article 3. The Commission had found by 15 votes to one that there had been no violation of Article 3.

In contrast in *A v United Kingdom*,[207] the Court, having found a violation of Article 3, considered it unnecessary to examine whether the ill-treatment (a jury acquitted a stepfather of assault after he pleaded 'reasonable chastisement') was a violation of Article 8. Similarly, in *Z v United Kingdom*,[208] the Commission did not consider it necessary to examine Article 8 having found a violation of Article 3. We have seen an increasing confidence on the part of Strasbourg to subject state conduct to intensive scrutiny. Feldman has analysed the process by which international human rights law obligations and supervisory bodies gain authority and achieve a pull towards compliance on the part of Contracting States. The substance of rights is developed through a process of dialogue between states which build confidence on the part of states in the supervising institutions and it is not surprising that the jurisprudence under Articles 2 and 3 has grown.[209] The increased willingness of Strasbourg to analyse conduct through the lens of Article 3 rather than Article 8 reflects the evolving nature of the jurisprudence and the fact that the ECHR is a 'living instrument'.

The physical and psychological well-being of a person can be affected by the state of the environment and a number of claims brought under Article 8 have been based upon the failure of the state to protect the quality of life or amenity of

---

[205] (1986) 8 EHRR 235.
[206] See for example *A v United Kingdom* (n 112), *Z v United Kingdom* (n 39).
[207] *A* (n 112).
[208] *Z* (n 175).
[209] D Feldman, 'Human Rights Treaties, Nation States and Conflicting Moralities' (1995) 1 *Contemporary Issues in Law* 1.

property. Thus, in the well-known case of *Lopez Ostra v Spain*,[210] the applicants complained that the operation of a waste treatment plant caused noise, fumes and smells and that this affected their private and family life, although without seriously endangering the applicants' health. The authorities had not created the emissions, but they had permitted the plant to be built on their land, with the assistance of government funding. The Court found a violation of Article 8, but considered that although the conditions created by the plant made life difficult, they did not reach the level of seriousness contemplated by Article 3 so that there was no degrading treatment.

Importantly, there is no need to have any interest in property in order to bring a complaint under Article 8. As far as English law is concerned, in *Hunter v Canary Wharf Ltd*, the House of Lords confirmed that private nuisance is a property tort, the essence of which is that the enjoyment of property rights is infringed. Lord Hoffmann observed that:

> Once it is understood that nuisances 'productive of sensible personal discomfort' do not constitute a separate tort of causing discomfort to people but are merely part of a single tort of causing injury to land, the rule that the plaintiff must have an interest in the land falls into place as logical and, indeed, inevitable (see *St Helen's Smelting Co v Tipping* (1865) HL Cas 642 at 650, 11 ER 1483 at 1486).[211]

Clearly, it cannot be said that the land has suffered 'sensible' injury; rather, its 'utility has been diminished by the existence of the nuisance'.[212] *Hunter* exposes a *lacuna* in English law. The claimants' lives were made a misery over an extensive period because their homes were infiltrated by dust from the Docklands development. They did not suffer physical injury. There could be no claim in negligence in the absence of physical injury; there could be no claim in nuisance in the absence of an exclusive right to possession.

Lord Cooke was the sole dissenting voice in *Hunter*, arguing for a test of 'residence' as a sufficient basis for standing in such cases. He identified the nub of the claim as interference with the amenity of the home, an interest protected by a range of international instruments, including Article 16 of the United Nations Convention on the Rights of the Child, as well as Article 12 of the Universal Declaration on Human Rights and Article 8 of the Convention. For the reasons discussed in Chapter 3 we do not consider that sound interpretation of the HRA *requires* English courts to fashion the tort of nuisance to meet such claims.[213] The most that can be said is that without action the United Kingdom will on appropriate facts be in breach of her international obligations by failing to ensure an appropriate remedy at domestic level.

---

[210] (1995) 20 EHRR 277.
[211] [1997] AC 655 [452].
[212] *Ibid* [451] (Lord Hoffmann).
[213] See Chapter 3, section entitled 'Interpreting the Section 6 Obligation: "Compatibility" and "Convention Rights"'.

In *Khatun v United Kingdom*, the group of residents who lost their appeal in *Hunter* petitioned Strasbourg, alleging that the excessive dust violated their right to respect for private and family life and their home. The Commission considered that Article 8(1) applied to all the applicants and, although none alleged that they had suffered ill-health as a result of dust contamination, 'the fact that they could not open windows or dry laundry outside for a period of three years severely impaired their right to enjoy their homes and private or family lives'.[214] Therefore, there was an interference with Article 8(1) rights which needed to be justified under Article 8(2) by demonstrating that it corresponded to a pressing social need and was proportionate. Interference with Article 8 rights requires justification under Article 8(2) which includes the 'economic well-being of the country' among the legitimate aims for interference. The Commission held that the construction of the Limehouse Link road as part of the London Docklands development scheme pursued the legitimate aim of serving the well-being of the country. The Commission also held that the construction of the road was essential to the development of the area and fulfilled an important public interest. The Commission found that although the dust was unpleasant, there were no health problems associated with it. On the facts, therefore, a fair balance had been struck between the interests of the community and the individuals. Attention was also drawn to the fact that the works took three years and no proceedings were instituted while they were in progress and the applicants were probably affected to different degrees.

A person's right to privacy in the sense of the right to be let alone against unreasonable intrusion by others and the right to prevent the dissemination of private information is contemplated by Article 8, and this issue is discussed in detail in Chapter 8.

Parental/Family Rights

In *F v Wirral Metropolitan Borough Council*,[215] the Court of Appeal held that a parent has no right at common law to seek damages for interference with parental rights. The only remedies available were public law remedies, and for the parents, the tort of misfeasance in public office. This tort is of extremely limited scope, confined to cases where a claimant can show that a public officer has acted in bad faith, either by intending to injure the claimant or with reckless indifference to the illegality of his act and in the knowledge of or with reckless indifference to the probability of his causing damage to the claimant.[216]

Claims for interference by a public authority with parental/family rights are now met through Article 8 ECHR; the HRA has effectively introduced a statutory

---

[214] *Khatun v UK* (1998) 26 EHRR CD 212, 215.
[215] [1991] 2 All ER 648.
[216] *Three Rivers District Council v Governor and Company of the Bank of England* [2000] 3 All ER 1.

tort to protect parents and families against interference with family relationships by public authorities. The notion of family life has been interpreted to include relationships between parent and child, both legitimate and illegitimate,[217] as well as more extended family relationships.[218] The Court has held that the 'mutual enjoyment by parent and child of each other's company constitutes a fundamental element of family life'.[219] Many of the claims brought before Strasbourg relate to child protection procedures.

In *TP and KM v United Kingdom*[220] (the English proceedings were *M (A Minor) v Newham London Borough Council*, appeal consolidated with *X (Minors) v Bedfordshire County Council*[221]), a mother and child alleged that the local authority was negligent in its removal of the child into the care of the local authority and that the right to respect for private and family life had been violated. The Court held that the removal of the child did not violate Article 8, as there were strong suspicions of abuse and well-founded fears that the mother could not protect the child. Thus, the removal of the child pursued a legitimate aim and was proportionate. However, subsequently, the authority had failed to disclose to the mother the transcript of an interview at which the abuser was correctly identified as a person other than her mother's boyfriend by the daughter until a year later—if the mother had been adequately involved in decisions regarding her daughter's care on an ongoing and regular basis the error regarding mis-identification of the abuser as the mother's boyfriend would have come to light much sooner. Article 8 had been violated by the failure to involve the mother sufficiently in the decision-making process.

Where Article 8 is engaged, the state must demonstrate that decisions are justified by 'relevant and sufficient reasons' and that actions are proportionate.[222]

Article 9—Freedom of Thought, Conscience and Religion

There are two aspects to Article 9: the right to freedom of thought, conscience and religion (including the right to change that religion or belief) and the right to manifest one's religion or belief. Limitations on the right under Article 9(2) are permitted only in relation to the manifestation of religion or belief.

---

[217] *Marckx v Belgium* (1979–80) 2 EHRR 330.
[218] *Boyle v United Kingdom* (1995) 19 EHRR 179 concerning right of access by an uncle to his nephew after the child had been taken into care.
[219] *Olsson v Sweden* (1989) 11 EHRR 259.b.
[220] [2001] 2 FLR 549. See also *MAK v United Kingdom* (2010) 51 EHRR 14.
[221] *X (Minors)* (n 94).
[222] *Olsson* (n 219). See also *D v East Berkshire Community NHS Trust* (n 184).

Like freedom of speech, protected under Article 10, this right has been described as one of the essential foundations of a democratic society:

> It is, in its religious dimension, one of the most vital elements that go to make up the identity of believers and their conception of life, but it is also a precious asset for atheists, agnostics, sceptics and the unconcerned. The pluralism indissociable from a democratic society, which has been dearly won over the centuries, depends on it.[223]

Article 9 has occasionally featured in tort claims. In *Church of Jesus Christ of the Latter Day Saints v Price*,[224] the defendant argued that his proselytising behaviour which involved targeting occupants of church buildings, following church members down the street and making persistent phone calls were all justified under Article 9 as lawful manifestations of his religion. Beatson J held that the activities constituted a nuisance and in his conclusion took account of the right of church members to practise their religion and their rights of association and assembly without unlawful interference. He cited the well-known case of *Otto-Preminger v Austria*[225] to support the need for those manifesting their religion to have regard to the rights of others. For example, cases that relate to educational provision will be considered under Article 2 of Protocol 1; matters relating to public protest will be considered under Article 11 and so on.

Article 10—Freedom of Expression

Article 10 guarantees the right to freedom of expression, which includes freedom to hold opinions and to receive and impart information and ideas without interference by a public authority and regardless of frontiers. Two areas of English tort law that engage Article 10 are defamation and privacy which are discussed in detail in Chapters 7 and 8, respectively.

Article 11—Freedom of Assembly and Association

The Strasbourg Court has acknowledged the special affinity of Article 11 with freedom of expression, describing it as *lex specialis* in relation to the *lex generalis* of Article 10. It will be recalled that the right of peaceful demonstration is protected by Article 11. In *Plattform 'Ärzte für das Leben v Austria*,[226] the Court held that this right may impose positive obligations on the state to protect those who

---

[223] *Kokkinakis v Greece* (1994) 17 EHRR 397.
[224] (2004) EWHC 3245, 2004 WL 3222620.
[225] (1995) 19 EHRR 34.
[226] (1991) 13 EHRR 204.

wish to protest from counter-demonstrators. Any restriction on or interference with the right must pursue a legitimate aim and correspond to a pressing social need, as well as being proportionate to the aim pursued.

Article 11 features rarely in HRA claims; any claims generally being dealt with under Article 10.[227] There has been a growing tendency for claimants whose activities are targetted by protestors to seek injunctions under the Protection from Harassment Act 1997. The campaign against Huntington Life Sciences by Stop Huntingdon Animal Cruelty (SHAC) was resisted by the use of injunctive relief.[228] The campaign took the form of threatening letters, phone calls, malicious allegations, letters containing offensive material, criminal damage, intimidation, protest camps; the Court found that directors and employees were unquestionably subjected to harassment of a very serious nature intended to intimidate and terrify. In what has been described as merely a 'nod',[229] the Court acknowledged that it must act compatibly with ECHR rights, but there is no discussion of the HRA or ECHR jurisprudence; freedom of expression and association are mentioned but noting the importance of the qualifications in Articles 10(2) and 11(2).

Article 14—Prohibition of Discrimination

Article 14 ECHR requires states to secure the enjoyment of Convention rights and freedoms without discrimination on any ground and a non-exhaustive list of possible grounds of discrimination is set out. This Article has featured in claims brought under the HRA but it is beyond the scope of this work to examine these in detail and readers' attention is drawn to specialist texts.[230] Suffice to say that in a series of judgments the Court of Appeal has devised what it has called a structured approach to such questions, so that the Court will ask:

1. Do the facts fall within the ambit of one or more of the Convention rights?
2. Was there a difference in treatment in respect of that right between the complainant and others put forward for comparison?
3. If so, was the difference in treatment on one or more of the proscribed grounds under Article 14?
4. Were those others in an analogous situation?
5. Was the difference in treatment objectively justifiable in the sense that it had a legitimate aim and bore a reasonable relationship of proportionality to that aim?[231]

---

[227] Amos (n 2) 590.

[228] *Daiichi Pharmaceuticals UK Ltd v SHAC* [2003] EWHC 2337, [2004] 1 WLR 1503; see KD Ewing, *Bonfire of the Liberties* (Oxford, Oxford University Press, 2010) 121 et seq.

[229] Ewing, *ibid.*

[230] Harris, O'Boyle and Warbrick (n 2); Amos (n 5) and Jacobs, White & Ovey (n 107).

[231] *R (on the application of Carson) v Secretary of State for Work and Pensions* [2003] EWCA Civ 797, [2003] 3 All ER 577, quoted by Amos (n 5) 606.

Article 1, Protocol 1—Protection of Property

Article 1 contains three distinct rules. First, every natural or legal person is entitled to the peaceful enjoyment of his possessions. Second, a person may be deprived of his possessions in the public interest in accordance with the law and general principles of international law. Finally, nothing within Article 1 of Protocol 1 shall in any way impair the right of a state to control the use of property in accordance with the general interest or to secure the payment of taxes or other penalties. In *Aston Cantlow and Wilmcote with Billesley Parochial Church Council v Wallbank*, the House of Lords held that the Church Council was not a public authority within section 6 HRA and therefore not subject to the requirement to act compatibly with ECHR rights. The claimant sought successfully to enforce liability for chancel repairs under the Chancel Repairs Act 1932. Lord Hope observed that in a case that engages Article 1 of Protocol 1, a balance must be struck between the rights of the individual and the public interest to determine whether the interference was justified. These rules are not unconnected as, before considering whether the first rule has been complied with, the court must first determine whether the last rules are applicable ... the second and third rules are concerned with particular instances of interference with the right to peaceful enjoyment of property. They should be construed in the light of the principle enunciated the first rule.[232] The House of Lords held that the burden of chancel repairs was a private law burden which ran with the land and of which the defendants had notice when they acquired the property. Thus, the defendants were not being subject to an arbitrary form of taxation and nor was their peaceful enjoyment of possessions the subject of interference.

In *AXA General Insurance Ltd v HM Advocate*,[233] insurers challenged the enactment of the Damages (Asbestos-Related Conditions) (Scotland) Act 2009 under Article 1 Protocol 1 on the basis that it was outside the legislative competence of the Scottish Parliament. Sections 1 and 2 of the Act reversed the House of Lords' decision in *Rothwell v Chemical & Insulating Co Ltd*[234] so that pleural plaques, pleural thickening and asbestosis now constitute actionable harm in Scotland. The UK Government indicated in the course of debate in the House of Commons that it did not consider it appropriate to legislate. The Supreme Court held that the insurers were victims within Article 34 as the expectation was that they would bear the burden of meeting the claims made actionable by the Act and the fund from which payments would be made constituted a possession within Article 1,

---

[232] *Aston Cantlow and Wilmcote with Billesley Parochial Church Council v Wallbank* [2003] UKHL 37, [2004] 1 AC 546 [67] (Lord Hope).
[233] [2011] UKSC 46, [2012] UKSC 1 AC 868.
[234] [2008] AC 281. The House of Lords held that the development of asymptomatic pleural plaques on the lungs as a result of exposure to asbestos did not constitute physical damage that could ground a claim for stress and anxiety.

Protocol 1. Such interference had to comply with the principle of lawfulness and pursue a legitimate aim through proportionate means.

The Court held that according to ECHR jurisprudence the national court would regard measures involving political, social or economic issues as falling within the legislature's discretionary area of judgment and respect that decision unless it was manifestly unreasonable. The Scottish Parliament was entitled to regard the consequences of recent case law as a social injustice in Scotland. Furthermore, although the Act was retrospective, the legislature was not precluded from interfering with existing contracts if special justification could be shown. In an observation that raises concerns for those who worry about the effective separation of powers and the rule of law, Lord Hope stated that judges are best placed to protect the rights of individuals but elected members of the legislature are best placed to judge what is in the country's best interests as a whole.[235]

Article 2, Protocol 1—The Right to Education

The leading authority in relation to the right to education is the *Belgian Linguistics* case.[236] The gist of the complaint was that the children of French speakers did not have access to mother-tongue education unless they travelled a considerable distance from their homes. The main challenge failed and the case laid down the basic principle that a person has the right to avail himself of the system of education that has been put in place by the state. There is no right under the ECHR to demand a particular form of education, except that to the extent that the state does make provision, such provision should not be made on a discriminatory basis as this would violate Article 14. A number of applications have been made by the parents of children with special educational needs, but these have not been successful, Strasbourg refusing to interfere with assessments made by the state. Thus, a claim by parents of a severely disabled child for a place in a mainstream school was denied.[237] Similarly, the parents of a dyslexic child could not insist on special, rather than mainstream schooling.[238] The Supreme Court has confirmed that the positive obligation under Article 2 of Protocol 1 is limited to regulating access to the education system that is provided without discrimination.[239] Thus, the value of the right depends upon the quality and resources of the education system provided by the relevant state.

---

[235] *AXA* (n 232) [49].
[236] *Case Relating to Certain Aspects of the Laws on the Use of Languages in Education in Belgium* (1968) 1 EHRR 252.
[237] *PD v United Kingdom* (1989) D & R 292.
[238] *Simpson v United Kingdom* (1989) 64 D & R 188.
[239] *A (Appellant) v Essex County Council (Respondent)* [2010] UKSC 33, [2011] 1 AC 280.

5

Public Authority Liability
Part 1—The Impact of the ECHR
on the Common Law

Introduction

A centrepiece of the Law Commission's Ninth Programme of Law Reform was consideration of remedies against public bodies, during the course of which a Consultation Paper on *Administrative Redress: Public Bodies and the Citizen* was published. This chapter suggested that the interests of justice were poorly served by the existing framework of tort law: negligence is unpredictable, and the torts of misfeasance in public office and breach of statutory duty failed properly to balance the interests of claimant and public authority in a 'clear and predictable manner'.[1] The Consultation Paper proposed that the conduct of public bodies should be measured in accordance with the principles of 'modified corrective justice': compensation should only be available in cases of serious misconduct where the state is respondent and the principle would apply only to 'truly public activity'.[2]

After wide-ranging consultation, the proposals were kicked into the long grass having been rejected across Government.[3] It is telling that one of the major criticisms raised by Government was the Law Commission's inability to assess and predict the economic impact of its proposals.[4] The Law Commission accepted that it needed to consider the extent to which reforms might divert resources from the delivery of public services to compensation payments. However, not even the first stage of any such quantitative analysis could be undertaken due to the fact that 'obtaining even basic figures for current compensation' proved impossible. The Law Commission therefore attempted to salvage something from the exercise by recommending that data on compensation payments should routinely be collected

---

[1] Law Commission, *Administrative Redress: Public Bodies and the Citizen A Consultation Paper*, Consultation Paper No 187 (2008) 4.92.

[2] *Ibid* 33.

[3] Law Commission Report No 322, *Administrative Redress: Public Bodies and the Citizen* (2010).

[4] In a similar vein, see Stevens regarding the lack of empirical data that guides the judiciary in its assessment of policy considerations: R Stevens, *Torts and Rights* (Oxford, Oxford University Press, 2007) Chapter 14 on 'Policy'.

in order for public bodies to fulfil 'their duties of 'accountability and transparency'. That the project apparently foundered for want of such basic information is especially ironic given that the stated goals were to 'improve administrative action and decision-making, promoting good governance and achieving accountability and transparency in public administration [consistent with the Government's … service transformation agenda]'.[5]

It is a basic feature of a society governed by the rule of law that citizens should be able to understand and predict, if need be with legal advice, the legal consequences that flow from their acts and omissions. Common law rules regarding the liability of public authorities in negligence do not always seem to meet this basic principle. In its Consultation Paper, the Law Commission stated that: 'The uncertain and unprincipled nature of negligence in relation to public bodies, coupled with the unpredictable expansion of liability over recent years, had led to a situation that serves neither claimants nor public bodies'.[6] Stevens has remarked on the endless stream of cases against public bodies in negligence, as liability 'has expanded, retreated and expanded again'.[7] The Commission also expressed the view that, the long-term trend is likely to be an expansion of liability.[8] The Consultation Paper came out in 2008, just before the key House of Lords' decision in *Smith v Chief Constable of Sussex*[9] and the rejection of the idea that the common law should reflect the positive obligations that are inherent in the European Convention on Human Rights (ECHR). In fact, contrary to the views expressed by the Law Commission, it is arguable that negligence law has become much more predictable since 2008; the courts have confirmed that actions that can be characterised as nonfeasance (and many claims against public authorities are premised upon failures to act) will fail. The most recent incarnation of this approach is *Michael v Chief Constable of South Wales*.[10] The courts are effectively consigning claims that engage ECHR rights to the action under the Human Rights Act 1998 (HRA). To that extent, recent developments in the tort of negligence have betokened greater certainty of outcome; such developments can be subject to attack, however, on the basis that, arguably, in some cases they offend the basic equality principle[11] and do not give citizens the protection they need and deserve when they rely upon the state to deliver on promises of protection. As we shall see in Chapter 6, the police force, for example, has been excused liability even in cases of commission.

As the first edition of *Tort Law & Human Rights* was completed, the European Court of Human Rights (ECtHR) in *Z v UK*[12] resiled from its decision in

---

[5] Law Commission (n 1) 3.7.
[6] Law Commission (n 1) 2.7.
[7] Stevens (n 4) 310.
[8] Law Commission (n 1) 4.52.
[9] [2008] UKHL 50, [2009] 1 AC 225.
[10] [2015] UKSC 2, [2015] AC 1732.
[11] See discussion of Dicey's equality principle in T Cornford, *Towards a Public Law of Tort* (Aldershot, Ashgate Publishing Ltd, 2008) Chapter 2.
[12] [2001] 2 FLR 612.

Osman v UK[13] that the striking out of the action in negligence against the police force in *Osman v Ferguson*[14] was a violation of the Article 6 right of access to a court; in *Z*, the ECtHR held that the failing of English law lay in the absence of an effective remedy to redress the breach of other substantive rights (in *Z*, Article 3 and in *Osman*, Article 2). It is unnecessary here to revisit the detail of those two judgments which are examined in Chapter 4.[15] What is of interest for the purposes of the present discussion is the impact that *Osman v UK* has had on the development of the law relating to public authority liability in negligence. *Osman v UK* had many critics, but despite its analytical flaws its mark upon English law has been significant. It should also be noted that, in common with other areas of law, notably privacy, *Osman* has shaped English law despite there being no acknowledged mechanism for giving effect to the judgment at domestic level. This author argued in the pre-HRA era that the common law presumption in *Derbyshire County Council v Times Newspapers Ltd*[16] provided a gateway through which the ECHR could infuse the action for negligence where claims against a public authority engaged the state's human rights obligations.[17]

In fact, English courts responded to their perception of the demands of the judgment of the ECtHR, but without justifying their decisions in terms of the HRA; it has been another example of the common law's pragmatic response to international standards. The effect of *Osman* on English law was immediate and it was twofold. English courts began to subject so-called 'immunities' to a much more searching examination in order to test the supposed rationale for their recognition. Secondly, English courts displayed a marked reluctance to strike out claims in negligence, emphasising that decisions should be made upon the basis of certain facts.

This chapter will examine the impact that the ECHR, including *Osman v UK* (rather than the HRA *per se*) has had on public authority liability. This distinction is important for at least two reasons: (i) the HRA is likely to be repealed; and (ii) the existence of a body of common law human rights jurisprudence informed by the ECHR provides a model for the influence of other international standards, not limited in their application by the restrictive rules of the HRA on limitation, non-retrospectivity and measure of damages. As cases continue to be brought against public authorities based on historical facts, this is not merely of academic interest.

[13] (2000) 29 EHRR 245, [1999] FLR 193.

[14] [1993] 4 All ER 344.

[15] For a detailed critique of the decision in *Z v UK*, see J Wright, 'The Retreat from *Osman*: *Z v United Kingdom* in the ECtHR and Beyond' in D Fairgrieve, M Andenas and J Bell (eds), *Tort Liability of Public Authorities in Comparative Perspective* (London, British Institute of International and Comparative Law, 2002).

[16] [1992] 1 QB 770. The House of Lords did not disagree with the Court of Appeal's view regarding the scope of the common law presumption, but decided that a local authority could not bring an action in defamation without the need to rely on the ECHR: [1993] AC 534. Lord Keith, giving the principal speech, relied upon US jurisprudence and agreed with Lord Goff in *Att-Gen v Guardian Newspapers (No 2)* [1990] 1 AC 283-84, that there was no difference in principle between English law and Article 10 ECHR.

[17] J Wright, 'Local Authorities, the Duty of Care and the European Convention on Human Rights' (1998) *Oxford Journal of Legal Studies* 1.

This chapter does not examine in detail the issue of omissions. Chapter 6 focuses on positive obligations as they have developed under the jurisprudence of the ECtHR and how English courts have responded to demands that the common law should develop parallel remedies. It is necessary for the purposes of exposition to separate the issue of omissions from other areas of public authority liability as the distinction between omission and commission is firmly entrenched in the common law; on the other hand, the extent and scope of positive obligations under the ECHR and therefore the basis of a claim under section 7 HRA has grown significantly since the first edition. There is the potential therefore for increasing tension between the common law and the demands of the human rights obligations undertaken by the UK. Apart from the problem area of non-retrospectivity of the HRA, the common law and the HRA case law can develop in tandem. Repeal of the HRA could potentially undermine the current twin-track approach where breaches of positive obligations on public authorities under the ECHR are remedied through the HRA and not the common law.

The Impact of *Osman v UK*

The impact of *Osman* was immediate and profound. Booth and Squires observed with some prescience that

> It is difficult to imagine the law of public authority negligence developing as it did in the UK at the end of the 1990's, and in the following years, had it not been for the decision of the ECtHR in the case of *Osman v United Kingdom*.[18]

Although *Osman* was eventually to be overruled by the ECtHR, its legacy has been enduring. It is curious looking back to the early decisions of *Arthur JS Hall v Simons*,[19] *Barrett v Enfield London Borough Council*[20] and *Phelps v Hillingdon London Borough Council*[21] that the cases are completely bereft of any argument as to the domestic legal basis for applying the ruling in *Osman*. There is no reference to any of the traditional common law presumptions, nor obviously to the HRA because it was not in force. In *Barrett*, Lord Browne-Wilkinson observed that if Mr Barrett's claim had been struck out he would in all likelihood petition Strasbourg, but that is not a justification grounded in common law rules. It is true that cases such as *Reynolds v Times Newspapers Ltd*[22] were also decided on the basis that the HRA applied, even though it was not in force. But, there was a long

---

[18] C Booth and D Squires, *The Negligence Liability of Public Authorities* (Oxford, Oxford University Press, 2006) 3.65.
[19] [2000] 3 All ER 673.
[20] [1999] 3 WLR 79.
[21] [2000] 3 WLR 776, [2001] 2 AC 619.
[22] [1999] 3 WLR 1010.

pre-HRA pedigree of referring to the ECHR requirements under Article 10 in the context of defamation even though the ECHR was not part of English law.

The first case decided at the highest level and which bore the imprint of *Osman* was *Arthur JS Hall v Simons*[23] in which the House of Lords finally dispatched the immunity of advocates in both civil and criminal proceedings. While commonly attributed to the House of Lords' decision in *Rondel v Worsey*, advocates had enjoyed immunity for their conduct in performing duties in court for more than two centuries.[24] The principal cogent argument used to support the immunity was that it prevents collateral attacks on decisions in civil and criminal cases, but the House was satisfied that this aim is served by the jurisdiction to strike out a civil challenge to a criminal conviction as an abuse of process. Likewise, the principles of res *judicata*, issue estoppel and abuse of process satisfied concerns regarding collateral attacks on civil proceedings.

The House was much influenced (in keeping with the practice which continues today of referring to the common law world when looking for inspiration, rather than our European neighbours, despite the supremacy of EU law)[25] by the empirical evidence from Canada which had rejected the immunity,[26] and which demonstrated that fears that the possibility of actions in negligence against barristers would tend to undermine the public interest were unnecessarily pessimistic. The compatibility of the immunity with Article 6 was considered only by Lords Hope and Hutton in dissent who considered that the core immunity in criminal cases should be retained. Lord Hope was concerned that an advocate's independent judgment would be influenced by the fear of litigation to the detriment of the efficient administration of justice; with echoes of Lord Keith in *Hill*[27] he worried that advocates would adopt a defensive approach. Regarding proportionality, he was satisfied that the client was not significantly disadvantaged because there is a range of mechanisms that address miscarriages of justice: the availability of compensation under section 133 of the Criminal Justice Act 1988 and advocates are subject to professional disciplinary procedures. Lord Hobhouse justified retention of the immunity in criminal cases on the basis of his 'perception' that such advocates are more likely to be subject to harassment from vexatious proceedings because 'unpleasant, unreasonable and disreputable persons' are more likely to be defendants in criminal rather than civil cases. It would also be invidious to single out one of the participants at trial when all others (at that time)[28] were in the public interest immune.

---

[23] *Arthur JS Hall* (n 19).

[24] *Rondel v Worsley* [1969] 1 AC 191; S William, 'Immunity in Retreat' (1999) 2 *Professional Negligence* 15.

[25] See P Gilliker, 'The Influence of EU and European Human Rights Law on English Private Law' (2015) *International and Comparative Law Quarterly* 64(2), 227–65.

[26] *Demarco v Ungaro* (1979) 95 DLR (3d) 385.

[27] *Hill v Chief Constable of West Yorkshire* [1989] AC 53.

[28] The immunity of expert witnesses was subsequently abolished in *Jones v Kaney* [2011] UKSC 13, [2011] 2 AC 398.

Lord Steyn was extremely sceptical that in 'the world of today', as he put it, that immunity was required to ensure a barrister performed his or her duty to the court; he pointed out that many professional people will at times face conflicting duties and he cited the confidentiality obligation that doctors owe to their patients which may at times conflict with the public interest. Lord Browne-Wilkinson agreed and Lord Hoffmann also pointed out that professional people generally owe duties of care in negligence. It is striking that the same arguments do not seem to have been accepted with regard to the police force.[29]

Lord Millett, the sole member of the majority to refer to Article 6, stated that a blanket professional immunity would be hard to defend in terms of the Convention and that he could find no compelling reasons to support it 'based on more than instinct or tuition'. Whatever the merits of the *Osman* reasoning, the effect was immediate; the removal of a long-established professional immunity demonstrated the power of the Strasbourg decision to interrogate the justification for long held positions.

The immunity of witnesses giving evidence as to facts remains, but recent authorities demonstrate that the rule of law requires that it should be narrowly construed. In *Darker v Chief Constable of West Midlands Police*,[30] the House of Lords held that police officers against whom allegations of conspiracy and misfeasance in public office had been made, were not entitled to absolute immunity except in relation to allegations relating to statements they would be giving at trial. It was alleged that police officers had fabricated statements in collaboration with an informer and the trial was stayed for abuse of process. Counsel argued that absolute immunity covering the whole range of police investigative functions was too rigid and over inclusive. Furthermore, such an immunity would be a disproportionate restriction on a victim's right of access to a court under Article 6. This immunity is not the same as the *Osman*-type immunity which went to the substance of tort law principles of negligence. Lord Cooke alone referred to the ECHR and held that the approach in *Darker* which would exclude conduct relating to the investigatory function from the immunity was supported by *Osman*, the effect of which was to reject blanket immunities for the police. It should be noted, though, that the ruling in *Darker* pre-dated the ECtHR's judgment in *Z v UK* and the rejection of the Article 6 element of *Osman v UK*.

Other members of their Lordships did not cast their judgments in terms of the ECHR, but they spoke of the importance of the rule of law. Lord Hope observed that:

> The purpose of the immunity is to protect witnesses against claims made against them for something said or done in the course of giving or preparing to give evidence. It is not to be used to shield the police from action for things done while they are acting as law enforcers or investigators. The rule of law requires that the police must act within the law

---

[29] See discussion in Chapter 6.
[30] [2001] 1 AC 435. For recent discussion and application, see *Daniels v Chief Constable of South Wales* [2015] EWCA Civ 680.

when they are enforcing the law or are investigating allegations of criminal conduct. It also requires that those who complain that the police have acted outside the law in the performance of those functions, as in cases alleging unlawful arrest or trespass, should have access to a court for a remedy.

The most significant decisions regarding public authority liability in the light of the right of access to a court during the immediate post-*Osman* phase were *Barrett v Enfield London Borough Council*[31] and *Phelps v London Borough of Hillingdon*,[32] each decided before the HRA came into force, but clearly influenced by *Osman*.

In *Barrett*, the House of Lords distinguished *X (Minors) v Bedfordshire County Council*[33] on the narrow basis that the relevant policy considerations were different when a child has actually been taken into the care of the local authority and therefore the action for damages for personal injury should proceed to trial. Lord Browne-Wilkinson observed that if the strike out decision was upheld the claimant would petition Strasbourg. The ECtHR would then apply *Osman* (somewhat prophetically His Lordship observed that, assuming the European Court still believes *Osman* to be correct), and hold that the plaintiff had been deprived of his right to have the balance struck between hardship suffered by him and damage to the public purse if an order is made against the defendant. Thus, the House of Lords held that Mr Barrett's claim should go to full trial.

In *Phelps*,[34] three consolidated appeals were taken to the House of Lords in order to determine whether a local education authority could be directly or vicariously liable for a failure to provide appropriate educational services. *Phelps* was the only case in which there had been a trial and the House of Lords reversed the Court of Appeal's decision and upheld the first instance judge's award of damages. It was held in *Jarvis v Hampshire County Council*[35] and *G v Bromley London Borough Council*[36] that both matters should proceed to trial.

In *Phelps*, Lord Slynn and Lord Clyde gave separate speeches with which the five other members of a specially constituted House agreed. In relation to *Phelps*, Lord Slynn began by approving Auld LJ's 'valuable' analysis in *G*, and his observations that 'the law is on the move and much remains uncertain' and he stressed the importance of considering actual rather than assumed facts. Applying *Barrett*, he held that there was no ground for holding that Pamela Phelps' claim was not justiciable and that ordinary *Caparo* principles should be applied to determine whether there is a duty of care. Where an educational psychologist is requested to advise in relation to a particular child and it is clear that parents and teachers will follow that advice, then prima facie a duty of care will arise. A casual remark and an isolated act would not create sufficient nexus. Lord Slynn implicitly rejected the approach of Stuart-Smith LJ regarding assumption of responsibility and in a

---

[31] *Barrett* (n 20).
[32] *Phelps* (n 21).
[33] [1995] 2 AC 633.
[34] *Phelps* (n 21).
[35] [2000] 3 WLR 776, [2001] 2 AC 619.
[36] [2000] 3 WLR 776, [2001] 2 AC 619.

view reminiscent of Lord Griffiths in *Smith v Eric S Bush*[37] he observed that the phrase simply means that 'the law recognises a duty of care. It is not so much that the responsibility is assumed as that it is recognised or imposed by the law'.[38] In Lord Slynn's view, damage of the nature of loss of employment or wages through a failure to diagnose dyslexia can constitute damage recognised by the common law, even if difficult questions of causation and quantum have to be addressed.

In *G*, Lord Slynn approved the views of Auld LJ in the Court of Appeal that it would be wrong to strike out the claim because Stuart-Smith LJ's views (the injury was purely economic and the claim should be rejected for the same reasons that the House had denied a duty of care in *X (Minors)* must now be read in the light of *Barrett* and the claim in *Jarvis* should, by analogy with the reasoning in *Phelps*, proceed to trial.

Lord Clyde alone considered *Osman* explicitly, highlighting the fact that broader considerations alone of policy may not be determinative of the duty issue: regard is had, *inter alia*, to the gravity of the negligence and the seriousness of the harm. In the instant appeals there were not sufficient grounds to exclude liability on public policy grounds alone and he took the same view as Lord Slynn that there was quite clearly proximity in *Phelps*; the appeal in *Jarvis* must therefore be allowed.

In *W v Essex County Council*,[39] the House of Lords evinced a willingness to reconsider the circumstances in which a duty of care will arise in the context of psychiatric damage suffered by secondary victims and declined to strike out claims against a local authority following a foster placement that went disastrously wrong. A 15-year-old boy who had been cautioned for an indecent assault and was the subject of investigation on suspicion of rape was placed with a foster family. The family had made it clear that they would not accept a foster child known or suspected to be a sexual abuser. They were not informed of the boy's history and within one month of placement he had sexually abused all the claimants' children. The House of Lords held that the local authority arguably owed the parents a duty of care. The leading speech was given by Lord Slynn who omitted any explicit reference to *Osman* but the thrust of his speech is animated by the spirit of *Osman* when he described the caution that should attend any decision to strike out and quoted Lord Brown-Wilkinson in *Barrett*; 'the development of the law should be on the basis of actual facts found at trial "not on hypothetical facts assumed (possibly wrongly) to be true"'.[40]

The trend towards more intensive interrogation of the policy reasons that arguably justify immunities has continued and in *Jones v Kaney*[41] the Supreme Court

---

[37] [1990] AC 473.

[38] *Phelps* (n 21) 791.

[39] [2000] 2 All ER 237.

[40] Craig and Fairgrieve described how *Osman*, like Banquo's ghost, hovered over the decision in *W v Essex County Council*: D Fairgrieve and P Craig, 'Barrett, Negligence and Discretionary Powers' [1999] *Public Law* 626.

[41] *Jones* (n 28).

abolished the immunity of expert witnesses who are instructed by parties to litigation. On the other hand the immunity of witnesses giving evidence as to facts
within their knowledge remains.[42] In *Smith v Ministry of Defence*,[43] the Supreme
Court held that the doctrine of combat immunity should be construed narrowly
and only applied to action taken in the course of actual or imminent armed conflict. With echoes of the post-*Osman* reluctance to strike out claims on the basis
of assumed facts, Lord Hope for the majority recited the authorities that have
denied a duty of care in negligence on the grounds of public policy including
Stovin v Wise,[44] *Hill*,[45] *Brooks v Metropolitan Police Commissioner*,[46] *Eguzouli-Daf
v Commissioner of Metropolitan Police*[47] and *Mulcahy v Ministry of Defence*[48] and
stated that

> the question whether a duty should be held to exist depends on the circumstances—
> on who the potential claimants are and when, where and how they are affected by the
> defendant's acts. The circumstances in which active operations are undertaken by our
> armed services today vary greatly from theatre to theatre and from operation to opera-
> tion. They cannot all be grouped under a single umbrella as if they were all open to the
> same risk, which must of course be avoided, of judicialising warfare. For these reasons,
> I think that the question whether the claims in this case fall within the exclusion recog-
> nised in *Mulcahy* or any extension of it cannot properly be determined without hearing
> evidence.[49]

All of the decisions described above were influenced by *Osman* and were not the
product of interpretation of the HRA. What is striking is that our most senior
courts applied the *Osman* ruling by the ECtHR even though the HRA was not
in force and in the absence of any argument regarding the application of the old
common law presumptions regarding the applicability of international law. In
Lawrence v Pembrokeshire County Council,[50] a case based upon post-HRA facts, the
claimants argued that the Court should recognise a duty of care on a local authority owed to parents regarding the exercise of child protection responsibilities by
social workers. This was an attempt to persuade the Court of Appeal to reject the
clear authority of the House of Lords in *JD v East Berkshire Community Health
NHS Trust*,[51] denying a duty of care to parents, the distinguishing feature being

---

[42] *L (A Child) v Reading Borough Council* [2001] 1 WLR 1575; *Darker* (n 30).
[43] [2013] UKSC 41, [2013] 3 WLR 69. Lord Hope cited Elias J in *Bici v Ministry of Defence* [2004]
EWHC 786 who described combat immunity as 'an exception to the principle that was established in
Entick v Carrington (1765) 19 St Tr 1029 that the executive cannot simply rely on the interests of the
state as a justification for the commission of wrongs. In his opinion the scope of the immunity should
be construed narrowly. That approach seems to me to be amply justified by the authorities', Smith, *ibid*
at [90].
[44] [1996] AC 923.
[45] *Hill* (n 27).
[46] [2005] 1 WLR 1495.
[47] [1995] QB 335.
[48] [1996] QB 732.
[49] *Smith* (n 43) [98].
[50] [2007] 1 WLR 2991.
[51] [2005] 2 AC 373.

that the claim in *JD* was based upon pre-HRA facts. Counsel argued that by virtue of sections 6, 2 and 11 HRA, Parliament clearly contemplated a parallel remedy at common law to reflect ECHR provision. Auld LJ giving judgment for the Court repeated the assertion of Richards LJ during the hearing that neither Strasbourg jurisprudence nor responsiveness of the common law to the needs of the time requires the Court to secure harmonisation of the two systems.

Privacy

In *Wainwright v Home Office*,[52] the House of Lords held that there was no common law tort of invasion of privacy where a mother and son had been searched in a manner that constituted a violation of the prison's internal rules and was not protected by statutory authority. Mrs Wainwright and her son had been strip searched as part of the prison's campaign to reduce the amount of drugs being smuggled into the prison. Mrs Wainwright's son who had physical and learning difficulties suffered a battery and was so distressed that he suffered post-traumatic stress disorder. Mrs Wainwright suffered emotional distress but no recognised psychiatric illness. No action could be brought directly against the Home Office under section 7 HRA as the facts occurred before 2 October 2000. Counsel for the claimants argued that in order to enable the UK to conform to its international obligations under the ECHR, the House should declare that there is a tort of invasion of privacy under which damages for emotional distress are recoverable. Both the Court of Appeal and the House of Lords held that the claimants had no cause of action prior to the coming into force of the HRA. There does not appear to have been any argument in relation to the obligation of the court as a public authority under section 6 HRA.

In the Court of Appeal, Lord Woolf rejected the argument that the ECHR should be relied upon to change English substantive law and also suggested that where this is in issue, 'it is by no means clear that the ECtHR will provide a remedy when our courts do not do so'. With regard to the search itself, the Court of Appeal declared the HRA irrelevant as it was not in force at the time, but held that the first instance judge was wrong to take the view that the search was disproportionate. Buxton LJ described the treatment of Mrs Wainwright as deplorable and pointed out that had the facts occurred at different times there might have been a claim under the Protection from Harassment Act 1997 or the HRA.[53] He did allude to the question of whether the recognition of the courts as 'public authorities' could be used to create private law rights, but declined to consider the matter further in the absence of much fuller argument.

Buxton LJ anticipated the ECtHR's judgment when he observed that the policy of searching was not in itself unreasonable but was a violation of Article 8 because

---

[52] [2003] UKHL 53, [2004] 2 AC 406.
[53] *Ibid* [62].

of the manner in which it was carried out. With regard to section 6 he said the following:

> Some have argued that, with the advent of the Human Rights Act, it is possible to use the recognition of the courts as 'public authorities' by s 6(3)(a) thereof to create private law rights broadly in the same verbal terms as the wording of the Articles of the ECHR. There are many difficulties about that contention: I readily adopt the observation of Sedley LJ in para 128 of *Douglas* that this also is not the place, at least without much fuller argument, in which to resolve such a large question. But the present importance of that issue is that it is seen to be the terms of the Human Rights Act, and not, as the judge thought, the direct application of the terms of the ECHR, that render it even arguable that the ECHR creates new torts in private law.[54]

The Court of Appeal was unanimous that the HRA did not apply, since the facts took place before 2 October 2000 and, applying *R v Lambert*[55] and *R v Kansal*,[56] took the view that the existence of section 22 HRA indicated that when Parliament wanted the Act to apply retrospectively it said so. However, it is highly arguable that *Lambert* and *Kansal* did not decide the point: in both cases the relevant 'acts' had occurred prior to 2 October 2000. In *Wainwright*, the argument would have been that the Court was obliged to 'act' (all the litigation postdated the Act) in its determination of substantive law after the HRA had come into force. While it might be objectionable to introduce a new tort, the recrafting/development of recognised nominate torts would not ordinarily be regarded as offending against the general principle of non-retroactivity. On the other hand, in what sense could English courts be acting incompatibly with Article 8 ECHR? It may be argued that in denying a remedy to Mrs Wainwright, English courts are not acting incompatibly with the Convention rights that are given effect by the HRA. The prison officers clearly acted in a manner that is incompatible with Article 8, but the courts arguably, do not act in a manner that is incompatible with Article 8. Any act or omission of the court that is incompatible with the ECHR, is incompatible with the Article 13 right to an effective remedy, which was not included in Schedule 1 to the HRA. As we have previously observed, Article 13 was excluded because the HRA itself provides the remedial structure for any ECHR violation. Arguably, however, sending Mrs Wainwright away emptyhanded (her son was awarded damages for battery), having been on the receiving end of deplorable treatment, is to fail to fulfil the positive obligation inherent in the requirement to 'secure the right to respect for private life'.

As we have seen in Chapter 3, various dicta have emphasised the court's obligation under section 6 to ensure compatibility with the ECHR as encompassing only existing causes of action. It is arguable that extending the ambit of *Wilkinson v Downton*[57] seems no more of a jurisprudential leap from its present boundaries

[54] *Ibid* [92].
[55] [2001] UKHL 37, [2002] 2 AC 545.
[56] [2001] UKHL 62, [2001] 3 WLR 1562.
[57] [1897] 2 QB 57.

than developing the new tort of misuse of private information by removing the existence of a relationship of a confidence from the prerequisites for an action for breach of confidence.[58]

It has been suggested that English courts should now take a small incremental step and protect the 'physical' dimension of privacy, either by removing the need for physical damage from *Wilkinson v Downton* or by extending the new 'misuse of information' action to cover breach of privacy situations more generally.[59] Now that the judiciary is identifying the interests that privacy aims to protect in terms of human autonomy and dignity[60] and the free development of the individual,[61] the further development of privacy is inevitable, although it seems unlikely that extension of *Wilkinson* will be the vehicle through which this is achieved. In view of the fact that the courts seem inclined to confine claimants to their HRA claim against public authority defendants, the permeation of the common law by the ECHR will likely occur through horizontal situations in cases of physical privacy, in similar fashion to the breach of confidence/privacy claim.

The Court of Appeal has taken a significant step in the phone hacking litigation in *Gulati v MGN Ltd*,[62] to further the protection of autonomy. In the case of one claimant whose phone had been hacked over a period of seven years but without any publication of private information taking place, a substantial award of damages was made for loss of autonomy over information.[63] This is much closer to the sort of interest protected by a general privacy tort and an argument could be made by analogy that Mrs Wainwright and her son should be protected from unwanted conduct that is unlawful and which violates their autonomy over their bodies without the need to prove that they have suffered physical harm. Furthermore, in the context of patient advice and decision making, the Supreme Court has rejected the medical paternalism inherent in *Sidaway v Board of Governors of Bethlem Royal Hospital*,[64] and has effectively introduced a reasonable patient standard for the disclosure of information.[65] On balance, in view of the recent developments under the umbrella of the emergent privacy tort,[66] it seems unlikely that *Wilkinson* will have a significant role to play in future.

Lord Hoffmann gave the leading speech for a unanimous House of Lords, which rejected the claimants' appeals, declaring that there is no tort of invasion of privacy and there is no remedy for the infliction of distress which falls short

---

[58] *Campell v MGN Ltd* [2004] UKHL 22, [2004] 2 AC 457.

[59] N Moreham, 'Privacy in the Common Law: A Doctrinal and Theoretical Analysis' (2005) 121 *Law Quarterly Review* 628.

[60] *Campbell* (n 58) [51] (Lord Hoffmann), quoted by Moreham, *ibid*, 635.

[61] *Campbell* (n 58) [12] (Lord Nicholls), quoted by Moreham, *ibid*, 634. See now *Gulati v MGN Ltd* [2015] EWCA Civ 1291, [2016] 2 WLR 1217, discussed in Chapter 8.

[62] *Gulati, ibid.*

[63] *Ibid.*

[64] [1985] AC 871.

[65] *Montgomery v Lanarkshire Health Board* [2015] UKSC 11, [2015] AC 1430, see Chapter 8, text accompanying n 103.

[66] See discussion of *Gulati* in Chapter 8 *Privacy—From Misuse of Private Information to Autonomy*.

of recognised psychiatric injury. According to Lord Hoffmann, while privacy is a value that can be seen to underlie common law rules, that is not the same as identifying privacy as a value in itself. He gave as an example of an underlying value, freedom of speech, which supported the decision in *Derbyshire County Council v Times Newspapers Ltd*[67] that a local authority could not sue in libel. Further, he concluded that there was nothing in the Strasbourg jurisprudence which 'suggests that the adoption of some high level principle of privacy is necessary to comply with Article 8 of the Convention'.[68] This is a curious observation. In common with bills of rights everywhere, domestically and internationally, the ECHR consists of statements of rights that must be secured by the machinery of the state. The precise scope of the rights is fleshed out over time as the supervisory bodies adjudicate complaints. The principles of law that emerge must be made real for citizens. The notion of 'private life', as interpreted by Strasbourg, embraces many facets of a person's private sphere and is much closer to a right such as the German right to free development of the personality than the informational autonomy issues that have dominated English litigation and jurisprudence.

Counsel also attempted to run a similar argument to the one Lord Browne-Wilkinson had accepted in *Barrett*: it was inevitable that Strasbourg would find a violation of Article 8. Lord Hoffmann was not convinced. However, he did not evaluate the prison officers' conduct for legitimacy and proportionality, tests which quite obviously failed before the ECtHR.

His Lordship took the view that the coming into force of the HRA

> [weakened] the argument for saying that a general tort of invasion of privacy is needed to fill gaps in existing remedies. Sections 6 and 7 of the Act are in themselves substantial gap fillers; if it is indeed the case that a person's rights under Article 8 have been infringed by a public authority, he will have a statutory remedy.[69]

On the question of whether the prison officers could be liable on the basis that their acts were calculated to cause distress on the basis of imputed intention as in *Wilkinson v Downton*,[70] Lord Hoffmann did not resile from his observation in *Hunter v Canary Wharf Ltd*, that 'the policy considerations which limit the heads of recoverable damage in negligence do not apply equally to torts of intention'.[71] However, he warned that if damages are to be available for mere distress, 'imputed intention will not do. The defendant must actually have acted in a way which he knew to be unjustifiable and intended to cause harm or at least acted without caring whether he caused harm or not'.[72] This was not the case here. On the facts as found by the first instance judge, the prison officers were guilty of sloppiness but no intention to humiliate. Lord Hoffmann did say that even if an intention to

---

[67] [1993] AC 34.
[68] *Wainwright* (n 52) [32].
[69] *Wainwright* (n 52) [34].
[70] *Wilkinson* (n 57).
[71] [1997] 2 All ER 426, [1997] AC 655, 707.
[72] *Wainwright* (n 52) [45].

cause distress could be shown, he reserved his opinion as to whether compensation could be recoverable, given that 'in institutions and workplaces all over the country, people constantly do and say things with the intention of causing distress and humiliation to others'.

At Strasbourg, the ECtHR found violations of both Articles 8 and 13.[73] The fact of the search did not violate Article 8, but the manner in which it was carried out was not proportionate to the legitimate aim of fighting the drugs problem in prison and thereby seeking to prevent crime and disorder within Article 8(2). The Court stressed the importance of complying with safeguards rigorously in order to protect the dignity of those being searched. As for Article 13, the Court referred to the fact that the House of Lords found no ground of civil liability, 'in particular as there was no general tort of invasion of privacy' and held that 'in these circumstances' there was no means of securing redress under Article 13.[74] Interestingly, the Court paid no explicit attention to the fact that arguably there would have been a remedy under section 7 HRA, if the facts had occurred post-2 October 2000.

Misfeasance in Public Office

In *Watkins v Secretary of State for the Home Department*,[75] the House of Lords was required to reconsider the principles of the tort of misfeasance in public office, namely whether special damage is required in order to found a claim. Mr Watkins' correspondence with his legal advisers had been opened in breach of the Prison Rules on three separate occasions, two of which occurred before 2 October 2000, the day on which the HRA came fully into force, one after. It was uncontested that the prison officers had deliberately and in bad faith broken the prison rules by opening and reading Mr Watkins' correspondence. The Home Office appealed against the Court of Appeal's decision that wilful breach of the claimant's constitutional right to receive unopened correspondence from his legal advisers amounted to misfeasance in public office that was actionable without proof of special damage. The first instance judge found that although the prison officers acted in bad faith, the tort was not actionable *per se* and dismissed the claims. The Court of Appeal, applying *Ashby v White* (which concerned the wrongful denial of the claimant's right to vote by a returning officer),[76] held that where the defendant has infringed a constitutional right there is no need to prove material damage.

Counsel for Mr Watkins did not attempt to argue that either the ECHR or section 6 HRA should inform the development of the common law. It was argued

---

[73] *Wainwright v United Kingdom* (2007) 44 EHRR 809.
[74] *Ibid* [55].
[75] [2006] 2 AC 395.
[76] (1703) 92 ER 710.

that the right of access to correspondence with legal advisers is a basic right protected by the common law and can be called a constitutional right.

The House of Lords allowed the Home Secretary's appeal. It was held that proof of material damage had been an essential ingredient of the tort for over 300 years and that to treat the character of the right invaded as determinative of what material damage was needed would be too imprecise and controversial. Moreover, it was to be inferred that Parliament intended infringement of the rights protected by the HRA to be remedied by the Act rather than by the creation of parallel remedies. Only Lord Rodger discussed in detail the ECHR dimension, observing how in cases against the United Kingdom the scope of the prisoner's right to correspond with his lawyers was gradually clarified by the ECtHR in *Silver v UK*[77] and *Campbell v UK*.[78] While the Prison Rules changed, it took time, however, for 'the message', as his Lordship put it, to filter through to front-line officers. This would be the most charitable view of the defendants in *Watkins* who treated the Prison Rules with flagrant disregard.

Their Lordships' opinions ranged widely. Lord Rodger emphasised the origin of the tort in the action on the case which always required proof of material damage as in such actions (which of course includes negligence), damage is 'the gist of the action'. He cited *Three Rivers District Council v Governor and Company of the Bank of England (No 3)*,[79] where Lord Hobhouse stated that as an action on the case, in the absence of material damage, misfeasance in public office is not actionable by any member of the public.

Stevens has argued that the concept of a constitutional right is too vague to ground the action for misfeasance in public office and if the claimant genuinely has a right against the defendant that right should found the claim. If there is no particular right, the requirement of special damage makes the necessary connection between the defendant's conduct and the claimant.[80] There is much to be said for Chamberlain's view that the relevant 'right' is the right not to be harmed by the deliberate and unlawful action of a public officer.[81]

Lord Walker acknowledged that the respondent was entitled to feel real indignation at the deliberate affront that he had suffered. He was sceptical that the avenues of redress provided by public law gave adequate protection and was troubled by the case. He included the possibility of a claim under the HRA as a reason not to extend misfeasance in public office to cases where no monetary loss has been suffered. Legal history, he said, should not be a bar to recovery, given that the libel action developed from the action on the case and awards of over £100k have been

---

[77] (1983) 5 EHRR 347.
[78] (1992) 15 EHRR 137.
[79] [2003] 2 AC 1, 231.
[80] Stevens (n 4) 90.
[81] E Chamberlain, 'Misfeasance in a Public Office: A Justifiable Anomaly to the Rights-Based Approach', unpublished conference paper, but see critique: J Murphy, 'Misfeasance in Public Office: A Tort Law Misfit' (2012) 1 *Oxford Journal of Legal Studies* 51–75.

made for a single libel without proof of any monetary loss whatsoever. However, he said that 'deliberate abuse of public office directed at an individual citizen calls for an effective sanction enforceable as of right by that citizen'.[82]

Lord Carswell was highly critical of the continuing influence of the old distinction between trespass and case and suggested that,

> It might not unreasonably be said that any civil wrong should carry damages and that those who deliberately flout the law and deprive others of their rights by abusing their position should be liable to the victims of such acts. The common law is capable of accommodating changes necessary to allow it to adapt to modern needs, as your Lordships recognised in the recent torture case *A v Secretary of State for the Home Department (No 2)*… . it might therefore [be] theoretically possible to abolish the distinction and hold that all torts are actionable without proof of material damage.[83]

This of course though begs the question: what is the 'tort'?

All their Lordships expressed some discomfiture that public servants who had clearly not acted for the 'public good' could not be held accountable through tort. Lord Bingham acknowledged that there is an 'obvious public interest in bringing public servants guilty of outrageous conduct to book. Those who act in such a way should not be free to do so with impunity'.[84] However, there were a number of reasons why the common law should not be adapted to accommodate the claim including the fact that it was 'undesirable to introduce by judicial decision, without consultation, a solution which the consultation and research conducted by the Law Commission may show to be an unsatisfactory part of what is in truth a small part of a wider problem'.[85] Furthermore, in a widely cited observation he stated that it could reasonably be inferred with the advent of the HRA, that Parliament intended human rights protected by the Act to be remedied under it and not by parallel remedies.[86]

The Law Commission has expressed serious doubts about the utility of the action and misgivings that public bodies would be concerned at being accused of malice or knowingly acting outside their powers.[87] Consultees, however, felt that the action fulfilled two useful functions. First, it can act as a marker for 'particularly opprobrious' conduct by public officials. It is used in cases of serious wrongdoing and exemplary damages are available.[88] In *Kuddus v Chief Constable of Leicestershire*, Lord Hutton noted that the action 'serves to uphold and vindicate the rule of law'.[89] Second, the action provides the opportunity to hold officers personally responsible. The action under the HRA only lies against the public authority, not against individual officials. The Law Commission was not convinced by

---

82 *Watkins* (n 75) [75].
83 *Watkins* (n 75) [80].
84 *Watkins* (n 75) [8].
85 *Watkins* (n 75) [26].
86 *Watkins* (n 75) [26] and to similar effect see also Lord Rodger [64] and Lord Walker [173].
87 Law Commission (n 1) 4.89.
88 Law Commission (n 3) 3.66.
89 [2001] UKHL 29, [2002] 2 AC 122 [79].

either argument, explaining that the functions of marking and the attribution of responsibility for conduct that is particularly reprehensible can be fulfilled through prosecution of the criminal offence of misfeasance in public office.[90]

False Imprisonment

The function of the trespass torts is to 'protect and vindicate the basic rights of the citizen against deliberate, even well-meaning invasion, whether or not any damage is caused'.[91] One of the most important torts to protect our fundamental rights is false imprisonment. It has always been actionable *per se*, that is the unlawful deprivation of liberty constitutes the tort without the need to prove loss. The claimant can recover damages simply for 'loss of liberty'.[92] However, somewhat presciently, Weir wrote of how the trespass torts have been infiltrated by 'negligence type thinking'.[93]

In the recent decision of *R (Lumba) v Secretary of State for the Home Department*,[94] a majority of the Supreme Court departed from this orthodoxy and held that although imprisonment was unlawful, compensatory damages were not recoverable because the claimants had suffered no loss. The crux of the matter was that the claimants had been imprisoned unlawfully because they had been imprisoned pursuant to an unpublished policy operated by the Home Office. In fact, the claimants would have been detained in any event had the defendant's statutory powers been exercised lawfully. The Supreme Court held that the detention was unlawful and the Home Secretary was liable for false imprisonment, but only nominal damages should be awarded as the claimants would have been imprisoned anyway. The Court effectively applied a causation test to determine whether the claimant had suffered any material loss. As Vauhas observed, 'a focus on material loss and the defendant's responsibility for that loss undermines the traditional vindicatory and protective nature of false imprisonment'.

It has been suggested that there are two possible explanations for *Lumba*.[95] First, the wrongdoing was conceptualised as 'public law' illegality rather than an action for breach of a personal, individual right. Second, the conceptualisation of loss as only material in nature. Admittedly unstated, there is an alternative explanation for *Lumba*. Not only has 'negligence' type thinking become pervasive, the approach of the ECtHR to awards of 'just satisfaction' may have influenced the

---

[90] Law Commission (n 3) 71.

[91] T Weir, *Tort Law* (Oxford, Oxford University Press, 2002) 123.

[92] *R v Governor of Brockhill Prison, ex p Evans (No 2)* [1999] QB 1043, 1060.

[93] T Weir, *An Introduction to Tort Law*, 2nd edn (Oxford, Oxford University Press, 2006) 134 discussed by J Varuhas, *Damages and Human Rights* (Oxford, Hart Publishing, 2016) 66–67.

[94] [2011] UKSC 12, [2012] 1 AC 245.

[95] Varuhas (n 93) 66.

Court. It is not uncommon for the ECtHR to hold that the finding of a violation of the applicant's right is in and of itself sufficient vindication and any award may be limited to costs and expenses.[96] This is particularly true in the case of breaches of procedural obligations in Article 6.

However, the authority of *Lumba* with regard to the nature of damages to be awarded is in some doubt. Baroness Hale, Lord Walker and Lord Hope all considered that there had been a serious abuse of power and nominal damages would not be sufficient to compensate the claimants. Lord Brown (with whom Lord Rodger agreed) found that the claimants had been lawfully detained, but held that substantial damages should be awarded for false imprisonment as a matter of course. This means that a majority of 5:4 in the Court agreed with the orthodox approach to the award of damages for false imprisonment.[97]

Nuisance

It has been suggested that apart from defamation and privacy, private nuisance is the tort that has felt the most influence of the HRA.[98] There are a number of ways in which the HRA impacts on the holder of a property interest. Where the claimant's enjoyment of his interest in land is adversely affected by the defendant's activity to the extent that would ground an action in private nuisance and the defendant is a public authority, the claimant now has two possible causes of action: an action against the public authority in private nuisance and an action against the public authority under section 7 HRA for acting incompatibly with the Article 8 right to respect for private life and the home, as well as the Article 1 Protocol 1 right to property. In a nuisance claim itself, whatever the status of the defendant, public or private, a claimant can argue that the court in its role as a public authority should not act in a manner that is incompatible with ECHR rights. Unlike privacy, which at the inception of the HRA was on the cusp of formal recognition as an independent tort, as an extant tort to the extent that the private rights recognised in English law engage ECHR rights, the common law rules in nuisance need to be compatible with the ECHR. This does not mean that the tort of nuisance must be shaped to accommodate the ECHR where there are gaps in the protection of ECHR rights. But, where legal rules exist they must not be incompatible with the ECHR.[99] Thus, the HRA has the capacity to impact at

---

[96] See generally D Harris, M O'Boyle, E Bates and C Buckley, *Harris, O'Boyle and Warbrick, Law of the European Convention on Human Rights*, 2nd edn (Oxford, Oxford University Press, 2009) 857.

[97] See discussion by A Ruck Keene and C Dobson, 'At What Price Liberty? The Supreme Court Decision in *Lumba* and Compensation for False Imprisonment' [2012] *Public Law* 628–38.

[98] D Nolan, 'Nuisance' in D Hoffmann (ed), *The Impact of the UK HRA on Private Law* (Cambridge, Cambridge University Press, 2011).

[99] See discussion in Chapter 3, text accompanying n 147 et seq.

both vertical and horizontal levels. Whichever route, it is necessary to identify the ECHR rights which are relevant to such claims.

Nuisance has traditionally been understood as concerning the rights and obligations of neighbouring landowners in relation to the use and enjoyment of their properties, with the function of the law to strike a fair balance between them.[100] In *Cambridge Water Co v Eastern Counties Leather Plc*,[101] Lord Goff spoke of the tort as reflecting the principle of give and take between neighbours of land. This is a realm in which the courts have traditionally held that a defence of public benefit will not prevent the defendant's use of land constituting a nuisance.[102] In the well-known case of *Miller v Jackson*[103] in which Lord Denning waxed lyrical on the subject of English cricket played on summer afternoons and how dear it is to us, the majority in the Court of Appeal held that public benefit was not relevant to the issue of liability in negligence, but could be considered at the remedies stage. In *Kennaway v Thompson*,[104] the Court held that public benefit was relevant at neither stage. However, this is not to deny the role that the locality or neighbourhood test has played in effectively promoting considerations of social utility when striking the balance between landowners.[105]

Human rights law is quite different and the constant refrain that runs through ECHR jurisprudence is the need to strike a fair balance between individual and community interests. Thus, in *Soering v United Kingdom*, the Court stated that 'inherent in the whole of the Convention is a search for a fair balance between the demands of the general interest of the community and the requirements of the protection of the individual's fundamental rights'.[106]

It is in the context of remedies that the ECHR has impacted most profoundly on the common law principles of nuisance. Under the influence of the ECHR English courts have applied public interest considerations in nuisance in order to mirror the remedy that would be available in an action against a public authority under section 7 HRA. The following discussion will draw out these themes. In order to examine the interplay of the ECHR and the common law, it is necessary to identify the scope of the relevant ECHR rights, namely the Article 8 right to respect for private life and the home, and Article 1 of Protocol 1 which protects property rights.

---

[100] For a discussion of how value-laden this exercise is, see J Conaghan and W Mansell in their critique of 'Nuisance: The Pale Green Tort' in *The Wrongs of Tort* (London, Pluto Press, 1993). They quote Lord Reid who observed that only 'those with a taste for fairy tales' would agree that judges merely discover law: Lord Reid, 'The Judge as Law-Maker' (1972) 12 *Journal of the Society of Public Teachers of Law* 22.

[101] [1994] 2 AC 264.

[102] *Bamford v Turnley* (1862) 3 B & S; 122 ER 27.

[103] [1977] QB 966.

[104] [1981] QB 88.

[105] See generally M Wilde, 'Nuisance Law and Damages in Lieu of an Injunction' in S Pitel, JW Neyers and E Chamberlain, *Tort Law: Challenging Orthodoxy* (Oxford, Hart Publishing, 2013) 386, citing JPS McLaren, 'Nuisance Law and the Industrial Revolution—Some Lessons from Social History' (1983) 3 *Oxford Journal of Legal Studies* 155.

[106] (1989) 11 EHRR 439 [89].

Article 8(1) protects the right to respect for both private life and one's home. It is not an absolute right and can be subject to interference provided this is in accordance with the law and necessary in one of the interests set out in Article 8(2). 'Private life' includes a person's physical and psychological integrity and a number of claims have been brought under Article 8 in respect of conduct which is damaging to the environment and which impacts detrimentally upon the applicant. Such claims would find their analogies in English law in nuisance provided that the claimant has the requisite interest in property. In *Hunter v Canary Wharf Ltd*, the House of Lords, by a 4:1 majority (Lord Cooke of Thorndon dissenting), confirmed that private nuisance is a tort against land so that a claimant must have an interest in the land affected by the nuisance. Lord Hoffmann observed that:

> Once it is understood that nuisances 'productive of sensible personal discomfort' do not constitute a separate tort of causing discomfort to people but are merely part of a single tort causing injury to land, the rule that the plaintiff must have an interest in land falls into place as logical and, indeed, inevitable (see *St Helen's Smelting Co v Tipping* (1865) HL Cas 642 at 650, 11 ER 1483 at 1486).[107]

The test for identifying a person's home under Article 8 is a simple, factual test and it is not necessary for a person to have a property interest in the premises. As Lord Millett stated: a person's home 'is an important aspect of his dignity as a human being, and is protected as such and not as an item of property'.[108] The fact that no property right is needed means that a person can choose as his home a place where he has no right to be and conversely may choose not to make his home in the place where he does have a right to live.[109] Essentially, the right is one of quiet enjoyment; the sorts of activity that found an action in private nuisance such as flooding, the emission of smells and noise may amount to violations of the Article 8 right.

Article 1, Protocol 1, on the other hand, protects the right to peaceful enjoyment of possessions and contains three distinct rules. The first rule is set out in the first sentence, which is of a general nature and enunciates the principle of the peaceful enjoyment of property. The Article then identifies two possible forms of legitimate interference with a person's possessions by the state: deprivation of possessions in the public interest which it subjects to certain conditions, and control of the use of property in accordance with the general interest. In each case a balance must be struck between the rights of the individual and the public interest to determine whether the interference was justified. A reduction in the value of property will constitute a deprivation for the purposes of the Article.

Possessions have been defined broadly by Strasbourg to encompass a wide range of rights and interests which may be classified as assets.[110] On the important

---

107 *Hunter* (n 71).
108 *Harrow London Borough Council v Qazi* [2003] UKHL 43, [2004] AC 983 [89].
109 *Ibid* [97] (Lord Millett).
110 B Rainey, E Wicks and C Ovey, *Jacobs White and Ovey: The ECHR*, 6th edn (Oxford, Oxford University Press, 2014) 496.

question of whether an interest in land is necessary to come within Article 1 of Protocol 1, the Strasbourg authorities suggest that a proprietary interest is required, but stress that the concept of a 'possession' is autonomous and independent of domestic classification. In *Önerylidiz v Turkey*,[111] the defendant state argued that the unlawful occupation of land and building a home upon it could not found a claim under Article 1, Protocol 1. The applicants' home at a refuse tip was destroyed by an explosion of methane gas killing nine members of the same family and giving rise to a violation of Article 2. The Court held that the applicant's proprietary interest in his dwelling was of a sufficient nature and sufficiently recognised to constitute a substantive interest and hence a 'possession' within the meaning of the rule laid down in the first sentence of Article 1 of Protocol No 1, the provision of which is therefore applicable to this aspect of the complaint. The key elements were that the authorities had long known of the slum settlements and had not only tolerated them but had levied council tax on the applicant as well as providing the slum homes with public services.

In *Powell and Rayner v United Kingdom*,[112] the applicants lived under the flight paths of aircraft operating out of Heathrow Airport. Their claim was brought under Article 13 in conjunction with Article 8, on the basis that the United Kingdom had failed to provide an effective remedy in connection with the violation of their right to respect for private life and home. The applicants were prevented from bringing a claim in nuisance against the airport operator by the Noise Abatement Act 1960 which specifically exempted aircraft noise from the scope of common law protection, further limited by section 76(1) of the Civil Aviation Act 1982 (must be flying at a reasonable height above the ground).

The ECtHR held that aircraft noise could amount to a violation of Article 8 and that in both cases the applicants' private life and scope for enjoying the amenities of their home had been adversely affected. The fact that the airport is operated by a private company made no material difference. The Court held that whether the case was analysed as a failure to fulfil the positive obligation to secure the right (as would need to be the case where the perpetrator of the nuisance is a non-state actor) to respect for private life and the home under Article 8(1), or an interference by a public authority under Article 8(2), the same considerations apply. In both contexts, regard must be had to the fair balance that has to be struck between the competing interests of the individual and of the community as a whole; and in both contexts the State enjoys a certain margin of appreciation in determining the steps to be taken to ensure compliance with the Convention. The Court held that the operation of the airport was without doubt necessary for the economic well-being of the country and the airport authorities had taken steps to reduce the level of noise. Therefore, the interference was justified and there was no violation of Article 13 (the right to an effective remedy) when read in conjunction with Article 8.

---

[111] (2005) 41 EHRR 325.
[112] (1990) 12 EHRR 355.

Mr Rayner had also complained of a violation of Article 1 Protocol 1. In its decision on admissibility, the Commission held that:

> This provision is mainly concerned with the arbitrary confiscation of property and does
> not, in principle, guarantee a right to the peaceful enjoyment of possessions in a pleas-
> ant environment. It is true that aircraft noise nuisance of considerable importance both
> as to level and frequency may seriously affect the value of real property or even render
> it unsaleable and *thus amount to a partial taking of property*, necessitating payment of
> compensation.[113]

Thus, claims under Article 1, Protocol 1 relate to the economic value of property
and Mr Rayner's claim failed because he did not establish that his house had suffered any loss of value. Claims that relate to amenity and interferences with the
aesthetic or environmental qualities pertaining to property are addressed through
Article 8. In *S v France*,[114] the applicant was the owner of a French chateau, near
to which a nuclear power station was constructed. The power station caused per-
manent noise, industrial style lighting at night and microclimatic change with the
result that the property value was allegedly halved. The French Court had awarded
250,000 francs in compensation. The Commission drew upon the Court's judgment in *Sporrong and Lönnroth v Sweden*,[115] where it held that for the purposes
of Article 1 Protocol 1 it had to determine whether a fair balance had been struck
between the demands of the interests of the community and the requirements of
protection of the individual's fundamental rights. Here the compensation paid
could not be described as disproportionate in relation to the prejudice to the
applicant and thus there had been no violation of the ECHR.

The balance between individual and community was struck differently in *Lopez
Ostra v Spain*,[116] where the applicant complained of violations of Articles 3 (inhuman and degrading treatment) and 8, as a result of the operation of a waste treatment plant situated a few metres from her home. The plant had emitted smells,
noise and fumes over a number of years. The case engaged positive obligations
under Article 8 due to the fact that the plant was operated by a private company.
The Strasbourg Court held that:

> severe environmental pollution may affect individuals' well-being and prevent them from
> enjoying their homes in such a way as to affect their private and family life adversely,
> without, however, seriously endangering their health. Whether the question is analysed
> in terms of a positive duty on the State to take reasonable and appropriate measures to
> secure the applicant's rights under paragraph 1 of Article 8, as the applicant wishes in her
> case, or in terms of an 'interference by a public authority' to be justified in accordance
> with paragraph 2, the applicable principles are broadly similar. In both contexts regard
> must be had to the fair balance that has to be struck between the competing interests of
> the individual and the community as a whole, and in any case the State enjoys a certain

---

[113] *Ibid.*
[114] (1990) DR 250.
[115] (1982) 5 EHRR 35.
[116] (1995) 20 EHRR 277.

margin of appreciation. Furthermore, even in relation to the positive obligations flowing from the first paragraph of Article 8, in striking the required balance the aims mentioned in the second paragraph may be of a certain relevance.[117]

The Court held that, despite the margin of appreciation, the state had not struck a fair balance between the interests of the town's economic well-being and the applicant's rights under Article 8. The claim under Article 3 was rejected on the ground that although living conditions were very difficult, they did not meet the level of severity required by Article 3.

More recently, in *Khatun v United Kingdom*,[118] the group of residents who lost their appeal before the House of Lords in *Hunter*,[119] petitioned Strasbourg. The proceedings in *Hunter* were based, *inter alia*, on the nuisance caused by the excessive dust created by the construction of the Limehouse Link Road which was built to provide access from the Docklands area to Central London. The residents alleged that their Article 8 rights to respect for private and family life had been violated and that they had suffered discrimination, contrary to Article 14, on the grounds of poverty, 'in that the amount of compensation they may receive for dust nuisance depends on the difference in value between the property as affected by dust and the property as not so affected'. Since the properties concerned were at the lower end of the scale in terms of amenity and cost, the presence of the dust had little effect on the value of the property, although causing significant personal discomfort. They also complained that their Article 13 right to an effective remedy was violated because the decision of the House of Lords in *Hunter* meant that they had no remedy for the Article 8 violation.

The Commission observed that the notion of 'home' is an autonomous concept and is determined by factual circumstances, such as the existence of sufficient and continuous links, and no distinction is drawn between those applicants with a proprietary interest in land and those without. Even where occupation is illegal this will not prevent the occupation falling within Article 8(1).[120] Although the applicants did not claim that they had suffered ill-health as a result of the dust, their right to enjoy their homes and private and family life was held to have been impaired. Therefore, there had been an interference with rights in Article 8(1) which required to be justified under Article 8(2) by demonstrating that the interference corresponded to a pressing social need and was proportionate to the aim pursued. The Commission determined that the construction of the road pursued the legitimate aim of serving the economic well-being of the country. This interference was necessary in a democratic society as it was essential to the development of the area and fulfilled an important public interest, against which the applicants' position must be weighed. The Commission found that, although the dust was unpleasant, there were no health problems associated with it. On the

---

[117] *Ibid* [51].
[118] (1998) 26 EHRR 212.
[119] *Hunter* (n 71).
[120] *Buckley v United Kingdom* (1997) 23 EHRR 597.

facts, therefore, a fair balance between the interests of the community and the individuals had been struck.

Remedies in Nuisance—The Influence of the ECHR

At common law, in contrast with the ECHR, where as we have seen interference with the amenity of the home can be justified on economic grounds under Article 8(2), the orthodox position is that a defence of public benefit will not convert a defendant's conduct from being a nuisance into a lawful activity.[121] However, under the influence of the ECHR, there are signs that it is becoming increasingly relevant to the consideration of remedies. A claimant in nuisance will usually seek an injunction to prevent future activity amounting to a nuisance and damages for loss caused by the nuisance. The court's discretion to award damages in lieu of an injunction dates back to the Chancery Amendment Act 1858 (popularly known as Lord Cairns' Act).[122] In his well-known dictum in *Shelfer v City of London Lighting Company*,[123] AL Smith LJ deprecated the possibility for the perpetrator of a nuisance to buy off his neighbour's rights by paying damages and leaving his neighbour with the nuisance or, in that case, his lights dimmed. In *Shelfer*, a publican obtained an injunction to restrain the defendant company from causing excessive vibration even though the consequence was that many London residents were deprived of their electricity supply. AL Smith LJ set out four criteria that would indicate when damages might be appropriate: if the injury to the plaintiff's legal rights is small; it is capable of being estimated in money; it can adequately be compensated by a small monetary payment; and it would be oppressive to grant an injunction.

A tendency to too readily apply the *Shelfer* criteria, indicating when damages rather than an injunction may be an appropriate remedy, has been recently described, *obiter*, as 'slavish' and inappropriate. In *Lawrence v Fen Tigers Ltd*,[124] the Supreme Court held that in determining whether to award damages instead of an injunction and, in considering whether to do so, the Court was free to take account of the existence, and terms and conditions, of any planning permission for the land in question, as well as other matters of public interest such as the effect of any injunction on the viability of the defendant's business and on the public's enjoyment of the activities carried on by that business; that, by contrast,

---

[121] *Bamford* (n 102) *cf* Lord Denning in *Miller* (n 103) and see generally M Lunney and K Oliphant, *Tort Law Text and Materials*, 5th edn (Oxford, Oxford University Press, 2013) 659–63. But see the impact of social utility in striking the balance between landowners, text accompanying n 104.

[122] See generally M Wilde, 'Nuisance Law and Damages in Lieu of an Injunction: Challenging the Orthodoxy of the *Shelfer* Criteria' in Pitel, Neyers and Chamberlain (n 105) 356. The discretion is now enshrined in section 50 Senior Courts Act 1981.

[123] [1895] 1 CH 287.

[124] [2014] UKSC 13, [2014] AC 822.

the Court could also take account of the effect on persons other than the claimant who would remain badly affected by the nuisance if an injunction were not granted; but that in all cases it was for the Court to weigh up all competing factors in the exercise of its unfettered discretion. Lord Sumption stated:

> [*Shelfer*] was devised for a time in which England was much less crowded, when comparatively few people owned property, when conservation was only beginning to be a public issue, and when there was no general system of statutory development control. The whole jurisprudence in this area will need one day to be reviewed in this court. There is much to be said for the view that damages are ordinarily an adequate remedy for nuisance and that an injunction should not usually be granted in a case where it is likely that conflicting interests are engaged other than the parties' interests. In particular, it may well be that an injunction should as a matter of principle not be granted in a case where a use of land to which objection is taken requires and has received planning permission.[125]

Striking the balance between the individual and the community is at the core of two important decisions, each of which was influenced in its outcome by the HRA: *Marcic v Thames Water Utilities Ltd*[126] and *Dennis v Ministry of Defence*.[127] *Dennis* is of particular interest in view of the fact that the issue of liability was determined entirely by common law rules, there being no defence of statutory authority available to the defendant. It has been strongly asserted that judges have no legitimate role to play in determining issues of public policy, and that 'our rights should not be decided, or altered, according to a judge's personal assessment of the balance of a basket of policy concerns'.[128] Some judges may conclude that an activity is not a nuisance; others may conclude that it is, but then refuse injunctive relief. It is possible to discern in many cases the judge determining where the public interest lies, taking into account factors that are quite clearly external to the parties. The incorporation of the ECHR and its explicit reference to issues such as 'the economic well-being of the country' as a justification for interference with property rights under Article 8(2) does at least have the merit of transparency so far as such a goal is possible to achieve.

The question at the heart of *Dennis* is to what extent can the fact that an activity be claimed to be furthering the public interest be raised in order to defeat a claim in nuisance. The claimant was the owner of Walcott Hall, a large country estate adjoining the RAF base at Wittering in Lincolnshire. Wittering is used to train pilots to fly Harrier jets which have vertical takeoff and landing capacities and are extremely noisy. The claimant argued that the noise amounted to a nuisance at common law or, alternatively, that his right to respect for private life and the home under Article 8 ECHR and his right to property under Article 1, Protocol 1 had been breached.

---

[125] *Ibid* [161].
[126] [2003] UKHL 66, [2004] 2 AC 42.
[127] [2003] EWHC 793, [2003] Env LR 34.
[128] Stevens (n 4) 309.

Regarding the locality, counsel argued that flying Harriers had become a usual activity within the patterns of life of the community. Buckley J rejected this, finding that the neighbourhood was essentially rural in character. He accepted evidence that the physical requirements of landing and the prevailing winds meant that unacceptable levels of noise for the occupants of Walcott Hall were unavoidable. He found that the claim in nuisance was established; the claim was governed entirely by the common law, as there is no statutory defence.

While the public importance of the activity did not prevent liability, Buckley J held that it was relevant to the issue of remedies and he exercised his discretion under section 50 Senior Courts Act 1981 to award damages in lieu of an injunction. He recognised that if the public interest is weighed in the scale to determine whether liability exists, great injustice may ensue: the greater the public interest, the greater may be the interference and one person may pay for the benefit of all. Better, therefore, if public interest is considered at the remedy stage and since the court has a discretion, the nuisance may continue but the public, in one way or another, pays for its own benefit.[129] He did express some concern that there was no analogous authority but he held that apart from situations where it might be more appropriate for the legislator to intervene, the common law should develop in a way that is consistent with human rights and that one individual should not bear the brunt of the public interest through the subjugation of his private rights. Accordingly, he said that

> The principles or policy underlying these considerations are that public interest should be considered and that selected individuals should not bear the cost of the public benefit. I am in favour of giving effect to those principles. I believe it is necessary to do so if the common law in this area is to be consistent with the developing jurisprudence on human rights.[130]

Buckley J did not explain in terms of the HRA how the common law was shaped by the ECHR. Having made an award of damages with regard to the common law claim, Buckley J declined to make an award in respect of the Article 8 and Article 1, Protocol 1 claims, but said that he would have done so had the common law claim not been successful.

Buckley J also held that the independent claim of Mrs Dennis under the HRA was satisfied by the nuisance claim brought by her husband. This feature of the judgment is open to criticism as the interests protected by Article 8(1) are not coterminous with the property interest protected by the tort of nuisance. We know from the House of Lords' decision in *Hunter v Canary Wharf* that the tort of nuisance protects interests in land, not the right to respect or one's 'home'; the right under Article 8 extends to all occupiers and there is no need for a victim to have a property interest. Equally, according to ECHR jurisprudence, Mrs Dennis had an

---

[129] *Dennis* (n 127) [46].
[130] *Dennis* (n 127) [47].

independent claim against the Ministry of Defence for the failure to respect the right to her home under Article 8 ECHR. It has been suggested that the judge's approach only makes sense, 'if it is considered as the infusion of the common law of nuisance with principles derived from the rights to be protected under the Convention, thus permitting departure from the strictures of the approach in *Hunter*'.[131]

Subsequently, in *Dobson v Thames Water Utilities Ltd*,[132] the Court of Appeal held that Buckley J was wrong on this point, there being no ECHR authority on the effect of the award of damages in nuisance on a separate claim under the ECHR. *Dobson* also confirmed that it is clear from the majority speeches in *Hunter* that damages in nuisance are recovered for injury to property and not the sensibilities of occupiers, although 'assessment of the common law damages for non-pecuniary loss of amenity on the basis of enjoyment of the estate "which envisages enjoyment by a family as opposed to one individual" was consistent with [*Hunter*]'.[133]

In *Marcic*, the House of Lords considered the impact of the statutory scheme of regulation set out in the Water Industry Act 1991 on the tort of nuisance and the right to bring a claim under section 7 HRA for a breach of Article 8 and Article 1, Protocol 1. Mr Marcic had lived for many years in a house in Stanmore which had been subject to repeated flooding. He sought a mandatory order to compel Thames Water to improve its sewerage system, as well as damages. The duty he sought to enforce was the duty contained in section 94(1)(a) 'to provide, improve or extend' the system of public sewers. It was common ground that the flooding which was caused by the failure to increase capacity by constructing more sewers engaged ECHR rights: a direct and serious interference of this nature with a person's home is *prima facie* a violation of the right to respect for private and family life and his entitlement to peaceful enjoyment of possessions. However, the House of Lords rejected both the claim in nuisance and the claim under the HRA.

The claim in nuisance failed as it was considered to be inconsistent with the statutory scheme. The House held that the sewerage undertaker was subject to an elaborate scheme of regulation under the 1991 Act, which included an independent regulator with powers of enforcement whose decisions were subject to judicial review; the statutory scheme provided a procedure for making complaints to the regulator which the plaintiff had chosen not to pursue; that a balance had to be struck between the interests of a person subject to sewer flooding and the interests of those, including other customers of the sewerage undertaker, who would have to finance the cost of constructing more sewers; that such a balancing exercise was better undertaken by an industry regulator than a court; that the common law should not impose on a sewerage undertaker obligations which would be inconsistent with the statutory scheme since that would run counter to the intention of

---

[131] S Deakin, A Johnston and B Markesinis, *Tort Law*, 6th edn (Oxford, Oxford University Press, 2008) 535.
[132] [2007] EWHC 2021, [2008] 2 All ER 362.
[133] *Ibid* [44].

Parliament and that a cause of action in nuisance would be inconsistent with the statutory scheme.

With regard to the claim under the HRA, the House applied the dicta in *Hatton v UK*,[134] decided shortly before *Marcic*, Lord Nicholls recalling the Strasbourg Court's observations in *Hatton* regarding the need to give special weight to the domestic policy-maker and the fact that the Convention is fundamentally subsidiary to the protection of human rights at domestic level. National authorities have 'direct democratic legitimation' and are in principle better placed than an international court to evaluate local needs and conditions. In matters of general policy, on which opinions within a democratic society may reasonably differ widely, 'the role of the domestic policy maker should be given special weight'. A fair balance must be struck between the interests of the individual and of the community as a whole. The House of Lords concluded that the statutory scheme struck the appropriate balance. It is important to note that Mr Marcic had not sought to engage the remedial machinery set out in the Water Industry Act, despite having been invited to do so.

Crucially, there exists a clear line of Court of Appeal authority which establishes that a failure to construct new sewers is not a nuisance and any statutory obligation should be enforced by way of public law remedies; thus there is no private right. As Lord Nicholls observed, however the claim might be put, it came down to a simple assertion that Thames Water should build more sewers because that would be the only way of preventing the flooding. Thus, the House of Lords held that the Court of Appeal had been in error to extend the principles of *Goldman v Hargrave*[135] and *Leakey v National Trust*[136] to the instant case as they clearly concerned the rights and obligations between ordinary neighbouring landowners and as such were not appropriate to the obligations of statutory undertakers, the discharge of whose responsibilities was appropriately overseen by a regulator.

Marcic can be criticised. The House of Lords determined that the claim was not justiciable but things had obviously gone very wrong. It is possible for a 'scheme' to be Convention compliant, but nonetheless the manner of its application to individuals may constitute violation(s) of ECHR rights. The difficulty for Mr Marcic was that he had not exhausted his remedies, such as they were under the Water Industry Act. The first instance judge found that there were repeated failures to record flooding incidents, despite repeated complaints (only one out of 16 recorded). There is no provision in the Act for compensating past damage once the regulator has upheld a complaint. This would suggest that the scheme is not compliant with the ECHR as an award of pecuniary damage will be made by the ECtHR in appropriate cases.[137] However, as Mr Marcic had not utilised the

[134] (2003) 37 EHRR 611.
[135] [1967] 1 AC 645.
[136] [1980] QB 485.
[137] H Wilberg, 'Public Resource Allocation, Nuisance and the HRA 1998' (2004) *Law Quarterly Review* 120, 574–79.

procedures set out in the Act, it would not be possible to determine that the manner of its application to him was incompatible with his ECHR rights.[138] It is quite clear that the fact that Parliament has created a framework which is intended to strike a balance between the interests of the individual and the community does not mean that a challenge cannot be made regarding the application of the policy in individual cases. It is beyond the scope of this work to examine in detail the shift that has occurred in judicial review.[139] The important point is that where there is a human rights challenge,

> the court is deciding whether or not the application of a policy to a particular individual is incompatible with a person's ECHR rights, and it is only concerned with that aspect of the primary decision-maker's decision which engages Convention rights.[140]

A different type of claim was brought, again against Thames Water, in *Dobson v Thames Water Utilities Ltd.*[141] This was a group action brought by local residents who claimed that the defendant had caused nuisance through its negligence in running the plant which caused unpleasant odours and infestations of mosquitoes, as well as breaches under the HRA. At first instance, Ramsey J held that the *Marcic* principle did not preclude the claimants from bringing claims in nuisance alleging negligence based upon the principle deriving from *Allen v Gulf Oil Refining Limited*[142] where as a matter of fact and degree the exercise of adjudication on that cause of action does not involve conflicts with the statutory processes under the Water Industry Act. At the trial of the action it was held that the company was liable for nuisance caused by odour and damages were awarded to the property owners. In line with the Court of Appeal's views,[143] the damages awards in nuisance were held to constitute just satisfaction for the purposes of the HRA and it was also held that the awards reflected loss to the whole family. For those claimants without a property interest, no damages were necessary to provide just satisfaction under the HRA since the damages awarded to property owners reflected the loss of amenity of the whole family and a declaration of rights had been made and other remedies were available under sections 80 and 82 of the Environment Protection Act and section 94 of the Water Industry Act 1991.

In *Hatton v United Kingdom*,[144] a group of claimants lived near Heathrow airport. They claimed that the Government's policy on night flights at Heathrow violated their rights under Article 8. The ECtHR found no violation because the policy struck a balance that was within the state's margin of appreciation. The

---

[138] See generally *Huang v Secretary of State for the Home Department* [2007] UKHL 11, [2007] 2 WLR 581 discussed M Amos, *Human Rights Law* (Oxford, Hart Publishing, 2014) 91 *et seq.*

[139] See Amos, *ibid.*

[140] Amos, *ibid* 127.

[141] The trial of the action is reported at [2011] EWHC 3253, 140 Con LR 135, the Court of Appeal's decision on preliminary issues is reported at [2009] EWCA Civ 28, [2009] HRLR 19.

[142] [1981] AC 1001.

[143] See n 141.

[144] *Hatton* (n 134).

Court emphasised 'the fundamentally subsidiary nature' of the Convention. National authorities have 'direct democratic legitimation' and are in principle better placed than an international court to evaluate local needs and conditions. In matters of general policy, on which opinions within a democratic society may reasonably differ widely, 'the role of the domestic policy maker should be given special weight'.[145] A fair balance must be struck between the interests of the individual and of the community as a whole. It should be also noted that in contrast in cases like *Lopez Ostra*, the public body has failed to comply with domestic legal rules.

The Right to Respect for Private Life and Home of those without a Property Interest—does the Tort of Private Nuisance Fulfil the UK's obligations under the ECHR?

As we have seen, through the development of its positive obligations jurisprudence, the ECHR requires states to take action to ensure that rights are respected as between non-state actors, although with a margin of appreciation allowed to the state in determining the need for any interference with a right. Two distinct principles emerge from the Strasbourg jurisprudence which are problematic for English law. First, the ECHR does not require a claimant to have a proprietary interest in order to claim a violation of the right to respect for private and family life and the home. In *Hunter*, the House of Lords affirmed the longstanding requirement for a proprietary interest in land to found a claim in nuisance. Second, according to Strasbourg jurisprudence a claim can be made for loss of amenity[146] and for inconvenience and unpleasantness, which cannot be redressed in English law through negligence in the absence of physical injury.

In the first edition, we argued that the fact that a person cannot use nuisance law as a vehicle for protecting Article 8 rights means that the tort of private nuisance is incompatible with the ECHR. This is an overstatement; instead we have a *lacuna* in the law which means that only a property owner can effectively vindicate the amenity of his home where the defendant is a non-state actor. In *Hunter*, Lord Cooke dissenting, argued that the right to sue should be extended in the light of Article 8.

Lord Cooke's speech in *Hunter* demonstrated a desire to cast off the historical technicalities of the nuisance action, in order to render the law reflective of contemporary values, in particular the standards of international human rights law. He began by pointing out that while the majority opinions achieved a 'symmetry' in the law of nuisance, this did not necessarily strengthen the 'utility' or 'justice' of the common law. In what would be anathema to the corrective justice and rights-based theorists, he stated that 'the choice in the end is a policy one between two

---

[145] *Hatton* (n 134) [97].
[146] *Lopez Ostra* (n 116).

competing principles'.[147] He observed that legal analysis does not assist in identifying what the policy of the law should be and held in the light of *Lopez Ostra*
and comments by Harris, O'Boyle and Warbrick[148] that a test of 'residence' would
be an acceptable basis for standing in cases such as *Hunter*. He also surveyed academic opinion, the preponderance of which (then) rejected confining the tort to
those with proprietary interests and stated that:

> The reason why I prefer the alternative advocated with unwonted vigour of expression
> by the doyen [Fleming in *The Law of Torts*, 8th edn (1992)] of living tort writers is that it
> gives better effect to widespread conceptions concerning the home and family.[149]

The issue of standing to sue arose at first instance in *McKenna v British Aluminium
Ltd*.[150] The claimants complained that emissions, noise pollution, and invasion of
privacy from British Aluminium's neighbouring factory had caused damage, in
terms of mental distress and physical harm, to each of them so far as their occupation and/or enjoyment of their respective homes were concerned. The claims were
brought in nuisance and strict liability under *Rylands v Fletcher*.[151] The defendant
applied to strike out the claims brought by children who argued, relying on *dicta*
in *Douglas v Hello! Ltd*,[152] that the common law should be developed in a manner that is compatible with ECHR rights. Neuberger J was persuaded by Counsel's argument based upon the Court of Appeal's decision in *Douglas* that the case
should proceed on the basis of the need to render the common law Convention-
compliant, a point that was conceded by defendant counsel. Neuberger J cited
Keene LJ in *Douglas* who observed that the court's obligation under section 6(1)
HRA arguably included their 'activity in interpreting and developing the common
law' between non-state actors. He went on to say that:

> To my mind, that is a powerful argument, and it may very well turn out to be right. But
> assuming, which I should and do for today's purposes, that it is the duty of the court to
> extend the common law to enable the relevant claimants to have a claim in the present
> case (provided, of course, that the factual basis for their claim is made out) then how the
> court decides to achieve that is a matter of speculation. We are in the early days of the
> HRA 1998 and of its application to the common law.

However, Neuberger J accepted that to change the rule on standing would be
inconsistent with nuisance as a property tort. There is obviously a powerful case
for saying that the right to respect for private life and the home enshrined in
Article 8 have not been properly effected if a person with no interest in the home,
but who has lived in the home for some time and had his enjoyment of the home
interfered with, is at the mercy of the person who owns the home as the only

---

[147] *Hunter* (n 71) 456.
[148] Harris, O'Boyle and Warbrick, *Law of the European Convention on Human Rights* (London, Butterworths, 1995) 319.
[149] *Hunter* (n 71) 462.
[150] [2002] Env LR 30.
[151] [1866] LR 1 Ex 265, [1868] LR 3 HL 330.
[152] [2001] 2 WLR 992.

person who can bring the proceedings. There is no support in subsequent authority for such a radical change; nor is there sustained support for the argument that we made in the first edition regarding such an interpretation of section 6(3) HRA. Nolan must surely be correct to observe that horizontal effect under the HRA is simply not powerful enough to 'require such radical change to be made to a long-standing cause of action'.[153]

Concluding Remarks

The HRA now provides a remedy for those who are harmed by the acts of public authorities which are incompatible with the ECHR rights set out in Schedule 1 HRA. Thus, Mrs Wainwright and her son would now have a claim against the prison authorities for the violation of their Article 8 rights as a result of the distressing and humiliating searches that were carried out in breach of the Prison Rules. Mr and Mrs Jain whose nursing home business was ruined by the local authority's ex parte application to cancel the home's registration would have a claim against the local authority for a violation of their property rights under Article 1 of Protocol 1.[154] Having initiated proceedings against the UK Government under the ECHR, they subsequently recovered £750,000 in a settlement with the UK Government.

In general terms, the action under the HRA has not informed the development of the common law. There has been no leaching of principle from the statutory action to the common law, apart from the isolated case of *D v East Berkshire Community NHS Trust*. Thus, it remains the case that damages in negligence against a public authority can only be recovered for material damage; on the other hand the action under the HRA redresses heads of damage such as grief, distress and frustration. Ricochet damage suffered by third parties is redressed more extensively both in terms of standing and heads of damage under the HRA.

However, it is arguably in the field of omissions that the relative impermeability of the common law to the ECHR is at its starkest, as the following discussion in Chapter 6 will illustrate. It is important to separate the discussion of 'omissions' from other areas of public authority liability because the distinction between omission and commission underpins much of the reasoning in English law. It is also important because there is a burgeoning jurisprudence of positive obligations under the ECHR which is now accessible to English claimants under the HRA. As we shall see, English courts have been prepared not only to accommodate but to move beyond the positive obligations developed by Strasbourg.

---

[153] D Nolan, 'Nuisance' in D Hoffmann (ed), *The Impact of the UK Human Rights Act on Private Law* (Cambridge, Cambridge University Press, 2011) 188.
[154] *Jain v Trent Strategic Health Authority* [2009] UKHL 4, [2009] 1 AC 359.

6

Public Authority Liability
Part 2—Positive Obligations
and Omissions

Introduction

English tort lawyers are accustomed to considering 'omissions' (often referred to as non-feasance) in the context of negligence. The distinction between an omission and commission has become firmly embedded in the English common law and many tort claims brought against public authorities are premised upon failures to act. Such actions generally fail, unless the claimant can demonstrate an assumption of responsibility towards the defendant. In contrast, where European Convention on Human Rights (ECHR) rights are engaged, the same set of facts may give rise to a positive obligation to act. After initial wariness, there is a growing body of English case law where positive obligations under Article 2 ECHR have been recognised and in situations where the tort of negligence is for various reasons to no avail.

This chapter considers the positive obligations/omissions dimension to liability because the treatment of such obligations under the Human Rights Act 1998 (HRA)/ECHR has significant impact upon public authority liability; if the HRA is repealed, there could be a remedial gap if the structure of remedies is not configured appropriately. The fact that there is a remedy under section 7 HRA for failures to act under the various Articles of the ECHR means that the pressure to deliver effective remedies consequent upon the failures of public authorities has been taken off the common law. But, the incidence of positive obligations under the ECHR has grown considerably since the first edition of *Tort Law & Human Rights*; somehow those obligations must be met by English law and in the absence of any statutory remedy, it would fall to the common law to secure the Article 13 right to an effective remedy, as well as the remedial elements that have been recognised within the substantive Articles themselves.

The reluctance of English tort law to impose liability for omissions is a foundational principle[1] of English law. The traditional justifications are that imposing a

---

[1] *Smith v Littlewoods Organisation Ltd* [1987] AC 241 (Lord Goff). See D Nolan, 'Negligence and Human Rights Law: The Case for Separate Development' (2013) 76(2) *Modern Law Review* 286, 304;

positive duty to act for another's benefit would unduly restrict individual liberty by unfairly singling out one defendant from many others who might have assisted the claimant; and, secondly, the challenge of determining what the limits upon such altruism should be.[2] If I have a duty to rescue someone from drowning, why would I also not have a duty to give alms to the homeless living on the street? Such liability could be 'impossibly burdensome'.[3] Thus, in the absence of a special relationship, English law generally imposes no duty upon a person to come to another's rescue even where assistance could be provided with little or no effort on the part of the rescuer. This rule applies to both public and private parties alike, the most common exceptions being situations where one party has made an 'assumption of responsibility' to the other or has created a source of danger or occupies a special relationship or position of responsibility in relation to the third party, for example parent/child, employer/employee, teacher/pupil. Non-liability for an omission can also be seen as the corollary of rules about causation; the relevant (non) actor has not caused the damage suffered by the claimant.

Many claims in negligence that are brought against public authorities are based upon allegations of failures to act, many premised upon failures to discharge statutory or common law obligations. It seems almost too obvious to state that arguments from liberty and limitless altruism have no application in the case of public authorities, which are tasked with discharging a myriad of duties and responsibilities in the public interest. Contrary to the view expressed by Megarry J in *Malone v Metropolitan Police Commissioner*,[4] public authorities have no 'liberty' interest and exist only to further the aims for which they have been established; 'any action taken must be justified by positive law'.[5] Without drawing any distinction between public and private bodies, Megarry VC stated that, 'England it may be said, is not a country where everything is forbidden except what is expressly permitted: it is a country where everything is permitted except what is expressly forbidden'.

The distinction between misfeasance and non-feasance is hard-wired in English tort law, as its formal application to both public and private parties alike. It seems that the introduction of the HRA rather than being a factor that would support the extension of the duty of care into new situations has generally had quite the opposite effect. The attitude of English courts confronted with arguments to recognise new duties of care in negligence has hardened; it will now be very difficult for a claimant to bring claims in negligence against public authorities premised upon a failure to act, or in other words, what some commentators have described

---

R Bagshaw, 'Tort Design and Human Rights Thinking' in D Hoffmann (ed), *The Impact of the Human Rights Act on Private Law* (Cambridge, Cambridge University Press, 2011) 129; F Du Bois, 'Human Rights and the Tort Liability of Public Authorities' (2011) *Law Quarterly Review* 127, 589–609.

[2] *Stovin v Wise* [1996] AC 923 (Lord Hoffmann).
[3] T Cornford, *Towards a Public Law of Tort* (Aldershot, Ashgate Publishing Ltd, 2008) 139.
[4] [1979] Ch 344.
[5] *R v Somerset CC Ex p Fewings* [1995] 1 All ER 513, 524 (Laws J).

as a 'failure to confer a benefit'.[6] In the first edition, we noted that English courts rarely reasoned in terms of omissions analysis in public authority cases, preferring instead to rely on 'policy' arguments.[7] English courts have at least demonstrated greater conceptual clarity in recent decisions, but the consequence for the claimant has been that the development of new duty situations has been restricted and, unfortunately, some cases that actually engage acts of commission have been miscategorised as omissions. Clearly, the answers we get depend upon how we frame our questions.

The ECHR can broadly be described as enshrining the obligation of states to accord their citizens full enjoyment of their *civil and political* rights, as opposed to economic, social and cultural rights. Civil and political rights are essentially those rights which guarantee the liberty of the citizen against unlawful and arbitrary state action and the right to participate in a democratic polity. Civil and political rights are drafted in such a way that they impose immediate obligations on the state; there is no allowance or concession to reflect differential states of development or wealth. Thus, Article 1 ECHR states that the High Contracting Parties 'shall secure to everyone within the jurisdiction' the rights and freedoms set out.

Economic, social and cultural rights on the other hand relate to the right to those goods that broadly support human physical flourishing, the right to housing, food, work and so on. These rights were borne of the struggle between the working classes and the dominant elites, and their realisation became central to the programmes of the socialist governments of the twentieth century. The treaty obligations in relation to economic, social and cultural rights are cast in terms of requiring states to achieve 'progressively the full realisation of the rights recognised [in the International Covenant on Economic, Social and Cultural Rights] by all appropriate means'. The revised European Social Charter states that the parties 'accept as the aim of this policy, to be pursued by all appropriate means ...'. There is no clear and neat dividing line between economic rights and civil and political rights; for example, there is a right to education in the ECHR and many of the civil and political rights have an economic dimension, the right to legal assistance for example.

Implementing economic, social and cultural rights can be perceived as challenging for states because of their financial implications: if the rights to food, health and housing are to be made real, states must put in place programmes to ensure these goods are delivered. In contrast, civil and political rights are sometimes portrayed as the more readily realisable because in many instances they are negative in character; they require the state to refrain from interfering with the liberty of the citizen. Clearly, though, in economic terms there is no watertight division between the two. Civil and political rights cost money too. Take for example the Article 6

[6] D Nolan, 'The Liability of Public Authorities for Failing to Confer Benefits' (2011) *Law Quarterly Review* 127, 260–87.
[7] J Wright, *Tort Law & Human Rights* (Oxford, Hart Publishing, 2001) 139.

right to a fair trial which requires states to expend significant resources in the provision of courts, judges, interpreters and legal aid.

Notwithstanding the principally negative nature of rights under the Convention, in the sense that the state is required to abstain from treatment that would
violate the rights and freedoms, the Strasbourg organs have developed a body
of jurisprudence, the essence of which is that the state may be required to take
positive steps to secure the enjoyment of the right. These obligations, commonly
referred to as positive obligations, were once thought of as the exception rather
than the rule but there are 'now hardly any provisions ... under which positive
obligations have not been recognised'.[8] For the purposes of our discussion, there
are two key points to note in relation to the positive obligations jurisprudence.

First, by Article 1 ECHR the Contracting States agree to 'secure to everyone
within their jurisdiction the rights and freedoms defined in Section I of [the]
Convention'. Taken together with the text of later Articles dealing with particular
rights, Article 1 has been interpreted as imposing both negative and positive obligations.[9] A leading example is afforded by *Z v United Kingdom*[10] which concerned
the positive obligation on the state under Article 3 to protect children from inhuman and degrading treatment at the hands of their parents. The ECtHR held that
the obligation on High Contracting Parties under Article 1 of the Convention to
secure to everyone within their jurisdiction the rights and freedoms defined in
the Convention, taken together with Article 3, requires states to take measures
designed to ensure that individuals within their jurisdiction are not subjected to
torture or inhuman or degrading treatment, including such ill-treatment administered by private individuals. These measures should provide effective protection,
in particular, of children and other vulnerable persons and include reasonable
steps to prevent ill-treatment of which the authorities had or ought to have had
knowledge. A similar approach to positive obligations is manifest under Article 2,
discussed below.

In other cases, the Court has established that there may be positive obligations
upon the state to act in order to prevent third party, non-state actors from interfering with Convention rights. This dimension of positive obligations jurisprudence
has its origins in *X and Y v The Netherlands*,[11] where owing to a *lacuna* in Dutch
criminal law there could be no criminal prosecution of the person who had sexually assaulted the applicant. The Strasbourg Court held that although the essential
object of Article 8 is the protection of the individual against arbitrary interference
by public authorities, there may be positive obligations and these obligations 'may

---

[8] B Rainey, E Wicks and C Ovey, *Jacobs, White and Ovey, The European Convention on Human
Rights* (Oxford, Oxford University Press, 2014) 102.
[9] See A Mowbray, *The Development of Positive Obligations under the European Convention on
Human Rights by the European Court of Human Rights* (Oxford, Hart Publishing, 2004).
[10] (2002) 34 EHRR 97.
[11] (1985) 8 EHRR 235 [23].

involve the adoption of measures designed to secure respect for private life even in the sphere of the relations of individuals between themselves'.[12] Accordingly, there had been a violation of Article 8. The right to privacy, as understood to mean the right to prevent the dissemination of private information, is derived under the Convention from the positive obligations inherent in Article 8. We have also seen that the right to demonstrate peacefully may require state authorities to act to prevent others from interfering with that right.[13]

It will be apparent that many sets of facts in case law that relate to 'omissions' to act on the part of public authorities in the sense employed by the common law, would now be recognised as potentially giving rise to positive obligations to act on the part of a public authority through the medium of section 6 HRA, read together with the relevant Article in the ECHR. Much speculation attended the advent of the HRA, in particular whether the recognition of positive obligations under the ECHR and consequent claims arising under the HRA would lead to any relaxation in the non-liability for omission rule of the common law. In the first edition, we observed that the introduction of an action under section 7 HRA against a public authority that acted incompatibly with a Convention right might well act as a brake on the development of the common law.[14] At the time that *Osman v UK* was decided, there was no effective legal mechanism by which the negligent actions of the police could be challenged and accountability sought. The legal landscape has changed completely and recent decisions of our most senior courts demonstrate a distinct reluctance to see the common law adapt to keep pace with developments under the HRA. In fact, the remedies can be seen as occupying entirely separate domains.

In complete contrast to the judicial reticence to expand the boundaries of the tort of negligence, our most senior courts have taken a proactive stance in accommodating public authority liability under sections 6 and 7 HRA in new situations, even going beyond the situations and instances recognised by Strasbourg: the notion of a 'mirror' approach seems especially redundant here.

The following discussion will set out the extent to which positive obligations have been recognised by the European Court of Human Rights (ECtHR), how English courts have responded to the demands of the HRA and the ECHR and then assess the impact of the ECHR and the HRA on the common law. Academic commentators and the courts have tended to view the remedy under section 7 HRA, on the one hand, and recognised causes of action under the common law, on the other, as fulfilling similar roles and effectively being substitutive of one another. In fact, they occupy different domains with their own rules regarding standing, limitation, causation, standard of care and heads of damage.

---

[12] *Ibid.*
[13] *Plattform 'Ärzte für Das Leben' v Austria* (1988) 13 EHRR 204.
[14] Wright (n 7) Chapter 2.

Positive Obligations on Public Authorities under the ECHR

In Chapter 5 we reviewed what many have regarded as the *Osman* debacle. As we have seen, *Osman* excited English lawyers because it seemed that the ECtHR was intruding upon our legal sovereignty by attempting to shape the substance of tort law against the grain of the common law. There was the decision by the ECtHR in *Osman v United Kingdom*[15] that the Court of Appeal's refusal to recognise a duty of care in *Osman v Ferguson*[16] amounted to a restriction on the right of access to the court in violation of Article 6; this was tantamount to holding there should be a duty of care on such facts. This was followed by the retreat from *Osman v UK* in *Z v United Kingdom* where the Court resiled from its previous holding and determined instead that the relevant mischief lay in the state's failure to afford an effective remedy to the children as required by Article 13 for the violation of the positive obligation to protect the vulnerable children from inhuman and degrading treatment under Article 3.

The potential impact of positive obligations far outweighs the narrow Article 6 point. We shall see that far from applying the 'mirror' principle, English courts have taken positive obligations under the HRA far beyond any situations recognised as requiring protection under the ECHR. There are three dimensions to the positive obligations inherent in Articles 2 and 3. First, the state must put in place an appropriate legal framework to secure the rights; second, there may in some circumstances be a positive operational obligation to protect the right; finally, there is a procedural duty to investigate where the substantive right is engaged. The reader is invited to consider the discussion in conjunction with Chapter 4.

Legal and Administrative Framework

Article 2(1) ECHR provides that 'everyone's right to life shall be protected by law'. In *LCB v United Kingdom*,[17] the applicant claimed that her leukaemia had been caused by her father's exposure to radiation at the Christmas Island tests before she was born. The Court found that the expert evidence did not establish a causal link between parental exposure to radiation and childhood cancer and nor could she establish that had the Government provided her family with more

---

[15] (1998) 29 EHRR 245.
[16] [1993] 4 All ER 344.
[17] (1998) 27 EHRR 212.

information about the tests and their consequences earlier, medical intervention might have mitigated her illness. However, in *LCB*, the ECtHR recognised for the first time that the Article 2 obligation enjoins a state not only to refrain from the intentional and unlawful taking of life, but also has an obligation to take appropriate steps to safeguard the lives of others. From this flows a 'primary duty on the state to secure the right to life by putting in place an appropriate legal and administrative framework to deter the commission of offences against the person, backed up by law enforcement machinery for the prevention, suppression and punishment of breaches of such provisions.[18] Thus, in *Önerylidiz v Turkey*, the ECtHR stated that 'The positive obligation ... entails above all a primary duty on the State to put in place a legislative and administrative framework designed to provide effective deterrence against threats to the right to life'.[19]

There needs to be 'an effective judicial system' to enforce the criminal and other laws required by Article 2. Criminal laws will normally be required, but where the taking of life is unintentional a civil remedy may be sufficient. In *Calvelli and Ciglio v Italy*,[20] a baby had died, allegedly as a result of medical negligence and criminal proceedings against the doctor for involuntary manslaughter became time-barred due to delays during the police inquiry and judicial investigation. The ECtHR did not consider it necessary to decide whether the state had breached Article 2 due to the delays in the police inquiry and judicial investigation which led to the barring of the prosecution. This was because the applicants could bring a civil action for damages which could be followed by disciplinary proceedings. This obligation under Article 2 extends beyond protection from threat to life from agents of the state and criminality of third parties and includes dangers posed by industrial and commercial activity, whether public or private.

In *Öneryildiz*, the following observations were made by the ECtHR regarding Article 2 after 39 people were killed following a methane gas explosion at a waste tip that had been tolerated by the authorities. The public health authorities had allowed the operation of the tip notwithstanding an expert report that highlighted the dangers and furthermore had not acted to prevent the construction and occupation of unauthorised slum dwellings nearby. The Court stated that:

> The Court considers that this obligation must be construed as applying in the context *of any activity, whether public or not, in which the right to life may be at stake*, and *a fortiori* in the case of industrial activities, which by their very nature are dangerous, such as the operation of waste-collection sites.

While there should be civil remedies available against wrongdoers, the question arises whether there should in principle be a civil remedy against the state where the principal wrongdoer, as in *Osman v United Kingdom*, is a non-state actor. In

---

[18] *Makaratzis v Greece* (2005) 41 EHRR 1092 [57].
[19] (2005) 41 EHRR 325.
[20] (2002) Application No 32967/96 I (ECtHR Grand Chamber).

cases such as *McCann v United Kingdom*[21] (the so-called death on the 'rock' case concerning the lethal shooting of three alleged terrorist members of Provisional IRA by SAS soldiers in Gibraltar) and *Osman v United Kingdom*, this question was left open on the basis that any claim to such a remedy should be considered under Articles 6 and 13.[22]

In *Mastromatteo v Italy*,[23] the Court indicated that Article 2 does require the possibility of a civil remedy against the state in the case of a murder where the state is at fault. The applicant's son had been murdered by prisoners who had been granted prison leave and who then absconded. The Grand Chamber found that there was no violation of the substantive obligation under Article 2 as there was nothing in the material before the national authorities to alert them to the fact that the release of the prisoner would pose a real and immediate threat to life, still less that it would lead to the death of the applicant's son. It should be noted that the English Court of Appeal has now held that the Article 2 duty may be owed to the public at large.[24] However, with regard to the complaint that the applicant had not received compensation from the state, the Court agreed to consider the application from the standpoint of Article 2 as the applicant had not invoked Article 13 in his application. The Court found no violation of this procedural dimension of Article 2 because he could have brought an action in negligence against the state under Article 2043 of the Civil Code and an action could have been brought against the judges.

The case is clear authority for the proposition that in principle there should be a civil remedy available against the state in cases regarding the alleged violation of the operational obligation under Article 2. This point is important in light of the United Kingdom's decision not to give further effect to the Article 13 right to an effective remedy within the HRA. In cases that fall outside the HRA (for example historic abuse claims that pre-date the HRA), it could be argued that the courts should in response to their obligation as a public authority develop a common law remedy based upon breach of the ECHR.[25]

P v United Kingdom[26] also confirms that the possibility of bringing proceedings in negligence may be a vehicle for securing the procedural dimension of Article 3. This case concerned a claimant detained at a young offenders' institution who was prone to extreme self-harming behaviour and who alleged that a failure to treat him appropriately was a violation of Articles 2 and 3. The claim before the ECtHR

---

[21] (1995) 21 EHRR 97.
[22] D Harris, M O'Boyle, E Bates and C Buckley, *Harris, O'Boyle and Warbrick, Law of the European Convention on Human Rights*, 2nd edn (Oxford, Oxford University Press, 2009) 41.
[23] Reports of Judgments and Decisions 2002-VIII, 151 (GC).
[24] *Sarjantson v Chief Constable of Humberside Police* [2013] EWCA Civ 1252, [QB] 411. Cf *Osman v UK* (n 15) where the ECtHR held that the risk to life needed to be a 'real and immediate risk to the life of an identified individual or individuals', see Chapter 4.
[25] See discussion text accompanying n 134.
[26] (2014) 58 EHRR SE7 [69].

failed due to a failure to exhaust domestic remedies, namely negligence against the custodial authority which could have addressed the procedural dimension of Article 3. In *P*, the Court stated that:

> It is also recalled that a procedural obligation arises under art.3 requiring a thorough and effective investigation capable of establishing facts and attributing responsibility as regards allegations of serious ill-treatment falling within the scope of this Article. However, if the infringement of the right to physical integrity is not caused intentionally, the positive obligation to set up an effective judicial system does not necessarily require criminal proceedings to be brought in every case and may be satisfied if civil, administrative or disciplinary remedies were available to the victims.

Preventive Operational Measures to Protect the Right to Life—the Operational Obligation

Quite apart from the need for appropriate law enforcement machinery to secure effective protection for the right to life, the Strasbourg organs have also developed an extensive jurisprudence regarding the state's obligation to take operational measures to protect the right to life, in particular, but not limited to, situations where one person's life is at risk from the criminal conduct of another. So, there will be cases where a duty to act on the part of a public authority will be recognised under Article 2 ECHR, but in circumstances where a duty of care would be denied at common law. The leading Strasbourg authority remains *Osman v United Kingdom*.[27] For ease of reference, a brief summary of the facts is given.

The decision of the Court in *Osman v United Kingdom* had its genesis in the bizarre behaviour of a schoolteacher, Paget-Lewis, who developed an obsession for a pupil, Ahmet Osman. Paget-Lewis subjected Ahmet and his family to an escalating campaign of harassment and intimidation over an extended period which culminated in the shooting and death of Ahmet's father, Ali, and the wounding of Ahmet himself. Paget-Lewis also shot and killed the deputy headmaster's son and wounded the deputy headmaster. The Osman family repeatedly raised concerns with the police regarding Paget-Lewis' bizarre and frightening behaviour and the police were aware of statements that he intended to commit a murder. However, in relation to the positive obligation under Article 2, the ECtHR held that:

> It must be established … that the authorities knew or ought to have known at the time of a real and immediate risk to the life of an identified individual or individuals from the criminal acts of a third party and that they failed to take measures within the scope of their powers which, judged reasonably, might have been expected to avoid that risk.[28]

---

[27] *Osman v UK* (n 15).
[28] *Osman v UK* [116].

The ECtHR added an important caveat:

> bearing in mind the difficulties involved in policing modern societies, the unpredictability of human conduct and the operational choices which must be made in terms of priorities and resources, such an obligation must be interpreted in a way which does not impose an impossible or disproportionate burden on the authorities.

This is somewhat different from the considerations that influence the standard of care in negligence. While the cost of precautions is a relevant consideration in determining whether there has been a breach of duty,[29] generally the defendant's personal resources are not.[30] On the facts, the Court held by seventeen votes to three, that there was no decisive stage in the series of events when the police knew, or ought to have known, that there was a real and immediate risk to the Osman family: thus, there was no violation of Article 2.

On the other hand in *Opuz v Turkey*,[31] a violation of the Article 2 positive obligation was found. The applicant alleged that the Turkish authorities had failed to protect her and her mother from domestic violence which led to her mother's death. The victims' situations were known to the authorities and the mother had requested the police to take immediate action, stating that her life was in danger. The only steps taken by the authorities consisted of taking statements from the perpetrator. Two weeks later the applicant's mother was killed. The Court held that the lethal attack could have been foreseen and the responsibility to take reasonable steps to mitigate the harm was therefore engaged.

These cases are extremely fact-sensitive and it may be difficult for an applicant to establish the precise circumstances surrounding a death and therefore what the state authorities should reasonably have done. In *Mikyail Mamamdov v Azerbaijan*,[32] the ECtHR held that the self-immolation of the applicant's wife as a protest tactic (the family were about to be evicted from their home) did not constitute reasonable or predictable behaviour. The Court did say that once the situation became clear, the Article 2 obligation would kick in—on the facts though it had not been established that any additional steps should have been taken by the authorities.

In view of the common law's resistance to recognising affirmative duties of action, other than in extremely limited circumstances, it might have been thought that the Article 2 operational obligation will prove fertile ground for claimants who wish to render public authorities accountable for 'omissions' type cases. Few claims

---

[29] *Latimer v AEC Ltd* [1953] AC 643, cf E Weinrib, *The Idea of Private Law* (Cambridge, Massachusetts, Harvard University Press, 1995) 149 discussed in M Lunney and K Oliphant, *Tort Law Text and Materials*, 5th edn (Oxford, Oxford University Press, 2013) 168 *et seq*. See generally discussion in J Fleming, 'The Economic Factor in Negligence' (1992) 108 *Law Quarterly Review* 9.

[30] An exception is *Goldman v Hargrave* [1967] 1 AC 645.

[31] (2010) 50 EHRR 28.

[32] Application No 4762/05, 17 December 2009.

have been brought under the HRA on *Osman* type facts and the indications are that establishing liability under section 7 HRA will be challenging. That said, there are signs that English courts are becoming willing to contemplate liability under Article 2 in an expanding range of situations. Furthermore, it is clear that 'but for' causation rules do not apply. The aim of human rights is the promotion and realisation of human rights standards in which all citizens have a stake; individual loss must be compensated but is certainly not the 'gist' of the action.

Causation

In *E v United Kingdom*,[33] a breach of Article 3 was found after the authorities had failed to protect children from abuse by their stepfather. The authorities had failed to monitor the situation after a stepfather had been convicted of sexual abuse and it was held that they should have found out he was abusing children and acted to protect them. In terms of causation, as with Article 2, the obligation is one of means, not results, so that 'a failure to take reasonably available measures which could have had a real prospect of altering the outcome or mitigating the harm is sufficient to engage the responsibility of the state'.[34]

Similarly, in *Kilic v Turkey*,[35] a case with extreme facts, a journalist was murdered by or with the connivance of the security forces. Finding a breach of Article 2, the Court gave no consideration to whether the steps that should have been taken would actually have saved the applicant brother's life.

In *E v Chief Constable of the RUC*,[36] Baroness Hale said she was troubled by the rejection of the 'but for' test in *E v United Kingdom*. However, the 'but for' test was rejected by the ECtHR in *Osman*. The UK Government had argued that it must be established on sound and persuasive grounds that there is a causal link between the failure to take preventive action of which the authorities are accused and that that action, judged fairly and realistically, would have been likely to have prevented the incident. The Court held that the applicant must show that the authorities failed to take measures within the scope of their powers, which judged reasonably, might have been expected to avoid that risk.[37] This is a very much weaker test than the standard 'but for' test, but it is consistent with the aims of the ECHR which are the promotion and protection of human rights standards and the rule of law, rather than compensation for damage dependent upon proof of loss.

---

[33] (2002) 36 EHRR 519.
[34] *Ibid* [99].
[35] (2001) 33 EHRR 1357.
[36] [2008] UKHL 66, [2009] 1 AC 536.
[37] *Osman* (n 15) [116].

Article 2 in English Law

The leading authority in English law following the enactment of the HRA is *Van Colle v Chief Constable of Hertfordshire Police*.[38] The claimants' son, Giles Van Colle, was murdered by his former employee, Brougham. Brougham had been charged with the theft of items belonging to Van Colle and he also faced charges in relation to two other thefts. He was bailed unconditionally. In the period leading up to the trial he attempted to dissuade witnesses including Giles Van Colle from giving evidence against him. He telephoned Van Colle twice and made threats against him and his family. These calls were reported to the investigating officer. There were incidents concerning other victims of theft by Brougham including cars catching fire and property being set alight. It has been remarked that the report of the facts in the Court of Appeal and House of Lords illustrate how different a story sounds when told by different storytellers: the Court of Appeal judgment screams negligence, the House of Lords emphasised that this was a petty criminal whose record of violence involved only a seven-year-old conviction for petty assault.[39]

The House of Lords applied the *Osman* test and held that to establish a violation of the positive obligation under Article 2 of the Convention it had to be shown that a public authority had, or ought to have, known at the time of the existence of a real and immediate risk to the life of an identified individual from the criminal acts of a third party and that it had failed to take measures within the scope of its powers which, judged reasonably, might have been expected to avoid that risk. As confirmed by Lord Carswell in *Re Officer L*,[40] the test remained constant and was to be applied whatever the particular circumstances of the case, and no lower test applied where the risk to an individual's life arose from the state's decision to call him as a witness; that the claimants' son's status as a witness, although a relevant factor, was not significant, given the minor character of the offences with which the accused was charged; that since neither his criminal record nor his approaches to witnesses indicated that the accused was given to violence and since some incidents had not been reported and the reported incidents had not involved explicit death threats, it could not reasonably have been anticipated from the information available to the police officer at that time that there was a real and immediate risk to the claimant's son's life.

The ECtHR came to the same conclusion in *Van Colle v United Kingdom*.[41] The Court held that the risk factors were no greater than those in *Osman* and it could not be said that there was a decisive stage at which the investigating officer

---

[38] [2008] UKHL 50, [2009] 1 AC 225.
[39] JR Spencer, 'Suing the Police for Negligence: Orthodoxy Revisited' [2009] *Cambridge Law Journal* 25–27.
[40] [2007] UKHL 36, [2007] 1 WLR 2135.
[41] (2013) 56 EHRR 23.

knew or ought to have known of a real and immediate risk to Van Colle's life from Brougham.[42]

A key element of the *Osman* test is whether the public authority *knew or ought to have known* of the real and immediate risk. In *Van Colle*, Lord Bingham cautioned against the use of hindsight in evaluating whether events presented the necessary level of risk. He said that

> the test depends not only on what the authorities knew, but also on what they ought to have known. Thus stupidity, lack of imagination and inertia do not afford an excuse to a national authority which reasonably ought, in the light of what it knew or was told, to make further inquiries or investigations: it is then to be treated as knowing what such further inquiries or investigations would have elicited.[43]

He concluded that the police could not have been expected to conduct an investigation of the kind that would follow a murder when all they were dealing with was a minor theft.

Lord Phillips in *Van Colle* identified the following as the key question:

> Does the state of knowledge refer to: (i) what the public authority ought to have appreciated on the information available to them?; or (ii) what the public authority ought, had they carried out their duties with due diligence, to have acquired information that would have made them aware of the risk?.[44]

He believed that (i) was intended; this would seem to reject Lord Bingham's comment to the effect that the police cannot plead their own inertia as a defence.

Certainly the outcome in *Van Colle* tends to support the approach suggested by Lord Phillips. A disciplinary tribunal found the investigating officer, DC Ridley, guilty of failing to perform his duties conscientiously and diligently in connection with improper approaches to witnesses. It found that the events amounted to an escalating situation of intimidation in respect of the witnesses Panayiotou and Van Colle. DC Ridley was in a unique position during this time with the fullest picture of the developing situation. DC Ridley was fined five days' pay. Arguably, had DC Ridley acted with due diligence he would have been able to put the pieces of the jigsaw together and appreciated the danger to Mr Van Colle. The inference from *Van Colle* is that there is therefore a subjective element to the *Osman* test because knowledge is subjective and not inferred. Furthermore, as in the case of policy arguments deployed in common law claims in negligence, English courts are clearly fighting shy of taking a view as to how a criminal investigation should be conducted and seem keen to avoid any sense of directing the police service in their allocation of resources. This approach is to be contrasted with Laws LJ in *DSD v Commissioner of Police for the Metropolis*.[45]

---

[42] *Ibid* [103][105].
[43] *Van Colle v Chief Constable of the Hertfordshire Police* (n 38).
[44] *Ibid* [86].
[45] [2015] EWCA Civ 646.

Subsequently, senior courts have confirmed that the *Osman* test sets a high hurdle. In *Mitchell v Glasgow City Council*,[46] Drummond and Mitchell had been neighbours and tenants of the local authority for many years. Drummond was a threatening and aggressive man who had threatened to kill Mitchell at least once a month for a long period and had committed criminal damage to Mr Mitchell's property. Things came to a head when Drummond was summoned to a meeting with the Council to discuss his anti-social behaviour and proceedings for eviction. After the meeting, Drummond attacked Mitchell and caused the injuries from which Mr Mitchell died. A unanimous House of Lords found that there was no duty of care owed in negligence and that the local authority had not acted incompatibly with Article 2 ECHR. However, their Lordships' reasoning differed somewhat.

Lord Hope emphasised that the *Osman* test is 'a high one' and, echoing Lord Bingham, that we should beware the dangers of hindsight.[47] There was nothing on the facts to suggest a real and immediate risk to the life of Mr Mitchell: Drummond had threatened to kill Mitchell on countless occasions, he had not made any threats at the meeting and nor was he armed at the meeting. In short, he did not say or do anything to alert the defenders to the risk of the imminent and fatal attack.

Lord Rodger took a different approach and held that even if Glasgow City Council had been aware of a real and immediate risk to Mr Mitchell, they would not have been under any Article 2 obligation to prevent it for the simple reason that the prevention of crime is the responsibility of the police, not a landlord. The local authority does not have the responsibility nor the resources to act as a general policeman under Article 2; in fact a local authority will frequently be trying to place difficult tenants who may have histories like that of Mr Drummond. This view clearly militates strongly against the development of any generalised conception of affirmative duties of action under Article 2 HRA.

In *Sarjantson v Chief Constable of Humberside Police*,[48] the Court of Appeal held that the scope of the operational duty under Article 2 was not limited to circumstances where a real and imminent risk to the life of an *identified or identifiable* individual was or should have been known. The essential question was whether the police had known or ought to have known of a real and immediate risk to the life of the victim of violence and whether they had done all that could reasonably be expected of them to prevent it from materialising. Where the police had been informed about an incident of violent disorder, it was sufficient that they had known or ought to have known that there were actual or potential victims of the criminal activity regardless of their names or identities. In this case, therefore, the duty had arisen when the first emergency call had been made, informing the police

---

[46] [2009] UKHL 11, [2009] 1 AC 874.
[47] *Ibid* [31] and [33].
[48] *Sarjantson* (n 24).

that there were individuals in the vicinity of the street where the men were causing mayhem and where to find those individuals so as to protect them if it was reasonably necessary to do so.

Furthermore, it was no answer to the claim in *Sarjantson* that it would have made no difference to the outcome in terms of the injuries suffered if the police had responded to the 999 call in a timely fashion. Since there had been no reason at the time when the first emergency call had been made for the police to believe that immediate attendance was not required and the tone and content of the emergency calls suggested there was an immediate likelihood that the men would injure or kill one or more persons in the vicinity, the question whether a response would have made a difference was not relevant to liability.[49] However, the but for question would be relevant to determining *quantum* of damages.

In a key development in *Rabone v Pennine Care NHS Trust*[50] the Supreme Court extended the ambit of the operational obligation under Article 2 to a voluntary patient receiving treatment for depression. Melanie Rabone, who was 24-years-old, committed suicide by hanging herself from a tree during two days' home leave from Stepping Hill Hospital where she was undergoing treatment as a voluntary psychiatric patient (that is, she had not been detained under the Mental Health Act 1983). She had been admitted to the hospital as an emergency patient following a suicide attempt and assessed as being at high risk of a further suicide attempt. Despite this assessment, and in the face of serious parental concern, the treating physician bowed to Melanie's wish to go home for the weekend. Having told her parents that she was going to meet friends, Melanie went to Lyme Park where she took her own life. Her parents brought claims in negligence against the defendants under the Law Reform (Miscellaneous Provisions) Act 1934, which provides for the survival of causes of action for the benefit of the estate of a deceased, and under section 7 HRA for breach of the Article 2 right to life. The Trust admitted negligence and paid £7500 to settle the 1934 Act claim: some £2,500 for funeral expenses and the balance for Melanie's pain and suffering prior to death.

Building on Strasbourg jurisprudence recognising the operational duty to protect prisoners from other inmates[51] and from suicide,[52] as well as the Supreme Court's decision in *Savage v South Essex Partnership NHS Foundation Trust*[53] concerning a psychiatric patient detained under the Mental Health Act 1983, the Supreme Court held that the operational duty arose and had been breached in Melanie's case. The key factors were the assumption of responsibility by the state for the individual's welfare and safety (including by the exercise of control) and the

---

[49] *Sarjantson* (n 24) [29] Lord Dyson MR.

[50] [2012] UKSC 2, [2012] 2 AC 72. This discussion draws on J Wright, 'The Operational Obligation under Article 2 of the European Convention on Human Rights and Challenges for Coherence: Views from the English Supreme Court and Strasbourg' (2016) *Journal of European Tort Law* 7(1) 1–14.

[51] *Edwards v United Kingdom* (2002) 35 EHRR 487.

[52] *Keenan v United Kingdom* (2001) 33 EHRR 913.

[53] [2009] 1 AC 681, [2008] UKHL 74.

particular vulnerability of the victim, noting that in circumstances of 'sufficient vulnerability' the ECtHR has been prepared to find a breach of the operational duty even where there has been no assumption of responsibility, such as the failure of a local authority to protect children at risk of abuse. Indeed, the whole point of the operational duty in many cases is to delineate when there has been a failure to take responsibility when circumstances require it. The operational obligations apply to all detainees, but are particularly stringent in relation to those who are especially vulnerable by reason of their physical[54] or mental[55] condition.

The operational obligation under Article 2 was considered most recently by the English Supreme Court in a strike out application by the Ministry of Defence in *Smith v Ministry of Defence*.[56] The claimants were family members of British soldiers who had been killed by improvised explosive devices which were detonated at the roadside as they travelled in Snatch Land Rover vehicles. The claimants alleged a breach of Article 2 in the failure to provide suitably safe equipment. By a narrow 4:3 majority, the Supreme Court held that the claims should go to trial. The Court held that the application of the operational obligation under Article 2 to military operations will vary and that an unrealistic and disproportionate positive obligation in relation to the planning or conduct of military operations should not be imposed. However, where it is reasonable to expect an individual to be afforded the protection of Article 2, then Article 2 should be given effect. Allegations relating to either matters of procurement, training or the conduct of operations linked to the exercise of political judgement or issues of policy, or to acts or omissions occurring during actual operational engagements, would be beyond the reach of Article 2. However, the trial should establish the facts to determine whether the claims raised fall between these two areas and any decision on liability should be deferred until the conclusion of that factual inquiry.

Smith is a remarkable case. It is the clearest example yet of the rejection of the 'mirror' principle.[57] As Lord Hope, giving the leading judgment for the majority, observed, Strasbourg has not yet examined the extent to which Article 2(1) offers protection to armed forces engaged in operations such as those in Iraq in 2006. This did not deter the Supreme Court. Rather, Lord Hope drew upon 'straws in the wind' such as they are to inform his thinking. First, he noted the authorities that suggest it would not be compatible with the characteristics of military life to expect the same standard of protection as would be afforded to civilians, at least in the context of military discipline when on active service. However, he considered that as a general rule service personnel should receive the same protection from death or injury by the provision of appropriate training and equipment as other members of the police, fire and emergency services. However, it is different when

---

[54] *Tarariyeva v Russia* (2006) 48 EHRR 609.
[55] *Keenan* (n 52).
[56] [2013] UKSC 41, [2014] AC 52. This discussion also draws on Wright (n 50) 1–14.
[57] See discussion of section 2(1) HRA obligation in Chapter 3.

service personnel move to active operations at home or overseas and he stated that 'it is here that the national interest requires that the law should accord the widest measure of appreciation to commanders on the ground who have the responsibility of planning for and conducting operations there'.[58]

Lord Hope asserted that *Stoyanovi v Bulgaria* supports his analysis. In fact, *Stoyanovi*, which is the only direct authority from Strasbourg on the death of a serviceperson on active duty, points in the other direction and would generally seem to deny the protection of the operational obligation under Article 2. Lord Hope quoted from the ECtHR in *Stoyanovi*:

> Whenever a state undertakes or organises dangerous activities, or authorises them, it must ensure through a system of rules and through sufficient control that the risk is reduced to a reasonable minimum. If nevertheless damage arises, it will only amount to a breach of the state's positive obligations if it was due to insufficient regulations or insufficient control, but not if the damage was caused through the negligent conduct of an individual or the concatenation of unfortunate events.

He then went on to contrast that situation and the instant case of

> operations undertaken in a situation where it was known or could reasonably have been anticipated that troops were at risk of attacks from insurgents by unconventional means such as the planting of IEDs. Regulation of the kind contemplated in *Stoyanovi* is likely to be very difficult, if not impossible, to achieve on the ground in situations of that kind. Even where those directing operations are remote in place and time from the area in which the troops are operating, great care is needed to avoid imposing a burden on them which is impossible or disproportionate.[59]

Lord Hope's identification of an area of potential state responsibility that lies between issues of policy and procurement on the one hand and combat operations on the other seems fraught with difficulty. Procurement decisions take place far from the theatre of war, but commanders on the battlefield or otherwise engaged in challenging security situations such as the patrols in Iraq, must deploy the equipment they have, often in fast developing and unpredictable situations. Lord Carnwath in the minority described the majority view as an inadequate response; having heard full argument he considered that the Court should have been able to determine whether or not the claims were viable or at the very least determine what questions of fact would need to be determined for a favourable result following trial.[60]

Lord Mance who sat in *Rabone*, a decision which he had supported on the basis of the factors outlined by Lord Dyson, delivered a powerful dissenting judgment in *Smith*. He referred to the lack of Strasbourg guidance on the question of whether a state should be liable for the death of a soldier due to the negligence of

---

[58] *Smith* (n 56) [71].
[59] *Smith* (n 56) [73].
[60] *Smith* (n 56) [154].

his commander or another soldier: the prospect of Strasbourg reviewing this was so striking that he could not give a positive answer and the domestic court should await clear guidance from Strasbourg. He could not countenance any extension of Article 2 obligations in the absence of prior Strasbourg authority or the court otherwise being confident in what Strasbourg would decide. In a hark back to the 'mirror principle', he stated that:

> If the European court considers that the Convention requires it to undertake the retrospective review of armed conflicts to adjudicate on the relations between a state and its own soldiers, without recognising any principle similar to combat immunity, then it seems to me that a domestic court should await clear guidance from Strasbourg to that effect.[61]

He also deprecated what would appear to be the development of an independent 'substantive law of tort overlapping with domestic tort law but limited to cases involving death or the risk of death'. For Lord Mance, there is no Strasbourg authority that points in the direction of positive operational obligations arising in such situations; indeed, the reasoning in *Stoyanovi* highlights the inherently dangerous nature of military life and concludes that there is no operational duty to prevent that danger.

The Duty to Investigate

The third dimension to the positive obligation under Article 3 is the requirement to conduct an effective investigation where there are well-founded allegations of ill-treatment that constitutes a violation of Article 3. In *DSD v Commissioner of Police of the Metropolis*,[62] the Court of Appeal upheld the findings of the first instance judge that the police investigation into over 100 rapes and sexual assaults was seriously deficient and what is more had been impaired by a failure to allocate appropriate resources. The police force had focussed on the 'easy to clear up' cases in order to meet targets.

The Impact of the HRA on the Common Law

As we have seen, the remedy under section 8 HRA and an action for damages in the tort of negligence are incommensurable. The range of claimants, burden of proof, limitation period, heads of damage, measure of damages, standard of care and causation rules are different and so one should not be considered substitutive

---

[61] *Smith* (n 56) [142].
[62] *DSD* (n 45). See discussion in Chapter 4.

of the other. It has been said that English courts do not reject recognition of a duty of care in negligence on the ground that there is an alternative form of redress.[63] In fact there are numerous examples of judges citing the existence of alternative remedies as a factor that tells against duty.[64] As Tofaris and Steel point out, such remedies serve different aims: for example, criminal injuries compensation will not render the police accountable for their actions and judicial review will not provide a remedy for past wrongs.[65] It is clear, though, that in negligence and in other areas of law, the courts will generally refuse to extend the common law when Parliament has enacted legislation in an area of law.[66]

The *Hill* Principle, *Osman v United Kingdom* and their Effects

English law has reached the position that, despite a general trend towards rejecting immunity from suit in negligence for members of what might broadly be described as professional groups, the position of the police appears to be unassailable at least in terms of the negligent investigation of crime. Such cases can frequently be classified as cases of omission, although the *Hill* principle has been applied in cases of misfeasance too.[67] While the possibility of a claim under the HRA led the Court of Appeal to reject *X (Minors) v Bedfordshire County Council* and to permit claims by children in negligence based upon the failings of social workers,[68] the police have successfully resisted such attempts by claimants. Our senior judiciary generally has been unwilling to extend the common law so that claimants have a remedy under both the tort of negligence and under the HRA.

It has been suggested that the section 6 duty on the court not to act incompatibly with ECHR rights may translate into a duty to develop the law in a manner that is 'consistent with such rights'.[69] Such arguments have not prevailed. As we have suggested in Chapter 3, it is arguable that such developments are only tenable where a substantive right requires the provision of a civil remedy, given that the ECHR draws a clear distinction otherwise between the substantive rights

---

[63] See the discussion by Nolan (n 1) 316.

[64] *Rowling v Takaro Properties* [1988] AC 473 (judicial review); *X (Minors) v Bedfordshire County Council* [1995] 2 AC 633 (statutory complaint); *Hill v Chief Constable of West Yorkshire* [1989] 1 AC 53 (Criminal Injuries Compensation); *Brooks v Commissioner of Police* [2005] UKHL 24, [2005] 1 WLR 1495 (police complaints procedure).

[65] S Tofaris and S Steel, 'Police Liability in Negligence for Failure to Prevent Crime: Time to Rethink', Cambridge, Legal Studies Research Paper Series paper no 39/2014.

[66] See for example, *R (Keyu) v Secretary of State for Foreign and Commonwealth Affairs* [2015] UKSC 69, [2015] 3 WLR 1665.

[67] *Brooks* (n 64); *Robinson v Chief Constable of West Yorkshire Police* [2014] EWCA Civ 15, [2014] PIQR 14. See C McIvor, 'Getting Defensive about Police Negligence: The *Hill* Principle, the Human Rights Act 1998 and the House of Lords' (2010) *Cambridge Law Journal* 69(1) 133–50.

[68] *D v East Berkshire Community Health NHS Trust* [2004] QB 558.

[69] McIvor (n 67) 150.

and the right to an effective remedy in Article 13;[70] in any event, that remedy is now provided by the HRA. Hickman's prediction that the remedy under section 7 would have no more than a residual effect[71] has not come to pass; the courts have relied extensively on the HRA as a justification for continuation of the non-liability for omissions rule as the following discussion will demonstrate. As Arden LJ has put it,

> The position would seem to be that English courts are not necessarily going to develop the common law in the field of tort by reference to Convention rights and values, but will do so only in specific cases where that is appropriate for domestic reasons.[72]

This bifurcation is amply illustrated by the fate of the rules laid down by *X (Minors)* and *Hill*.

The Fate of *X (Minors)* and *Hill* Following the Enactment of the HRA

The two key authorities that most amply demonstrated the common law rule that there can be no liability for an omission at common law in the pre-HRA era were *X (Minors) v Bedfordshire County Council*[73] and *Hill v Chief Constable of West Yorkshire*.[74] Both decisions have achieved a level of notoriety and it is instructive to consider the story of their progeny side by side as the courts' attitude to liability of the police on one hand and social workers on the other have been so different and arguably create incoherence within the common law.

The facts of *X (Minors)* are well-known but for the sake of completeness, a brief summary is provided here. Five siblings who had suffered serious ill-treatment and neglect by their parents alleged that the local authority had failed properly to discharge their statutory obligations to enter the children's names on the child protection register and to remove them into the care of the local authority with due expedition. The children sought damages for their physical and psychological injuries.

The leading speech was given by Lord Browne-Wilkinson. After holding that the decisions made by the social workers were justiciable on the basis that they were practical decisions about the welfare of the children and that the decisions were conceivably outside the ambit of local authority discretion, his Lordship

---

[70] TR Hickman, 'Tort Law, Public Authorities and the HRA 1998' in D Fairgrieve, M Andenas, and J Bell, *Tort Liability of Public Authorities in Comparative Perspective* (London, British Institute of International and Comparative Law, 2002) 18.

[71] *Ibid* 25.

[72] Lady Justice Arden, 'Human Rights and Civil Wrongs: Tort Law under the Spotlight' [2010] *Public Law* 140.

[73] *X (Minors)* (n 64).

[74] *Hill* (n 64).

proceeded to consider the criteria set out in *Caparo Industries Plc v Dickman*.[75] The local authority accepted that the harm was foreseeable and that a relationship of proximity existed between the local authority and the claimants. However, the House concluded that it was not fair, just and reasonable to recognise a duty of care in negligence. A raft of reasons was given, including the difficulty of apportioning responsibility when the scheme of child protection is multi-disciplinary, the delicate nature of the task and the risk of over caution and defensiveness, the risk of costly and vexatious litigation and the availability of complaint under the statutory complaints procedure and application to the local government ombudsman.[76]

Lord Browne-Wilkinson said the closest analogies to *X (Minors)* were *Hill v Chief Constable of West Yorkshire*[77] and *Yuen Kun-Yeu v AG of Hong Kong*[78] in which a duty was denied. 'In my judgment' he said, 'the courts should proceed with great care before holding liable in negligence those who have been charged by Parliament with the task of protecting society from the wrongdoings of others'. 'Omissions' language is much more explicit in *Michael v Chief Constable of South Wales Police*, where Lord Toulson giving judgment for the majority stated that

> English law does not as a general rule impose liability on the defendant (D) for injury or damage to the person or property of a claimant (C) caused by the conduct of a third party ... the fundamental reason [as Lord Goff explained in *Smith v Littlewoods Organisation Ltd*], is that the common law does not generally impose liability for pure omissions. It is one thing to require a person who embarks on action which may harm others to exercise care. It is another matter to hold a person liable in damages for failing to prevent harm caused by someone else.[79]

The children in *X (Minors)* took their case to the ECtHR where the UK Government conceded that its positive obligation under Article 3 ECHR to protect the children from inhuman and degrading treatment had been violated, but successfully resisted the argument that the Article 6 right to a fair trial had been violated, an issue that is fully discussed in Chapter 5.[80] Furthermore, the UK Government conceded that the Article 13 right to an effective remedy had been breached and the ECtHR made the then highest ever awards of just satisfaction for psychological and physical damage, totalling £320,000. The Government accepted that, in the particular circumstances of the case, the range of remedies available (compensation from the Criminal Injuries Compensation Board, invocation of the complaints procedure under the Children

---

[75] [1990] 2 AC 605.
[76] J Wright, 'Local Authorities, the Duty of Care and the European Convention on Human Rights' (1998) 18 *Oxford Journal of Legal Studies* 1.
[77] *Hill* (n 64).
[78] [1988] AC 175.
[79] [2015] UKSC 2, [2015] WLR 343 [97].
[80] *Z v United Kingdom* (n 10).

Act 1989 and complaint to the Local Government Ombudsman) was insufficient to satisfy the demands of Article 13. In view of the seriousness of the violation of one of the most important Convention rights, the Government accepted that a legally enforceable right to compensation should be available and pointed out that such a right would exist on the coming into force of the HRA.

The House of Lords decision in *X (Minors)* and the ECtHR decision in *Z v United Kingdom* were revisited by the Court of Appeal in *D v East Berkshire Community NHS Trust.*[81] In *D*, three consolidated appeals concerned claims that allegations of abuse that eventually proved to be unfounded were made against parents by professionals (doctors and social workers) charged with the welfare of the children. In one case, the child was removed from its parents. In each case, the first instance court had held that no duty of care was owed to either parent or child because it was 'not fair, just and reasonable' to impose such a duty, applying the principles laid down by the House of Lords in *X (Minors)* and *Newham*. It is important to note that no claim against any public authority could be brought under the HRA in any of the three cases as the facts pre-dated the coming into force of that Act which generally does not have retrospective effect. Apart from the exception created by s 22(4), which is not relevant to the present discussion, it has been held that the HRA does not apply to the acts of courts, tribunals or public authorities which took place prior to 2 October 2000.[82] Thus, the general route for a claim under section 7 HRA relying on Article 8 ECHR available to a parent aggrieved by a public authority decision was not available. Where the HRA does apply and a decision is taken by a local authority (acting through its social workers and other professional advisers) to take a child into the care of the local authority, the removal of the child is an interference with family life under Article 8(2) ECHR. The interference must then be justified in accordance with the criteria laid down in paragraph 2 of Article 8.

In *D*, counsel argued that the law had moved on since *X (Minors)* and placed emphasis on *Barrett v Enfield London Borough Council*[83] and *Phelps v London Borough of Hillingdon.*[84] Lord Phillips, giving judgment for the Court of Appeal, noted that in neither case did the House of Lords purport to depart from *X (Minors)* but 'it is always possible for the House of Lords to reduce the impact of a previous decision by distinguishing it or confining it narrowly to its particular facts'.[85] Neither *Barrett* nor *Phelps* were cases of non-feasance. In *Barrett*, Lord Slynn giving the leading speech took the view that the policy factors applied in *X (Minors)* did not have the same force, cumulatively or separately, once a child

[81] [2003] EWCA Civ 1151, [2003] 4 All ER 796. See generally, J Wright, 'Immunity No More: Child Abuse Cases and Public Authority Liability in Negligence after *D v East Berkshire Community NHS Trust*' (2004) 20 *Journal of Professional Negligence* 58.

[82] *R v Lambert* [2001] UKHL 37, [2002] 2 AC 545 and see generally M Amos, *Human Rights Law*, 2nd edn (Oxford, Hart Publishing, 2014) 60.

[83] [1999] 3 WLR 79.

[84] [1999] 1 WLR 500.

[85] *D* (n 81) [34].

has been taken into care. In *Phelps*, the House concluded that individual professionals called in to advise the local education authority regarding the educational needs of children could owe a duty of care for which the local education authority could be vicariously liable. The question of whether a direct duty of care could be owed was left open.[86]

The Court of Appeal in *D* found that the effect of *Barrett* and *Phelps* was to restrict *X (Minors)* to a core proposition that decisions whether or not to take a child into care could not be the subject of an action in negligence. Furthermore, the Court held that the core proposition could not survive the coming into force of the HRA because where a claim against a local authority is made under section 7 HRA, there will now be litigation involving factual inquiries into the conduct of the professionals involved. The Court was influenced by the need to address cases of historic abuse, a problem that applies with especial force in the light of the very high profile historic abuse cases that have emerged since this litigation. Lord Philips stated that

> In these circumstances [the claim under section 7 HRA based upon Article 8 ECHR], the reasons of policy that led the House of Lords to hold that no duty of care towards a child arises, in so far as those reasons have not largely been discredited by the subsequent decisions of the House of Lords, will largely cease to apply. Substantial damages will be available on proof of individual shortcomings which will be relevant alike to a claim based on breach of section 6 and a claim based on breach of the common law duty of care … the decision in [*X (Minors)*] cannot survive the 1998 Act … the absence of an alternative remedy for children who were victims of abuse before October 2000 militates in favour of the recognition of a duty of care once the public policy reasons have lost their force.[87]

In relation to the parents' claim, however, the Court held that there are strong public policy reasons to deny the claim as there is an inherent potential conflict of interest between parent and child as it will always be in the parent's interests that the child is not removed. The Trust did not appeal the decision in favour of the children and the House of Lords assumed its correctness. The parents' appeal was rejected by a 4:1 majority in the House of Lords.[88] Lord Bingham dissented and could see no ground for distinguishing between parent and child—in either case a duty of care would help to instil a due sense of professional responsibility. Given that a parent, as well as a child, now has a claim under section 7 HRA and Article 8, the argument that the policy reasons for denying a duty of care have lost their force apply equally to a parent.

Lord Nicholls recited the Article 8 obligation to respect family life which is owed to both parents and children. He said,

> Family life is to be guarded jealously. … Interference with family life requires cogent justification, for the sake of children and parents alike. So, public authorities should so

---

[86] D Fairgrieve, 'Pushing Back the Boundaries of Public Authority Liability; Tort Law Enters the Classroom' [2002] *Public Law* 288.

[87] *D* (n 81) [81]–[83].

[88] *JD v East Berkshire Community NHS Trust* [2005] 2 AC 373.

far as possible cooperate with the parents when making decisions about their children. Public authorities should disclose matters relied upon by them as justifying interference with family life. Parents should be involved in the decision-making process to whatever extent is appropriate to protect their interests adequately.[89]

Where a public authority acts incompatibly with a parent's Article 8 rights a claim will lie under section 7 HRA. Following *D*, the father and daughter in one of the appeals petitioned Strasbourg on the basis that their enforced separation violated Article 8. The ECtHR upheld the claims in *MAK v United Kingdom* and awarded both parent and child compensation for non-pecuniary damage.[90] The Court held that while there were relevant and sufficient reasons for the authority to suspect abuse, the delay in consulting a dermatologist (who would have made a correct diagnosis of illness rather than intentional injury) extended the interference with the right to respect for family life and was not proportionate to the legitimate aim of protecting the child from harm.

In *D*, the Court of Appeal departed from the House of Lords' decision in *X (Minors)*. In terms of the doctrine of precedent, it is clear that decisions of the House of Lords bind the Court of Appeal. An otherwise binding precedent may be departed from when it is inconsistent with intervening legislation. But, it is difficult to see that that applies here.[91] The common law and the HRA are not substitutes for one another and public authorities may owe duties under the common law and the HRA. The Court of Appeal did not attempt to justify its decision by reference to any provision of the HRA.

This looks very like *de facto* retrospective effect and the House of Lords has previously held that the HRA does not have retrospective effect. In fact the House of Lords in the subsequent appeal by the parents cast no doubt on the correctness of the Court of Appeal's decision with regard to the children and the extreme facts of *X (Minors)* have been recognised as providing an exception to the general application of the doctrine of precedent.

This author suggested[92] that some support for the Court of Appeal's conclusion might arguably have been found in sections 6(1) and 6(3) of the Act by invoking the Court's own obligation to develop the common law in line with the Convention. The difficulty, though, with this argument is that whether or not a claimant has a common law remedy in the tort of negligence arguably does not engage the substance of the relevant right, in *D*, Article 8. The Court itself is not proposing to interfere with the right to family life. That said, the remedial dimension to individual rights could include Article 8. In *X and Y v The Netherlands*, the failure to provide a means by which a rapist could be prosecuted was a failure to respect private life. A lack of a civil remedy could amount to a failure to respect private life;

---

[89] *Ibid* [73].
[90] (2010) 51 EHRR 14.
[91] *Miliangos v George Frank (Textiles) Ltd* [1976] AC 443 (Lord Simon).
[92] Wright (n 81).

however, that failure is a failure by the state. As we have seen, Strasbourg does not generally indicate *how* remedies should be effected at domestic level. This means that a refusal to recognise a duty of care on these facts does not mean that the *Court* would be acting incompatibly with Article 8, although the United Kingdom might be.

In *Z v United Kingdom*, on the other hand, Article 3 was engaged and this Article imports a clear remedial obligation upon the part of the state that is independent of Article 13. Thus, arguably, a court that does not ensure a civil remedy for a violation of Article 3 would be acting incompatibly with Article 3 and therefore unlawfully. The ECtHR has held that where an allegation has been made that there has been a failure to protect someone from the acts of others there should be a mechanism for establishing liability and, in the case of Articles 2 and 3, compensation, should in principle include non-pecuniary damage. However, the Court declined to make any finding whether on these facts only court proceedings could provide effective redress, 'though judicial remedies indeed furnish strong guarantees of independence, access for the victim and enforceability in compliance with Article 13'.[93]

In *Kay v Lambeth London Borough Council*,[94] the House of Lords held that following the enactment of the HRA courts should follow the ordinary rules of precedent, save in an extreme case where the decision of the superior court could not survive the introduction of the HRA. Lord Bingham emphasised in *Kay*, that the facts in *X (Minors)* were of an 'extreme' character that justified the Court of Appeal's approach. The extreme facts were: judgment was given in 1995, well before the HRA came into force; no reference was made to the ECHR in any of its opinions; the children succeeded in establishing a violation of Article 3 recovering very substantial reparation.[95]

The local authority did not appeal in *JD*. The House of Lords (Lord Bingham dissenting) rejected the parents' appeal on the ground that a duty to the parent would conflict with the duty owed to the child and 'these decisions should not be clouded by imposing a conflicting duty in favour of parents or others suspected of having abused the child'.[96] In complete contrast with the Court of Appeal's approach, the House found that the new remedy under the HRA militated against recognising a duty to the parent.[97] Lord Bingham alone wished to see the contours of negligence develop to accommodate the parents' claim:

> The question does arise whether the law of tort should evolve, analogically and incrementally, so as to fashion appropriate remedies to contemporary problems or whether it should remain essentially static, making only such changes as are forced upon it, leaving

---

[93] *Z v United Kingdom* (n 10) [139].
[94] [2006] 2 AC 465.
[95] *Ibid* 498.
[96] *JD* (n 88) [86] (Lord Nicholls).
[97] *JD* (n 88) [94] (Lord Nicholls).

difficult and, in human terms, very important problems to be swept up by the Convention. I prefer evolution.[98]

The Court of Appeal in *D* was in a bind. No claim lay under the HRA, in *Z v United Kingdom* the ECtHR had found that the United Kingdom was in violation of the Article 13 right to an effective remedy and, according to *X (Minors)* no duty of care was owed to children by a public authority. There is an important difference between *X (Minors)* and *D*, but not one that was identified by counsel or the Court of Appeal. *X* was a case of an omission, *D* quite clearly was an act of misfeasance—the removal of a child without justification.

D occupies a lone outcrop of the common law; here the existence of a remedy under the HRA told in favour of a duty of care in negligence. The general approach of the courts has been exactly the reverse: the cause of action under the HRA negates any argument to develop the common law.[99] *D* is a case where the availability of the remedy under the HRA militated in favour of a duty of care on the basis that the policy arguments which had been determinative in *X (Minors)* had lost their force as a result of the HRA. Quite the opposite position has been taken in relation to the police.

The leading authority on negligence liability of the police arising during the investigation of crime remains *Hill v Chief Constable of West Yorkshire.*[100] However, a case that arose on very particular facts that quite clearly evinced an omission to act has now been taken to signify a no-liability rule in a much wider sphere of application, and has even been extended to cover cases that are quite clearly examples of misfeasance. Unlike *X (Minors)*, the possibility of the HRA claim has served to bolster a restrictive approach to the development of the common law rules.

Hill v Chief Constable of West Yorkshire

It is instructive to remind ourselves of what the House of Lords decided in *Hill*. The claim in negligence was brought by the mother of the final victim murdered by the serial killer Peter Sutcliffe, commonly known as the Yorkshire Ripper. Mrs Hill alleged that the police had been negligent for failing to identify and capture the killer before he murdered her daughter. The claim failed for a want of proximity—there was no special relationship between either the victim and the police or the killer and the police. According to Lord Keith, the characteristics which led to liability in *Home Office v Dorset Yacht Co Ltd*[101] (another example of an omission) were missing. Unlike the owners of the yachts moored at Brownsea Island, who were at risk from known inmates under the control of the dozy prison officers, Miss Hill was one

---

[98] *JD* (n 88) [50] (Lord Bingham).
[99] *Smith v Chief Constable of Sussex Police* [2008] UKHL 50, [2009] 1 AC 225; *Jain v Trent Strategic Health Authority* [2009] 1 AC 853.
[100] *Hill* (n 64).
[101] [1970] AC 1004.

of a 'vast number of the female general public who might be at risk' from Sutcliffe's activities and Sutcliffe had never been in the custody of the police. Thus, the element of proximity was missing. On this basis, *Hill* is defensible according to common law rules; Lord Keith could have stopped there but he did not, moving on to set out a raft of policy arguments that have become 'received thinking' in many cases.

It is the *obiter dicta* that have assumed significance in subsequent authority. Lord Keith listed the policy arguments that further justified the no duty finding because it would not be 'fair, just and reasonable to recognise a duty of care'. Lord Keith considered that imposing a duty of care might lead the police to carry out their functions in a 'detrimentally defensive' frame of mind, a great deal of time, trouble and expense would attend preparing legal defences, police manpower and attention would be diverted from their most important function, that of the suppression of crime. It can equally be argued that the threat of liability will encourage professionals to do their jobs properly and improve standards. Lord Keith however concluded that

> the general sense of public duty which motivates police forces is unlikely to be appreciably reinforced by the imposition of such liability so far as concerns their function in the investigation and suppression of crime. From time to time they may make mistakes in the exercise of that function, but it is not to be doubted that they apply their best endeavours to the performance of it.[102]

This view has been criticised on a number of occasions,[103] most recently by the Supreme Court in *Michael v Chief Constable of South Wales Police*,[104] where Lord Toulson for the majority accepted the force of counsel's criticisms of *Hill* in this regard.[105]

In *Michael*, a claim was brought both under the HRA and at common law based upon the alleged negligence of the police in failing to respond in a timely manner to a 999 call made by Ms Michael following which she was stabbed to death by her ex-boyfriend. The Supreme Court considered that the one consequence of which the Court could be confident if liability were imposed would be potentially significant financial implications for the police force. However, on the right facts successful claims may be brought against the police under the HRA, although as we have seen the bar is high. While this remedial reality militated in favour of a duty of care in *D*, the majority in *Michael* was not persuaded that consistency between the common law and the Convention should be encouraged. Baroness Hale on the other hand having referred to *D*, considered that,

> [T]he issues under the Human Rights Act 1998 are not identical to the issues under the law of negligence, but the existence of a human rights advanced against the imposition of

[102] *Hill* (n 64) [63] (Lord Keith).
[103] See *Brooks* (n 64) [28] (Lord Steyn), [37] (Lord Roger), [39] (Lord Brown); *Van Colle* (n 38) [48] (Lord Bingham).
[104] *Michael* (n 79).
[105] *Michael* (n 79) [121].

a duty in negligence claims have also 'largely ceased to apply' in a case such as this, where it is alleged that a tragic death would have been averted had the police reacted appropriately to Ms Michael's emergency call.[106]

Hill is a classic case of an omission with the alleged negligence consisting of a failure to apprehend a prolific murderer and a case in which it was completely unnecessary for Lord Keith to embark upon his much-cited enumeration of policy arguments. Classic omissions analysis would have sufficed. However, English courts have not always applied the distinction between acts and omissions clearly or consistently. Lord Keith failed to apply that distinction and the result has been that the policy considerations described above have also been applied to negate a duty of care on facts that related to the negligent acts of the police themselves towards the claimant, rather than being parasitic on the positive misconduct of a third party.

Thus, *Brooks* concerned a negligence action against the police for psychiatric harm caused by their alleged mistreatment of a witness to murder, Duwayne Brooks, the friend of Stephen Lawrence who was at his friend's side when he was killed in a brutal racist attack. Therefore, the gist of the claim was quite different from *Hill*; one commentator has gone so far as to say that the current major obstacle to the proper interpretation of *Hill* is *Brooks*.[107] As McIvor has observed, as a 'straightforward misfeasance, Brooks should not have been dealt with under the *Hill* principle'. A frequently overlooked limitation in Lord Keith's speech is the fact that in discussing policy, he was explaining why an action for damages should not lie against the police 'in circumstances such as those of the present case'.[108] Lord Keith also stated that 'there is no question that a police officer, like anyone else, *may be liable in tort to a person who is injured as a direct result of his acts and omissions*', citing the well-known examples of *Knightley v Johns*[109] and *Rigby v Chief Constable of Northamptonshire*.[110]

In *Robinson v Chief Constable of West Yorkshire Police*,[111] the Court of Appeal applied the *Hill* principle on very different facts where the claimant alleged that she suffered personal injury as a direct result of the negligent way in which a drug dealer had been arrested on a high street. This set of facts is far removed from *Hill* and bodes ill for effective accountability by one of our key public services. The essence of the claim was clearly negligence in a police operation that caused direct physical injury to the claimant and there is therefore a clear analogy with cases such as *Knightley v Johns*[112] and *Rigby v Chief Constable of Northamptonshire*[113]—it

---

[106] *Michael* (n 79) [196] (Baroness Hale).
[107] For an excellent discussion, see McIvor (n 67).
[108] *Hill* (n 64) 62.
[109] [1982] 1 WLR 349.
[110] [1985] 1 WLR 1242.
[111] *Robinson* (n 67).
[112] *Knightley* (n 109).
[113] *Rigby* (n 110).

is not a case of a failure to confer a benefit or a failure to prevent an unknown or indeed known third party from causing harm to another. Singling out the police force for immunity (*Robinson* is a case of immunity as individuals in professional and personal capacities owe duties not to cause direct physical harm to others), especially at a time when the courts are tending to restrict immunities[114] calls for inquiry into the scope of responsibility that the keepers of the peace owe to individual members of the public who suffer physical harm as a direct result of their operational negligence.

Smith v Chief Constable of Sussex Police

Smith[115] is a case that exemplifies the courts' 'hands off' approach to the potential liability of the police in negligence. It is a 'third party' case, but based upon a set of facts that are much stronger than either *Hill* or *Dorset Yacht*. The claimant had been in a live-in relationship with his attacker, Jeffrey. After the relationship had ended and after receiving a stream of violent, abusive and threatening telephone, text and internet messages including death threats, he dialled 999 and reported a history of violence and threats. The police assigned two officers to the case who visited Mr Smith that day, but did not examine the messages, made no entry in their notebooks and took no statement from Mr Smith. Further threatening communications were reported but there was very little follow up. It was a strike out application and facts therefore assumed to be true; the escalating sense of intimidation and terror suffered by Smith is manifest. Finally, the claimant was attacked with a claw hammer and suffered brain damage. Jeffrey was convicted of grievous bodily harm with intent and sentenced to 10 years' imprisonment. The facts pre-dated the HRA and Mr Smith brought issued proceedings against the Chief Constable in negligence.

Apart from a killing in custody by an inmate, it is hard to imagine a stronger set of facts than *Smith*. Counsel argued that the facts displayed a high degree of proximity, that there had been an assumption of responsibility by the police, that Article 2 would be engaged on the facts and that by analogy with *D* the public policy considerations in *Hill* were undermined. Furthermore, the decision in *Brooks* in which their Lordships had refused to endorse the full breadth of the *Hill* policy considerations was distinguishable on the facts. All to no avail.

The House of Lords by a 4:1 majority, Lord Bingham dissenting, held that there was no duty of care owed on the ground that in the absence of special circumstances, it was a core principle that the police owed no common law duty

---

[114] *Jones v Kaney* [2011] UKSC 13, [2011] 2 AC 398; *Arthur JS Hall v Simons* [2000] 3 All ER 673. For discussion of whether the level of immunity of superior court judges should be lowered, see J Murphy, 'Rethinking Tortious Immunity for Judicial Acts' (2013) *Legal Studies* 455–77.

[115] *Smith v Chief Constable of Sussex Police* (n 99).

of care to protect individual members of the public from harm caused by criminals; such a duty would encourage defensive policing and divert manpower and resources from their primary function of suppressing crime and apprehending criminals in the interests of the community as a whole.

On the impact of the ECHR, Lord Bingham considered that the existence of a Convention right does not call for 'instant manufacture of a common law right where none exists'.[116] However, he went on to say that one would normally expect to see conduct that violates fundamental rights reflected in the common law and that in some areas the common law has evolved in a direction signalled by the Convention.[117] Thus, 'there is a strong case for developing the common law action for negligence in the light of Convention rights'. Developing common law rights would also strengthen the protection of human rights at national level. The HRA is not entrenched and likely to be repealed; there is much to be said for the common law, honed over centuries and arguably less susceptible to changing political moods.

Lord Bingham as sole dissenting voice put forward a basis for liability in third party situations as follows: if a member of the public (A) furnishes a police officer (B) with apparently credible evidence that a third party, whose identity and whereabouts are known, presents a specific and imminent threat to his life or physical safety, B owes A a duty to take reasonable steps to assess such threat and, if appropriate, take reasonable steps to prevent it being executed.[118] He concluded that the principle he put forward as the liability principle was satisfied, that on the facts there had been an assumption of responsibility and that public policy pointed strongly in favour of a duty of care.

Lord Hope began his remarks regarding *Smith* by referring to 'the highly regrettable failure to react to a prolonged campaign by Jeffrey threatening the use of extreme criminal violence'. Some of Lord Hope's remarks can be read as sceptical of some complaints of domestic abuse, 'those that are genuine must be sorted from those which are not'.[119] Police work would, he said, be impeded if every report imported a duty of care—some will require more immediate action than others.[120] These concerns would be better addressed through breach, rather than the all or nothing duty of care. On the question of the HRA, Lord Hope considered that the common law should continue its separate development, 'on its own feet'. To the extent that there is any shortfall in how it addresses cases which meet the *Osman* threshold, a claim can now be brought under the HRA.

---

[116] Citing *Wainwright v Home Office* [2003] UKHL 53, [2004] 2 AC 406.

[117] Citing *D* and Pill LJ in the Court of Appeal in *Smith* [2008] HRLR 600 [53], *ibid* [45] (Rimer LJ).

[118] *Smith* (n 99) [44].

[119] This observation drew implicit criticism from Baroness Hale in *Michael* (n 79) [198].

[120] It has been argued by some commentators that there should be a shift from duty of care to breach as the locus for determining liability. See generally, D Fairgrieve, *State Liability in Tort: A Comparative Law Study* (Oxford, Oxford University Press, 2003).

Lord Phillips expressed discomfiture: the issues of policy raised by the case are not readily resolved by a court of law. His Lordship alluded to the Law Commission's work on *Administrative Redress: Public Bodies and the Citizen*[121] and suggested that the ambit of the common law would be better determined by Parliament. As we have seen,[122] the Law Commission's proposals were rejected by all parties. Lord Carswell also felt *Smith* is a hard case, and highlighted the lack of professionalism and dismissive attitude that the police service displayed towards Mr Smith. However, he concluded that the interests of the wider community are best served by the no duty rule. For Lord Brown, it was quite unnecessary to develop the common law to provide a cause of action parallel to sections 7 and 8 of the HRA, although he acknowledged that it might have been otherwise if the *Osman* line of authority had become established before the HRA came into force.

Many commentators have expressed concern that our senior judiciary engage in law- making exercises on the basis of 'policy' arguments that are largely a matter of impression and have no basis as a matter of empirical fact;[123] or if such arguments would be verifiable empirically, supporting evidence is not cited by either counsel or the judges. Reporting on its recent project to investigate *Administrative Redress: Public Bodies and the Citizen*, the Law Commission accepted that it needed to consider the extent to which any reform might divert resources originally allocated for public purposes to individuals as compensation payments. However, it proved impossible to create a dataset outlining the current position on compensation payments as obtaining even basic figures proved impossible. The lack of robust information made it impossible to rebut the concerns of consultees, particularly government. As a result, the Law Commission recommended, subject to the successful completion of any pilot study, that the costs of compensation to central government bodies are regularly collated and published.[124]

In *Michael v Chief Constable of South Wales Police*, the Supreme Court by a 5:2 majority (Baroness Hale and Lord Kerr dissenting) applied the full rigour of *Hill*, *Brooks*, and *Smith* and held that the police did not owe a duty of care to a woman murdered in her home by her former partner. Ms Michael dialled 999 after her ex-boyfriend turned up at her house in the middle of the night, found her with another man and hit her. He took the man from the house and said that when he came back he would hit her. It was necessary for the call to be re-routed by the call handler and at this point the call was downgraded from requiring immediate

---

[121] Law Commission, *Administrative Redress: Public Bodies and the Citizen A Consultation Paper* Consultation Paper No 187 (2008), for discussion see Chapter 5.
[122] Law Commission Report No 322, *Administrative Redress: Public Bodies and the Citizen* (2010), for discussion see Chapter 5, text accompanying n 3.
[123] See R Stevens, *Torts and Rights* (Oxford, Oxford University Press, 2007) especially 306–19; A Beever, *Rediscovering the Law of Negligence* (Oxford, Hart Publishing, 2007), see discussion in Chapter 2, text accompanying n 62.
[124] Law Commission Report (n 122) 6.14, 69.

response to 'G2', meaning that the officers should respond to the call within 60 minutes. Ms Michael called 999 again, she was heard to scream and the line went dead. When the police officers arrived at her home eight minutes later she was dead.

Lord Toulson, giving judgment for the majority, acknowledged the scale of the tragedy, Ms Michael lost her life in the most violent fashion and her children had lost their mother and breadwinner. Her parents had lost their daughter and had taken on the work and responsibility for bringing up their grandchildren. An investigation by the Independent Police Complaints Commission led to a lengthy report that contained serious criticisms of both police forces for individual and organisational failures. However, the Supreme Court held no duty of care was owed by the police to Ms Michael. Lord Toulson cast his reasoning firmly in the language of non-feasance. English law does not as a general rule, he said, impose liability on the defendant for injury or damage to the person or property of the claimant caused by the conduct of a third party. The fundamental reason, as explained by Lord Goff in *Smith v Littlewoods Organisation Ltd*,[125] is that the common law does not impose liability for a pure omission. There are exceptions, such as obligations that arise from a duty to control another, *Dorset Yacht* being the classic example, and responsibilities to safeguard another based upon the *Hedley Byrne* principle,[126] often described as an 'assumption of responsibility'.[127]

Lord Toulson stated that the refusal of the courts to recognise a duty of care in favour of victims or potential victims of crime except in cases where there has been a representation and reliance does not involve giving special treatment to the police, citing *Yuen Kun Yeu v Attorney General of Hong Kong*,[128] *Murphy v Brentwood*[129] and *Gorringe v Calderdale Metropolitan Borough Council*.[130] The question is not whether the police should have special immunity, but whether an exception should be made to the ordinary application of common law principles which would cover the facts of the case.

Counsel for the claimant argued that the court should adopt the liability principle put forward by Lord Bingham in *Smith*, as this would improve the performance of the police in dealing with cases of actual or threatened domestic violence. Lord Toulson was concerned that the court had no way of judging the consequences of such a change: 'it is speculative whether the addition of potential liability at common law would make a practical difference at an individual level to the conduct of police officers and support staff'.[131]

---

125 *Smith* (n 1).
126 *Hedley Byrne & Co Ltd v Heller & Partners Ltd* [1964] AC 465.
127 *Michael* (n 79) [99]–[100] (Lord Toulson).
128 [1987] 2 All ER 705.
129 [1991] 1 AC 398.
130 [2004] UKHL 15, [2004] 1 WLR 1057.
131 *Michael* (n 79) [121].

Counsel argued that the court should develop the common law to encompass the duties of the police under the ECHR, relying in particular on the observations of the Court of Appeal in *D v East Berkshire NHS Trust*. This argument was given short shrift, Lord Toulson saying he could see no basis for 'gold plating' the claimant's Convention rights by providing compensation on a different basis from the claim under the HRA. Lord Toulson was clear that civil actions are designed to compensate claimants for losses, Convention claims are intended to uphold minimum human rights standards and to vindicate those rights.[132] Like Lord Phillips in *Smith*, Lord Toulson considered that the question of introducing public compensation for victims of crime above that provided by the Criminal Injuries Compensation scheme should be a matter for Parliament. This view misses the point of litigation such as *Michael, Smith* and *Ashley v Chief Constable of Sussex Police*[133] where a principal concern is frequently an attempt to render accountable the body which is charged with the preservation of the Queen's peace.[134] The creation of a statutory cause of action under the HRA does not of itself provide a sufficient reason for the common law to duplicate or extend it.

The Supreme Court agreed that the claim under Article 2, in particular the question of what the call handler ought to have made of the 999 call was properly a matter for investigation at trial. This finding sits rather unhappily alongside the determination, without any further fact-finding, that there had been no assurance such as to give rise to an assumption of responsibility on the *Hedley Byrne* principle as amplified in *Spring v Guardian Assurance Plc*.[135]

Lord Kerr in the minority would have placed greater emphasis on 'proximity' as an indicator of a duty of care; he pointed out that the reasons given by the majority in *Smith* consist mostly of policy reasons and the question of whether it is fair, just and reasonable to recognise a duty of care is better considered against the background of whether a sufficiently proximate relationship exists.[136] He was highly critical of the idea that the 'incidence of liability should depend upon the happenstance of the telephonist uttering words that can be construed as conveying an unmistakeable undertaking that the police will prevent the feared attack is surely unacceptable'.[137] It is the common law as shaped by the courts that determines our rights and obligations; the effect of *Michael* is that a key emergency service can circumscribe its obligations to individual members of the public through carefully worded exchanges—this approach takes us to Kafkaesque levels of formalism. Furthermore, as Lord Toulson has pointed out, 'assumption of responsibility' is in

---

[132] *Michael* (n 79) [127].

[133] *Ashley v Chief Constable of Sussex Police* [2008] 1 AC 962 where an action in negligence was permitted to proceed notwithstanding that the defendant had admitted liability in battery.

[134] *Halsbury's Laws of England*, fifth edn (LexisNexis Butterworths, 2013), Vol 84, para 40, cited by Lord Toulson at [29].

[135] [1995] 2 AC 296.

[136] *Michael* (n 79) [156].

[137] *Michael* (n 79) [167].

many instances a misnomer because this is in fact a duty imposed by the court.[138] It should not be forgotten that section 11 HRA preserves other rights and claims that exist independently of the Act.

Implications of Non-Retrospectivity of the HRA and 'Omissions' Doctrine—the So-What Question?

Whether termed an immunity or non-recognition of a duty of care, English courts have circumscribed narrowly the potential for the police service to owe a duty of care to members of the public in their role in investigation/suppression of crime. Public authorities quite clearly may owe positive obligations to members of the public directly affected by their acts and omissions under the ECHR, including Article 2 and Article 3, and those who are victims of failures to discharge positive obligations may bring claims under section 7 HRA. However, the HRA is not retrospective.[139]

At the time of writing, it seems that barely a week goes by without fresh claims relating to historic sexual abuse of children emerging. According to the Jay Report into Child Sexual Exploitation in Rotherham, as a conservative estimate, approximately 1400 children were exploited over the Inquiry period from 1997–2013. The Report alludes to suggestions of a cover up following suppression of earlier reports. In some cases, there are allegations of a cover up by the police force. Clearly, where the perpetrators are still alive claims may be brought against them in the trespass torts, subject to satisfying the rules on limitation of actions. Since the important ruling in *A v Hoare*,[140] historic claims are likely to surface and be actionable for many years to come. In *A v Hoare*, the House of Lords departed from the restrictive approach to limitation as set out in *Stubbings v Webb*,[141] holding that the wording in section 2(1) of the Law Reform (Limitation of Actions) Act 1954, 'negligence, nuisance or breach of duty' was wide enough to include personal injury that resulted from battery. This means that the court has discretion to extend the limitation period under section 33 Limitation Act 1980. The action against a perpetrator of harm that reaches the level of severity protected by Article 3 is an important part of the remedial framework that is required by the positive obligation inherent in Article 3. However, it does not address the

---

[138] *Michael* (n 79) [174], to the same effect see Lord Griffiths in *Smith v Eric Bush* [1990] 1 AC 831.

[139] *R v Lambert* (n 82), *R v Kansal* [2001] EWCA Crim 1260, [2001] 3 WLR 751; *Porter v Magill* [2001] UKHL 67, [2002] 2 WLR 37 and in *JA Pye (Oxford) Ltd v Graham* [2002] UKHL 30, [2002] AC 467 it was conceded that the HRA did not apply as the original decision was made before 2 October 2000.

[140] [2008] 1 AC 844.

[141] [1993] AC 498.

requirement for accountability of agencies, such as the police who may be responsible for discharging operational obligations to protect those at risk of ill-treatment under Article 3, especially the most vulnerable, such as child victims of sexual abuse. However, as far as actions in negligence against the child protection agencies are concerned, currently the ruling in *D v East Berkshire Community NHS Trust* suggests that local authorities may be sued for the negligence of social workers (although a cautionary note must be repeated, as *D* was a case of commission not omission), but according to *Hill* and progeny no duty of care will be owed by the police unless it can be demonstrated that there was an assumption of responsibility by officers to victims.

The important question arises whether in cases with facts arising (often years) before 2 October 2000, claimants should be able to argue successfully that the obligation on the court as a public authority under section 6 not to act incompatibly with ECHR rights means that the court should recognise a duty of care in negligence on facts that would engage positive obligations under Articles 2 and 3. In this way victims of historic abuse would have a civil remedy against those public authorities that should arguably be held accountable. In order to make good the claim, it must be shown that the court is potentially acting in a way which is incompatible with a Convention right by refusing to shape the common law by reference to the ECHR.

In Chapter 3, we explored the interpretation of section 6(1) and (3) HRA to determine what it means to say that a court is acting incompatibly with a Convention right. Unlike the case of privacy which was the focus of speculation before the HRA came into force, we are not here considering whether English courts may recognise a new cause of action. Rather, the question we must consider is whether it can be argued that section 6(1) read with section 6(3) HRA means that the court is obliged to recognise a duty of care on the part of the police following failures to respond to credible allegations of child grooming and sexual abuse that pre-date the HRA. In other words, could the HRA force the courts to extend the boundaries of negligence on omissions type facts that engage the Article 3 right to be free from inhuman and degrading treatment?

As we have observed in Chapter 3, it is the nature of the substantive obligation that is critical here. In order to make good the argument we would need to show that the court's failure to develop the common law is incompatible with Article 3. The court itself is not going to subject anyone to inhuman and degrading treatment,[142] but the remedial framework obligation inherent within Article 3 requires that victims should be able to bring civil actions against public bodies that fail to protect them. In this way, a victim might be able to overcome the fact that the HRA is not retrospective. In Chapter 3 we saw that it has been argued that the court should, in observing its obligation under section 6 HRA, recognise

---

[142] See Lord Hoffmann's comments in *Jones v Saudi Arabia* [2006] UKHL 26 [44].

a duty of care in negligence.[143] In *A v United Kingdom*, the ECtHR stated that [the obligation in Article 1 taken together with Article 3]:

> requires states to take measures designed to ensure that individuals within the jurisdiction are not subjected to torture or inhuman or degrading treatment or punishment administered by private individuals. Children and other vulnerable individuals, in particular, are entitled to State protection, in the form of effective deterrence, against such breaches of personal integrity.[144]

Baroness Hale in *Campbell v MGN Ltd* discussed the injunction upon the courts in the HRA: 'The 1998 Act does not create any new cause of action between private persons. But if there is a relevant cause of action applicable, the court as a public authority must act compatibly with both parties' Convention rights'.[145] A little further on she said that the courts would not 'invent a new cause of action to cover types of activity which were not previously covered': see *Wainwright v Home Office* [2003] 3 WLR 1137. ... [Having described the treatment of Mrs Wainwright and her son as 'a gross invasion of their privacy', Baroness Hale continued]:

> That case indicates that our law cannot, even if it wanted to, develop a general tort of invasion of privacy. But where existing remedies are available, the court not only can but must balance the competing Convention rights of the parties.[146]

The tort of negligence is an established cause of action and one that is frequently invoked against professionals who fail to meet the standards expected of them. Where facts pre-date the HRA and the police conduct would ordinarily engage the ECHR obligations, there are strong arguments for saying that the courts should remedy the remedial gap. The observations made by the Court of Appeal in *D v East Berkshire Community NHS Trust* (effectively approved by the House of Lords in *JD* and *Kay v Lambeth Borough Council*) to the effect that the credibility of the 'old' policy arguments to deny a duty of care has been lost now that there is the possibility of an action under the HRA apply here *mutatis mutandis*.

We shall now consider further, first, the argument that non-retrospectivity of the HRA would be a complete bar to relying upon section 6 HRA to require the court to accommodate claims in relation to abuse that would engage Article 3 ECHR, by way of the development of the common law; and, second, the remedial obligations inherent within ECHR jurisprudence. These remedial obligations are important to support arguments that 'acting incompatibly' with an ECHR right extends to a failure to afford appropriate remedies for such rights violations.

[143] *Lawrence v Pembrokeshire County Council* [2007] EWCA Civ 446, [2007] 1 WLR 2991, see generally J Wright, 'A Damp Squib? The Impact of Section 6 HRA on the Common Law: Horizontal Effect and Beyond' [2014] *Public Law* 289.
[144] *A v United Kingdom* (1999) 27 EHRR 611 [22].
[145] *Campbell v MGN Ltd* [2004] 2 WLR 1232 [132].
[146] *Ibid* [133].

The Non-Retrospectivity Hurdle

It is clear that, save for the exception in section 22(4) HRA, that the Act does not have retrospective effect.[147] Clearly, no claims can be brought against a public authority directly under section 7 HRA. It is arguable that this does not prohibit the court from its role as a public authority from developing the common law to ensure that those who have been victims of rights violations, should in appropriate cases, be afforded a remedy through the tort of negligence. As we are aware, the police generally owe no duty of care to victims of crime in their investigations. The duty to investigate under Articles 2 and 3 HRA is separate from the operational obligation to protect and is a 'freestanding duty, detached from the substantive obligation'.[148] The House of Lords held that where there has been an historic failure to comply with a procedural obligation to investigate under Article 2, it doesn't follow that there can be a continuing obligation. However, the House held that if a decision is taken post October 2000, to investigate pre-HRA facts, then any such investigation must comply with the procedural obligations of Article 2.[149] The jurisprudence under the ECHR is much more nuanced than the decision in *Re McCaughey* would suggest and in the case of historic abuse, in which it is alleged that the police 'turned a blind eye' to such ill-treatment, it is arguable that the procedural obligation is a continuing one. The golden thread that runs through the ECHR is the need to make rights practical and effective and the jurisprudence under Article 3 continually stresses the need to protect the most vulnerable. This protection is rendered illusory when a responsible public authority can shrug off the obligation to investigate, especially when there is credible evidence of historic collusion in the suppression of facts that would have led to investigation and protection of other likely victims.

Remedial Obligations in the ECHR

It might be objected that there could be no obligation on the court to develop common law remedies where public authorities have violated ECHR rights for the simple reason that the Article 13 right to an effective remedy was not included in the rights scheduled to, and given further effect by, the HRA. Article 13 was deliberately omitted, the explanation being that section 8 provides the domestic analogy for Article 13.[150] English courts have taken the view that the remedial structure set

---

[147] See *R v Lambert* (n 82), *R v Kansal* (n 139), see Chapter 3, text accompanying n 243.

[148] Amos (n 82) 69, citing *Silih v Slovenia* (2009) 49 EHRR 996.

[149] *Re MeCaughey* [2011] UKSC 20, [2012] 1 AC 725.

[150] See generally G Marshall, 'Patriating Rights—With Reservations' in J Beatson, C Forsyth, and I Hare (eds), *Constitutional Reform in the United Kingdom: Practice and Principles* (Oxford, Hart Publishing, 1998) at 75.

out in sections 7–9 HRA is the vehicle through which the Article 13 obligation is satisfied. However, the exclusion of Article 13 from the HRA is not in itself a justification for refusing to recognise other remedies.

Under a number of ECHR rights, the state has an obligation to ensure appropriate remedies *inherent in the right itself.* Therefore, in considering the court's obligation under section 6 HRA, regard should be paid to the remedial elements of the substantive rights that are included in the HRA. These obligations, while not apparent on the face of the text, have been recognised in the Strasbourg jurisprudence regarding states' positive obligations under the ECHR. Thus, in connection with the positive obligation to take all appropriate steps to safeguard life for the purposes of Article 2, a state has

> a primary duty to put in place a legislative and administrative framework designed to provide effective deterrence against threats to the right to life … . if the infringement of the right to life is not intentional, the positive obligation to set up an 'effective judicial system' does not necessarily require criminal proceedings to be brought in every case and may be satisfied if civil, administrative or even disciplinary remedies were available.[151]

Indeed, in *Oneryildiz v Turkey*, a First Section Chamber held that it was unnecessary to consider the Article 13 complaint in view of its conclusion on the complaint under Article 2 that domestic legal proceedings (criminal and administrative) had not complied with procedural obligations under Article 2, nor proved capable of affording appropriate redress.[152] Similarly in *Mastromatteo v Italy*, where the applicant's son had been murdered by a prisoner on leave from prison, a Grand Chamber examined the complaint that no compensation had been paid by the state under the procedural head of Article 2.[153]

Recent case law shows an increasing awareness of the remedial dimension of positive obligations under the ECHR. In *R (B) v Director of Public Prosecutions*,[154] the claimant alleged that the discontinuation of the prosecution of his attacker was a breach of Article 3 ECHR. The claimant, who had a long history of psychotic illness, was attacked and part of his ear was bitten off. On the basis of a medical report that concluded that his mental condition might affect his perception and recollection of events, the CPS decided that they could not put the claimant before the jury as a reliable witness and that there was no realistic prospect of securing a conviction. The High Court held that by 'depriving the claimant of the opportunity of proceedings running their proper course and causing him to feel that he was beyond the protection of the law, the decision was a breach of Article 3 ECHR'.

---

[151] *Oneryildiz v Turkey* (2004) 41 EHRR 325 and see also *Calvelli and Ciglio v Italy* (n 20), where civil proceedings were found to satisfy the Article 2 procedural obligation after the applicants' child was stillborn due to the negligence of a doctor—the applicants had argued that the doctor should have been held criminally responsible.

[152] *Oneryildiz, ibid* [141].

[153] Application No 377703/97 decision of a Grand Chamber of the European Court of Human Rights dated 24 October 2002.

[154] [2009] EWHC 106, [2009] 1 WLR 2072.

The provision of appropriate remedies at domestic level is an important aspect of securing the right to respect for private life under Article 8 'even in the sphere of the relations of individuals between themselves': as we have seen, in *X and Y v The Netherlands*, due to a gap in Dutch law, no criminal charge could be brought against an alleged sex offender. On the facts, the availability of civil law remedies did not discharge the Article 8 obligation, but the Court made the following important observation:

> ... the Court, which on this point agrees in substance with the opinion of the Commission, observes that the choice of the means calculated to secure compliance with Article 8 in the sphere of the relations between themselves is in principle a matter that falls within the Contracting States' margin of appreciation. In this connection, there are different ways of ensuring 'respect for private life', and the nature of the State's obligation will depend on the particular aspect of private life that is at issue. Recourse to the criminal law is not necessarily the answer.[155]

Clearly, the remedial obligation under Article 8 falls upon the state; not only is the choice of remedy a matter for the state, the ECtHR does not prescribe which arm of the state should fulfil the positive obligation. In a common law system, where large areas of substantive law have been developed by the courts, it is surely not illegitimate to expect that that should continue. It is also within the spirit of the White Paper which aimed to 'bring rights home' that this should be so. Courts have been unreceptive to arguments that the common law should be expanded where a public authority defendant is before the court[156] and the claimant cannot proceed under section 7: for example, in cases where the claimant cannot sue because the relevant facts predate 2 October 2000. Thus, in *Wainwright v Home Office*, the House of Lords held that there was no common law tort of invasion of privacy where a mother and son had been searched in a manner that constituted a violation of the prison's internal rules and were not protected by statutory authority. Lord Hoffmann gave the leading speech, with all other law Lords expressing full agreement. He took the view that the coming into force of the HRA

> [weakened] the argument for saying that a general tort of invasion of privacy is needed to fill gaps in existing remedies. Sections 6 and 7 of the Act are in themselves substantial gap fillers; if it is indeed the case that a person's rights under Article 8 have been infringed by a public authority, he will have a statutory remedy.[157]

In *Wainwright*, Buxton LJ alone in the Court of Appeal referred to section 6(3) HRA and remarked that there are many difficulties with the argument that the recognition of the court as a public authority could be used to create private law

---

[155] *X and Y* (n 11).
[156] This is not to deny the impact that *Osman v UK* (n 15) has arguably had upon recent developments in negligence, but it is beyond the scope of the present discussion to consider that issue here.
[157] *Wainwright* (n 116) [34].

rights in broadly the same terms as ECHR rights:[158] the question could not be resolved without much fuller argument.

It is arguable that where a person has suffered a violation of a Convention right by a public authority and the HRA does not apply, then English courts in refusing to develop the common law may be acting incompatibly with a Convention right, particularly in relation to those rights that impose positive obligations to afford domestic remedies, and we are not talking here of the Article 13 right. It is extremely unusual for the Strasbourg Court to indicate that it is the *courts* that should provide a remedy so it would be difficult to argue that the courts have violated a right: it could on the other hand be argued that they have acted incompatibly with an ECHR right, in the event that they fail to afford relief by way of the common law, if a remedy is called for and does not otherwise exist.

In *McKenna v British Aluminium Ltd*, an application to strike out claims in nuisance and strict liability by 30 claimants, not all of whom had an interest in land, was dismissed. Neuberger J, refused to strike out the claims on the basis that

> there is a real possibility of the court concluding that in the light of the different land-scape, namely Article 8.1 now being effectively part of our law, it is necessary to extend or change the law, even though, in circumstances where the Convention was no part of English law [*Hunter v Canary Wharf*], the majority of the House of Lords thought otherwise.[159]

Having reviewed the various dicta referred to above regarding the nature of the court's obligation under section, Neuberger J was persuaded that he should 'proceed on the basis that the court should, as it were, develop the common law so as to be Convention-compliant'.[160] In *Dennis v MOD*, Buckley J held that to allow a human rights claim under the HRA, but deny a remedy in nuisance would be a solution to the difficult question of how to take account of the undoubted public interest in operating a training base for Harrier Jump Jets at RAF Wittering. However, he took the view that this would reflect adversely on the 'flexibility of the common law' which should be 'consistent with the developing jurisprudence on human rights'.[161] Thus, he concluded that nuisance was established, public interest being no defence to the claim, but that the flying should continue and that compensation should be awarded. He could have reached the same conclusion in practical terms through the HRA claim alone, but clearly felt that the extant common law cause of action should be rendered compatible with the ECHR.

The argument that section 6 requires English courts to act compatibly with ECHR rights in developing *parallel* remedies at common law was put squarely before the Court of Appeal in *Lawrence v Pembrokeshire County Council*,[162] where

---

[158] *Wainwright* (n 116) [92].
[159] [2002] Env LR 30 [52].
[160] *Ibid* [36].
[161] *Dennis v Ministry of Defence* [2003] EWHC 793 (QB) [47]–[48].
[162] *Lawrence* (n 143).

the principles established by the House of Lords in *JD* were revisited, but on post-HRA facts. The claimant sought damages for psychiatric injury after her children were placed on the Child Protection Register as being at risk of physical and/or emotional harm by the claimant and/or their father. Claims were brought in negligence and under section 7(1)(a) HRA.[163] This case was very different from claims under Articles 2 and 3 and in any case the inherent conflict of interest between parent and child would lead to denial of a duty of care at common law. The Court of Appeal was unanimous that the principles applied by the Court of Appeal and House of Lords and *JD* applied and that the inherent conflict of interest between parent and child where suspected abuse is investigated precludes a duty of care being owed to the parent, whether the professional involved is a doctor or a social worker. The only new feature of the instant case was that the facts had occurred post HRA but that made no material difference. Auld LJ alone gave a fully considered judgment and he examined the argument that the common law should be modified to accommodate the Article 8 claim at some length, citing two principal difficulties that stood in the way.

First, he was concerned that the recognition of a duty of a care might lead to defensiveness as any justification for intervention could not be established until the breach inquiry, necessarily after the event: essentially he was alluding to a fear that authorities might be too wary of intervening where children are at *risk* of abuse:

> the whole point of the East Berkshire solution is to forestall by robust and timely intervention, if at all possible, the greater possible harm when a local authority suspects parental abuse of children in the context of their family life together.[164]

This argument is fallacious given that where a public authority does interfere with family life, it will have to justify its actions under Article 8(2). The threat of legal proceedings and consequent forensic inquiry exists whichever cause of action is relied upon. This factor was key in Phillips LJ's reasoning in *D v East Berkshire* that it no longer made sense to deny a duty of care.

Second, it seems to have been argued by counsel, that if a duty of care were recognised, a public authority would be able to raise the issue of conflict of interest during the breach inquiry which should be modelled to reflect the criteria laid down under Article 8(2) ECHR. In other words, the criteria developed to justify an interference with family life under Article 8(2) would determine whether a duty of care had been breached. Auld LJ was concerned that this would distort negligence principles. Certainly, if tort principles were to be changed by mapping Article 8 ECHR directly this would be objectionable. Counsel clearly went too far. Auld LJ went on to say, 'As Richards LJ observed in the course of [counsel's]

---

[163] The claim under s 7 HRA was out of time and the question of whether it would be equitable to extend the period under s 7(5)(b) HRA had not been determined.

[164] *Lawrence* (n 143).

submissions, neither the Strasbourg jurisprudence nor responsiveness of the common law to the needs of the time requires the court to secure harmonisation of the two systems'.[165]

One of the objections that may be raised against the development of the common law to meet what may be termed 'remedial gaps' in the protection of ECHR rights in English law is the argument from coherence. We have previously identified the challenges for coherence generally in English law that are presented by the framework of remedies and the wide category of 'victims' under the ECHR/HRA on the one hand, and the much narrower class of claimants recognised under the Fatal Accidents Act 1976. It must be remarked that fairness and the promotion of human rights standards, especially where the most vulnerable are concerned, should not be sacrificed on the altar of certainty and formalism. Coherence did not deter the Court of Appeal from securing the rights of children in *D v East Berkshire Community NHS Trust*.[166] The issue of coherence is examined further in the following section.

Coherence

Academic commentators rightly point out that adapting the common law on an *ad hoc* basis may have serious repercussions for the wider coherence of private law.[167] It is frequently pointed out that if a positive obligation to act is imposed on the police by the common law, this would in principle apply as much to property damage as personal injury/life.[168] In *Michael*, Lord Toulson stated that

> it is hard to see why the [putative] duty should be confined to potential victims of a particular kind of breach of the peace. Would a duty of care be owed to a person who reported a credible threat to burn down his house? Would it be owed to accompany which reported a credible threat by animal rights extremists to its premises if not, why not.[169]

For Lord Kerr, the answer was almost too obvious to state: 'it is entirely right and principled that the law should accord a greater level of importance to the lives and physical well-being of individuals than it does to their property'.

One answer to the non-retrospectivity issue could be for English courts to recognise a common law action for breach of the HRA analogous to the developments

---

[165] *Lawrence* (n 143) [39].
[166] *D* (n 81).
[167] Hickman (n 70) 51; Nolan (n 1) 286–318.
[168] See *Van Colle v Chief Constable of Hertfordshire Police* (n 38) [100] (Lord Phillips) and Lord Bingham raises the same question following his discussion of his 'liability' principle at [55].
[169] *Michael* (n 79) [119] (Lord Toulson).

that have taken place in New Zealand following *Attorney General v Simpson (Beignets Case)* and *Carmichael* in those cases where there is a remedial require-ment within the substantive right. In each case, the courts responded to a gap in the law by recognising a constitutional claim based upon the relevant bill of rights. As we have seen, the tort of negligence is very different from the action under the HRA which is linked to the ECHR in terms of standard of care, causation, heads of damage, burden of proof. In order to really bring rights home, victims of ECHR violations should not need to take their cases to Strasbourg. The HRA provides in section 11 that a person's reliance on a Convention right does not restrict his right to make any claim or bring any proceedings which he could make or bring apart from sections 7 to 9. It can be argued that if English courts are to fulfil the obliga-tion in section 6 HRA not to act in a way which is incompatible with a Convention right, then in appropriate circumstances the courts should develop the common law. In such cases, the courts would not be developing new causes of action, but adapting the existing framework of remedies and imposing widely accepted pro-fessional standards on the police force.[170] The difficulty with this argument is the *dicta* that unequivocally state that the courts are not required to recognise new causes of action. These *dicta* however can be distinguished because none of the cases relate to the vertical effect of the HRA and in any event such observations have been made in cases where a new cause of action has effectively been intro-duced, although it could not be plausibly argued that this was required by the HRA.[171]

Furthermore, where the section 7 action is not available because facts pre-date 2 October 2000, the objection that the courts should not intrude where Parliament has legislated has no application. Adapting the common law would in fact further the aim of the HRA which was to bring rights home. There is no question either of 'gold-plating' the ECHR rights which was the objection raised by Lord Toulson in *Michael*.

One objection to such an approach is that even if the ECHR obligation (typi-cally under Articles 2 and 3) does import a remedial element that is separate from the Article 13 right to an effective remedy, there is nothing in the ECHR to say which branch of government should effect the grant of the remedy. Bagshaw is surely right to observe that the Convention does not contain a general obligation for every emanation of the state to do what it can to reduce the likelihood of viola-tions of the Convention.[172] However, the Strasbourg jurisprudence speaks about 'effective frameworks of laws' to deter violations of Articles 2 and 3. Given that typically in English law, it has fallen to the common law to redress violations of Articles 2 and 3 through negligence and the trespass torts, it is not unreasonable to

[170] *Michael* (n 79) (Lord Kerr).
[171] Wright (n 143).
[172] Bagshaw (n 1) 123.

suggest that within this limited field a cause of action based upon breach of ECHR rights should be recognised.

Furthermore, in *Z v United Kingdom*, in its discussion of Article 13, the ECtHR highlighted the principle of subsidiarity: it is for states to enforce Convention rights in 'whatever form they happen to be secured in the domestic legal order'.[173] However, there is a limit to the discretion afforded to the state and the scope of Article 13 will vary depending on the nature of any violation. The Court held that where an allegation is made that there has been a failure to protect someone from the acts of others, there should be a mechanism for establishing liability and in the case of breaches of Articles 2 and 3, compensation should in principle be available for non-pecuniary damage. However, while acknowledging that judicial remedies are effective in terms of access for the victim, enforceability and independence, the Court declined to make any finding as to whether on these facts only court proceedings could provide effective redress for the purposes of Article 13.

Nolan has argued trenchantly that liability in negligence and under the HRA should develop independently of each other;[174] in the other camp are those who argue equally forcefully for convergence.[175] As we have seen, our senior judiciary has generally taken the view that the case for convergence cannot be made since there is now a direct remedy under the HRA for the violation of Convention rights. Lord Bingham it seems could not quite make up his mind; in *JD* he considered that 'one would ordinarily be surprised if conduct which violated a fundamental right or freedom did not find a reflection in ... the common law'. On the other hand, in *Watkins*, His Lordship observed that 'Parliament intended infringements of the core human (and constitutional) rights protected by the Act to be remedied under it and not by development of parallel remedies'.[176]

Nolan's case for separate development rests on the 'implausibility' of two key assumptions that he suggests underpin the arguments by the convergence proponents: first, the functional equivalence assumption, that is that negligence and human rights law serve the same purposes; and, second, that the norms of human rights are more important or more fundamental than those of negligence law. On the first, there are many examples of claimants utilising the tort of negligence to seek accountability of public bodies. As we have discussed in Chapter 2, it is thorough tort rules that many states give effect to internationally agreed human rights standards. This does not mean that they serve the same purposes. Human rights need to be protected and this occurs through the complex framework of rights and remedies at national level, of which tort law is a part. Mrs Hill, the mother of the last victim of the Yorkshire Ripper, did not want compensation; she considered

---

[173] *Z v United Kingdom* (n 10) [108].

[174] Nolan (n 1).

[175] Fairgrieve (n 120) 80; J Steele, 'Damages in Tort and under the Human Rights Act: Remedial or Functional Separation?' [2008] *Cambridge Law Journal* 606.

[176] *Watkins v Secretary of State for the Home Department* [2006] UKHL 17, [2006] 2 AC 395 [26].

that she had been let down by the public service charged with protecting her daughter. Trevor Hicks was left bereft by the needless and negligent deaths of his daughters. Whether we like it or not, these were cases about human rights; formalistic reasoning can cast dust in our eyes and prevent us from seeing the real issues.

On the question of norm superiority, the HRA is an über statute. It is an ordinary statute in the sense that it is not entrenched and can be repealed, but it is not subject to the doctrine of implied repeal and all law is subject to it. It is fundamental and in the event of norm conflict it is superior, although the court may only issue a declaration of incompatibility and may not strike down legislation.

Nolan's strongest argument for separate development is the argument from coherence. He castigates commentators and counsel who fail to articulate clearly exactly how the substance of negligence should be shaped by the Convention. As we have seen there are extensive differences between ECHR norms and the tort of negligence and introducing damages for emotional distress to an extended list of victims would lead to a tort that is very different from the one we know, unbounded by both categories of damage and clear categories of claimant with relaxed rules on causation and clear and explicit elements of distributive justice. In an otherwise comprehensive analysis, Nolan omits the possibility for public services to plead a lack of resources as justifying a failure to act under Articles 2 and 3 ECHR; with the exception of property torts, a lack of resources will not generally impact on the standard of care. The standard of care in private nuisance is measured by the abilities and resources of the defendant.[177]

Arguments for coherence, based upon a supposed public/private divide in English law are disingenuous. The Diceyian heritage means that those who have sought and continue to seek to make public bodies accountable for harm suffered through their acts and omissions and the vindication of their rights have relied upon torts, especially negligence and the trespass torts.

Conclusion

English courts are urging counsel to rely on common law rights 'first' before resorting to HRA arguments. The life of the HRA currently hangs in the balance. In this chapter we have explored the great fault-line that runs through the common law and separates those who suffer as a result of misfeasance but refuses to recognise liability in favour of those who suffer harm through 'omissions'. The notion of an 'omission' should be highly contested in a world of professional people responsible for delivering services to those who rely upon them for safety and protection. This point was well made by Lord Kerr in *Michael*; it is to be hoped that others will follow his lead when fairness and justice demand it.

---

[177] *Goldman* (n 30).

7

Defamation and Freedom
of Expression

Introduction

It is often remarked by commentators that the 'constitutionalisation' of freedom
of expression through its inclusion in bills of rights has the effect of forcing courts
to engage with the philosophical justifications for free expression in order that
they can tease out the boundaries between expression and legitimate restrictions
upon it.[1] Regarding the scope of freedom of expression, Barendt has drawn upon
Dworkin and suggested that 'the particular understandings or conceptions of [a
freedom] are best elucidated by an examination of the moral and political reasons
justifying its protection and an appreciation of the significance in the constitution
as a whole'. Under the influence of the European Convention on Human Rights
(ECHR) we have seen such a trend in the English courts. Freedom of expression
has undergone a transformation in English law from being a Diceyian 'residual
liberty' to becoming a 'constitutional right' recognised by the common law and a
right under the Human Rights Act 1998 (HRA).

Even before the enactment of the HRA, the common law recognised the right to
freedom of expression in *Derbyshire County Council v Times Newspapers Ltd*[2] and
in *R v Secretary of State for the Home Department ex parte Simms*[3] and *Reynolds
v Times Newspapers Ltd*[4] the starting point for analysis was the right to freedom of
expression; in *Reynolds*, Lord Steyn described freedom of expression as a constitutional right. He noted that there are three ways in which freedom of expression is protected: as a liberty in the sense that a person can do whatever is not
prohibited by law; as a constitutional right; and finally, through Article 10 which is
given further effect through the HRA.

---

[1] See generally E Barendt, *Freedom of Speech* (Oxford, Clarendon Press, 2007); H Fenwick and
G Phillipson, *Media Freedom under the Human Rights Act* (Oxford, Oxford University Press, 2006).

[2] [1993] AC 534 (House of Lords), [1992] 1 QB 770 (Court of Appeal).

[3] [2000] 2 AC 115.

[4] [1999] 4 All ER 609.

Protection for freedom of expression has been further enhanced by the enactment of the Defamation Act 2013 which makes a number of substantive changes to the law of defamation, but which is not designed to codify the law into a single statute. Like all statutes, the Defamation Act 2013 must be interpreted in accordance with section 3 HRA; however, this seems unlikely to make any real practical difference to the substance of the law given that in this area of law English courts have consistently sought to interweave the values and principles of ECHR jurisprudence regardless of the particular enacting mechanism through which this is achieved; in other words, despite all the rhetoric and academic preoccupation with the concept of 'horizontality', English courts have merely applied the ECHR in defamation claims.

A number of 'justificatory' theories have been advanced in support of the notion that freedom of speech is deserving of constitutional protection.[5] First, this freedom is essential if there is to be dissemination of political information which fosters political debate, such that people can exercise their right to vote in accordance with the democratic ideals of an open society. Few would disagree that freedom of expression is at the core of a democratic society. When a people exercise its right to self-determination, it must be properly informed about the choices before it. The European Court of Human Rights (ECtHR) rarely refers to Article 3 of Protocol 1 ECHR (the obligation to hold elections under conditions that will ensure the free expression of the people) in its jurisprudence on Article 10, but the case law is replete with the need for Article 10 to underpin democracy. Articles 10, 11 and Article 3 of Protocol 1 can be seen as a triumvirate that guarantees effective political democracy. In a recent decision of the Grand Chamber, it was noted that:

> [e]expression of the opinion of the people [under Article 3] is inconceivable without the assistance of a plurality of political parties representing the currents of opinion flowing through a country's reputation. By reflecting those currents, not only within political institutions but also, thanks to the media, at all levels of life in society, they make an irreplaceable contribution to the political debate which is at the very core of the concept of a democratic society.[6]

Second, freedom of expression enables the full development of the human person and should be a fundamental aspect of individual autonomy, enabling the full development of the human personality. Then there is the argument propounded

---

[5] For discussion see G Marshall, 'Press Freedom and Free Speech Theory' [1992] *Public Law* 40; Barendt (n 1).

[6] *Yumak and Sadak* hudoc (2008) quoted by DJ Harris, M O'Boyle, EP Bates, CM Buckley, *Harris, O'Boyle & Warbrick: Law of the European Convention on Human Rights*, 2nd edn (Oxford, Oxford University Press, 2009) 713.

by John Stuart Mill, that freedom of speech will lead to the discovery of truth and enhance scientific and social progress.[7]

There is a fourth justification advanced by Schauer,[8] and discussed by Barendt, which is premised upon the idea that regulation of speech by government and other bodies (such as the Church) is a bad thing and to be distrusted. The natural inclination of governments is to suppress new ways of thinking that may be antithetical to the established social and political order. The treatment of Galileo by the Roman Catholic Church would be apposite here. Barendt has criticised Schauer's argument on the basis that it is parasitic on the first three positive arguments for free speech and cannot therefore avail the judge or the philosopher in explaining why speech is special and deserving of protection.

The positive theories all find support in the Strasbourg jurisprudence but it is clear that the highest degree of protection has been allotted to political speech. As the ECtHR has reiterated on many occasions, freedom of expression is at the very core of a democratic society; without freedom of expression there can be no free flow of political information which is so essential if the polity is to be informed on matters of public debate and free to form opinion in a meaningful way. Not only that, freedom of expression augments self-fulfilment and enables the development of the human person. The Court in *Handyside v UK* encapsulated both these ideals:

> The Court's supervisory functions oblige it to pay the utmost attention to the principles characterising a 'democratic society'. Freedom of expression constitutes one of the essential foundations of such a society, one of the basic conditions for its progress and for the development of every man.[9]

Examples can also be found in Strasbourg jurisprudence to support the Mill thesis in that they are cases expounding the necessity for protection from state interference where a speaker is contributing to a debate on matters of public interest.[10] Ultimately, where there is uncertainty over scientific matters, public discussion may lead to discovery of the truth.

The right to freedom of expression enshrined in Article 10 shares the structure of the other personal freedom Articles contained in Articles 8–11. Each sets out the substantive right in the first paragraph and then lists the grounds upon which states may restrict the right in the second paragraph. Included within the

---

[7] JS Mill, *On Liberty and Other Essays* (Oxford, Oxford University Press, 1991).
[8] F Schauer, 'Must Speech be Special?' (1983) 78 *North Western University Law Review* 1284, 1305.
[9] *Handyside v United Kingdom* (1979–80) 1 EHRR 737 (n 8) [48].
[10] *Hertel v Switzerland* (1998) EHRR 534.

scope of restrictions which may be permitted, assuming that they satisfy the other qualifying requirements of Article 10(2), are restrictions in the interests of 'the protection of the reputation or rights of others, for preventing the disclosure of information received in confidence'. Much of the jurisprudence that has developed under Article 10 concerns the compatibility of state defamation laws with the right to freedom of expression. It is fair to say that the Court continues to be vigilant to guard the free speech interest, particularly in the realm of political speech, but also where speech relates to matters considered to be in the public interest generally. In contrast, where an applicant has complained that artistic expression has been curtailed on the grounds of obscenity or blasphemy, a greater margin of appreciation has been allowed to states in assessing the need for restrictions upon the right.[11]

It will be noted that 'reputation' is not listed as a protected right under the ECHR. However, action to protect this interest is one of the justifications set out in Article 10(2) ECHR for limiting freedom of expression. Furthermore, the ECtHR has held that reputation is protected by Article 8 as one element of private life.[12] This does not mean that an attack on a person's reputation will necessarily have an effect on an individual's private life such that there is a violation of Article 8. Whether publication of information affecting reputation will impact on private life will depend upon the facts. In *re Guardian News and Media Ltd*,[13] members of the press challenged anonymity orders granted in favour of individuals who were challenging measures taken against them by the Treasury under the Terrorism (United Nations Measures) Order 2006. The Supreme Court found that publication of the claimant's name would seriously affect his private life because of the impact on his reputation in the community in which he lived. The anonymity orders were discharged by the Supreme Court on the basis that a full account of the proceedings was a matter of legitimate public concern, particularly given the inability of the claimant to challenge the substance of the allegations on which the Treasury order was made.

In contrast, Tugendhat J relying on *Pfeifer v Austria*,[14] has suggested that where a defamatory statement engages only a person's professional attributes, then it is

---

[11] See for example *Otto-Preminger-Institut v Austria* (1994) 19 EHRR 34, where the seizure of a film depicting 'God as a senile, incompetent idiot, Christ as a cretin and Mary as a wanton lady' (Innsbrück Regional Court) was justified on the grounds that it was necessary to uphold the right to freedom of religion of others, notwithstanding that the applicant was a private cinema club, no entry was permitted to those under 17 and advertising material for the film carried a warning of unsuitability for those of religious persuasion, and *Wingrove v United Kingdom* (1996) 24 EHRR 1 which concerned the refusal to grant a classification certificate for a video on the ground that it infringed the criminal law of blasphemy, pursued the legitimate aim of protecting the rights of others and was consonant with the aim of the protections afforded by Article 9 to religious freedom, a decision upheld on the basis that it pursued the legitimate aim of protecting the rights of others and was consonant with the aim of the protections afforded by Article 9 to religious freedom. The common offence of blasphemous libel was abolished by s 79 Criminal Justice and Immigration Act 2008—this was a crime of strict liability. The public order offences criminalising acts that stir up racial hatred have been amended by the Racial and Religious Hatred Act 2006.

[12] *Radio France v France* (2005) 40 EHRR 706 [31].

[13] [2010] UKSC 1, [2010] 2 AC 697.

[14] (2009) 48 EHRR 8 [35]; see also *Karako v Hungary* Application No 39311/05, 29 April 2009 [22]–[23].

less likely that their Article 8 rights will be engaged.[15] A close reading of *Pfeifer* does not support this assertion and indeed it is worth noting that one of the earliest cases on the meaning of 'private life' actually held that the personal relationships in business contexts could be protected by 'private life'.[16]

All forms of expression are included within the umbrella of Article 10, thus paintings, books, cartoons, films, video recordings, statements in radio interviews, information pamphlets, and the internet; and with any content, including incitement to hatred and pornography.[17] In principle, expression which is offensive or shocking to the population or sections of it is protected. Thus, in a frequently quoted *dictum*, the Court stated that: Article 10 is applicable not only to 'information' or 'ideas' that are favourably received or regarded as inoffensive or as a matter of indifference, but also to those that offend, shock or disturb the State or any sector of the population. Such are the demands of that pluralism, tolerance and broadmindedness without which there is no 'democratic society'.[18]

However, freedom of expression is not an unqualified good; it can be used to incite racial hatred, to promote violence, to intimidate and harass and to spread intimate details of another's private life and health which the public has no legitimate interest in knowing. Thus, Article 10(2) recognises uniquely among the Convention rights that the exercise of freedom of expression carries with it duties and responsibilities. The right to freedom of expression is not absolute and shares the structure of the other personal freedoms contained in Articles 8–11. Each of these Articles sets out the substantive right in the first paragraph and then the grounds upon which states may restrict the right in the second paragraph. Included within the list of restrictions that may be permitted under Article 10, assuming that they satisfy the other criteria of legality and proportionality are restrictions in the interests of 'the protection of the reputation or rights of others, for preventing the disclosure of information received in confidence'.

Any action for defamation represents an attempt to restrict freedom of expression in order to protect the reputation of another, which is a legitimate aim under Article 10(2), and permissible provided that two conditions are satisfied. First, the restriction must be 'prescribed by law' and, second, the restriction must be 'necessary in a democratic society'. In order to satisfy the first requirement, it must be shown that the law is adequately accessible:

the citizen must be able to have an indication that is adequate in the circumstances of the legal rules applicable to a given case ... a norm cannot be regarded as 'law' unless it is formulated with sufficient precision to enable the citizen to regulate his conduct.[19]

[15] *Thornton v Telegraph Media Group Ltd* [2010] EWHC 1414, [2011] 1 WLR 1985 [38].

[16] *Niemitz v Germany* (1998) 16 EHRR 97.

[17] B Rainey, E Wicks and C Ovey, *Jacobs, White & Ovey: The European Convention on Human Rights*, 6th edn (Oxford, Oxford University Press, 2014) 435.

[18] *Handyside* (n 9) [48].

[19] *Sunday Times v United Kingdom* (1979–80) 2 EHRR 245.

Whether, and the extent to which, interest in reputation should be protected by a legal system is fiercely contested. A leading academic commentator railed against what he perceived as the invidious nature of the tort of defamation because prior to the Defamation Act 2013 there was no need to show any loss whatsoever: a claimant could

> get damages (swingeing damages!) for a statement made to others without showing that the harm was untrue, without showing that the statement did him the slightest harm, and without showing that the defendant was in any way wrong to make it (much less that the defendant owed him any duty of any kind[20]

It has been suggested that the fact that there was no need to present evidence of damage was based upon the fact that reputation has been perceived as a form of property and defamation is an interference with that interest. This extrapolation flows from the fact that interference with property is actionable without proof of damage.[21]

It is clear that the HRA requires English courts to ensure that defamation laws are compatible with ECHR rights. *Reynolds* was decided before the HRA came into force, but it was common ground that the House of Lords should proceed upon the basis that the Act would soon be in force. The impact of the ECHR upon the tort of defamation has been profound. Even before the HRA came into force, English courts had recognised the need for common law principles in this field to march hand in hand with the ECHR. The importance of Article 10 in shaping the common law[22] was recognised by English courts long before the enactment of the HRA, and so it is not surprising that it was the fields of defamation and privacy that were scrutinised for compliance with the ECHR and felt the constraining influence of the Convention early on and have continued to do so.

In the ground breaking case of *Derbyshire County Council v Times Newspapers*,[23] in a decision that was affirmed by the House of Lords, the Court of Appeal held that a local authority could not bring an action in libel. The Court of Appeal took its decision in reliance on the ECHR, all members agreeing that where the common law was uncertain (as in this case)[24] or ambiguous then the Court should have regard to Article 10 to decide the case. However, Butler-Sloss LJ alone engaged with the detail of ECHR jurisprudence, citing extensively from the leading judgment of the ECtHR in *Lingens v Austria* which concerned the criminal prosecution for libel of a journalist. In *Lingens*, the ECtHR highlighted not just the right to freedom of expression, but the obligation upon the press *to ensure* that the public are properly informed on matters of public concern. Thus,

---

[20] A Weir, *A Casebook on Tort*, 8th edn (London, Sweet & Maxwell, 1996) 525.
[21] P Cane, *The Anatomy of Tort Law* (Oxford, Hart Publishing, 1997) 73.
[22] See discussion of *Attorney-General v Guardian Newspapers* [1990] 1 AC; Chapter 1 *Introduction*.
[23] *Derbyshire County Council* (n 2).
[24] There were two conflicting decisions on the point: *Manchester Corp v Williams* [1891] 1 QB 94 and *Bognor Regis UDC v Campion* [1972] 2 QB 169.

Whilst the press must not overstep the bounds set out, inter alia, for the 'protection of the reputation of others', it is nevertheless incumbent on it to impart information and ideas on political issues just as on those in other areas of public concern. Not only does the press have the task of imparting such information and ideas: the public also has the right to receive them.[25]

Furthermore, in *Sunday Times v United Kingdom (No 2)*, the Court stressed the 'vital' role that the press plays as 'public watchdog'.[26] English courts too have long stressed the important role that the press plays on behalf of the public and the right of the public to 'know' under Article 10 ECHR.[27]

In *Derbyshire County Council*, the House of Lords found no need to rely upon the ECHR, but agreed that no action by the public authority could lie. Lord Keith declared that it is of the highest public importance that a 'democratically elected governmental body, or indeed any governmental body, should be open to uninhibited public criticism'.

Any action for defamation constitutes an attempt to restrict freedom of expression in order to protect the reputation of another, which is a legitimate aim under Article 10(2), and capable of being justified provided that two conditions are satisfied. First, the restriction must be 'prescribed by law', and, second, the restriction must be 'necessary in a democratic society'. In terms of the first requirement, the ECtHR has developed a three-fold test.[28] First, the restriction must have some basis in national law, which may be statutory or unwritten common law,[29] and will extend to professional rules[30] and treaty obligations.[31] Second, the law must be accessible: 'The citizen must be able to have an indication that is adequate in the circumstances of the legal rules applicable to a given case'. Finally, the law should enable the citizen to foresee the consequences that will flow from his conduct. In *Sunday Times* the Court stated that 'a norm cannot be regarded as a "law" unless it is formulated with sufficient precision to enable the citizen to regulate his conduct'.[32]

In order to demonstrate that a restriction on freedom of expression is 'necessary in a democratic society', it must correspond to a pressing social need and must be proportionate to the legitimate aim pursued. Leading commentators on ECHR jurisprudence have alluded to the 'great complexity' of Article 10 cases and the

---

[25] *Lingens v Austria* (1986) 8 EHRR 407.

[26] (1992) 14 EHRR 229.

[27] *In Re Guardian News and Media* [2013] EWCA Crim 2367, [2014] 1 WLR 3326, (disclosure of identity of marines during trial by Court Martial); *In re S (A Child)* [2004] UKHL 47, [2005] 1 AC 593 (disclosure of identity of parent on trial for murder of sibling permitted in interests of open justice).

[28] See generally, *Jacobs, White & Ovey* (n 18) 310.

[29] *Sunday Times v UK* (n 19), which held that the common law rules on contempt of court satisfied the prescribed by law requirement.

[30] *Barthold v Germany* (1985) 7 EHRR 383 concerned the rules of the Veterinary Surgeons' Council.

[31] *Slivenko v Latvia* (2004) 39 EHRR 490.

[32] *Sunday Times v UK* (n 19) [26].

difficulty of drawing general inferences from a large and diverse body of law. Harris, O'Boyle and Warbrick remark that, 'the nature and form of expression, together with the position of persons exercising their right to free speech, will continue to be the lynchpin for assessing the standard of review and the choice of methodologies'.[33] However, this observation should not be taken to mean that the Court has adopted the US 'public figures' doctrine whereby a public official will succeed in a defamation action only upon demonstrating malice.[34] Rather, the ECtHR has developed a 'public status doctrine' according to which the limits of acceptable criticism will be substantially greater in the case of public figures. In assessing proportionality of domestic measures, the Court will examine:

> (i) the nature of the interference; (ii) the position of the applicant and the status of the victim of defamation or insult; (iii) the subject matter of the contested statements; and (iv) the reasons for the interference provided by the national authorities.[35]

For the English Press a major concern at the time the HRA bill was introduced was the likelihood that the HRA would herald an English privacy law. Government responded by introducing what became section 12 HRA, the intention being to recognise the particular importance of freedom of expression. The then Home Secretary stated that:

> [s]o far as we are able, in a manner consistent with the convention and its jurisprudence … [to say] to the courts that whenever there is a clash between Article 8 rights and Article 10 rights, they must pay particular attention to the Article 10 rights.[36]

Section 12 applies where the court is considering whether to grant any relief which, if granted, might affect the exercise of the Convention right to freedom of expression. Section 12(4) provides that

> (4) The court must have particular regard to the importance of the Convention right to freedom of expression and, where the proceedings relate to material which the respondent claims, or which appears to the court, to be journalistic, literary or artistic material (or to conduct connected with such material), to—(a) the extent to which—(i) the material has, or is about to, become available to the public; or (ii) it is, or would be, in the public interest for the material to be published; (b) any relevant privacy code.

However, in *Douglas v Hello! (No 1)*, Sedley LJ observed that it was not possible to have regard to Article 10 without having equally particular regard to Article 8 since Article 10 is qualified in favour of the reputation and rights of others and the protection of information received in confidence. In *Campbell v MGN Ltd*, several

---

[33] *Harris, O'Boyle & Warbrick* (n 6) 511.
[34] *New York Times v Sullivan* 376 US 254 (1964); see generally *Harris, O'Boyle & Warbrick* (n 6) 501.
[35] *Harris, O'Boyle & Warbrick* (n 6) 499.
[36] *Hansard*, HC Deb 2 July 1998, vol 315, col 543, Secretary of State for the Home Department, Mr Jack Straw, quoted by M Amos, *Human Rights Law* (Oxford, Hart Publishing, 2014) 561.

of their Lordships concurred with this interpretation.[37] It has been stated in an oft-cited dictum by Lord Steyn that in every case that concerns conflict between Articles 8 and 10 neither has as such precedence over the other and where the values are in conflict the courts will undertake an intense focus on the specific rights being claimed.[38] In their Report on the draft Defamation Bill, the Joint Committee on Human Rights implicitly criticised these observations and remarked that section 12 has not had the effect in practice that Parliament had envisaged. The Committee acknowledged that the ECtHR has included the right to reputation within Article 8 ECHR and held that Article 8 should be given equal weight with freedom of expression. The Committee noted that international publishers considered English defamation law to be a threat to their freedom of expression and stated that the Committee wished to see the expressed will of Parliament on freedom of expression, 'upheld to the full extent this is possible, in cases where the competing rights are finely balanced'.[39]

The text of the HRA itself has arguably had very little to do with what might be termed the modernisation of defamation. Barendt has described the changes wrought by the HRA as little more than 'cosmetic'.[40] As we have seen, the precise meaning of section 6 HRA and the extent of 'horizontal effect' has never been resolved by the courts, but the impact of ECHR values and principles on common law rules that engage the Article 10 right to freedom of expression has been pervasive. Lord Phillips seemed to downgrade the obligation of the courts in *Flood v Times Newspapers Ltd*[41] to an obligation 'to have regard to' the requirements of the Convention. However, the fact is that, beginning with *Derbyshire County Council*, there has arguably been a significant shift in English common law, informed by the ECHR, to buttress freedom of expression. Over the same period, the courts have developed the tort of misuse of private information, which is analysed in the following chapter. In practical terms, we see that areas of defamation law which were previously extremely complex have been simplified, and enhanced protection has been given to certain forms of expression; the contemporary challenge for courts and legislator is to delimit the scope of private life appropriately, views about which tend to become polarised around the concept of subject matter that is of legitimate 'public interest'.

In view of the fact that defamation really 'has seen the emergence of a common law human rights jurisdiction',[42] developments which have now been consolidated

---

[37] [2004] UKHL 22, [2004] 2 AC 457 [55] (Lord Hoffmann), [111] (Lord Hope), [138]–[141] (Baroness Hale).

[38] *Re S (A Child) (Identification: Restriction on Publication)* [2005] 1 AC 593 at [17]. See Chapter 8 *Privacy—From Misuse of Private Information to Autonomy.*

[39] Joint Committee on the Draft Defamation Bill Session 2010–12 Report, together with formal minutes, HL Paper 203 HC 930-1 published 19 October 2011 [18].

[40] Barendt (n 1) 39.

[41] [2012] UKSC 11, [2012] 2 AC 273 [46] (Lord Phillips).

[42] M Hunt, *Using Human Rights Law in English Courts* (Oxford, Hart Publishing, 1997) 205. See *ex parte Simms* (n 3); *In re Guardian News and Media* (n 27).

and further developed by the Defamation Act 2013, the repeal of the HRA would be of little significance. The Defamation Act is described as an Act to 'amend' the law of defamation; in fact, as the Joint Committee commented on the draft Bill, it is not always clear when the Act is making changes of substance to the law and when it is simply codifying the common law.[43] The Defamation Act was enacted in response to concerns regarding substantive and procedural elements of the law and, according to a Ministry of Justice press release, 'reverses the chilling effect on freedom of expression current libel law has allowed, and the prevention of legitimate debate we have seen in the past'.[44]

The following discussion will examine ECHR jurisprudence and then move on to critique recent developments in English law, in particular the changes wrought by the Defamation Act 2013, in the light of that analysis. For ease of exposition, each is treated separately with cross-referencing as appropriate.

The View from Strasbourg—Article 10 Jurisprudence

The ECtHR has carved out a special role for political comment and comment on matters of public interest so that a strict scrutiny approach is applied to any interference with such speech. Although Strasbourg has not gone so far as to require that states should introduce a *Sullivan* type defence[45] to political defamations, it is clear that political speech serves a critical role in the pursuit of a democratic society governed by the rule of law. It is entirely consonant with the spirit of the Convention that this should be so. It is only through an 'effective political democracy' that Convention rights and freedoms will be upheld.

The case that set the tone for Strasbourg jurisprudence and which continues to be much-cited by English courts is *Lingens v Austria*.[46] Immediately after the Austrian general elections in 1975, Lingens had published two articles that were critical of the behaviour of Bruno Kreisky, the retiring Chancellor and President of the Austrian Socialist Party. In a television interview Kreisky had described the Jewish Documentation Centre (run by the renowned 'Nazi hunter' Simon Wiesenthal) as a political mafia and its activities as employing 'mafia methods'. These accusations had been prompted by Wiesenthal's accusation that the President of the Austrian Liberal Party had served in the SS during the Second World War. Against this background, Lingens wrote an article criticising Kreisky's attitude to the Liberal Party

---

[43] Joint Committee (n 39) [21].

[44] Ministry of Justice, *Defamation Laws Take Effect* (31 December 2013).

[45] In *Sullivan v New York Times* [1964] 376 US 254, the US Supreme Court decided that no action for defamation would lie in respect of political speech, unless the plaintiff could prove actual malice on the part of the disseminator. For a comparative account see I Loveland, *Political Libels* (Oxford, Hart Publishing, 2000).

[46] *Lingens* (n 25).

President and said that had Kreisky's comments about Wiesenthal 'been made by someone else this would probably have been described as the basest opportunism'. The second article in which he described Kreisky's behaviour as 'immoral; undignified' was a development of the first.

Lingens was convicted of the crime of defamation, but in view of his good faith no damages were awarded. Lingens petitioned Strasbourg that the conviction was a violation of his Article 10 rights. According to the Austrian Criminal Code, proof of truth was a defence to the action. There was no dispute between the parties that the conviction was 'prescribed by law' and that it was aimed at protecting 'the reputation or rights of others', thus fulfilling two of the conditions laid down by Article 10(2). Disagreement centred on whether the conviction was 'necessary in a democratic society'. The Court quoted from its judgment in *Handyside* and continued:

> These principles are of particular importance so far as the press is concerned ... it is incumbent on it to impart information and ideas on political issues just as on those in other areas of public interest. Not only does the press have the task of imparting such information and ideas: the public also has the right to receive them ... freedom of political debate is at the very core of a democratic society which prevails throughout the Convention ... Article 10(2) enables the reputation of all individuals to be protected, and this protection extends to politicians too, even when they are not acting in their private capacity; but in such cases the requirements of such protection have to be weighed in relation to the interests of open discussion of political issues.[47]

In an important passage, that was conclusive for the applicant, the Court held that:

> a careful distinction needs to be made between facts and value-judgments. The existence of facts can be demonstrated whereas the truth of value-judgements is not susceptible of proof ... As regards value-judgements [the requirement to prove truth] is impossible of fulfilment and it infringes freedom of opinion itself, which is a fundamental part of the right secured by Article 10 ....[48]

The distinction between facts and value-judgements is crucial and pervasive in ECHR jurisprudence. However, the indications as to how statements are to be classified are few; there is a general trend towards classifying a statement as a value-judgement if it is a statement of opinion. In *De Haes and Gijsels v Belgium*,[49] the applicants, an editor and a journalist, had published five articles in which they accused three judges and the Advocate-General of bias, after they awarded custody to a father who was suspected of having committed child abuse. The applicants based their allegation of bias on the fact that the judges were part of the same social circle as the child's father and shared the same right-wing political views. The journalists were convicted of the crime of defamation. Strasbourg found

---

[47] *Lingens* (n 25) [41]–[42].
[48] *Lingens* (n 25) [46].
[49] (1997) 25 EHRR 1.

a violation of Article 10. It was held that the views regarding bias amounted to opinion, which was not susceptible of proof, but held that such an opinion may be impugned in the absence of *any* factual basis. Proof of bias based upon the ideological leanings of the judges could not be established but there were facts in the articles regarding the father's behaviour to his children that were capable of justifying the decisions taken by the judges. Thus, a lack of factual basis may lead to the view that an opinion is excessive, but will not per se justify a restriction on such expression. In *Lavric v Romania*,[50] the Court emphasised that a 'person's status as "politician or other public figure" does not remove the need for a sufficient factual basis for statements which damage reputation, even where such statements are considered to be value-judgements'.

De Haes and Gijsels has been described as confirming the extension of Article 10's public-private defamation divide that was introduced in *Thorgeirson v Iceland*, from matters affecting just politicians to all information raising a legitimate matter of public interest.[51] The applicant had been convicted of defamation after he published two articles in which he made allegations of brutality against the police force. The Court refused to accept the Government's argument that the wide limits of acceptable criticism did not apply to other matters of 'public interest'. The Court held that it was unreasonable, if not impossible, for the applicant to establish the truth of his statements in view of the fact that he was reporting others' statements regarding police brutality. The motive of the applicant was to encourage a public investigation and having regard to that fact the Court did not find the language excessive.

The margin of appreciation allowed to states in deciding whether there is a pressing social need to restrict freedom of expression is generally greater in the fields of artistic and commercial speech. However, the margin will be reduced where the restriction affects freedom to contribute to debate on matters of public interest. In *Hertel v Switzerland*,[52] the applicant had been banned under unfair competition legislation from publishing results of research that allegedly showed hazardous effects on food heated in microwave ovens. A violation of Article 10 was found.

In *Bladet Tromso and Stensaas v Norway*, the Norwegian courts had found that statements of fact published by the applicants were defamatory and not proved to be true. The statements were taken from a report about seal hunting by an inspector. The newspaper had not verified the information through independent research. The Court said that account must be taken of the overall background and public controversy surrounding seal hunting when the statements were made. The reporting was fair and balanced, since different views were presented. The chilling effect of defamation laws was highlighted: The most careful scrutiny on the part of

---

[50] Unreported,
[51] Loveland (n 45) 154.
[52] (1998) 28 EHRR 534. See also *Barthold v FRG* (1985) 7 EHRR 583 [54] and [58].

the Court is called for when, as in the present case, the measures taken or sanctions imposed by the national authority are capable of discouraging the press in debates over matters of public interest.[53]

The Court held that whether the newspaper could be dispensed from the ordinary obligation of verifying the information depended on two factors: the 'nature and degree of the defamation … and the extent to which the newspaper could reasonably regard the report as reliable'.[54] As to the first, a number of allegations were not serious, those that were could be understood as being exaggerated. More importantly, none of those committing the 'reprehensible acts' were named, the ship was named. The report had been drawn up by an inspector appointed by the Ministry of Fisheries and the press should normally be entitled to rely on the contents without undertaking independent research.[55]

The Court will inquire into the good faith of the speaker in determining the necessity for a restriction on freedom of expression as measured by two factors: the motive of the speaker and whether the speaker exercised due care in disseminating the information. In *Bladet Tromso and Stensaas*, the aim of the publication was to stimulate debate and it was reasonable for the newspaper to rely on the inspector's report. In *Lingens*, the Court noted that the good faith of the speaker was undisputed by the Austrian courts, his motive was to voice criticism of politicians on political questions and politicians were expected to show a greater degree of tolerance of defamation than other individuals. Similarly, in *Thorgeirson* the Court was not convinced that the aim of the articles was to besmirch the reputation of the police force; rather, the journalist's aim was to urge the Minister of Justice to establish an official investigation into the allegations. On the other hand, the journalist applicant in *Prager and Oberschlick v Austria*, who defamed a judge, was unable to demonstrate good faith because the research he had undertaken was not adequate to substantiate the seriousness of the allegations made.[56] He had not attended a single criminal trial before the judge and he had not given the judge any opportunity to comment on the accusations levelled against him.

The Court has emphasised on a number of occasions that the context against which defamatory words are spoken is important, even though that context may not be fully articulated by the applicant.[57]

To summarise, the following points emerge:

(i)   motive and due diligence of the speaker are relevant considerations as they will speak to the issue of good faith; the court will examine whether the

---

[53] (1999) 29 EHRR 125 [64].

[54] *Ibid* [66].

[55] *Ibid* [68].

[56] (1996) 21 EHRR 1.

[57] *Lingens* (n 25) [40]. Cf *Telnikoff v Matusevich* [1992] AC 243, see discussion text accompanying n 127.

speaker did a reasonable amount of research and whether allegations are presented in a balanced manner;[58]

(ii)   the court will examine the nature and purpose of the speech; and

(iii)   the context of publication is important.

The Response of English Courts to the Demands of Article 10

Serious Harm

The response by English courts to the demands of the HRA and the ECHR was immediate and profound. English law has now moved away from the position that a claimant could bring an action in defamation and recover damages without showing that any harm at all had been suffered. English courts responded to the need to establish proportionality for interference with the right to freedom of expression by imposing a requirement that the claimant establish seriousness of harm in order to bring a successful claim in defamation. In an important decision, the Court of Appeal in *Jameel v Dow Jones & Co Inc*, held that the bringing of a defamation action

> in circumstances where [the claimant] reputation has suffered no or minimal actual damage … may constitute an interference with freedom of expression that is not necessary for the protection of the claimant's reputation. In such circumstances the appropriate remedy for the defendant may well be to challenge the claimant's resort to English jurisdiction or to seek to strike out the action as an abuse of process.[59]

Furthermore, Lord Phillips attributed the increased willingness of the courts to consider that a libel action may be an abuse of process where there has been no unlawful damage to reputation to the introduction of the new Civil Procedure Rules, as well as the coming into force of the HRA. Thus, he said that:

> There have been two recent developments which have rendered the court more ready to entertain a submission that pursuit of a libel action is an abuse of process. The first is the introduction of the new CPR. Pursuit of the overriding objective requires an approach by the court to litigation that is both more flexible and more proactive. The second is the coming into effect of the Human Rights Act 1998. Section 6 requires the court, as a public authority, to administer the law in a manner which is compatible with Convention rights, in so far as it is possible to do so. Keeping a proper balance between the Article 10 right of freedom of expression and the protection of individual reputation must, so it seems to us, require the court to bring to a stop as an abuse of process defamation

---

[58]   See *Jacobs, White & Ovey* (n 17) 447.

[59]   [2005] EWCA Civ 75, [2005] QB 946.

proceedings that are not serving the legitimate purpose of protecting the claimant's reputation, which includes compensating the claimant only if that reputation has been unlawfully damaged.[60]

This principle was applied by the judges hearing most of the defamation cases: in *Kaschke v Osler*[61] and *Brady v Norman*,[62] Eady J struck out the claims and in *Lonzim Plc v Sprague*, Tugendhat remarked that: 'the fact of being sued at all is a serious interference with freedom of expression ...'.[63]

In *Jameel*, it was accepted by the claimant that there had been only minimal publication of an internet news article within the jurisdiction. While the Court struck out the defamation claim as an abuse of process, it upheld the claimant's contention that it is an irrebuttable presumption of English law that the publication of a defamatory article causes damage to the person defamed. Citing *Handyside v United Kingdom, Sunday Times v United Kingdom* and *Prager and Oberschlick v Austria*, the defendant had argued that the presumption of damage is incompatible with Article 10 ECHR. Giving judgment for the Court of Appeal, Lord Phillips MR remarked upon the longevity of the rule and the fact that neither the Faulks Committee,[64] nor Sir Brian Neill's Report[65] had recommended abolition of the rule. Accordingly, convincing evidence of incompatibility with Article 10 would be required to justify its elimination and by inference this was not apparent.[66]

In a rejection of the orthodox position on the presumption of damage, Tugendhat J held in *Thornton v Telegraph Media Group Ltd*, that a threshold of seriousness is required in accordance with the true interpretation of *Sim v Stretch* and by the HRA need to have regard for Article 10 ECHR and the principle of proportionality. Lord Atkin's speech in *Sim v Stretch* has for many years been regarded as the classic test for determining what is defamatory in the question: 'Would the words tend to lower the plaintiff in the estimation of right-thinking members of society generally?'[67] However, Tugendhat J drew upon a further observation to justify requiring a threshold of seriousness. Lord Atkin had also said

> that juries should be free to award damages for injuries to reputation is one of the safeguards of liberty. But the protection is undermined when exhibitions of bad manners or discourtesy are placed on the same level as attacks on character and are treated as actionable wrongs.[68]

---

[60] *Ibid* [40].
[61] [2010] EWHC 1075.
[62] [2010] EWHC 1215.
[63] [2009] EWHC 2838 [22].
[64] Report of the Committee on Defamation (1975) (Cmnd 5909).
[65] Supreme Court Committee Report on Practice and Procedure in Defamation, July 1991.
[66] *Jameel* (n 59) [37].
[67] *Sim v Stretch* [1936] 2 All ER 1237 [40].
[68] Lord Atkin, *ibid* at 1242.

Tugendhat J's decision to adopt a new definition of defamation was described as 'bold' and justified by only the slightest authority: bad manners and discourtesy need not involve any reputational harm and the issue in *Jameel* was one of civil procedure rather than related to the substantive law of defamation.[69] Nevertheless, his approach to proportionality has been followed and built upon by section 1 Defamation Act 2013 which has introduced a threshold test of 'serious harm' for claims that arise on or after 1 January 2014.

Section 1(1) of the Defamation Act 2013 provides that: 'A statement is not defamatory unless its publication has caused or is likely to cause serious harm to the claimant'. The draft Bill would have replaced the common law tests with a requirement for the claimant to prove 'substantial harm' to their reputation. The Parliamentary Joint Committee on the draft Defamation Bill criticised the lack of clarity in the proposed test: the Secretary of State for Justice thought the new test raised the bar, while the Minister of State thought it reflected existing law. Overall, the Joint Committee was concerned that free speech is being threatened, or 'chilled', to an unacceptable degree and expressed concern that the requirement to show that a real and substantial tort had been committed was interpreted as met whenever more than minimal harm was caused to a person's reputation.[70] Furthermore, the Joint Committee in its Report expressed regret that section 12 HRA had not in practice had the effect that Parliament had envisaged and wished to see the expressed will of Parliament on freedom of expression upheld.[71]

The Committee was guided in its work by four principles:

(i)   some aspects of current law and procedure should provide greater protection to freedom of expression. This is a key foundation of any free society. Reputation is established over years and the law needs to provide due protection against unwarranted serious damage;

(ii)   costs in defamation actions should be reduced to limit the chilling effect of such actions;

(iii) defamation law should be easier for the ordinary citizen to understand and afford; and

(iv)   defamation law should adapt to 'modern commercial culture' which can be instant, global, anonymous, very damaging and potentially out of the courts' reach.[72]

The Joint Committee proposed that the test of 'substantial harm' should be replaced by the stricter threshold of 'serious and substantial harm'. The ECtHR has also held that in order for the right to reputation protected by Article 8 to come into play, an attack on a person's reputation must attain a certain level of seriousness.[73]

---

[69] M Lunney and K Oliphant, *Tort Law Text and Materials*, 5th edn (Oxford, Oxford University Press, 2013) 699.

[70] Joint Committee (n 39) 26–27.

[71] Joint Committee (n 39).

[72] Joint Committee (n 39) [16].

[73] *Axel Springer AG v Germany* (2012) 55 EHRR 183 [83].

In *Ames v The Spamhaus Project Ltd*,[74] Warby J considered the test set out in section 1 and the connection between 'serious harm' and the *Jameel* test which requires a tort to be 'substantial'. In his view, section 1 does not abolish the *Jameel* test, it introduces an additional requirement. The use of the word 'serious' obviously distinguishes the statutory test from the common law as stated in *Thornton*. The threshold identified in *Thornton* was that the statement should 'substantially' affect attitudes in an adverse way, or has a tendency to do so. The *Jameel* test also requires a tort to be 'substantial'. These matters, together with issues about meaning, should be considered by way of preliminary issue.

The first judgment regarding 'serious harm' was given by Bean J in *Cooke v MGN Ltd.*,[75] who held that the relevant date for the purposes of deciding whether the threshold of serious harm is met is the date of issue of proceedings. He held that it is not sufficient for the purpose of 'serious harm' to demonstrate serious distress or injury. However, he held that evidence will not be required in every case to satisfy the serious harm test, as some statements such as accusing a person of being a paedophile or a terrorist are obviously likely to cause serious harm to reputation. The nature and effect of any subsequent apology is a factor to be taken into account in considering whether serious harm is likely.

Bean J's finding regarding distress or injury is open to challenge on a number of grounds. Reputation is now recognised both under the ECHR and the HRA as an aspect of private life and protected by Article 8 ECHR. The award of damages (just satisfaction) in respect of distress is well-established in ECHR jurisprudence and under the HRA.[76] It seems likely therefore that claimants will argue in accordance with section 3 HRA that section 1 Defamation Act 2013 should be 'read and given effect in a way which is compatible' with Article 8. The fact that section 1(2) requires a corporation to prove actual or likely 'serious financial loss' also implies that lesser forms of harm are within the purview of section 1(1) for the non-corporate claimant'.

Subsequently in *Lachaux v Independent Print Ltd*,[77] Warby J held that the Court could look at what happened after publication and that serious harm could be proved by inference. He found that serious harm had occurred having regard to the seriousness of the topic (alleged domestic abuse) and defamatory meanings, the reputable nature of the publishers and the inherent likelihood that the publications had reached a significant number of people who knew the claimant. This last point is important as the circulation of the relevant article was small; but its impact in terms of reach to a readership who knew the claimant was significant. The relevant date for making the assessment is the date when the issue is determined

---

[74] [2015] EWHC 127.

[75] [2014] EWHC 2831, [2015] 1 WLR 895.

[76] See for example *Campbell v MGN Ltd*; [2004] UKHL 22; [2004] 2 AC 457; *Rabone v Pennine Care NHS Foundation Trust* [2012] UKSC 2, [2012] 2 AC 72.

[77] [2015] EWHC 2242, [2016] QB 402.

by the judge, not the date of issue of proceedings. This means that an action in defamation may be inchoate at the time the statement is made and a statement may move from being defamatory to non-defamatory and vice-versa.

Serious Harm and Corporations

Consultation on the Defamation Bill revealed concerns regarding the inequality of arms that may arise where a trading company sues an individual or a non-governmental organisation to stifle criticism of the company's behaviour and activities through the threat of costly and lengthy litigation.[78] A well-known example of such inequality of arms is the case of *McDonald's Corporation v Steel*[79] (often known as the '*McLibel* case', brought by the 'McLibel Two') where the fast food chain brought an action in defamation against the applicants based upon criticisms of McDonalds contained in a leaflet that was part of a Greenpeace campaign. The litigation lasted many years, but the defendants were litigants in person because legal aid is not available for defamation. The Consultation suggested that the introduction of the requirement to show substantial harm should help to adjust the balance and section 1(2) of the Defamation Act provides that for the purposes of section 1, 'harm to the reputation of a body that trades for profit is not "serious harm" unless it has caused or is likely to cause the body serious financial loss'.

At first blush, the ECHR does not impose such a restriction on the ability of a trading corporation to defend its reputation. In *Steel & Morris v United Kingdom* (the Strasbourg proceedings following *McDonald's Corporation v Steel*, above),[80] the applicants argued that the reasons under English law for permitting wider criticism of government bodies applied equally to criticism of large multinationals, particularly given that their vast economic power was coupled with a lack of accountability. In this regard, the applicants prayed in aid the principle in English law that local authorities, government-owned corporations and political parties could not sue in defamation. However, the ECtHR was not persuaded:

> The Court further does not consider that the fact that the plaintiff in the present case was a large multinational company should in principle deprive it of a right to defend itself against defamatory allegations or entail that the applicants should not have been required to prove the truth of the statements made. It is true that large public companies inevitably and knowingly lay themselves open to close scrutiny of their acts and, as in the case of the businessmen and women who manage them, the limits of acceptable criticism are wider in the case of such companies (see *Fayed v. the United Kingdom*, judgment of 21 September 1994, Series A no. 294-B, p. 53, § 75). However, in addition to the public interest in open debate about business practices, there is a competing interest in protecting

---

[78] Draft Defamation Bill Consultation [138].
[79] Unreported 31 March 1999, Civil Transcript No 720.
[80] (2005) 41 EHRR 403.

the commercial success and viability of companies, for the benefit of shareholders and employees, but also for the wider economic good. The State therefore enjoys a margin of appreciation as to the means it provides under domestic law to enable a company to challenge the truth, and limit the damage, of allegations which risk harming its reputation (see *Markt intern Verlag GmbH and Klaus Beermann v. Germany*, judgment of 20 November 1989, Series A no. 165, pp. 19–21, §§ 33-38).[81]

A bare majority of the House of Lords in *Jameel v Wall Street Europe Sprl*[82] rejected the argument that the common law presumption of damage in a libel action brought by a trading corporation is inconsistent with the HRA. Baroness Hale and Lord Hoffmann in a minority accepted that trading corporations should be required to prove special damage in order to succeed in a libel claim. In a trenchant call to protect democratic values, Baroness Hale reminded us of the power of trade:

> these days the dividing line between governmental and non-governmental organisations is increasingly difficult to draw. The power wielded by the major multi-national corporations is enormous and growing. The freedom to criticise them may be at least as important in a democratic society as the freedom to criticise the government.[83]

The speeches of Lord Bingham (in the majority) and Baroness Hale (in the minority) may usefully be contrasted. Citing *Steel & Morris*, Lord Bingham observed that the state enjoys a generous margin of appreciation as to the way in which a company may challenge the truth of, and limit the damage from, allegations which risk harm to reputation. This is indeed what the ECtHR stated in *Steel & Morris* but the fallacy of Lord Bingham's reasoning is revealed by Baroness Hale when she points out that the reason the damages against the defendants in the *McLibel* case were found to be disproportionate was precisely because English law did not require the company to establish any financial loss. Of course, even if the company were to be prevented from suing in the absence of special damage, individual directors could still take proceedings to vindicate their individual, personal reputations. This influenced Lord Bingham's conclusion that any increase in the chilling effect was likely to be minimal. However, how many members of the public would be able to identify the directors of most major corporations; probably very few. Equally, how many members of the public will have access to the resources necessary to defend such actions (the 'McLibel Two' were litigants in person).

English law has now taken a stronger position than the ECtHR in that a corporation that trades for profit can only sue in defamation if it has suffered or is likely to suffer serious financial loss. In practical terms, it may be very difficult for a corporation to establish financial loss. In *Collins Stewart v The Financial Times Ltd*, Tugendhat J struck out a claim for special damages based on a fall in share value following the publication of the article in question. He held that movement

---

[81] *Steel & Morris v United Kingdom* ibid [94].
[82] [2006] UKHL 44, [2007] 1 AC 359.
[83] *Ibid* [158].

in share price was too uncertain to be acceptable as a legal basis for assessing damages: 'the reasons why a share is traded at a particular price … are unknown, or at best matters of conjecture'.[84] In any event, as the Joint Committee's Report observed, a fall in share price is a loss suffered by shareholders rather than the corporation itself.[85]

Defences

It is through the defences to defamation that English courts have traditionally struck a balance between the conflicting interests of freedom of expression and reputation. The extension of qualified privilege in the shape of the so-called *Reynolds* defence was an early response by the English courts to the perceived demands of the ECHR and the HRA. This litigation took place before the HRA had come into force, but 'it was common ground that the House should act on the reality that the Human Rights Act [would] soon be in force'.[86] Returning to *Reynolds* is instructive, in view of more recent English case law under Article 10, because the clear view of a majority of the House of Lords was that freedom of expression is the starting point for analysis. Most trenchant was Lord Steyn, who remarked that

> The starting point is now the right of freedom of expression, a right based on a constitutional or higher legal order foundation. Exceptions to freedom of expression must be justified as being necessary in a democratic society. In other words, freedom of expression is the rule and regulation of speech is the exception requiring justification.[87]

Exceptionally, Lord Hobhouse denied that the case had anything to do with freedom of expression and opinion.[88]

Publication on a Matter of Interest

Section 4 of the Defamation Act 2013 creates a new defence to an action for defamation of 'publication on a matter of public interest'. Section 4 Defamation Act 2013 provides that:

1. It is a defence to an action for defamation for the defendant to show that –
   (a) the statement complained of was, or formed part of, a statement on a matter of public interest; and
   (b) the defendant reasonably believed that publishing the statement complained of was in the public interest.

---

[84] *Collins Stewart v Financial Times Ltd* [2004] EWHC 2337, [2005] EMLR 5.
[85] Joint Committee (n 39) [115].
[86] *Reynolds* (n 4) 208 (Lord Steyn).
[87] *Reynolds* (n 4) 208.
[88] *Reynolds* (n 4) 237.

2. Subject to subsections (3) and (4), in determining whether the defendant has shown the matters mentioned in subsection (1), the court must have regard to all the circumstances of the case.

3. If the statement complained of was, or formed part of, an accurate and impartial account of a dispute to which the claimant was a party, the court must in determining whether it was reasonable for the defendant to believe that publishing the statement was in the public interest disregard any omission of the defendant to take steps to verify the truth of the imputation conveyed by it.

4. In determining whether it was reasonable for the defendant to believe that publishing the statement complained of was in the public interest, the court must make such allowance for editorial judgement as it considers appropriate.

5. For the avoidance of doubt, the defence under this section may be relied upon irrespective of whether the statement complained of is a statement of fact or a statement of opinion.

Furthermore, section 4(6) abolishes the common law defence known as the *Reynolds* defence.

The drafting of section 4(1) reflects the fact that the common law contained both a subject element—what the defendant believed was in the public interest; and an objective element—whether that belief was reasonable. As the Explanatory Notes state, the defence is based on the common law defence of *Reynolds* and is intended to reflect those principles as developed in subsequent case law. The questions of 'public interest' and 'reasonableness of belief' will be informed by principles that have been developed over many years. It is important therefore to return to *Reynolds* which paved the way for what might reasonably be termed a general public interest defence.

Reynolds was a momentous decision in English law, directly shaped by the ECHR, even though the HRA was not yet in force. Before this, a journalist needed to establish that the requirements of qualified privilege (the duty and interest test) were satisfied if a plea of justification could not be made out. Qualified privilege will apply to

> an occasion where the person who makes a communication has a duty, legal, social or moral, to make it to the person to whom it is made, and the person to whom it is so made has a corresponding interest or duty to receive it.[89]

In *Reynolds*, counsel for the defendant newspaper led by one of the country's leading advocates for free speech, Lord Lester QC, argued that the time had come for English courts to recognise a generic category of 'political information' that would attract qualified privilege, defeasible upon proof of malice. It was argued that the *ex post* analysis in any case regarding whether a communication of political information attracted privilege, contributed to the chilling effect of defamation law upon the media. *Reynolds* was decided shortly after both the High Court of

---

[89] *Adam v Ward* [1917] AC 309, 334 (Lord Atkinson).

Australia[90] and the New Zealand Court of Appeal[91] had taken the step of recognising political expression as deserving of qualified privilege, although in each system the scope and reach of such expression is treated differently. The House of Lords declined to introduce a generic category of speech that would attract qualified privilege, instead opting for a test of 'responsible journalism'.

The defendant argued that the time had come for English law to recognise political speech as a generic category of expression deserving of qualified privilege, specifically that English law should adopt the scope of such speech indicated by the formulation laid down by Brennan J in *Lange v Australian Broadcasting Corporation*, namely the dissemination of 'information, opinions and arguments concerning government and political matters affecting the people of the United Kingdom'.[92] However, Lord Lester argued that, unlike Australia, English law should not subject the speaker to a requirement to prove reasonableness, proof of malice being a sufficient brake on the effect of the defence.

This argument was rejected by the House of Lords in a speech by Lord Nicholls which seems completely out of step with what would be desirable in the interests of the 'common convenience and welfare of society'[93] (the traditional justification for qualified privilege) as this might presently be understood. Although His Lordship stated that his starting point was freedom of expression and he noted that 'freedom to disseminate and receive information on political matters is essential to the proper functioning of the system of parliamentary democracy cherished in this country', he proceeded on the basis that he was addressing two interests of equal importance. He rather swiftly moved from freedom of speech to stating that:

> Protection of reputation is conducive to the public good. It is in the public interest that the reputation of public figures should not be debased falsely. In the political field, in order to make an informed choice, the electorate needs to be able to identify the good as well as the bad. Consistently with these considerations, human rights conventions recognise that freedom of expression is not an absolute right. Its exercise may be subject to such restrictions as are prescribed by law and are necessary in a democratic society for the protection of the reputation of others.[94]

According to Strasbourg, the starting point for analysis is freedom of expression. Freedom of expression, particularly political expression, is deserving of the highest degree of protection: the interests in speech and reputation are not accorded equal weight. Any restriction on freedom of expression must be *convincingly justified*. In a recent Grand Chamber judgment, the Court could not have been plainer on the question of priority: 'The Court reiterates that there is little scope under

---

[90] *Lange v ABC* (1997) 71 ALJR 818.
[91] *Lange v Atkinson* [1998] 3 NZLR 424.
[92] *Reynolds* (n 4) 200.
[93] *Toogood v Spyring* (1834) 1 CM & R 181, 193 (Parke B).
[94] *Reynolds* (n 4) 201.

Article 10 § 2 of the Convention for restrictions on political speech or, as in this case, on debate of questions of public interest'.[95]

Lord Nicholls concluded that recognising 'political information' as a new 'subject matter' category of qualified privilege would not ensure adequate protection for reputation; further it would be unsound to distinguish political discussion from discussion of other matters of public concern. In terms of ECHR compliance, on this issue His Lordship was right; as the dicta above illustrate, the ECtHR will treat matters of public interest with the same priority as discussion on political issues. He concluded that the elasticity of the common law allowed the courts to give appropriate weight to the importance of freedom of expression by the media on all matters of public concern. He then set out the well-known list of 10 matters to be taken into account, emphasising that they 'are illustrative only'.[96] The matters to be taken into account included: the seriousness of the allegation; the nature of the information, and the extent to which the subject-matter is a matter of public concern; the source of the information; the steps taken to verify the information; the status of the information; the allegation may have already been the subject of an investigation which commands respect; the urgency of the matter; whether comment was sought from the [claimant]; whether the article contained the gist of the [claimant's] side of the story; the tone of the article; and the circumstances of the publication, including the timing.

It was not clear from the speeches in *Reynolds* whether *Reynolds* introduced a new defence or whether the decision could simply be interpreted as an extension to qualified privilege as traditionally understood. This question was confronted, without being resolved, in *Jameel v Wall Street Journal Europe Sprl*.[97] Lord Hoffmann and Baroness Hale both took the view, echoing the Court of Appeal in *Loutchansky v Times Newspapers Ltd (Nos 2–5)*,[98] that *Reynolds* privilege was a different jurisprudential creature from the traditional duty/interest test for qualified privilege. It derived from the general obligation of the press, media and other publishers to communicate 'important information upon matters of general public interest and the general right of the public to receive such information'.[99] For Lord Hoffmann, this proposition should be treated as a matter of law and not have to be decided as a question of fact in every case.[100] For Lord Bingham and Lord Scott, *Reynolds* had built upon the tradition duty/interest test to cover information that the public as a whole, as opposed to specific individuals, was entitled to know. Does it matter, we may ask, whether we treat *Reynolds* as *sui generis* or merely an extension of traditional qualified privilege?

---

[95] *Verein gegen Tierfabriken v Switzerland (no 2)* (2011) 52 EHRR 8.
[96] *Reynolds* (n 4) 205.
[97] *Jameel* (n 82).
[98] [2002] QB 783, 806.
[99] *Jameel* (n 82) [146].
[100] *Jameel* (n 82) [50].

Lord Hoffmann rightly pointed out that the effect of *Reynolds* was that the test of legitimacy focused upon the content of the material rather than the occasion of publication. It is, he says, not the occasion which is privileged, but the material.[101] The consequence of *Reynolds* was that there were effectively two different vehicles for protecting communications: the traditional duty/interest test which once established is defeasible by the claimant proving malice; and the new *Reynolds* privilege which required the speaker to establish that the public interest requires publication of the material and that the various factors listed by Lord Nicholls are satisfied. Thus, *Reynolds* imposed a burden upon the defendant to demonstrate that the 'responsible journalism' standard has been met. On the latter, the House of Lords in *Jameel*, emphasised that the factors identified by Lord Nicholls in *Reynolds* were indicative only and not to be treated as a checklist of hurdles, where a failure to comply with each and every one would remove the defence. The House of Lords set aside the Court of Appeal's decision[102] that failure to obtain the claimants' side of the story meant that the test of responsible journalism had not been met.

It was held that the 'responsible journalism' test applied more widely than the press and broadcasting media so that the defence was in principle available whenever a person published material of public interest provided that the conditions of responsible journalism were satisfied.[103] It was clear from *Seaga v Harper* that publication of information to the public at large may in principle attract *Reynolds* privilege, without satisfying the traditional reciprocity of duty and interest test for qualified privilege. In such a case, the speaker must conform to the responsible journalism test, rather than the claimant proving malice. In *Seaga v Harper*, the defendant failed to take sufficient care to check the accuracy of information and the defence of qualified privilege failed.

Reynolds was clearly a manifestation of a 'liberalising intention'[104] towards freedom of expression and one that was arguably inspired by the impending effect of domestic incorporation of the ECHR. There was then something of a conundrum now at the heart of this area of law: it is possible that the defendant's need to prove that she has acted responsibly and in accordance with good journalistic practice may have placed more of an obstacle to asserting freedom of expression than using qualified privilege, defeasible only by malice, a point that was made by Lunney and Oliphant.[105]

While section 4(6) has abolished the *Reynolds* defence, section 4 says nothing about 'qualified privilege' which remains to cover those cases where a claimant can

---

[101] *Jameel* (n 82) [50] (Lord Hoffmann).

[102] *Jameel (Yousef) v Dow Jones* (n 59).

[103] *Seaga v Harper* [2008] UKPC 9, [2009] 1 AC 1. Cf *Kearns v General Council of the Bar* [2003] EWCA Civ 331, [2003] 1 WLR 1357, where the Court of Appeal expressed the view that Reynolds privilege was confined to media publications.

[104] *Jameel* (n 82) [35] (Lord Bingham).

[105] M Lunney and K Oliphant, *Tort Law Text and Materials*, 4th edn (Oxford, Oxford University Press, 2010) 752.

establish the traditional duty/interest test is satisfied. This is important as many statements are made within the context of particular relationships, for example references given to employers, and these will continue to be covered by qualified privilege.

The Explanatory Notes state that section 4 is intended to reflect the existing common law as set out most recently by the Supreme Court in *Flood v Times Newspapers Ltd.*[106]

A Statement on a Matter of 'Public Interest'

Lord Phillips in *Flood* noted with approval Lord Bingham's observations in the Court of Appeal in *Reynolds*:

> By [public interest] we mean matters relating to the public life of the community and those who take part in it, including within the expression public life activities such as the conduct of government and political life, elections (subject to section 10 of the Defamation Act, so long as it remains in force) and public administration, but we use the expression more widely than that, to embrace matters such as (for instance) the governance of public bodies, institutions and companies which give rise to a public interest in disclosure, but excluding matters which are personal and private, such that there is no public interest in their disclosure.[107]

In *Flood*, Lord Phillips, with whom Lord Mance agreed, expressed support for Lady Hale's formulation in *Jameel*'s case,[108] that the *Reynolds* defence sprang from 'the general obligation of the press, media and other publishers to communicate important information on matters of public interest and the general right of the public to receive such information'. She added that 'there must be some real public interest in having this information in the public domain'. The role and obligation of the press as watchdog is repeatedly stressed in ECHR jurisprudence.

'Reasonable Belief' that Publication was in the Public Interest

Apart from the requirement for the statement to be on a matter of public interest, the defendant must have a reasonable belief that publication was in the public interest. It is noteworthy that the list of factors set out by Lord Nicholls in *Reynolds* which were included in the Bill did not make it into the statute book; both Houses of Parliament expressed concern that such a list would lead to a checklist approach being taken by the courts and the general 'circumstances of the case' wording was substituted. However, the Nicholls factors will clearly form the sort of considerations that the court will take into account under section 4(2) which requires the

---

[106] *Flood* (n 41).
[107] *Reynolds* (n 4) [176]–[177] (Lord Bingham), cited by Lord Phillips, *Flood* (n 41) [33].
[108] *Jameel* (n 82).

court to have regard to 'all the circumstances of the case', and which will include allowance for 'such editorial judgement as it considers appropriate' (section 4(2)). Lord Brown pointed out in *Flood* that in reality the publication on a matter of public interest or *Reynolds* defence is really a single question: Could the publisher, given whatever they knew (and did not know) and whatever they had done (and not done) to guard against the publication of untrue defamatory material properly have considered the publication to be in the public interest?[109] Both section 4 and recent case law emphasise that determining public interest and appropriateness of publication need to be looked at 'in the round'[110] and the fact that a journalist may have fallen short in some respects of the standards to be expected of a reasonable journalist will not preclude recognition of public interest privilege.[111]

In *Flood*, Lord Mance examined in detail relevant ECHR jurisprudence whose influence has shaped the new defence. The key issue in *Flood* went to identification of DS Flood as an officer being investigated for allegations of corruption and the extent to which there is a duty of verification. According to ECHR standards, the press not only has a right, but also an obligation to report on matters of public interest: 'journalists are both 'public' and social watchdogs'.[112] The ECtHR has tolerated a degree of exaggeration or even provocation in the way the press expresses itself and the bounds of press criticism in respect of politicians and officials 'though not necessarily to the same extent' are larger than they are in relation to private individuals.[113] As far as private individuals are concerned,

> special grounds are required before the media can be dispensed from their ordinary obligation to verify factual statements that are defamatory of private individuals. Whether such grounds exist depends in particular on the nature and degree of the defamation in question and the extent to which the media can reasonably regard their sources as reliable with respect to the allegations ...

The criteria set out in *Reynolds* reflect the approach taken by the ECtHR in assessing the necessity of any interference with freedom of expression. Thus, the Court will examine whether the defendant did a reasonable amount of research before publication,[114] whether the allegations were presented in a reasonably balanced manner[115] and whether the claimant was given the chance to give their side of the story.[116]

As to the naming of DS Flood, without names any article would have been 'very much disembodied, would have been unlikely to be readable or publishable and

---

[109] *Flood* (n 41) [113].
[110] *Flood* (n 41) [131] (Lord Mance).
[111] *Bonnick v Morris* [2003] 1 AC 300.
[112] *Jersild v Denmark* (1994) 19 EHRR 1.
[113] *Flood* (n 41) [139] (Lord Mance), citing *Vides Aizardzibas Klubs v Latvia* Application No 57829/00 (unreported) given 27 May 2004 and *Flux v Moldova (No 7)* [2007] ECHR 28700/03 (23 October 2007).
[114] *Prager and Oberschlick* (n 56).
[115] *Bergens Tidende v Norway* (2001) EHRR 430 [57].
[116] *Ibid* [58].

would not have fulfilled the journalists' purpose of stimulating diligent investigation by the police'.[117] In terms of verification, the press cannot disclaim all responsibility for checking their sources as far as practicable, 'provided the report is of real and unmistakeably public interest and is fairly presented, [journalists] need not be in a position to produce primary evidence of the information given by such sources'.[118] In conclusion, Lord Mance returned to the fundamental shift identified in *Jameel* and *Reynolds* which is that freedom of the press has been liberalised and the balance shifted in favour of the press to publish stories of genuine public interest.

There is a marked difference between the CA and the Supreme Court in *Flood*, the former taking the view that the journalists should have verified or at least taken steps to verify the truth of the details of the alleged corruption upon which they reported. As Lord Mance pointed out, this was at odds with Lord Nicholls' views in *Reynolds*, that the source of information might well be informants with no direct knowledge of the events.[119] For Lord Clarke, where the case concerns denunciation of a public officer, a strong circumstantial case will justify the defence.

In conclusion, the court will take account of all the circumstances, the starting point being that any interference with freedom of expression should be 'necessary' in the circumstances of the case.[120]

From 'Fair Comment' to 'Honest Opinion'

As we have seen, the distinction between facts and value-judgements pervades the ECHR jurisprudence: 'the existence of facts can be demonstrated whereas the truth of value-judgments is not susceptible of proof'.[121] A requirement for a defendant to prove the truth of a value judgement will violate the Article 10 right to freedom of expression.[122] The classification of a statement as a fact or value judgement falls within the margin of appreciation of the national authorities, in particular the courts. However, even in the case of a value judgement, there must be a sufficient factual basis to support it.[123]

Section 3 Defamation Act 2013 has abolished the defence of fair comment on a matter of public interest and replaced it with a new defence of 'honest opinion' which requires the defendant to show that three conditions are met. First, the

---

[117] *Flood* (n 41) [168] (Lord Mance).
[118] *Flood* (n 41) [158].
[119] *Reynolds* (n 4) [23].
[120] *Reynolds* (n 4) (Lord Nicholls); Flood (n 42) [193] (Lord Dyson).
[121] *Lingens* (n 25) [46].
[122] *Lingens* (n 25); *Oberschlick v Austria* (1994) 19 EHRR 389.
[123] *Lindon, Otchakovsky-Laurens and July v France* (2007) 46 EHRR 761.

statement must be a 'statement of opinion' (section 3(2)). There is no requirement for the opinion to be on a matter of public interest. Second, the impugned statement should indicate, 'in general or specific terms, the basis of the opinion' (section 3(3)). Finally, the defendant must show that

> an honest person could have held the opinion on the basis of (a) any fact which existed at the time the statement complained of was published; (b) anything asserted to be a fact in a privileged statement published before the statement complained of.

The defence will be defeated if the claimant shows that the defendant did not hold the opinion (section 3(6)).

The statement must be recognisable as comment, as distinct from an imputation of fact. The Explanatory Notes assert that the assessment is on the basis of how 'the ordinary person' would understand it and as an inference of fact is a form of opinion this would be covered by the defence. The Joint Committee recommended that the term 'public interest' should be dropped from the draft Bill on the basis that the right to protection of personal privacy and confidentiality are now well established. The Committee also noted that it may be a breach of Article 10 to require a person to prove the truth of a value statement irrespective of whether it concerns a matter of public interest or not.[124]

The Explanatory Notes indicate that section 3(2) is intended to reflect the test approved by the Supreme Court in *Joseph v Spiller*. In *Joseph*, Lord Phillips, giving the leading speech for a unanimous Supreme Court, stated that:

> the comment must identify at least in general terms what it is that has led the commentator to make the comment, so that the reader can understand what the comment is about and the commentator can, if challenged, explain by giving particulars of the subject matter of his comment why he expressed the views that he did. A fair balance must be struck between allowing a critic the freedom to express himself as he will and requiring him to identify to his readers why it is that he is making the criticism.[125]

In *Joseph*, the Supreme Court disapproved the requirement set out by Lord Nicholls in *Tse Wai Chun v Cheng*,[126] for the speaker to identify matters with sufficient particularity to enable the reader to judge for herself whether the comment was well founded.

The requirement for a defendant to indicate in 'general or specific terms' the basis of her opinion is in tune with the ECHR and the need for a restriction on the freedom of expression to be 'necessary'; in the previous edition, the author criticised the view of a majority in the House of Lords in *Telnikoff v Matusevich*[127] that the defence was not made out where the defendant criticised an article written by the claimant in *The Daily Telegraph* in a letter that he wrote to the

---

[124] Joint Committee (n 40) [69(a)].
[125] *Joseph v Spiller* [2010] UKSC 53, [2011] 1 AC 852 [104] (Lord Phillips).
[126] [2001] EMLR 777 [19]
[127] *Telnikoff* (n 57).

same newspaper. The defendant argued that the views expressed were statements of opinion. The House of Lords considered that the letter should be examined on its own in determining whether the statements were fact or comment, with the result that the various statements must be regarded as fact not comment, and with regard to which the defendant had not pleaded any defence. This was a harsh approach, given that the defendant had been prompted to write by the polemical tone of the article and it was obvious from the letter that the defendant was responding to opinions the claimant had expressed. It seems extremely unlikely that a case such as this could be decided in the same way today. In *Telnikoff*, Lord Ackner, alone and in dissent, acknowledged the importance of freedom of expression and concluded that the essential question is clearly what is the 'context' in which the letter is to be construed. Such an approach accords with the ECHR.[128]

The opinion does not have to be reasonable or correct—what matters is that it is honest and one that an honest person could have held. The existing case law on the sufficiency of the factual basis for the opinion is encompassed by the requirement under section 3 that an honest person could have held the opinion on the basis of an existing fact or anything asserted to be a fact in a privileged statement. When assessing whether an honest person could have held the opinion on the basis of an existing fact, it seems likely that greater leeway will be allowed to the speaker where the comment touches upon the political sphere or other matters of public interest. ECHR jurisprudence is replete with the observation that 'the limits of acceptable criticism are wider in relation to politicians acting in their public capacity than in relation to private individuals'.[129] The same principle applies in relation to civil servants acting in an official capacity,[130] people who voluntarily enter the public arena, for example business people engaged in running large corporations[131] and those who participate in public debate.[132]

Although restricting himself to some very brief concurring remarks in *Joseph v Spiller*, Lord Walker arguably captured the real issue which is that the defence of fair comment developed to protect a small cadre of writers, artists and musicians who placed their works on a public platform and whose work was subject to criticism. Times have changed and we are all potentially publishers now, every time we complete a review on Trip Advisor we pass comment in a way that may affect reputation. Lord Walker observed that:

> millions now talk, and thousands comment in electronically transmitted words, about recent events of which they have learned from television or the internet. Many of the events and the comments on them are no doubt trivial and ephemeral, but from time to time (as the present appeal shows) libel law has to engage with them. The test for

---

[128] See generally *Lingens* (n 25).
[129] See for example, *Castells v Spain* (1992) EHRR 445. See also *Joseph v Spiller* (n 125) [79] (Lord Phillips).
[130] *July v France* (2013) 57 EHRR 28.
[131] *Fayed v United Kingdom* (1994) 18 EHRR 393.
[132] *Jerusalem v Austria* (2003) 37 EHRR 25 [38].

identifying the factual basis of honest comment must be flexible enough to allow for this type of case, in which a passing reference to the previous night's celebrity show would be regarded by most of the public, and may sometimes have to be regarded by the law, as a sufficient factual basis.[133]

Academic and Scientific Debate

The Joint Committee noted that there is convincing evidence that defamation law is used to silence members of the scientific and academic community in order to protect products and profits.[134] Among the notorious cases is that of Dr Simon Singh who was forced to defend costly and lengthy defamation proceedings after he published an article that passed comment upon the efficacy of treatments promoted by the British Chiropractic Association. The Joint Committee requested that a provision should be added to the Bill that would extend qualified privilege to peer-reviewed articles in scientific or academic journals and this has been effected by section 6 Defamation Act 2013. Section 6 requires that a statement should relate to a scientific or academic matter and that prior to publication the statement should have been subject to an independent review by the editor and one or more experts in the relevant field. This requirement accords with accepted academic practice.

In future, those who make comment upon important scientific or academic matters will have a number of avenues to seek protection, each of which has been directly informed by ECHR jurisprudence. The key concern is that freedom of expression on important matters affecting the public interest should not be chilled, and about which the public need to be informed so that they can make important choices affecting their own lives. As Lord Phillips stated in *British Chiropractic Association v Singh*, the litigation would almost certainly have chilled public debate which, had it taken place, would have assisted potential patients to make informed choices.[135]

Costs

The Defamation Act 2013 has made a number of changes to the substantive law of defamation that significantly shifts the balance in favour of freedom of expression. However, there remains an area as yet unaddressed which affects very significantly the extent to which a speaker is able to exercise the right to freedom of expression and that is costs. The Coalition Government 2010–2015 excluded publication

---

[133] *Joseph v Spiller* (n 125) [131] (Lord Walker).
[134] Joint Committee Report (n 39) [47].
[135] [2010] EWCA Civ 350, [2011] 1 WLR 33 [11].

and privacy proceedings (proceedings for defamation, malicious falsehood, breach of confidence involving publication to the general public, misuse of private information and harassment, where the defendant is a news publisher) from the implementation of reforms aimed at making the costs of civil litigation more proportionate following the Report by Lord Justice Jackson.[136]

The Jackson Reforms are directed at the mischief caused by Conditional Fee Agreements (CFAs). CFAs were introduced following the Woolf Report in the 1990s in order to improve access to justice for those of modest means and to shift the burden of litigation from the public purse as access to legal aid was reduced. However, the scope of CFAs was revised by the Access to Justice Act 1999 allowing the recovery of 100 per cent of success fees and After the Event insurance premiums from the losing party; thus, the cost of all CFA litigation was imposed upon unsuccessful defendants as a class. Losing defendants were to be required to contribute to the funds which would enable lawyers to take on other cases, which might not be successful, but which would provide access to justice for people who could not otherwise have afforded to sue. Therefore, the policy shifted the burden of funding from the state to unsuccessful defendants, which is arguably a rational social and economic policy.

However, an unwelcome by-product was the use by claimant lawyers of 'success fees' which might involve uplift of 100 per cent of base costs payable by the losing side. One of the most notorious examples of the practice is *Campbell v MGN Ltd*[137] where the High Court awarded damages in the sum of just £2500 for genuine distress and injury to feelings caused by the unjustified publication and disclosure of details of the claimant's therapy at Narcotics Anonymous and £1000 aggravated damages for 'trashing her as a person'. The total legal costs for this litigation were in the order of £1.1 million. The CFA provided that if the appeal to the House of Lords was successful, success fees at the rate of 95 per cent of base costs in respect of the solicitor's costs and 100 per cent of counsel's base costs would be payable. MGN Ltd challenged both the privacy claim and the award of success fees before the ECtHR, being successful regarding the costs but losing regarding the privacy violation. The ECtHR held that it must consider the proportionality of requiring an unsuccessful defendant not only to pay the reasonable and proportionate costs of the claimant, but also to contribute to the funding of other litigation and general access to justice, by paying up to double those costs in the form of recoverable success fees.[138] However, the Court held that the conditional fee arrangements with recoverable success fees pursued the legitimate aim of 'protecting the rights of others' under Article 10(2) by seeking to achieve the widest public access to legal

---

[136] See Article 4 of the Legal Aid, Sentencing and Punishment of Offenders Act 2012 (Commencement No 5 and Saving Provision) Order 2013 and the Jackson Report, *Reforming Civil Litigation Funding and Costs in England and Wales* (2010).

[137] *Campbell* (n 38).

[138] *MGN Ltd v UK* (2011) 53 EHRR 5.

services funded by the private sector. However, the requirement to pay success fees was disproportionate to the legitimate aims sought to be achieved by the success fee system and exceeded the broad margin of appreciation allowed to Government in such matters.

In *Coventry v Lawrence*, the Supreme Court held by a majority that the decision in *MGN Ltd v UK* did not compel the conclusion that the regime in the Access to Justice Act 1999 was incompatible with Article 6 or Article 1 Protocol 1. *MGN Ltd* concerned the question of whether the regime struck a fair balance between freedom of expression in Article 10 and the Article 6 right of access to a court. The balancing of Article 6 rights was a different exercise. Lord Neuberger and Lord Dyson, with whom Lord Sumption and Lord Carnwath agreed, distinguished *MGN Ltd*, saying that the context in which the Strasbourg Court had criticised the scheme was its effect in defamation and privacy cases stating:

> The right of freedom of expression is always given particular weight by the [ECtHR]. As the Court said at para 201, the most careful scrutiny is called for when measures are capable of discouraging the participation of the press in debates over matters of legitimate public concern: the balance of Article 6 rights is completely different.[139]

The Jackson Report provoked strong views among both claimant and defendant representatives. Media representatives objected strongly to the 'chilling' or 'ransom' effect of litigation funding on media defendants who may be forced to settle unmeritorious claims. On the other hand, access to justice for claimants who sought to vindicate reputation or other privacy rights had undoubtedly been enhanced. Lord Justice Leveson recommended in his Report that the reforms to 'no win no fee' arrangements should not be brought into force in privacy and defamation actions until a regime of costs protection was in place.[140] Furthermore, the Joint Committee on Human Rights welcomed the Government's acceptance of the Leveson recommendation but in its seventh and most recent report (March 2015) the Joint Committee has expressed concern that the *MGN Ltd* judgment remains unimplemented which may prolong the chilling effect on freedom of expression.[141] We have now reached the position where publication and privacy proceedings have been excluded from the implementation of the Jackson Reforms and there are currently no proposals to address the disproportionate awards of costs in such cases.

In *Miller v Associated Newspapers Ltd*,[142] Mitting J rejected a HRA challenge by the *Daily Mail* to the recoverability of both success fees and an After the Event insurance premium on the basis that they were incompatible with the newspaper's

---

[139] [2015] UKSC 50, [2015] 1 WLR 3485.

[140] Rt Hon Lord Justice Leveson, *An Inquiry into the Culture, Practices and Ethics of the Press*, Vol 4, HC 780 iv (November 2012).

[141] www.publications.parliament.uk/pa/jt201415/jtselect/jtrights/130/13002.htm accessed on 9 July 2016.

[142] [2016] EWHC 397.

Article 10 rights. The *Daily Mail* relied on *MGN Ltd v United Kingdom*, but, in the absence of exceptional circumstances and applying *Kay v Lambeth Borough Council*,[143] Mitting J considered himself bound by *Campbell v MGN Ltd (Costs)*[144] and issued a leapfrog certificate for the *Daily Mail* to appeal directly to the Supreme Court.

Injunctive Relief

The most intrusive form of restriction on freedom of expression is injunctive relief with its inherent danger of 'chilling' freedom of expression. The leading ECHR case on 'prior restraints' is *Observer and Guardian v United Kingdom*,[145] which concerned the injunctions granted against the publishers, editors and journalists of two newspapers in the infamous Spycatcher litigation. It was this case more than any other which arguably paved the way for the introduction of a right to privacy in English law. Peter Wright, a former British Security agent, had retired to Australia where he wrote his memoirs for publication in which he alleged that the Security Service had attempted to undermine the 1974–1979 Labour Government and that a former Head of the Service had spied for the Russians. It was explosive stuff and the British Government issued proceedings before the Australian courts. In the meantime, the applicant newspapers published articles based upon the book in the United Kingdom and the Attorney General thereupon sought injunctions before the English courts to restrain further publication. Interim injunctions were granted, upheld by the Court of Appeal, but by the time the proceedings reached the House of Lords (July 1987), the book had been published and was widely known in the USA. Nevertheless, the injunction was upheld by a majority of the House of Lords on 30 July 1987. The injunction was finally discharged by the House of Lords in October 1988, in view of the fact that secrecy[146] had been destroyed through the widespread publication of the book's contents.

The applicants challenged the compatibility of the injunction with Article 10 at Strasbourg. The Court was unanimous that the injunction between July 1987 and October 1988 was a violation of Article 10, as it was not necessary in a democratic society. The Court held that:

> For the avoidance of doubt, and having in mind the written comments that were submitted in this case by 'Article 19' ... the Court would only add to the foregoing that Article 10 of the Convention does not in terms prohibit the imposition of prior restraints on publication, as such. This is evidenced not only by the words 'conditions', 'restrictions',

---

[143] [2006] UKHL 10, [2006] 2 AC 465.
[144] [2005] UKHL 10, [2005] 1 WLR 3394.
[145] (1991) 14 EHRR 153.
[146] The distinction between 'secrecy' and 'privacy' is significant: see discussion of *PJS v News Group Newspapers Ltd* [2016] UKSC 26, [2016] 2 WLR 1253; Chapter 8 *Privacy—From Misuse of Private Information to Autonomy*.

'preventing' and 'prevention' which appear in that provision, but also by the Court's *Sunday Times* judgment of 26 April 1979 and its *Markt Intern Verlag GmbH* and *Klaus Beermann* judgment of 20 November 1989. On the other hand, the dangers inherent in prior restraints are such that they call for the most careful scrutiny on the part of the Court. This is especially so as far as the press is concerned, for news is a perishable commodity and to delay its publication, even for a short period, may well deprive it of all its value and interest.

As we have seen, the passage of the Human Rights Bill through Parliament was accompanied by significant concerns amongst the press that the introduction of Article 8 rights would have an adverse impact on the freedom of the press. There were concerns that the normal application of the conventional approach to interlocutory relief laid down in *American Cyanimid Co v Ethicon Ltd*[147] would lead to orders imposing prior restraint upon newspapers whenever applicants complained that publication would infringe their Article 8 rights. Section 12 HRA was enacted to allay these fears, by setting a 'higher threshold for the grant of interlocutory injunctions against the media'.[148] Section 12(3) provides that: 'No such relief is to be granted so as to restrain publication before trial unless the court is satisfied that the applicant is likely to establish that publication should not be allowed'.

In *Cream Holdings Ltd v Bannerjee*, the House of Lords held that 'likely' cannot have been intended to mean 'more likely than not' in all situations as this would set the bar too high. Rather, the intention must have been to require a claimant to demonstrate a likelihood of success that is higher than the *American Cyanimid* 'real prospect' standard but permits the court flexibility to dispense with this standard where circumstances require.[149] According to Lord Nicholls, the court should not make an interim restraint order unless the applicant's prospects of success at trial are 'sufficiently favourable to justify an order in the particular circumstances of the case'. He went on to say that this would generally mean that an applicant should satisfy the court that he will 'probably (more likely than not)' succeed at trial.

Cream Holdings was an action to restrain the publication of confidential information. The question arises whether section 12 HRA has any impact on the rule in *Bonnard v Perryman*,[150] given that reputation is an aspect of 'private life' under Article 8 ECHR. The Court of Appeal in *Greene v Associated Newspapers*,[151] held that the rule in *Bonnard v Perryman* was unaffected by s 12 HRA and the interpretation given in *Cream Holdings*. *Bonnard v Perryman* requires the court to deny injunctive relief where a defendant will justify his remarks, unless it is plain that the defence will fail. Traditionally, there are two reasons for the rule: first, the importance the court attaches to freedom of speech; and, second, because to grant

---

[147] [1975] AC 396.
[148] *Cream Holdings Ltd v Bannerjee* [2004] UKHL 44, [2005] 1 AC [15] (Lord Nicholls).
[149] *Ibid* [20] (Lord Nicholls).
[150] [1891] 2 Ch 269.
[151] [2005] 3 WLR 281, [2004] EWCA Civ 1462.

an injunction is to determine whether a statement is a libel and that question was a matter for the jury—granting an injunction would be tantamount to usurping the role of the jury in defamation cases.[152] This aspect of the rationale has now been undermined, as section 11 Defamation Act 2013 removes the presumption in favour of jury trial unless the court orders otherwise. It remains the case that it is rare for the court to grant interim injunctions in defamation cases, but will do so in an appropriate case.[153] Referring to the Strasbourg Court's judgment in *The Observer and Guardian* case,[154] the Court of Appeal held that using the *Cream Holdings* threshold for granting an injunction would seriously weaken the effect of Article 10.

---

[152] *Ibid* [57].
[153] *ZAM v CFW and TFW* [2011] EWHC 476 (QB).
[154] *Observer and Guardian* (n 145).

8

Privacy—From Misuse of Private Information to Autonomy

Introduction

Article 8(1) of the European Convention on Human Rights (ECHR) obliges the Member States of the Council of Europe to respect a wide range of personal interests: 'private and family life, home and correspondence'. The terms 'Privacy' and 'Private Life' are used in a wealth of different contexts to indicate interests deserving of protection from interference by the state as well as private parties.[1] The range of interests protected by Article 8 ECHR was outlined in Chapter 3, where it was observed that matters affecting one's sexual orientation, gender identity, physical and psychological integrity and the disclosure of personal information, including one's picture, are all encompassed under the umbrella of 'private life'. In the USA, privacy rights and interests are usually considered to refer to matters of individual autonomy, such as sexuality[2] and reproductive freedom,[3] which are protected as matters of constitutional law and the ability to restrict the dissemination of private information which is achieved through tort law.[4]

At the time the Human Rights Bill was debated in Parliament, English courts were on the cusp of recognising an action to protect the dissemination of private information. As we have seen in Chapter 3, significant parliamentary and academic attention focussed on the extent to which the Human Rights Act 1998 (HRA) would have horizontal effect and thereby impact upon rights and obligations between non-state actors. Apart from some piecemeal engagement with the horizontality issue, English courts have declined to give a definitive answer as to the extent to which section 6 HRA has horizontal effect. It may well be that this question is never answered. Nevertheless, this has not impeded the recognition of

---

[1] See E Barendt, 'Privacy as a Constitutional Right and Value' in P Birks (ed), *Privacy and Loyalty* (Oxford, Clarendon Press, 1997).
[2] *Bowers v Hardwick* 85 US 140 (1986).
[3] *Griswold v Connecticut* 381 US 479 (1965).
[4] *Melvin v Reid* 112 Cal app 285 (1931).

a new tort of misuse of private information grounded in the first instance upon the action for breach of confidence and then being recognised as a new and different tort in its own right.[5] Furthermore, following claims brought in relation to phone hacking, some of which were based upon publication but others of which related to 'loss of privacy or autonomy' over one's personal information,[6] as a result of phone hacking, awards of damages have been upheld by the Court of Appeal for the hacking itself. Arguably, this is a new tort of 'privacy'.[7]

Thus, 'privacy' embraces a number of different types of action beyond the transformed action for breach of confidence; it is an action that encompasses loss of control over personal information, but also arguably protects the individual from unwanted physical intrusion by others. As Moreham has argued, a 'superficial look' at English law would suggest that privacy in English law is just about restraining the dissemination of private information.[8] This held true until very recently, but English law is certainly on the march and many dimensions of 'autonomy' are now protected in English law.

The new tort of misuse of private information has been achieved by absorbing the values of Article 8 into the common law and does not stem from any particular interpretation of section 6 of the HRA. This means that the new body of legal principles is unlikely to be vulnerable to a repeal of the HRA and the introduction of any British Bill of Rights. The new tort of misuse of private information was not born of the HRA and will therefore not die with it.

The Article 8 right to respect for private life has the capacity to reach into the corners of most aspects of our lives. In *Peck v United Kingdom*, the European Court of Human Rights (ECtHR) stated that: 'Private life is a broad term not susceptible to exhaustive definition. The Court has already held that elements such as gender identification, name, sexual orientation and sexual life are important elements of the personal sphere protected by Article 8. That Article also protects a right to identity and personal development, and the right to establish and develop relationships with other human beings and the outside world and it may include activities of a professional or business nature. There is, therefore, a zone of interaction of a person with others, even in a public context, which may fall within the scope of 'private life…'.[9] It is difficult to imagine which area of a person's life is not caught by Article 8.

---

[5] In *Vidal-Hall v Google Inc* [2015] EWCA Civ 311, [2015] 3 WLR 309, the Court of Appeal took the important step of holding that insofar as a claim was based on the use of private information the legal wrong was the tort of misuse of private information at least in relation to service out of the jurisdiction.

[6] *Gulati v MGN Ltd* [2015] EWHC 148, [2016] FSR 12.

[7] *Gulati v MGN Ltd* [2015] EWCA Civ 1291, [2016] 2 WLR 1217. Permission to appeal was refused by the Supreme Court.

[8] NA Moreham, 'Beyond Information: Physical Privacy in English Law' (2014) *Cambridge Law Journal* 73(2), 350–77.

[9] *Peck v United Kingdom* (2003) EHRR 719, quoted by B Rainey, E Wicks and C Ovey, *Jacobs, White & Ovey: The European Convention on Human Rights*, 6th edn (Oxford, Oxford University Press, 2014) 362.

When it is borne in mind that the Strasbourg Court has frequently referred to positive obligations in the context of private life, subject to a state's margin of appreciation, it can readily be seen that there is scope for an expansive interpretation of this right. Harris, O'Boyle and Warbrick have observed that

> Typically, the Court applies Article 8(1) to the individual facts of each case and has avoided laying down general understandings of what each item covers. In some cases, the Court has utilized the co-terminancy of them to avoid spelling out precisely which individual interest is at stake.[10] Nonetheless, a survey of the case law shows a generous approach to the definition of the personal interests protected, and the lack of precision in Article 8(1) has allowed the case law to develop in line with social and technical developments. The disadvantage may be the absence of a theoretical conspectus, which makes an account of the jurisprudence inevitably descriptive and prediction about its likely progress hazardous.[11]

English courts too have resisted the notion that the jurisprudence of the European Court of Human Rights (ECtHR) requires the state to develop a high level principle of privacy.[12] However, many dimensions of privacy are now protected by English law. It has taken us around 100 years longer to get here, but it would seem we have now reached the same position that animated Warren and Brandeis when they argued in their seminal paper that there was a general 'right to be let alone' immanent in the common law.[13] Warren and Brandeis charted the development of the common law from its early preoccupation with physical interference with life and tangible property to the recognition of man's spiritual nature, his feelings and his intellect.

Over the centuries the common law had gradually extended the range of interests deserving of protection, from land and cattle to recognition of the legal value of 'sensations'. Gradually, the interest in reputation was protected through the actions for slander and libel. The development of copyright laws and the protection of trade secrets and trade marks were but aspects of the legal protection of intellectual and emotional life. Warren and Brandeis argued that the unifying general principle was the 'right to be let alone'. Their call for explicit recognition of privacy protection, initially unheeded, was gradually taken up by the states, which accorded privacy protection to individuals, either through the common law or statute.

---

[10] DJ. Harris, M O'Boyle, EP Bates and CM Buckley, *Harris, O'Boyle and Warbrick: Law of the European Convention on Human Rights*, 2nd edn (Oxford, Oxford University Press, 2009) cite the telephone tapping cases of *Klass v Germany* (1979–80) 2 EHRR 214 [41] and *Kopp v Switzerland* (1999) 27 EHRR 91 where the Court held that telephone conversations are part of 'private life', 'family life' and 'correspondence'.

[11] Harris, O'Boyle and Warbrick, *ibid* 361.

[12] *Wainwright v Home Office* [2003] UKHL 53, [2004] 2 AC 406, with Lord Hoffmann giving judgment for a unanimous House of Lords.

[13] S Warren and L Brandeis, 'The Right to Privacy' (1890) 4 *Harvard Law Review* 193.

In the sphere of reproductive rights there have been significant developments in the English law of obligations that arguably reflect a 'human rights based' approach. There has been a growing tendency to accommodate claims which could not be met through the application of orthodox tort principles. It must be acknowledged that these developments have not been formally shaped by the ECHR, nor the HRA, but they arguably signify a deepening of a common law human rights jurisdiction. As with the new tort of misuse of private information, these developments have grown organically from the rights established in the common law[14] and are therefore impervious to repeal of the HRA.

This chapter is divided into two parts. In the first the development of the new English privacy tort in the light of the ECHR is examined. In the second part, the new and broader protection of other aspects of autonomy are considered. The discussion in the first section will be conducted in three parts: first, the analysis will attempt to determine the scope of privacy of information as recognised by Strasbourg; second, we shall examine the response of English courts to the demands of the ECHR case law; and, finally, we shall draw together the emerging principles in order to reflect upon possible future directions. This chapter will not consider the large and much broader range of issues that fall to be determined under the HRA in connection with the public authority's obligation under section 6(1). The reader's attention is drawn to a range of excellent detailed treatments of the broader topic.[15] The focus here is on the (putative) impact of the ECHR on tort principles.

Privacy Jurisprudence under the ECHR

As we discussed in Chapters 2 and 3, the ECHR does not cast duties directly upon third parties; as an international treaty, it is states that agree to be bound to secure to everyone within the jurisdiction the rights and freedoms set out (Article 1 ECHR). The ECHR itself does not bind non-state actors in international law; it is states that secure 'human' rights to their citizens. In view of the fact that the present discussion focuses on the rights of private actors *inter se*, it is necessary to examine the Strasbourg jurisprudence regarding any positive obligation on states to control the behaviour of non-state actors, the jurisprudence regarding positive obligations. The Court has held that there may be positive obligations upon the state in relation to Article 8. Positive obligations are fully discussed in Chapter 6, and it will be recalled that they take two forms: first, they may be such that the state itself must take positive steps to fulfil the Article 8 obligations, for example,

---

[14] See for example the speech of Lord Scarman in *Sidaway v Board of Governors of Bethlem Royal Hospital* [1985] AC 871.
[15] See generally M Amos, *Human Rights Law* (Oxford, Hart Publishing, 2014).

by the enactment of legislation regarding illegitimacy,[16] or the provision of access to a decree of judicial separation;[17] or, second, the state may be required to take steps to secure that private parties behave in a way that is respectful of others' right to private life.[18] In a much cited *dictum*, the Court in *X and Y v The Netherlands* held that: '[positive obligations] may involve the adoption of measures designed to secure respect for private life even in the sphere of the relations of individuals between themselves'.[19]

Although a positive obligation is discovered through the interpretation of Article 8(1), the Court has held that the limitations set out in Article 8(2) may be relevant, since the permitted aims in Article 8(2) are relevant in shaping the content of the right. In *Rees v United Kingdom*, the Court stated that:

> In determining whether or not a positive obligation exists, regard must be had to the fair balance that has to be struck between the general interest of the community and the interests of the individual, the search for which balance is inherent in the whole of the Convention. In striking this balance the aims mentioned in the second paragraph of Article 8 may be of certain relevance, although this provision refers in terms only to 'interferences' with the right protected by the first paragraph—in other words is concerned with the negative obligation flowing therefrom.[20]

One of the grounds upon which interference with the rights enshrined in Article 8(1) is permitted is where such interference is necessary, 'for the protection of the rights and freedoms of others'. Clearly, in most cases of privacy intrusion, as understood in the context of the present discussion, the countervailing argument will be that the right to freedom of expression under Article 10 ECHR should prevail. It is clear as well that in relation to positive obligations states have a wide margin of appreciation in determining the steps that need to be taken to ensure compliance, having regard to the needs and resources of the community and individuals.

It is very unusual for Strasbourg to indicate which branch of government should secure a right. So, in terms of securing privacy from media intrusion in the UK, while English law was deficient in failing to secure the right to respect for private life, any violation of Article 8 was a violation by the United Kingdom. The Strasbourg jurisprudence on positive obligations under Article 8 requires that states take steps to protect ECHR rights as between non-state actors, but it generally does not indicate which branch of government should secure the right. Indeed, as is clear from *X and Y*, 'the choice of the means calculated to secure compliance with Article 8 in the sphere of the relations of individuals between themselves is in principle a matter that falls within the Contracting States' margin of

---

[16] *Marckx v Belgium* (1979–80) 2 EHRR 330.
[17] *Airey v Ireland* (1979–80) 2 EHRR 305.
[18] *X and Y v The Netherlands* (1986) 8 EHRR 235.
[19] *Ibid* [23].
[20] (1987) 9 EHRR 56.

appreciation'.[21] In *X and Y*, the Court did find that the availability of civil remedies was insufficient in the case of the wrongdoing (sexual assault) inflicted upon Miss Y. On the facts, the availability of civil law remedies did not discharge the Article 8 obligation, but the Court made the following important observation:

> ...the Court, which on this point agrees in substance with the opinion of the Commission, observes that the choice of the means calculated to secure compliance with Article 8 in the sphere of the relations between themselves is in principle a matter that falls within the Contracting States' margin of appreciation. In this connection, there are different ways of ensuring 'respect for private life', and the nature of the State's obligation will depend on the particular aspect of private life that is at issue. Recourse to the criminal law is not necessarily the answer.[22]

This is essentially a matter of subsidiarity and it is this principle that makes it very difficult to argue that an English court (as opposed to Parliament) is obliged by the terms of section 6(1) HRA to fashion new common law rights. That does not mean to say that the common law should not adapt and change to reflect contemporary human rights standards and values, but the HRA does not oblige this. As we argued in Chapter 3, it is difficult in terms of ECHR jurisprudence to make the argument that English courts can be required to recognise new causes of action in the common law. The obligation to secure the right is at the level of the state and it is up to the state to decide how to protect the right. A failure to develop the action for breach of confidence would have meant that English law was not compatible with the ECHR, not that English courts had failed to act compatibly with the ECHR since there is nothing in the jurisprudence to require English *courts* to act to protect the right.[23] Rather, it could be argued equally that Parliament had acted incompatibly with the ECHR in failing to enact a privacy law.

In terms of the substance of privacy of information, there have been significant developments in ECHR case law since the first edition. Strasbourg was initially slow to hold that the publication of true facts could amount to a violation of Article 8. In part, this was probably because privacy torts have been widely recognised within civilian jurisdictions[24] so there was simply little pressure to develop privacy case law in relation to private information. On the other hand, in those applications which were brought, the Commission was inclined to reject at the admissibility stage on the basis that the state had been acting within its margin of appreciation.[25] It has been suggested that Strasbourg's reticence in this field was a

---

[21] *X and Y* (n 18) [24].

[22] *Ibid.*

[23] See Chapter 3, text accompanying n 161.

[24] See generally BS Markesinis, *The German Law of Torts: A Comparative Treatise*, 4th edn (Oxford, Hart Publishing, 2002); H Kötz and K Zweigert, *An Introduction to Comparative Law*, 3rd revised edn (Oxford, Clarendon Press, 1998); BS Markesinis, 'Conceptualism, Pragmatism and Courage: A Common Lawyer Looks at Some Judgments of the Federal Supreme Court' (1986) 34 *American Journal of Comparative Law* 349.

[25] See for example the admissibility decision in *Winer v United Kingdom* (1986) 48 D & R 154.

manifestation of reluctance to impose positive obligations especially where there is a potential conflict with another right(s).[26]

The initial reluctance of Strasbourg to supervise Convention compliance in this field effectively is illustrated by *Winer v United Kingdom*.[27] Here, the applicant complained that the publication of a book containing intimate details of his married life constituted a violation of his right to respect for private life. In relation to parts of the book, which were accepted by the publishers as being defamatory, the applicant had settled a claim out of court. His application to Strasbourg related to parts of the book that contained true facts. The Commission took into account the Article 10 right to freedom of expression of both the author and publisher in establishing the extent of positive obligations under Article 8 of the Convention and alluded to the wide margin of appreciation allowed to states in fulfilling positive obligations: 'the way in which a high Contracting Party may meet such obligations is largely within its discretion'. The Commission concluded that the applicant's right to privacy was not wholly unprotected, as was shown by his defamation action and settlement, and his own liberty to publish. The Commission also took the view that, in the light of the uncertainty surrounding the action for breach of confidence, there was no necessity to bring such an action in the English courts; he had therefore exhausted domestic remedies. This decision failed to distinguish appropriately between the rights to reputation and the right to privacy of information and signified an undue deference to the state in determining whether a state has met its positive obligations. While reputation has now been recognised as an interest that falls within the scope of 'private life',[28] privacy and reputation are different interests and the protection of one will not afford protection to the other.

In *Spencer v United Kingdom*, the Commission considered the applications of Earl and Countess Spencer in relation to newspaper reports of the latter's stay at a private clinic for the treatment of bulimia and alcoholism, including the publication of photographs taken with a telephoto lens of Countess Spencer walking in the grounds of the clinic. The petitions alleged that the United Kingdom had violated Articles 8 and 13 (the right to an effective remedy) in failing to provide appropriate redress where private information and photographs had been published and re-published. The applications were declared inadmissible because, in failing to invoke an action for breach of confidence in the English courts, the Commission found that the applicants had failed to exhaust domestic remedies as

---

[26] H Fenwick and G Phillipson, *Media Freedom under the Human Rights Act* (Oxford, Oxford University Press, 2006) 667.

[27] *Winer* (n 25).

[28] *Pfeifer v Austria* (2007) 48 EHRR 175; *In the Matter of Guardian News and Media* [2010] UKSC 1, [2010] 2 AC 697.

required by the then Article 26 (now Article 35) ECHR. However, the Commission
gave a clear steer when it declared that:

> On the facts as presented by the parties, the Commission would not exclude that the
> absence of an actionable remedy in relation to the publications of which the applicants
> complain could show a lack of respect for their private lives. It has regard in this respect
> to the duties and responsibilities that are carried with the right of freedom of expres-
> sion guaranteed by Article 10 ... and to the Contracting States' obligation to provide a
> measure of protection to the right of privacy of an individual affected by the exercise of
> another's freedom of expression.[29]

In *Von Hannover v Germany (No 1)*,[30] the Court made it clear that an individual
whose privacy is violated by another individual must have a remedy in national
law and that the 'touchstone'[31] regarding the conflict between private life and freedom of expression is whether publication is justified by the contribution that is
made to a debate of general public interest.

Although it is clear that freedom of expression enjoys particular strength,
Strasbourg has not prioritised expression over other rights and other than confirming that some rights are absolute has not generally stratified rights.[32] Indeed,
in the recent Grand Chamber decision in *Von Hannover (No 2) v Germany*, the
Court reiterated that the outcome in a case should not in theory vary according
to whether it has been lodged with the Court under Article 8 by the person who
was the subject of the Article 8 violation or under Article 10 by the publisher. As a
matter of principle the rights deserve equal respect.[33]

In *Von Hannover (No 2)*, the Court set out the criteria that are relevant to balancing the right to freedom of expression against the right to respect for private
life, as follows:

(i)   the contribution the impugned articles or photos make to a debate of
         general interest;
(ii)   how well-known is the person concerned and what is the subject of the
         report?
(iii)   the prior conduct of the person concerned;
(iv)   the content, form and consequences of the publication; and
(v)   the circumstances in which photos were taken.

In addition, in *Axel Springer AG v Germany*, the Strasbourg Court added the
method of obtaining the information and its veracity and the severity of the
sanction.[34]

---

[29] (1995) 25 EHRR CD 105 [112].
[30] (2005) 40 EHRR 1.
[31] To borrow from Rainey, Wicks and Ovey (n 9) 375.
[32] Fenwick and Phillipson (n 26) 691.
[33] *Von Hannover v Germany (No 2)* (2012) 55 EHRR 15 [106].
[34] (2012) 55 EHRR 62.

The touchstone test of whether the impugned information contributes to a debate of general interest derives from *Von Hannover v Germany (No 1)*. The applicant was Princess Caroline of Monaco who complained that the failure of the German courts to grant relief regarding the publication of photographs of her going about her daily life, including in public spaces, was a violation of her Article 8 right to respect for private life. The Court held that:

> The Court considers that a fundamental distinction needs to be made between reporting facts—even controversial ones—capable of contributing to a debate in a democratic society, relating to politicians in the exercise of their functions, for example, and reporting details of the private life of an individual who, moreover, as in this case, does not exercise official functions. While in the former case the press exercises the role of 'watchdog' in a democracy by contributing to 'impart[ing] information and ideas on matters of public interest'; it does not do so in the latter case.[35]

The reasoning has been criticised for its unduly restrictive view of the press in that it rules out in advance the 'possibility of any speech value in private facts'.[36] In *Von Hannover v Germany (No 1)*, the Court equated the notion of a 'public figure' with someone who performs 'official functions': on that basis Princess Caroline was not a public figure and therefore information about her could not contribute to a debate of general interest. This is an extraordinarily narrow view of a' public figure'; Judge Barreto, while concurring that there had been a violation of Article 8 regarding certain images (those of Princess Caroline playing tennis and riding on horseback), dissented from the majority on this point. He stated that:

> Public figures are persons holding public office and/or using public resources and, more broadly speaking, all those who play a role in public life, whether in politics, the economy, the arts, the social sphere, sport or in any other domain'—paragraph 7 of Resolution 1165 (1998) of the Parliamentary Assembly of the Council of Europe on the right to privacy (see paragraph 42 of the judgment). It is well known that the applicant has for years played a role in European public life, even if she does not perform any official functions in her own country.

The corollary of the majority view would be that reporting private facts in relation to the private life of a private figure must amount to a violation of Article 8.

The Court did state that in certain special circumstances, the public's right to be informed can extend to the private lives of public figures, particularly politicians. It would seem also that oral submissions made to the European Court on behalf Princess Caroline emphasised the campaign of harassment conducted against her by the German media. Accordingly, the Court stated that the *context* in which photographs are taken is important—here it was without the applicant's knowledge or consent—and the harassment endured by many public figures in their daily lives

---

[35] *Von Hannover v Germany* (n 30) [63].

[36] Fenwick and Phillipson (n 26) 695 who state that: 'Such a view in ruling out almost in advance the possibility of any speech value in the discussion of private facts, amounts to a strikingly restrictive view of the role of the press. And this is not a position which is properly argued for in the judgment'.

cannot be fully disregarded.[37] The case is as much about intrusion through a climate of continual harassment as it is about the publication of private information. The element of harassment has also weighed significantly with English courts.[38]

In *Von Hannover (No 2)* the Court has effectively rowed back from the position it took in *Von Hannover (No 1)* so that it would seem 'the slenderest of threads'[39] may link to a debate of general interest. Strasbourg took the opportunity to restate the principles that govern the balancing act between Articles 8 and 10 and perceptibly shifted the ordering of priority towards freedom of expression. In *Von Hannover (No 2)*, Princess Caroline had complained of an article and accompanying photos of her skiing holiday and also of two articles that contained information regarding her father, Prince Rainier's illness, and the conduct of members of his family during his illness. The German Federal Court had found that the former did not contribute to a debate of general interest while the same could not be said of the information about Prince Rainier, the reigning sovereign of the Principality of Monaco. The Federal Court held that the reigning monarch's illness was an event of contemporary society and a matter of general interest and the press was therefore entitled to report on how the Prince's children reconciled their obligations of family solidarity with the legitimate needs of their private life, among which was the desire to go on holiday. The ECtHR agreed that the photos in question did contribute 'at least to some degree, to a debate of general interest'.[40] In a clear rejection of the reasoning in *Von Hannover (No 1)*, the Court stated that

> irrespective of the question whether and to what extent the first applicant assumes official functions on behalf of the Principality of Monaco, it cannot be claimed that the applicants, who are undeniably very well known, are ordinary private individuals. They must, on the contrary, be regarded as public figures.

Importantly, the ECtHR found that the national courts had carefully balanced the respective rights and had taken account of Strasbourg case law. The Court has reiterated on a number of occasions that where the national courts have undertaken the balancing exercise in conformity with the criteria laid down in Strasbourg case law that it would require 'strong reasons to substitute its view for that of the domestic courts'.[41] While the Federal Court of Justice had changed its approach since *Von Hannover (No 1)*, the Federal Constitutional Court had confirmed the approach and undertaken a detailed analysis of Strasbourg case law, in response to the applicants' complaints that the Federal Court had disregarded

---

[37] *Von Hannover v Germany* (n 30) [64].
[38] *Murray v Express Newspapers Plc*, also known as *Murray v Big Pictures (UK) Ltd* [2008] EWCA Civ 446, [2008] 3 WLR 1360 [59].
[39] E Reid, 'Rebalancing Privacy and Freedom of Expression' (2012) *Edinburgh Law Review* 16(2), 253–58.
[40] *Von Hannover (No 2)* (n 33) [118].
[41] *Von Hannover (No 2)* (n 33) [107], citing *MGN Ltd v United Kingdom* (2011) 53 EHRR 5.

Strasbourg jurisprudence. The Strasbourg Court was surely right to find that the applicants were public figures; this does not mean of course that they have no private life to protect, but it is an appropriate starting point for performing the balancing approach rather than shutting down immediately any argument that publication may be appropriate in the circumstances. It will be recalled that the litigation leading up to *Von Hannover (No 1)* took place over the period immediately following Princess Diana's death and with it the associated public repugnance at the baser antics of the paparazzi which manifested in the Parliamentary Assembly Resolution 1165. *Von Hannover (No 1)* probably represented the lowest point for freedom of expression and the more realistic and balanced approach of *Von Hannover (No 2)* is in line with Strasbourg jurisprudence generally and to be welcomed.

The following section will examine how English courts have responded to the demands of the ECHR, as well as growing public concerns that privacy should be protected appropriately, especially in the wake of the phone hacking scandal that led to the closure of the *News of the World* newspaper. While the ECHR itself has provided the foundation for the new tort of misuse of information, references to ECHR jurisprudence are fairly scant which is probably accounted for by the fact that the House of Lords forged ahead in *Campbell v MGN Ltd*,[42] before the seminal Strasbourg decision in *Von Hannover v Germany (No 1)*.

Developments in English Law

The scope of protection in English law afforded to aspects of what can be described in broad terms as personal privacy, has widened considerably since the first edition. Through incremental development of the action for breach of confidence, a new tort of 'misuse of private information' has been recognised, a cause of action that does not require a claimant to establish a relationship of confidence between the claimant and another. These developments have taken place through the incremental development of existing legal rules, rather than innovation premised upon any specific interpretation of the HRA. The future of the HRA is in doubt, but the tort of misuse of private information is here to stay. The new tort did not grow out of the HRA and does not depend upon it for its existence.[43] Increasingly, and, as we have seen, it may well be in an attempt to future proof aspects of the protection

---

[42] [2004] UKHL 22, [2004] 2 AC 457.
[43] See https://inforrm.wordpress.com/2015/05/11/will-the-tort-of-misuse-of-private-information-disappear-if-the-human-rights-act-is-repealed-hugh-tomlinson-qc/ accessed on 24 February 2016. *Cf* N Moreham, 'Privacy and Horizontality: Relegating the Common Law' (2007) *Law Quarterly Review* 123, 373; and T Bennett, 'Horizontality's New Horizons—Re-Examining Horizontal Effect: Privacy, Defamation and the Human Rights Act' (2010) *Entertainment Law Review* 21(3), 96 (Pt 1) and 145 (Pt 2).

of individual human rights, the judiciary speak of the need to rely upon rights that are recognised by the common law, rather than litigants turning first to the HRA. This does not amount to a judicial recognition that the common law should develop to accommodate rights that are protected under the ECHR.[44] What English law has not (yet) done is to recognise explicitly a wide-ranging 'privacy' tort.[45] Thus, intrusive and offensive behaviour such as a strip search that is carried out in a humiliating fashion and in breach of the prison rules will not yield a remedy other than by bringing an action against the prison authorities under section 7 HRA. However, this assertion seems less certain in light of recent developments to protect more generally what might be termed, 'autonomy' interests, which are discussed below.

There is no neat dividing line between intrusive behaviour that causes distress and publication itself; as in the case of Strasbourg case law, the general conduct of the publisher will be relevant to the question of whether publication should be permitted. The signal failure over many years of English law to protect privacy was exemplified by the facts in *Kaye v Robertson*.[46] Kaye, a well-known actor, was recovering in hospital following brain surgery. He was in a private room with a notice on the door restricting access by visitors. Journalists gained access to the room, conducted an 'interview', took photographs and left. Fifteen minutes later Mr Kaye had no recollection of their visit. In an action to restrain publication, Kaye could not argue that his privacy had been invaded, there being no cause of action or right. In *Malone v Police Commissioner*, Megarry J held that there is no general right to privacy in English law and stated that: 'No new right in the law, fully-fledged with all the appropriate safeguards, can spring from the head of a judge deciding a particular case: only Parliament can create such a right'.[47]

So, Kaye sought an injunction to prevent publication on the alternative grounds of: trespass, passing off, libel and malicious falsehood. While the Court of Appeal considered that it was certainly arguable that the plaintiff would establish a libel by innuendo at full trial, and that a jury would 'probably' find that Mr Kaye had been libelled, such a conclusion was not 'inevitable'. Thus, the injunction on the ground of libel was refused. Limited relief was granted on the basis of malicious falsehood: the newspaper was restrained from publishing anything which could be understood as conveying the impression that the plaintiff had consented to the interview or being photographed. The Court of Appeal was unanimous in its

---

[44] *A v British Broadcasting Corporation* [2014] UKSC 25, [2015] AC 588 [55]. See discussion of Omissions in Chapter 6 and P Bowen QC, who has welcomed the 'resurgence of common law constitutionalism'—'Does the Renaissance of Common Law Rights Mean that the Human Rights Act 1998 is Unnecessary?' (2016) *European Human Rights Law Review* 4, 361–77.

[45] *Wainwright* (n 12).

[46] [1991] FSR 62.

[47] [1979] Ch 344, 372.

criticism of the common law's inadequacy to protect the claimant's rights; in the words of Bingham LJ:

> This case ... highlights, yet again, the failure of both the common law of England and statute to protect in an effective way the personal privacy of the individual citizen. ... If ever a person has a right to be let alone by strangers with no public interest to pursue, it must surely be when he lies in a hospital bed recovering from brain surgery. ...

It is striking, at least to today's eyes, that there is no reference in *Kaye* to the ECHR, no argument appears to have been put to the effect that the Article 8 right to respect for private life was engaged on the facts, nor that there was any obligation of confidentiality in relation to the information obtained from Mr Kaye. It is well-established that information relating to health is private information both under the ECHR and under the common law.[48] It was the therapeutic dimension to the information in *Campbell v MGN Ltd*[49] which persuaded the majority in the House of Lords that the publication of the photographs of Miss Campbell leaving Narcotics Anonymous was a misuse of private information. Perhaps *Kaye* is not so surprising given that Megarry J in *Malone* had emphatically declined to extend the common law in the absence of a right to privacy.

In *Malone*, the claimant sought a declaration that the interception, monitoring and recording of telephone conversations was unlawful even if done pursuant to a warrant issued by the Home Secretary. Sir Robert Megarry VC gave a judgment of many parts, but ultimately held that the practice of telephone tapping was legal but was a 'subject which cries out for legislation'. He held that the ECHR was not justiciable in the English courts so he had no jurisdiction to make a declaration regarding Article 8, but equally it was clear to him that the practice in the UK was in violation of Article 8. However, he concluded that there could be no obligation of confidentiality on someone who overhears telephone conversations, whether accidentally through a crossed line or deliberately, through telephone tapping. His reasoning appears to have been premised on that fact that everyone is aware of the possibility that they may be overheard and therefore there is no reasonable expectation of privacy/confidentiality. He then went on to say that if, contrary to his finding, such a duty of confidentiality could arise, it would be discharged where certain criteria focusing on the disclosure of 'iniquity' were satisfied:

> first, that there should be grounds for suspecting that the tapping of the particular telephone will be of material assistance in detecting or preventing crime, or discovering the criminals, or otherwise assisting in the discharge of the functions of the police in relation to crime. Second, no use should be made of any material obtained except for these purposes. Third, any knowledge of information which is not relevant to those purposes should be confined to the minimum number of persons reasonably required to carry out the process of tapping. If those requirements are satisfied, then it seems to me that there will be just cause or excuse for carrying out the tapping, and using information obtained for those limited purposes.

---

[48] *X v Y* [1988] 2 All ER 648.
[49] *Campbell* (n 42).

These criteria correspond closely to the justifications for intrusion into private life set out in Article 8(2). Interestingly, the test of reasonable expectation of privacy applied by Megarry VC seems to be the test for establishing a breach of confidence as established in *Campbell*: the claimant will need to establish that she had a reasonable expectation of privacy.

The criteria for establishing when an obligation of confidence will arise were summarised by Megarry J in his well-known dicta in *Coco v A N Clark Engineers Ltd*, to the effect that:

> three elements are normally required if, apart from contract, a case of breach of confidence is to succeed. First, the information itself, in the words of Lord Greene M.R. in the *Saltman* case must have the 'necessary quality of confidence about it'. Secondly, that information must have been imparted in circumstances importing an obligation of confidence. Thirdly, there must be an unauthorised use of that information to the detriment of the party communicating it.[50]

A duty will arise even where information is given to the recipient without an express undertaking that it will remain confidential. Provided that the recipient of the information could reasonably have been expected to understand that the information was being given to him on the basis that it should be confidential, an obligation of confidence will arise.[51] Until the advent of the HRA it was difficult to determine precisely when information is imparted in circumstances importing an obligation of confidence; in particular whether it was necessary for a relationship of confidence (whether contractual or otherwise) to exist. Returning to *Kaye*, given the claimant's compromised health condition, as recognised by the Court, he quite clearly had not consented to the contact and therefore the information pertaining to his private life could reasonably have engendered such an equitable obligation, bolstered by the ECHR. However, applying the criteria set out in *Coco*, the claim would apparently have foundered for the lack of a relationship of confidence. All the judges in *Kaye* agreed that their inability to render a remedy that fitted the wrong committed manifested the signal shortcoming of English law; despite the 'monstrous invasion' of Mr Kaye's privacy, Glidewell and Leggatt LJJ were compelled to observe that the introduction of a privacy law was a matter for Parliament. Mr Kaye's complaint was of intrusion and privacy infringement; it really had nothing to do with falsity.

The first tentative steps towards recognition that the private nature of information itself can give rise to an obligation of confidentiality, rather than the obligation being premised upon a relationship of confidence *per se*, can be tracked through a series of cases beginning with Lord Goff's well known *obiter dictum* in *Attorney General v Guardian Newspapers Ltd (No 2)* (*'Spycatcher'*).

> ... a duty of confidence arises when confidential information comes to the knowledge of a person (the confidant) in circumstances where he has notice, or is held to have

---

[50] [1948] 65 RPC 203 at 215.
[51] *Ibid* (Megarry J).

agreed, that the information is confidential, with the effect that it would be just in all the circumstances that he should be precluded from disclosing the information to others. I have used the word 'notice' advisedly, in order to avoid the (here unnecessary) question of the extent to which actual knowledge is necessary; though I of course understand knowledge to include circumstances where the confidant has deliberately closed his eyes to the obvious. The existence of this broad principle reflects the fact that there is such a public interest in the maintenance of confidences, that the law will provide remedies for their protection.

He went on to clarify that he had expressed the circumstances in which the duty arises in broad terms:

not merely to embrace those cases where a third party receives information from a person who is under a duty of confidence in respect of it, knowing that it has been disclosed by that person in breach of his duty of confidence, but also to include certain situations ... where an obviously confidential document, such as a private diary, is dropped in a public place, and is then picked up by a passer-by.[52]

In *Shelley Films Ltd v Rex Features Ltd*,[53] the defendant photographic agency bought and supplied to a newspaper a photograph which had been taken without authorisation on the set of a film in closed and secret production. In fixing the agency with the requisite knowledge, the High Court referred to the defendant coming into possession of information in circumstances where he 'ought as a reasonable person' to know that the plaintiff intended to keep the information confidential. Furthermore, Mann J rejected counsel's argument that, absent some identifiable relationship, English law does not impose any such obligation not to impart information in such circumstances. Such a contention could no longer stand in the light of Lord Goff's observations in *Spycatcher*. There is no reference to the ECHR in *Shelley Films*.

In *Spencer v United Kingdom*, the European Commission concluded after detailed consideration of *Spycatcher*, *Shelley Films*, *Barrymore (Michael) v News Group Newspapers Ltd*,[54] *Francome v Mirror Group Newspapers Ltd*[55] and *Hellewell v Chief Constable of Derbyshire*[56] that the law relating to breach of confidence had been clarified considerably since *Winer v United Kingdom* and that this clarity meant that the failure by Countess Spencer to seek a remedy based upon breach of confidence meant there had been a failure to exhaust domestic remedies as required by the then Article 26 (now Article 35) ECHR. Accordingly, the Commission considered that the parties' submissions indicated that the remedy for breach of confidence (against the newspapers and their sources) was available to the applicants and that the applicants had not demonstrated that it was insufficient or ineffective in the circumstances of their cases.

---

[52] [1990] 1 AC 109, 281D-E.
[53] [1994] EMLR 134.
[54] [1997] FSR 600.
[55] [1984] 1 WLR 892.
[56] [1995] 1 WLR 804.

Douglas v Hello! Ltd (No 1)[57] marked a very significant turning point in the legal protection of privacy, but not as has sometimes been suggested for what it determined regarding the horizontal effect of the HRA. While Sedley LJ made a number of *obiter* remarks regarding horizontality and the role of the court under section 6 HRA, they have made no lasting impact on that particular debate. The Court of Appeal was confronted with the competing claims of Michael Douglas and Catherine Zeta-Jones on the one hand, and Hello! Ltd on the other, regarding the impending publication of photographs that had been taken surreptitiously at their wedding and distributed to the proprietors of Hello! magazine. The couple had sold the exclusive right to cover their wedding to the rival celebrity publication OK! Despite tight security, Hello! magazine obtained copies of the photographs and injunctive relief was sought by the claimants, including Northern & Shell Plc, the proprietors of OK! magazine in order to restrain publication by Hello! magazine.

The facts are well known, but important points to note are that at the wedding and reception only the claimants' photographer was permitted to take photographs, all guests were searched for cameras on arrival and the claimants' employees signed agreements not to take photographs. An injunction had been granted by Buckley J late in the evening, and continued by Hunt J on the basis that the images were confidential and that the defendants were in breach of confidence and probably breach of contract and malicious falsehood as well. The Court of Appeal was unanimous that the claimants would be likely to establish at trial that publication should not be allowed; however, the injunction was discharged because the balance of convenience as between the two magazines favoured Hello!, as it would be difficult to compute Hello!'s losses if publication were wrongfully prevented. The Court took the view that this was essentially a commercial dispute between two rival magazines in the same market which were not averse to adopting spoiling tactics against each other and that any damage to the claimants could be dealt with in monetary terms.

On the other hand, if OK! were to win at trial it would be able to pursue the equitable remedy of an account of profits or damages (Brooke LJ, Sedley LJ concurring) and any damage to the claimants could be adequately dealt with in monetary terms (Keene LJ). Sedley LJ also considered that while the celebrity couple would be likely to establish a breach of their privacy at trial, they had sold 'by far the greater part of that privacy [which] falls to be protected, if at all, in the hands of the third claimant. This can be done without the need of an injunction'.

In terms of the cause of action, both Brooke LJ and Keene LJ considered that it was arguable that the photographs constituted confidential information. For Brooke LJ there had been a real effort to inform those entering relevant parts of the wedding venue that the occasion had the characteristics of confidentiality. So far as the necessity for a confidential relationship was concerned, *Barrymore*

---

[57] [2001] QB 967.

v News Group Newspapers[58] and *Creation Records v News Group Newspapers Ltd*[59] demonstrated that an injunction would be granted where photographs had been taken surreptitiously and in circumstances in which the photographer would be taken to have known that the occasion was a private one where the taking of photos by outsiders was not permitted. Brooke LJ took into account the Commission finding in *Spencer* that the applicants had failed to exhaust their domestic remedies. Counsel for the UK Government in *Spencer* had argued that the applicants would have had a remedy in breach of confidence. In this respect, the Commission had relied heavily on the strong and detailed case of the applicants in the domestic proceedings which pointed to their former friends as the direct source of the essential confidential information that had been published. Thus, on the *Spencer* facts, the criteria set out by Megarry J in *Coco* appear to have been met. Brooke LJ accepted counsel's argument that the law is 'adequately configured to respect the Convention' by virtue of the action for breach of confidence.

Keene LJ considered the role of the court under section 6 HRA but held that it was unnecessary to determine whether the courts can create new causes of action because reliance was placed on the established cause of action for breach of confidence. Importantly, he stated that the obligation of confidentiality can arise as a result of the subject matter itself or the circumstances of the defendant's activities may suffice in some instances to give rise to liability.

Sedley LJ went further and declared that the claimants had a legal right to respect for their privacy which had been infringed. We have reached a point, he stated, where it can be said with confidence that the law recognises and will appropriately protect privacy. He was satisfied that the claimants would be likely to establish at trial a breach of their privacy. The arguments put forward by the UK in *Spencer* tended to support this conclusion, as did the remarks of Lord Nicholls in *R v Khan (Sultan)* regarding the developing principle of privacy protection, 'I prefer to leave open for another occasion the important question whether the present, piecemeal protection of privacy has now developed to the extent that a more comprehensive principle can be seen to exist.'[60]

To conclude the discussion of *Douglas v Hello! Ltd*, in relation to the need to recognise a privacy right, all members of the Court of Appeal proceeded on the basis that English law should now, in the light of Article 8 ECHR, protect privacy. Sedley LJ alone spoke of the claimants having 'a legal right to respect for their privacy'. Brooke LJ analysed the ECHR jurisprudence on positive obligations and implied that following *Spencer* English law should protect privacy, but he expressed no conclusion regarding the appropriate cause of action. He was open to the view that such protection might be otherwise than through the law of confidence:

> Whether they do so in future by an extension of the existing frontiers of the law of confidence, or by recognising the existence of new relationships which give rise to enforceable

---

[58] *Barrymore* (n 54).
[59] [1997] EMLR 444.
[60] [1997] AC 558, 582–83.

rights (as happened in relation to the law of negligence ever since the 3–2 decision of the House of Lords in *Donoghue v Stevenson*) is not for this court, on this occasion to predict.[61]

Finally, in a much-anticipated development,[62] in *Campbell v Mirror Group Newspapers Ltd*,[63] the House of Lords confirmed that it was no longer necessary to establish a relationship of confidence in order to restrain the publication of private information. The defendant newspaper had published details of Ms Campbell's drug addiction and the therapy she was undertaking with Narcotics Anonymous. The newspaper claimed that it was entitled to set the record straight by refuting her untrue claims that she did not take drugs. The defendant disclosed the fact of the claimant's drug addiction and that she was receiving treatment and published photographs of her leaving the treatment centre and hugging other clients. At trial the relevant information was categorised as follows:

(i)   the fact of Miss Campbell's drug addiction;
(ii)   the fact that she was receiving treatment;
(iii)   the fact that she was receiving treatment at Narcotics Anonymous;
(iv)   the details of the treatment—how long she had been attending meetings, how often she went, how she was treated within the sessions themselves, the extent of her commitment, and the nature of her entrance on the specific occasion; and
(v)   the visual portrayal of her leaving a specific meeting with other addicts and being hugged before such a meeting by other members of the group receiving treatment.[64]

It was conceded by counsel for Ms Campbell that her 'public lies' entitled *The Mirror* to publish the information in categories (i) and (ii). Ms Campbell challenged the newspaper's claim to be entitled to publish the information in (iii) to (v). By a majority of 3:2, the House of Lords held that Ms Campbell had a reasonable expectation of privacy in relation to this information. Although their Lordships disagreed as to the outcome, this was on a narrow point, and all agreed on the principles to be applied.[65] The significance of the case is that it is authority at the highest level rejecting the need for a relationship of confidence in order to found the cause of action. Lord Nicholls stated that the time had come to recognise that the values enshrined in Articles 8 and 10 are now part of the cause of action for breach of confidence[66] and that the 'touchstone of private life is whether in respect

---

[61] *Douglas v Hello! Ltd (No 1)* (n 57) 129.
[62] G Phillipson, 'Transforming Breach of Confidence? Towards a Common Law Right of Privacy under the Human Rights Act' (2003) 66 *Modern Law Review* 726.
[63] *Campbell* (n 42).
[64] *Campbell* (n 42) [23].
[65] *Campbell* (n 42) [36] (Lord Hoffmann).
[66] *Campbell* (n 42) [17].

of the disclosed facts the person in question had a reasonable expectation of privacy'.[67] In an observation that has particular significance regarding more recent developments, Lord Nicholls cautioned his fellow judges, in deciding what is the ambit of a person's private life, to 'be on guard against using as a touchstone a test which brings into account considerations which should more properly be considered at a later stage of proportionality'.[68]

Lord Nicholls stated that the cause of action has now firmly shaken off the limiting constraint of the need for an initial confidential relationship and he applied Lord Goff's formulation from *Spycatcher*—a duty of confidence will be imposed whenever a person receives information he knows or ought to know is fairly and reasonably to be regarded as confidential. However, he held that the essence of the tort is better encapsulated as misuse of private information.[69] Furthermore, he held that the values enshrined in Articles 8 and 10 are directly applicable between non-state actors. In so doing he stated that it was not necessary to 'decide whether the duty imposed on courts by section 6 of the HRA extends to questions of substantive law as distinct from questions of practice and procedure'. Instead, the time had come to recognise that the values enshrined in Articles 8 and 10 are now part of the cause of action for breach of confidence. Lord Nicholls cited the observation of Lord Woolf to the effect that the courts have been able to recognise the new tort by absorbing the rights protected by Articles 8 and 10 into the action for breach of confidence.[70] Further, Lord Nicholls observed, that it should now be recognised that for this purpose these values are of general application. The values embodied in Articles 8 and 10 are as much applicable in disputes between individuals or between an individual and a non-governmental body such as a newspaper as they are in disputes between individuals and a public authority.

Lord Nicholls described these developments as having been 'spurred by the enactment of the Human Rights Act 1998'.[71] With the greatest respect to Lord Nicholls, this rather overstates the case. As we have seen, the common law developments were anticipated by cases such as *Francome*, *Shelley Films*, *Creation Records* and the like and pre-dated the HRA. What is more, in *Spencer v UK*, it was counsel for the UK Government that had urged the Commission to find that the Spencers had not exhausted domestic remedies because they had not pleaded a claim in breach of confidence. As Sedley LJ remarked in *Douglas v Hello! Ltd (No 1)*, it would not be a happy thing if the national courts were without good reason to reject the UK's successful exegesis of its own law.

---

[67] *Campbell* (n 42) [21].
[68] *Campbell* (n 42) [21].
[69] *Campbell* (n 42) [14].
[70] *A v B Plc* [2003] QB 195, 202 [4].
[71] *Ibid* [11].

This survey has demonstrated that it is the ECHR mediated through the action for breach of confidence that has shaped the development of privacy in English law, English courts supporting the development of the law in a way that is consistent with the underlying values recognised through our treaty obligations. This is why the repeal of the HRA, whether replaced by a British Bill of Rights or not, will not make a significant impact on this area of the law. The Government has indicated that the British Bill will include all the ECHR rights and the United Kingdom will remain a party to the ECHR so it is reasonable to anticipate that this new tort will continue to develop, informed directly by ECHR jurisprudence under Articles 8 and 10 ECHR.

Two weeks after the House of Lords delivered judgment in *Campbell*, the ECtHR gave its judgment in *Von Hannover v Germany (No 1)*. The Court reiterated that the concept of private life extends to aspects relating to personal identity, such as one's name[72] or a person's picture.[73] Furthermore, in a familiar reference to *Niemitz v Swizerland*,[74] the Court stated that

> 'private life' includes a person's physical and psychological integrity; the guarantee afforded by Article 8 of the Convention is primarily intended to ensure the development, without outside interference, of the personality of each individual in his relations with other human beings …'

The Court also stated, citing *Peck v United Kingdom*, that 'there is therefore a zone of interaction of a person with others, even in a public context, which may fall within the scope of "private life"'. It is important to note that the jurisprudence of the ECtHR explains both the rationale for the right, as well as instancing the dimensions of private life, intrusion upon which will inhibit the capacity of an individual to shape his life and his relationships with others. English law has generally focused so far narrowly on the 'misuse of private information', rather than intrusion upon private life in a broader sense. However, a rider to this must be now be added.

In *Gulati v MGN Ltd*,[75] one of the claimants whose phone had been hacked for seven years, but without the publication of private information taking place, nevertheless received substantial damages for loss of autonomy over the information obtained. This is typical of the way in which the common law (including equity) develops; the reasoning is inductive rather than deductive. While this may mean that solutions to particular problems withstand analysis, charting the course of future developments in the absence of decisions grounded upon a sound theoretical basis becomes more of a challenge. Lord Hoffmann in *Campbell* does explore the more abstract question of why we should protect privacy. He said: 'what human rights law has done is to identify private information as something worth protecting as an aspect of human autonomy and dignity'.

---

[72] *Burghartz v Switzerland* (1994) 18 EHRR 101.
[73] *Schussel v Austria* Application No 42409/98 (unreported).
[74] (1993) 16 EHRR 97.
[75] *Gulati* (nn 6 and 7).

Reasonable Expectation of Privacy Test

As we have seen, the touchstone for engagement of Article 8 is whether the claimant has a 'reasonable expectation of privacy'. The answer to this question is highly fact dependent. In the words of Sir Anthony Clarke in *Murray v Express Newspapers Plc*,[76] and most recently applied by the Court of Appeal in *Weller v Associated Newspapers Ltd*,[77] and *K v News Group Newspapers Ltd*,[78] the question is

> a broad one which takes account of all the circumstances of the case. They include the attributes of the claimant, the nature of the activity in which the claimant was engaged, the place at which it was happening, the nature and purpose of the intrusion, the absence of consent and whether it was known or could be inferred, the effect on the claimant and the circumstances in which and the purposes for which the information came into the hands of the publisher.[79]

Details of a person's sexual life will be protected under Article 8. It is well-established that the publication of 'kiss and tell' stories which aim to satisfy the prurient interests of the public do not serve any 'legally protected public interest',[80] unless there is some element of setting the record straight. In *PJS v News Group Newspapers Ltd*,[81] publication of details of an adulterous sexual encounter was restrained because there was no public interest in publication; there was no false image to correct because while the couple were 'committed' it was accepted by the Court that commitment did may not entail monogamy. Furthermore, the fact that the information was already in the public domain and was widely known did not affect the claim; Article 8 in such cases protects privacy, not secrecy.[82]

There has been some uncertainty regarding the applicability of the test deriving from Lord Hope's speech in *Campbell* to the effect that where it is not obvious whether information is private, the broad test is 'whether disclosure of the information about the individual ("A") would give substantial offence to A, assuming that A was placed in similar circumstances and was a person of ordinary sensibilities'. Lord Hope drew upon the test that had been applied by Gleeson CJ in *Australian Broadcasting Corporation v Lenah Game Meats Pty Ltd*[83] and which was also applied by the trial judge in *Campbell*. The reference to a person of ordinary

---

[76] *Murray* (n 38).
[77] [2015] EWCA Civ 1176, [2016] EMLR 7.
[78] [2011] EWCA Civ 439, [2011] 1 WLR 1827.
[79] *Murray* (n 38) [36].
[80] *PJS v News Group Newspapers* [2016] UKSC 26 [41] (Lord Mance), citing *Couderc and Hachette Filipacchi Associates* Application No 41454/07 [100]–[101] and *Axel Springer* (n 34).
[81] *PJS*, ibid.
[82] *Cf* breach of confidence in *Spycatcher* where there may be no confidential information left to protect.
[83] (2001) 208 CLR 199.

sensibilities is, as Gleeson CJ acknowledged in his footnote on p 226, a quotation from an article by William L Prosser.[84] As William Prosser put it,

> the matter made public must be one which would be offensive and objectionable to a reasonable man of ordinary sensibilities, who must expect some reporting of his daily activities. The law of privacy is not intended for the protection of the unduly sensitive.[85]

Indeed, this formulation finds its way into the forefront of the headnote, but Lord Nicholls was rightly concerned that such an approach might confuse engagement of Article 8 with the issue of justification for interference under Article 8(2) and the need to seek a balance between 8 and 10. He pointed out that the American Law Institute uses the formulation of disclosure of a matter which 'would be highly offensive to a reasonable person'.[86] A similar approach has been taken in Australia.[87] However, in *Campbell*, Lord Nicholls cautioned that there are two problems with the 'highly offensive' test. First it sets the bar for establishing a reasonable expectation of privacy too high. Second, it is a formulation that suggests a conclusion derived from balancing the considerations which go more properly to issues of proportionality; for instance, the degree of intrusion into private life, and the extent to which publication was a matter of proper public concern. This could be a recipe for confusion.[88] Such confusion surfaced in an appeal from the Divisional Court of Northern Ireland.

In *JR38's Application for Judicial Review*,[89] a teenage boy appealed against the dismissal of his application for judicial review of a decision by the police to release a photograph of him alleging that he had been involved in public order offences. The police had tried to identify him by other means. A majority in the Divisional Court held that Article 8 was engaged on the facts, but the child's privacy had not been breached in the light of the safeguards that had been put in place prior to publication. However, somewhat disturbingly, a majority in the Supreme Court held that Article 8 was not even engaged on the facts; Lord Kerr and Lord Wilson dissented on this point. Lord Kerr took the view that the 'reasonable expectation of privacy' test is not or should not be the 'touchstone' for engagement of Article 8. Both Strasbourg and English courts have applied this test, although the precise wording may vary. The main plank of Lord Kerr's judgment is the obligation on the Court to give prominence to the child's best interests; there may therefore be conflict between the reasonable expectation of privacy test and the child's best interests. Lord Kerr was particularly concerned that the majority had not taken account of the applicant's age and urged the need to avoid stigmatisation and

---

[84] William L Prosser, 'Privacy' (1960) 48 *California Law Review* 383.
[85] *Ibid* 396–97.
[86] The American Law Institute, *Restatement of the Law*, Torts, 2d (1977), section 652D.
[87] *Australian Broadcasting Corporation* (n 83).
[88] *Campbell* (n 42) [22] (Lord Nicholls).
[89] [2013] NIQB 44, [2015] UKSC 42, [2015] 3 WLR 155.

criminalisation of children: children need to be protected from the consequences of their own foolishness.

In *Kinloch v HM Advocate*,[90] the police conducted covert surveillance of the applicant who was subsequently convicted of laundering criminal property. The applicant complained that his Article 8 right had been breached. In a judgment with which the other members of the Court agreed, Lord Hope stated that:

> There is a zone of interaction with others, even in a public context, which may fall within the scope of private life: *PG v United Kingdom*, 46 EHRR 1272, para 56. But measures effected in a public place outside the person's home or private premises will not, *without more*, be regarded as interfering with his right to respect for his private life. Occasions when a person knowingly or intentionally involves himself in activities which may be recorded or reported in public, in circumstances where he does not have a reasonable expectation of privacy, will fall into that category: *PG v United Kingdom*, para 57.

The big question is what is the '*more*' that will take the measures effected in a public place out of what is acceptable and into unacceptable incursion into private life territory. In *Campbell*, the photographs and the details regarding Miss Campbell's visits and treatment at Narcotics Anonymous were a violation because they were about an intensely personal issue, namely health. As Baroness Hale remarked, while some members of the public might like to see what Naomi Campbell looks like when she pops out for a pint of milk, there is nothing inherently private about that activity.[91]

In the *Peck* case, the applicant who was severely depressed was filmed on closed-circuit television in a shopping centre, carrying a kitchen knife which he subsequently used to slit his wrists. He was seen by the CCTV operator who called the police and, as Mr Peck accepted, may well have saved his life. The images were released to local press and other media as an example of the success of CCTV. The ECtHR noted that the monitoring itself, of which Mr Peck did not complain, did not give rise to an interference with private life; however, the release of the images was considered a violation as there was no attempt to obtain consent and his identity had not been disguised. The 'something more' referred to by Lord Hope is the fact that Mr Peck was in a state of mental ill-health. Arguably, in the case of *J38*, it was the fact that the appellant was a child and the need to consider rehabilitation and education and which had weighed so heavily with Lord Kerr that should mean that 'private life' is engaged; there may well be a justification for interference, as Lord Kerr in fact found, but to say that there is no reasonable expectation of privacy in the case of a juvenile is to disregard the rationale for the right: Lord Kerr quoted the important principle recapitulated by the ECtHR in *PG v United Kingdom*:

> 'Private life' is a broad term not susceptible to exhaustive definition. … Article 8 also protects a right to identity and personal development, and the right to establish and develop

---

[90] [2012] UKSC 62, [2013] 2 WLR 141.
[91] *Campbell* (n 42) [154]. See also *John v Associated Newspapers Ltd* [2006] EWHC 1611.

relationships with other human beings and the outside world. It may include activities of a professional or business nature. There is therefore a zone of interaction of a person with others, even in a public context, which may fall within the scope of 'private life'.[92]

These sentiments go beyond the notion of physical and psychological integrity long recognised as intrinsic to Article 8 and arguably extend to the need to consider the protection of the vulnerable such as Mr Peck and JR38 from the consequences of their own actions. Lord Clarke in *JR38* did say that had the photographs been published for some reason other than identification, Article 8(1) rights might have been engaged. Again, that is to confuse the issues of engagement of the right to respect for private life under Article 8(1) and justification for the interference in accordance with Article 8(2). This does matter because if engagement of Article 8 is not recognised, there can be no court supervision through the application of the criteria set out in Article 8(2) and in particular there will be no assessment of the proportionality of interference with the right to respect for private life.

In *Weller*, the claimants were the children of a famous musician who been photographed when out shopping with their father and relaxing at a cafe. Their father had remonstrated with the photographer who had given an assurance that any published photographs would be pixellated. In fact, the photos were published by the *Mail Online*, showing the children's faces and giving their names. Their father had not given interviews regarding his children or family life, although he had mentioned them in answers to questions in interviews. On the question of whether the children[93] had a reasonable expectation of privacy, the Court of Appeal applied the criteria laid down in *Murray* and *Von Hannover (No 2)*. Lord Dyson, giving judgment for the Court, laid considerable stress on the fact that although the children had been photographed in public, the occasion was a family outing which is an important aspect of the children's autonomy; it is not like the example given of Naomi Campbell popping out for a pint of milk or Elton John being snapped in the street with his chauffeur.[94] In considering the criteria set out in *Von Hannover (No 2)*, it was relevant, although not determinative, to consider whether the publication contributed to a debate of general interest and unsurprisingly the Court found that it did not.

Lord Dyson stated that the starting point is the place where the activity happened and the nature of the activity. In terms of the 'what is more' that takes an innocuous and commonplace event taking place in public into the private realm it is the element of family life which is protected by the broader right of personal autonomy. This added dimension distinguishes *Weller* from the example of Naomi Campbell popping out for a bottle of milk.[95]

---

[92] (2001) 46 EHRR 1272 [56].
[93] Their father made no claim *cf Von Hannover (No 1)* (n 30) and *(No 2)* (n 33).
[94] *John* (n 91).
[95] *Ibid.*

Lord Dyson cited the speech of Lord Sumption in *R (Catt) v Association of Chief Police Officers*. In *Catt*, the claimants had challenged the systematic retention of electronic data by the police. In one case, an elderly man had been active in the Peace movement for many years and had taken part peacefully in demonstrations organised by an extreme protest group. In the second case, the claimant had challenged the police practice of retaining data on harassment cases; the applicant had been involved in a minor altercation with a neighbour which had then been reported to the police. The Supreme Court held that Article 8, 'the most elastic of the rights protected by the Convention', was engaged in both cases. The collection and storage of the information was an interference with private life. However in the first case, it was a proportionate interference; in the second case the policy was lawful provided it was flexible enough to allow for deletion of the information when it was no longer required. Lord Sumption highlighted the fact that a feature of both the cases is that they related to acts of individuals in public spaces. Lord Sumption said this:

> [In light of the] expanded concept of private life in the jurisprudence of the Convention, the [reasonable expectation of privacy test] cannot be limited to cases where a person can be said to have a reasonable expectation about the privacy of his home or personal communications. It must extend to every occasion on which a person has a reasonable expectation that there will be no interference with *the broader right of personal autonomy* recognised in the case law of the Strasbourg court. This is consistent with the recognition that there may be some matters about which there is a reasonable expectation of privacy, notwithstanding that they occur in public and are patent to all the world. In this context mere observation cannot save in perhaps extreme circumstances, engage article 8, but the systematic retention of data may do.[96]

The Balancing Act

Where the applicant can establish that she has a reasonable expectation of privacy, at the next stage the court will apply what has been termed 'an intense focus' on the particular circumstances of the case, in order to arrive at a determination of where the balance lies between the competing rights concerned. This is intensely fact specific.[97] In a much-cited dictum, Lord Steyn stated in *Re S (A Child)*,[98]

> First, neither Article has *as such* precedence over the other. Secondly, where the values under the two Articles are in conflict, an intense focus on the comparative importance of the specific rights being claimed in the individual case is necessary. Thirdly, the justifications for interfering with or restricting each right must be taken into account. Finally, the

---

[96] [2015] UKSC 9, [2015] AC 1065 [10] (Lord Sumption).
[97] *Hutcheson v News Group Newspapers Ltd* [2011] EWCA Civ 808, [2012] EMLR 2.
[98] [2004] UKHL 47, [2005] 1 AC 593 [17].

proportionality test must be applied to each. For convenience I will call this the ultimate balancing test.

The case *Re S* concerned the application by a guardian in care proceedings of a young boy whose mother had been indicted for the murder of his older brother. The judge at first instance had granted an injunction restraining the identification of the child's mother. This injunction was lifted and S appealed. Lord Steyn carefully balanced the Article 8 right of the child and the Article 10 right of the press, but concluded overall that the balance came down in favour of the freedom of the press to report criminal trials; there is a strong public interest in maintaining public confidence in the impartial administration of justice.

Re S was decided before the important Strasbourg decision in *Neulinger and Shuruk v Switzerland*.[99] *Neulinger* concerned the question of whether an order that a child be returned to Israel by his mother who had fled to Switzerland should be enforced. The ECtHR held that the state's obligations under Article 8 could not be interpreted in a vacuum and should be interpreted in harmony with general principles of international law. The relevant rules here included the Hague Convention on the Civil Aspects of International Child Abduction 1980 and the UN Convention on the Rights of the Child. Article 3 of the latter states that 'In all actions concerning children, whether undertaken by public or private social welfare institutions, courts of law, administrative authorities or legislative bodies, the best interests of the child shall be the primary consideration'. It was held that to return the child to Israel in accordance with the Hague Convention would be incompatible with the child and mother's private lives.

In *K v News Group Newspapers*, the Court of Appeal referred to the need since *Neulinger* for a reappraisal regarding how the balance between competing rights under Article 8 and 10 should be struck.[100] Thus, in *K*, the defendant newspaper was injuncted from publishing details of an affair between two colleagues in the entertainment industry. The injunction was sought on the basis that neither party sought disclosure and the applicant wished to rebuild his family life in the absence of press intrusion. The Court held that it should accord particular weight to the Article 8 rights of any children likely to be affected by the publication, if that would be likely to harm their interests. Where a tangible and objective public interest tends to favour publication, the balance may be difficult to strike. The force of the public interest will be highly material, and the interests of affected children cannot be treated as a trump card.

Importantly, Ward LJ took into account the best interests of the children involved and the adverse impact of publicity upon them. In *K*, Ward LJ stated that a restriction can only be justified if it is proportionate and is no more than is necessary to promote the legitimate object of the restriction. To restrict publication

---

[99] [2011] FLR 122.
[100] *K v News Group* (n 78) [20].

simply to save the blushes of the famous, fame invariably being ephemeral, could have the wholly undesirable chilling effect on the necessary ability of publishers to sell their newspapers. We have to enable sales if we want to keep our newspapers. Unduly to fetter their freedom to report as editors judged to be responsible is to undermine the pre-eminence of the deserved place of the press as a powerful pillar of democracy. These considerations require the court to tread warily before granting this kind of injunction. In K, however, there was no demonstrable public interest in publication:

> there is no political edge to the publication. The organisation of the economic, social and political life of the country, so crucial to democracy, is not enhanced by publication. The intellectual, artistic or personal development of members of society is not stunted by ignorance of the sexual frolics of figures known to the public. As Lord Hope of Craighead said of Miss Campbell, 'it is not enough to deprive Miss Campbell of her right to privacy that she is a celebrity and that her private life is newsworthy'.[101]

In *Weller*, the Court of Appeal confirmed that a child's right is not a trump card in the balancing exercise, but it might require very 'powerful art 10 rights (for example, exceptional reasons in the public interest) to outweigh a child's art 8 rights where publication would be harmful to the child'.[102]

Injunctive Relief

Section 12 HRA applies whenever the court is considering whether to grant any relief which, if granted, might affect the exercise of the Convention right to freedom of expression. Section 12(3) applies to prior restraints and provides a threshold test: no relief should be granted 'unless the court is satisfied that the applicant is likely to establish at trial that publication should not be allowed'. Section 12(4) states that the court must have particular regard to the importance of the Convention right to freedom of expression. Section 12 was inserted to allay press fears that the introduction of Article 8 into domestic law would lead to extensive restrictions on freedom of expression. The then Home Secretary stated that, whenever there is a clash between Article 8 and Article 10 rights, '[the courts] must pay particular attention to the Article 10 rights'.[103] This has not happened; the Supreme Court

---

[101] *Campbell* (n 42) [120].
[102] *Weller* (n 77) [40].
[103] HC Deb 2 July 1998, vol 315, col 543, Secretary of State for the Home Department, Mr Jack Straw, quoted by Amos (n 15). See comments by the Joint Committee on Human Rights regarding the draft Defamation Bill, Chapter 7, text accompanying n 40.

has very recently confirmed that there is no presumptive priority in favour of Article 10. Different considerations apply in claims for injunctive relief based upon breach of confidence as opposed to privacy.

The Supreme Court's decision in *PJS*[104] is important on this point. Stories of the claimant's extra-marital affair had been widely published overseas, online and in the print media, but the injunction to restrain publication was granted. The Supreme Court emphasised the *qualitative* difference in terms of intrusion if unrestrained publication by the English media were permitted. If the claim had been based solely on breach of confidence, then the quantitative approach that asks how much has been published and what is there left to protect may be decisive.[105] Where there has been widespread publication, restraint cannot be justified as there is no 'confidence' left to protect.

In *PJS*, the interests of the claimant's children were also significant. Although not a trump card, section 12(4)(b) HRA requires the court to have regard to any relevant privacy code. The defendant is a member of the Independent Press Standards Organisation, whose code notes that 'editors must demonstrate an exceptional public interest to over-ride the normally paramount interests of children under 16'.

From Misuse of Private Information to Intrusion—*Gulati v MGN Ltd*

Arguably, one of the most important decisions in the last 10 years is *Gulati v MGN Ltd*,[106] a decision of the Court of Appeal from which permission to appeal was refused by the Supreme Court. The proceedings arose from the use of phone hacking by MGN Ltd on an industrial scale. It is difficult to know exactly what the case stands for because liability by MGN Ltd for infringements of privacy rights by obtaining confidential or private information from phone hacking was conceded. In every case, apart from one, the hacking had led to publication. The Court of Appeal upheld Mann J's awards of damages in respect of loss of privacy or autonomy resulting from the hacking itself, damages arising from publication of private information and damages for distress. The Court held that damages in respect of the invasion of privacy rights themselves would not amount to introduction of vindicatory damages for interference with a private right. It seems from *Gulati* that the act of interfering with the private sphere through *accessing* and intruding upon personal information such that the claimant loses their autonomy over that

---

[104] *PJS* (n 80).
[105] *PJS* (n 80) [25] (Lord Mance), citing *Sunday Times v United Kingdom (No 2)* (1991) 14 EHRR 229 [54]–[56].
[106] *Gulati* (n 7).

information is sufficient to ground the action; in other words, infringement of privacy rights is a tort that is actionable per se. Where phone hacking has occurred, then, according to the Court of Appeal, the victim has lost their autonomy over the information and will be able to recover damages for the distress caused in the absence of publication and/or material harm.

In *Catt*, Lord Sumption emphasised that Article 8 is about autonomy; however that was in an application by way of judicial review where ECHR rights are applied directly (vertically) to the claim against the public authority under the HRA. It is not authority for the mediation of ECHR rights into the private sphere; however, it is part and parcel of the growing recognition of the rationale for diverse interests protected by Article 8. In *PJS*, Lord Mance cited with approval the work of Moreham who has identified the core components of the right to privacy as 'unwanted access to private information and unwanted access to [or intrusion into] one's personal space'.[107] English law has travelled a great distance since the dark days of *Kaye*.

Damages

Claims brought in relation to the tort of misuse of private information or intrusion are private law claims. Their gestation has developed through the mediation of ECHR values into private law, but they are not claims under the HRA and as such are not governed by either section 8 HRA or Article 41 ECHR.[108] In *Gulati*, MGN Ltd appealed against damages awards ranging from £72,500 to £260,250 for misuse of private information, phone hacking and distress suffered as a consequence. MGN Ltd argued that the damages should be limited to distress but Mann J at first instance held that damages could also be awarded for the loss of privacy or autonomy over personal information resulting from the fact of the phone hacking. He awarded damages for each published article, the phone hacking itself and the distress caused by being hacked. Alan Yentob's mobile phone had been hacked at least twice a day for seven years, but there had been no publication. Mr Yentob suffered deep hurt and anger and was awarded £85,000 for the hacking plus an amount for distress and a small amount of aggravated damages. It was held that damages could be awarded for the loss of the right to control information, as well as for distress at information being exploited.

---

[107] NJ Moreham, *The Law of Privacy and the Media*, 2nd edn (Oxford, Oxford University Press, 2011).

[108] *Gulati* (n 7).

Concluding Remarks on the Tort of
Misuse of Private Information

The content of this tort is now informed directly by the Strasbourg jurisprudence under Articles 8 and 10. Furthermore, in terms of the balancing act, which has been described as analogous to a discretion, the court will take account of other international obligations, especially in relation to children. The development of privacy case law is evidence of a strengthening common law human rights jurisdiction. It is also a jurisdiction that is not dependent upon any particular interpretation of the HRA. It is striking that English courts have never determined precisely how the jurisprudence is mediated into English law. The bones of the new tort of misuse of private information have been fleshed out by the ECHR case law; while there has been some flirtation with principles derived from other jurisdictions, the approach is strongly influenced by Strasbourg. Where there are competing claims under Articles 8 and 10, neither takes precedence and determination of where the balance lies is a highly factually specific enquiry. The general principles have been established but it is not impossible to sympathise with newspaper editors who have expressed frustration regarding the lack of predictability and also the fact that this area of the law has been developed in the English courtroom by a small cadre of the judiciary. However, the latter point is easily overstated; the ECtHR is staffed by a judiciary from a wide range of backgrounds and perspectives and it was inevitable that the signal failure of English law to afford effective protection for privacy was bound eventually to be redressed.

A detailed examination of the Leveson Report and the follow up to recommendations is outside the scope of this work, but for the sake of completeness a number of observations will be made. Following a lengthy inquiry into the *Culture, Practices and Ethics of the Press* set up under Lord Justice Leveson, the Royal Charter on Self-Regulation of the Press was granted on 30 October 2013 and the Press Recognition Panel (PRP) which is established by the Charter came into being on the 3 November 2014. The PRP does not regulate the press; its task is to assess and review whether regulators that seek recognition meet the criteria set out in the Charter (Schedule 3). It is a completely voluntary system and the PRP cannot compel any regulator to apply for recognition. So far one application, from IMPRESS, has been received and is under consideration.

Against this background, the so-called Independent Press Standards Organisation (IPSO) started its work in September 2014 and in many respects looks very much like a re-brand of its forerunner, the much derided and discredited Press Complaints Commission.[109] Both the Board and the Complaints Committee are

---

[109] The Leveson Inquiry, *An Inquiry into the Culture, Practices and Ethics of the Press Executive Summary* (November 2012) www.gov.uk/government/uploads/system/uploads/attachment_data/file/229039/0779.pdf, see paras 41–46.

weighted 7:5 in favour of members who do not originate in the industry, but the Code itself is very closely based on the PCC Code of Practice and the remedies are toothless; as in the case of the Press Complaints Commission, remedies are limited to the possibility of requiring the publication of an adjudication and/or correction. In cases where the Complaints Committee finds that a publisher's arrangements for upholding standards and compliance were at fault, IPSO may require further remedial action to ensure that the publication meets the requirements of the Editors' Code.[110]

A key recommendation made by Leveson is that an arbitration service should be established—this would be an 'essential component'[111] of the system and would give claimants access to 'quick, fair low cost arbitration'.[112] The incentive for publishers would be that they would be deprived of their legal costs, even in successful cases, if claimants were deprived of such a right. As we go to press, it would seem that the Board has decided to pilot an arbitration scheme.

IPSO (whose members include News UK (*The Sun* and *The Times*), the *Daily Mail* and *Trinity Mirror*) has publicly stated that it will not apply to the PRP for recognition and nor can it be compelled to do so. It is hard to see that IPSO is going to make any meaningful contribution to the upholding of professional standards in journalism. Certainly, the well-heeled are likely to continue to access court-based remedies to secure effective protection of their privacy.

Autonomy

Although the precise effect of the section 6 obligation on the court has not been determined in relation to the development of the common law, and indeed the prospect of this happening recedes in view of the likely repeal of the HRA, the values that underlie the ECHR have undoubtedly had a significant impact on the development of the common law. This is another example of the ECHR itself, as opposed to the HRA, informing the development of the common law, but in a rather more nuanced fashion than might have been anticipated through an exercise in statutory interpretation. It will be recalled that during Parliamentary debates the Lord Chancellor noted that our courts 'will develop human rights throughout society. A culture of awareness of human rights will develop'.[113] Baroness Hale observed recently that the interest that the law of negligence protects

---

[110] See www.ipso.co.uk/IPSO/procedure.html#remedies accessed on 29 February 2016.
[111] See n 109 [66].
[112] *Ibid.*
[113] HL Deb 3 November 1997, vol 582, col 1228, quoted by Amos (n 15) 9.

is a person's interest in their physical and psychological integrity, an important feature of which is their autonomy.[114]

The right to respect for private life is engaged in cases concerning consent to medical treatment. In *Herczegfalvy v Austria*,[115] the applicant complained that he had been force-fed and forcibly administered drugs. It was found that he had been lawfully detained as a person of unsound mind under Article 5(1)(e) ECHR and the Court held that there was no violation of Article 8, because there was no evidence to disprove the authority's view that the applicant did not have capacity. Thus, where no valid consent is obtained from a competent patient there will at the very least be a violation of Article 8. Under English law, the action for battery will lie in the absence of consent.[116]

English courts have been reluctant to hold that an action in battery will lie where a medical professional has failed to advise the patient of risks or alternatives in treatment. Where the nub of the patient's complaint is that they were not properly informed about the risks of treatment, their legal remedy is confined to negligence. The disadvantage of the negligence action is that the patient must then prove that their physical injury has been caused by the doctor's breach of duty in failing to disclose risk in treatment. In battery on the other hand, it is not necessary to establish that inadequate disclosure has caused any harm, it is a tort that is actionable *per se*. It has been argued that the action for battery

> more accurately protects the patient's interest in self-determination because it is the violation of the patient's right to make an informed choice which is being compensated, rather than the materialization—through no one's fault—of a risk associated with treatment.[117]

The law on disclosure of risk has been substantially clarified in favour of patient autonomy since the first edition of *Tort Law & Human Rights*. In a decision that acknowledges how the stimulus of the HRA has led to the courts becoming 'increasingly conscious of the extent to which the common law reflects fundamental values', the Supreme Court in *Montgomery v Lanarkshire Health Board*[118] has formally departed from the medical paternalism of *Sidaway v Board of Governors of Bethlem Royal Hospital and Maudsley Hospital*[119] and adopted a clear reasonable patient standard.

---

[114] *Montgomery v Lanarkshire Health Board* [2015] UKSC 11, [2015] AC 1430.

[115] (1993) 15 EHRR 437.

[116] *Chatterton v Gerson* [1981] QB 432.

[117] E Jackson, *Medical Law, Text, Cases and Materials*, 3rd edn (Oxford, Oxford University, 2013) 173.

[118] *Montgomery* (n 114). See CP McGrath, 'Trust Me, I'm a Patient': Disclosure Standards and the Patient's Right to Decide' (2015) *Cambridge Law Journal* 74(2) 211–14; M Lyons, '*Montgomery v Lanarkshire Health Board*: Liability—Clinical Negligence—Defects' (2015) JPI Law 3, C130–C134; C Hobson, 'No (,) More *Bolam* Please: *Montgomery v Lanarkshire Health Board* (2016) (79) *Modern Law Review* 488–503.

[119] *Sidaway* (n 14).

In *Montgomery*, the applicant was a diabetic of small stature and in common with many diabetic patients was carrying a larger than average baby. The treating physician did not advise her that a vaginal delivery carried a 9–10 per cent risk of shoulder dystocia (the baby's shoulders are too large to pass safely through the birth canal). The applicant's son was born with severe disabilities caused by complications during the delivery as a result of shoulder dystocia. The applicant sought damages on behalf of her son, claiming that the injuries were attributable to the failure to warn of possible shoulder dystocia and the possibility of delivery by elective caesarean section.

A unanimous Supreme Court found for the applicant and rejected the approach of Lord Diplock in *Sidaway*, who had applied an unembellished *Bolam* test to all aspects of the doctor–patient relationship, whether diagnosis, treatment or advice in favour of Lord Scarman's approach who took as his starting point, 'the patient's right to make his own decision, which may be seen as a basic human right protected by the common law'.[120] Lord Scarman pointed out that in their decision-making a patient may be concerned with matters that are not solely medical considerations. In *Montgomery*, the Supreme Court noted that lower courts had 'tacitly ceased to apply the Bolam test'[121] and had effectively adopted the approach of Lord Scarman.[122] Furthermore, guidance on consent produced by the General Medical Council emphasises the patient's right to make decisions in partnership with their treating professionals. The Court held that:

> An adult person of sound mind is entitled to decide which, if any, of the available forms of treatment to undergo, and her consent must be obtained before treatment interfering with her bodily integrity is undertaken. The doctor is therefore under a duty to take reasonable care to ensure that the patient is aware of any material risks involved in any recommended treatment, and of any reasonable alternative or variant treatments. The test of materiality is whether, in the circumstances of the particular case, a reasonable person in the patient's position would be likely to attach significance to the risk, or the doctor is or should reasonably be aware that the particular patient would be likely to attach significance to it.

Essentially, this is a reasonable patient standard but it should be noted that the Court also discussed the importance of dialogue; the patient needs to be properly informed to understand the seriousness of their condition and risks and benefits of treatment and reasonable alternatives. Thus, the information must be comprehensible; it is implicit that the dialogue must be responsive to 'this' patient and their needs and concerns. Although *Montgomery* does not explicitly introduce a subjective patient standard, it is patient-centred and 'fact-sensitive, and sensitive also to the characteristics of the patient'.[123]

---

[120] *Sidaway* (n 14) 884–85.
[121] *Pearce v United Bristol Healthcare NHS Trust* [1999] ECC 167 (CA Civ).
[122] *Ibid* [63].
[123] *Montgomery* (n 114) [89].

Montgomery is to be welcomed; it has clarified an unclear area of law, provides effective protection for patient interests and manifests a commitment on the part of the courts to root fundamental values in the common law. It is another reminder that we do not necessarily need to rely upon the HRA to secure fundamental human rights for citizens in the United Kingdom. There is a clear human rights based jurisprudence that has emerged under the 'galvinising' impact of the HRA but a jurisprudence that does not depend upon the HRA for its existence or development. *Montgomery* can be seen as further proof that the courts are implicitly ensuring that the common law reflects the values set out in the ECHR (and indeed other human rights treaty obligations). This will apply in both the public and private spheres.

Montgomery exemplifies a human rights based approach to the development of the tort of negligence which could usefully be employed in other areas of tort. It is true that the tort of negligence has become more susceptible to rights based arguments, but the requirement for the claimant to prove 'damage', the so-called 'gist' of the action,[124] in order to ground a claim poses problems for the coherent development of the tort as claimants seek new forms of damage.[125] Nolan has cogently argued that a number of new forms of actionable damage have received recognition by the courts in recent years (negligent imprisonment, untreated learning disorders) and noted that 'the very existence of the requirement of actionable damage limits the utility negligence as a rights-vindication mechanism'.[126] Further, he states that 'if the law's aim is to provide a comprehensive mechanism for the vindication of a right, it may be necessary to employ a cause of action other than negligence'.[127]

Hickman has argued persuasively that rights based norms would in many cases more appropriately protect human rights than the tort of negligence with its requirement of damage and the onus upon the claimant to prove unreasonableness. In his paper on *Tort Law, Public Authorities and the HRA 1998*, he analysed the relationship between negligence principles and rights based norms; the latter he used to describe those

> fundamental interests which the law regards as unlawfully interfered with without the victim having to prove that the interference was unreasonable, and even though the interference caused no additional harm. It is simply enough that there has been an interference.[128]

[124] J Stapleton, 'The Gist of Negligence' (1988) 104 *Law Quarterly Review* 213, 389.

[125] D Nolan, 'New Forms of Damage in Negligence' (2007) 70(1) *Modern Law Review* 59–88. See also N Witzleb and R Carroll, 'The Role of Vindication in Torts Damages' (2009) 17 *Tort Law Review* 16.

[126] Nolan, *ibid* 88.

[127] Nolan, *ibid* 88.

[128] T Hickman, 'Tort Law, Public Authorities and the HRA 1998' in D Fairgrieve, M Andenas and J Bell (eds), *Tort Liability of Public Authorities in Comparative Perspective*, (London, BIICL, 2002).

Hickman is addressing the differences between trespass and case. It is a pity that the mantle he set down has not been picked up by the courts which, despite using the language of rights, have rooted claims in damage.

The challenge to established legal principle raised by utilising the negligence action to achieve redress in claims where the essence of the wrong is that personal autonomy has been infringed, is exemplified in the wrongful pregnancy/wrongful birth claims. In these cases, the claimant underwent sterilisation but nonetheless became pregnant and delivered a healthy child. The defendant has been negligent but the question is: what damage has the claimant suffered? Can the claimant recover damages for the pain and suffering of pregnancy and labour? Can the claimant recover the costs of bringing up the healthy child?

In *McFarlane v Tayside Health Authority*,[129] the House of Lords struggled with these questions. The claimants had four children and decided their family was complete so the husband underwent a vasectomy. They were advised that they no longer needed to use contraceptive measures as the husband's sperm count was negative. Mrs McFarlane became pregnant and both Mr and Mrs McFarlane sued for damages associated with pregnancy and childbirth and the costs of rearing the healthy, and, by now, much-loved child. The House of Lords by a majority held that the mother could, if negligence were to be established, recover damages for the pain, suffering, inconvenience and lost earnings flowing from the birth but not the costs of bringing up the child. All members of the House gave different speeches and the lack of a clear ratio[130] is testament to the limitations of the application of traditional negligence principles to these facts. Lord Steyn himself subsequently described reading the speeches in *McFarlane* as a 'gruesome task'.

All members of the House agreed that Mr and Mrs McFarlane had suffered a legal wrong and it can reasonably be argued that Lord Millett, despite his dissent from the decision, comes closest to identifying the real nature of the legal wrong. He said that

> [the claimants] have suffered both injury and loss. They have lost the freedom to limit the size of their family. They have been denied an important aspect of their personal autonomy. The decision to have no more children is one the law should respect and protect.

He advocated that in such cases the award of a conventional sum to the parents (of around £5,000) would reflect this loss. Lord Millett was opposed to the award of any damages related to the pregnancy or birth and stated that it was morally offensive to regard the birth of a normal healthy baby as 'more trouble and expense than it is worth'. All members of the House gave different reasons for denying the claim; for Lord Slynn it was not 'fair, just and reasonable' to make the award as the doctor had not assumed responsibility for the economic 'loss'; Lord Steyn

---

[129] [2002] 2 AC 59.

[130] L Hoyano, 'Misconceptions about Wrongful Conception' (2002) 65 *Modern Law Review* 883.

claimed to be rooting his decision in considerations of distributive justice. By this he meant that the public would find it hard to understand why parents with a much loved and healthy child should be compensated with its maintenance costs. He famously speculated that the commuter on the London Underground would consider that the law of tort 'has no business to provide legal remedies consequent upon the birth of a healthy child, which all of us regard as a valuable and healthy thing'. Lord Hope remarked on the 'disproportionality' of allowing such a claim; this observation of course is at odds with the basic premise of tort law that you take your victim as you find him and damages awards are not infrequently out of all proportion to the relevant breach of duty.

In *Parkinson v St James and Seacroft NHS Trust*,[131] a child was born with severe disabilities after a failed sterilisation. The case makes sad reading. The Parkinson family had modest means and lived in cramped accommodation. They had decided that they could not afford any more children. The pregnancy placed an intolerable strain on their marriage which ended. The Court of Appeal held that the extra costs associated with bringing up a child with a 'significant' disability were recoverable. Brooke LJ found that the birth of a disabled child was a foreseeable consequence of the surgeon's negligence, that the surgeon assumed responsibility in relation to damage within the scope of the duty and the award accorded with the principles of distributive justice and fairness.

In *Rees v Darlington Memorial Hospital NHS Trust*,[132] the claimant who suffered severe visual impairment became pregnant following a negligently performed sterilisation operation. The Court of Appeal had held that additional costs referable to the claimant's disability were recoverable but not the normal costs of raising the child. The House of Lords, confronted with *McFarlane* and *Parkinson*, took what has been described as 'an extraordinary position', and decided that where a healthy child is born a case of wrongful conception will attract a conventional award of £15,000, in effect adopting the approach advocated by Lord Millett in *McFarlane*.

This trilogy of cases exposes the incoherence that is created by pigeon-holing claims into causes of action that are ill-designed for the purpose. All commentators are seemingly uncomfortable with the analysis, although not necessarily the result. Objections may be raised against *McFarlane* on the basis that the logic of the view that the incalculable benefits of the child outweigh the costs would lead to the conclusion that the claimants had no overall loss at all. Thus, she should not have recovered for the pain and suffering of pregnancy and childbirth. Similarly in *Parkinson*, why are the benefits accruing from the birth of a disabled child commensurable with one head of loss but not another?[133] According to Weir, a healthy child cannot count as damage.[134] It is, however, unnecessary to regard the birth

---

[131] [2002] QB 266.
[132] [2004] 1 AC 309.
[133] R Stevens, *Torts and Rights* (Oxford, Oxford University Press, 2007) at 76.
[134] T Weir, *Tort Law* (Oxford, Clarendon Press, 2002) at 186.

of a child, whether able-bodied or disabled, as a loss or damage. Rather, attention should focus on what has happened to the woman/parent who has exercised a reproductive choice; she has suffered a loss as a result of the failure to respect her decision. Returning to *McFarlane*, Beever has suggested that in interpreting Lord Millett's position:

> Society must regard the birth of every person as a valuable event. This claim is surely right. But it is irrelevant to the issue that needed to be decided in *McFarlane* ... the issue there was not whether the child was valuable in himself, but whether his birth was a loss to the claimant.[135]

In terms of negligence, the damage is the moment of conception, not birth. At the moment of conception Mrs McFarlane's rights to determine the size of her family were violated and she suffered loss. Beever has argued that the approach in *Rees* is appropriate save that the £15,000 should be regarded as a tariff (which may then increase or decrease to reflect the circumstances of the claimant), rather than a conventional award which would be fixed. The interest which has been violated in these cases is freedom of reproductive choice and focusing on the consequences of that infringement to the right bearer is appropriate. The real loss to the mother is encapsulated in Lady Hale's judgment (as she then was) in *Parkinson*. She highlights that literally from the moment of conception a woman's life is not her own; she is subject to physical limitations during pregnancy, labour is hard work and when the child is born she is responsible for that child 24 hours a day until maturity.

Chester v Afshar[136] is another example of a claim that was successfully shoehorned into negligence, despite the fact that on orthodox principles the claimant could not establish that the defendant's negligence caused the damage of which she complained. The defendant surgeon negligently failed to advise his patient of the likelihood of an inherent risk in the procedure. Miss Chester was reluctant to undergo surgery for her back pain which carried a 0.9–2 per cent risk of cauda equine syndrome (which would involve pain, loss of sensation and impaired bowel and bladder function). Miss Chester went ahead with the surgery and the risk materialised, without any negligence in the conduct of the surgery. The surgeon's breach of duty to his patient lay in the failure to disclose the risk. The trial judge concluded that if she had been warned she would have wished to 'discuss the matter with others and explore other options'.[137] The judge did not find that if properly informed the claimant would never have undergone the operation. Thus, causation on traditional negligence principles was not established.

By a 3:2 majority (Lord Bingham and Lord Homann dissenting), the House of Lords accepted that the loss was 'coincidental'[138] but decided that the full damages

---

[135] A Beever, *Rediscovering the Law of Negligence* (Oxford, Hart Publishing, 2008) 392.
[136] [2004] UKHL 41, [2005] 1 AC 134.
[137] *Ibid* [7].
[138] Stevens (n 133) 165.

should be awarded to the claimant to reflect the wrong suffered. Clearly the claim cannot be accommodated according to the principles of negligence; as Lord Bingham observed it is trite law that damage is the gist of negligence and the damage was not caused by the breach of duty.[139] Lord Steyn held that the right of autonomy and dignity ought to be protected and referred to Lord Scarman's description of the patient's right as a 'basic human right protected by the common law'.[140] For Lord Hope, the function of the law is to enable rights to be vindicated.[141] Lord Walker commented that the advice is the foundation of consent and without consent, the surgery is an [assault], actually in terms of tort it is a battery.[142]

These observations by the majority point to trespass as the locus of liability. Proof of loss is irrelevant in the trespass torts;[143] it is the invasion of the right that grounds the action. It is preferable for the coherence of tort law for a claim to be 'pigeonholed' into the appropriate right and here it is the right to bodily integrity that has been violated. In such cases, the court should award 'substitutive' damages, ie damages that are awarded as a substitute for the right infringed; if there are consequential losses (which there were not in Miss Chester's case) they must be proved in the usual way.

In none of these cases was there any pleading, argument or discussion based upon the ECHR. All of the cases pre-date the HRA in terms of their facts and it is true that ECHR jurisprudence has developed in the period since *McFarlane*. In *Evans v United Kingdom*, the Grand Chamber agreed with the Chamber that 'private life', which is a broad term encompassing, inter alia, aspects of an individual's physical and social identity including the right to personal autonomy, personal development and to establish and develop relationships with other human beings and the outside world, incorporates the right to respect for both the decisions to become and not to become a parent.[144] It would not be unreasonable now for cases based upon such facts to be brought against public authorities on the basis that the right to respect for private life has been subject to interference. In cases between non-state actors, it would be preferable for the claims based upon the violation of autonomy to be addressed through trespass which protects bodily integrity, rather than negligence when proof of damage cannot be established.

> [T]ort Law can be employed to protect whatever interests are deemed worthy of protection in any particular society: the list of protected interests is not set in stone.[145]

---

[139] *Chester* (n136) [9].
[140] *Chester* (n 136) [24], citing Lord Scarman in *Sidaway* (n 14).
[141] *Chester* (n 136) [87].
[142] *Chester* (n 136) [93].
[143] In his discussion of substitutive damages, Stevens gives the example of being wrongfully detained which will ground a claim for substantial damages, *Huckle v Money* (1762) 2 Wils 205, 95 ER 768 but in cases of false imprisonment must be read subject to the Supreme Court decision in *R (Lumba) v Secretary of State for the Home Department* [2011] 2 WLR 671.
[144] (2008) 46 EHRR 728.
[145] K Oliphant, 'The Nature of Tortious Liability' in A Grubb (ed), *The Law of Tort* (London, Butterworths, 2002) [1.12].

9

Concluding Remarks

As we go to press, the political landscape is now dominated by 'Brexit', the challenges of which are considerable. The future of the Human Rights Act 1998 (HRA) is still uncertain but the capacity of government to cope with large programmes of legislation is not unlimited and from a pragmatic point of view the repeal of the HRA, if it is to happen, is not likely to be imminent. So, the HRA tort in its current form will remain with us for the foreseeable future. One significant and immediate change has been promised—the Conservative Party Conference has made clear that the legal responsibilities of British Armed Forces when abroad will be curtailed by legislation.

Our review of the influence of the HRA and the European Convention on Human Rights (ECHR) on the development of tort principles has revealed some findings that were perhaps unanticipated as the HRA came into force. First, public authority liability under the HRA has not been matched by developments in public authority liability under the common law. The judiciary has lately regretted the tendency of practitioners to focus claims for redress on the HRA, rather than common law rights. The common law though is a weak alternative to the HRA. We have only to look at the claim by the parents in *JD v East Berkshire Community NHS Trust*,[1] or the false imprisonment claim in *Austin v Commissioner of Police for the Metropolis*,[2] to see why a claimant will prefer the HRA route to a remedy. The same goes for *Michael v Chief Constable of South Wales Police*.[3]

That said, the Supreme Court has urged practitioners to look first to domestic law. Lord Toulson has regretted 'the baleful and unnecessary tendency to overlook the common law' and Lord Mance has asserted that in any dispute the starting point should be domestic law and should not be a 'focus on Convention rights, without surveying the wider common law scene'. These observations were both made in *Kennedy v Information Commissioner*[4] which concerned the scope of freedom of information, Lord Toulson remarking that his analysis was based solely upon the common law and not on Article 10 which 'adds nothing to the common law in the present context'. It is tempting in the light of such remarks to conclude

---

[1] [2005] 2 AC 373.
[2] [2009] 1 AC 564.
[3] [2015] UKSC 2, [2015] WLR 343.
[4] [2014] UKSC 20, [2014] 2 WLR 808.

that there is a resurgence in the common law, in the words of one commentator, 'a renaissance'.[5] However, claims that engage Article 10 rights have a long pedigree of cross reference between the ECHR and the common law and it would be misleading to draw wider lessons from such areas of the common law. Clayton has argued that the 'weak status' accorded to 'rights protection [by the common law] is a fundamental obstacle to their future development'.[6] This seems to be why there has arguably been a 'baleful tendency' to overlook the common law.

The issue of standing and remedies has contributed to this conundrum. Not only is the distinction between misfeasance and non-feasance fundamental in the common law; the difference between trespass and case is foundational too and informs how we think about rights and their actionability. *Watkins v Home Office*[7] has served to remind us that the distinction will not be disappearing any time soon. Furthermore, invocation of a 'constitutional' right will not necessarily yield anything other than a public law 'remedy'. Damages can only be secured by way of an established tort claim. This matters. As we know, the HRA can be repealed and it may be substituted by another statute which may or may not include a remedy analogous to sections 7 and 8 HRA. This takes us to the issue of 'constitutional resilience'.

A number of commentators have taken up their Lordships' baton and in a series of recent analyses have explored the qualities with which common law rights are endowed in order to interrogate such matters as their normative reach and their constitutional resilience. We need to do this in order to determine what weight can be attached to calls to heed the common law first, and in preference to the HRA/ECHR. In a valuable analysis, Elliott has examined common law rights through the lens of three vectors: the normative reach of the system; the rigour with which courts uphold such rights; and the constitutional resilience of such rights.[8]

Many constitutional rights are protected by both the common law and the ECHR and so in that sense their normative reach is comparable. So, for example, in the well-known case of *R (Daly) v Secretary of State for the Home Department*,[9] which concerned the right of confidential communication with one's legal adviser, Lord Bingham reasoned almost entirely on the basis of legal professional privilege which is well-established by common law. We have seen that our senior courts frequently invoked the comparability of the common law and Article 10 ECHR. In his valuable analysis, Elliott has cautioned against making extravagant

---

[5] P Bowen QC, 'Does the Renaissance of Common Law Rights Mean that the Human Rights Act 1998 is Now Unnecessary?' (2016) 4 *European Human Rights Law Review* 361–77.

[6] R Clayton QC, 'The Empire Strikes Back: Common Law Rights and the Human Rights Act [2015] *Public Law*, Jan, 3–12.

[7] [2006] UKHL 17, [2006] 2 AC 395.

[8] M Elliott, 'Beyond the European Convention: Human Rights and the Common Law (2015) 68 *Current Legal Problems* 85–117.

[9] [2001] UKHL 26, [2001] 2 AC 532.

claims regarding common law constitutional rights; it is 'far from clear' that the 'human rights values immanent within the common law [are] co-extensive with the [ECHR] rights'.[10] Our examination of positive obligations and the steadfast refusal of the courts to further extend duties of care in negligence shows us the limits of the common law in giving effect to ECHR rights. The common law has frequently acknowledged rights, but as Elliott acknowledges practical enforcement has been lacking.[11]

There are arguably dimensions too to the concept of normative reach that are additional to those considered by Elliot. Rules on standing are different for common law claims (including judicial review) and claims under the HRA; limitation periods are different too. The requirement to be a victim under the HRA is a narrower test than the sufficient interest test in judicial review. However, the European Court of Human Rights has allowed a claim by a non-governmental organisation (NGO) that could not reasonably have claimed to be a victim of a violation in the commonly accepted sense. In terms of the protection and promotion of human rights standards, standing is critical. We have seen that a much wider group of ricochet victims are protected under the ECHR/HRA than under the common law and the Fatal Accidents Act 1976 (FAA). Article 3 claims, for example, may enure for the benefit of ricochet victims who would have no claim under any cause of action recognised by the common law.[12] Similarly, parents of an adult child who dies in consequence of a violation of the positive obligation under Article 2 may have a claim as direct victims of both substantive, as well as procedural, violations. Under the FAA they would be limited to a claim for bereavement damages.

Remedies are different too. Damages are in principle available in a much wider range of circumstances under the HRA/ECHR. Heads of damage are much wider under the HRA than the common law. Furthermore, rules on causation are different. It is not necessary to show that harm could have been averted if the relevant human right had not been violated. As we have seen all that the claimant under the HRA has to show is that the action on the part of the public authority might have been expected to avert the risk of harm.

In his discussion of the 'protective rigour' applied by the courts to common law rights, Elliott has acknowledged that the common law has not always delivered 'tangible protection' of ECHR rights. On the question of 'constitutional resilience' of ECHR rights he has suggested that their 'legal bite' is enhanced through their occupation of the international legal plane; the United Kingdom is bound by the rights in the ECHR, as well as Strasbourg judgments. This is true, but as the

---

[10] Elliott (n 8) 89.

[11] Elliott (n 8) 89, citing *R v Secretary of State for the Home Department, ex parte Brind* [1991] 1 AC 696 and *R v Ministry of Defence, ex parte Smith* [1996] QB 517.

[12] *Cakici v Turkey* (2001) 31 EHRR 5, *cf Brooks v Commissioner of Police for the Metropolis* [2005] 1 WLR 1495.

common law yields to Parliament, it is not unknown for the UK Government to fail to adhere to Strasbourg judgments. Equally, as we have seen, the force of Strasbourg jurisprudence may be denied on the grounds that it is incompatible with a fundamental feature of English law or reflects misunderstanding by the Strasbourg Court.

A student of tort law could be forgiven for thinking that in terms of the structure of the law of torts, very little has changed in the last 30 years. I started my academic life in 1992 and at that time I drew upon Tony Weir's wonderful *Casebook on Tort* and the classic *Winfield and Jolowicz on Tort*, now in its 19th edition.[13] Many other excellent texts have since appeared, but, in terms of their arrangement of knowledge and exposition of principles, little has changed. A search for discussion of the HRA yields thin gruel. It generally appears almost as an afterthought under subheadings in chapters on General Principles and Public Authority Liability. But, we have a new public authority tort. As we have seen, the combined effect of section 7 and the rights set in Schedule 1 is that a whole raft of 'rights' enforceable under the HRA have been created. They are a species of statutory tort. Furthermore, the liability of our public bodies may extend to activities overseas.

However, the statutory tort has not generated an expansion of remedies under the common law; in fact, the contrary is true. The remedy under the HRA has weakened the cogency of arguments for parallel development common law. And yet, our senior judiciary, perhaps now fearful of the repeal of the HRA, has called for claimants to focus first on common law rights. This can only happen where such rights are extant.

Ultimately, the question of whether, and the extent to which, ECHR rights are protected by the common law is a policy decision for our courts. The corrective justice and rights theorists deny that 'policy' considerations have a legitimate role in shaping tort principles. Speaking extra-judicially, Lord Neuberger has eloquently refuted this position. In a recent speech he argued that all aspects of the law, especially issues in tort, are grounded on policy and 'any attempt to distil principles is fraught with problems'.[14] It is clear that the lived experience of the common law is experience, rather than logic. Every time a new head of damage is recognised in negligence, or the rules of causation are 'tweaked' to ensure practical justice, our courts make decisions based upon community welfare considerations. As we have seen, the most recent examples of judicial innovation in the law of torts have been the extension of new forms of privacy protection from the protection of private information and remedies for intrusion to autonomy over medical

---

[13] E Peel and J Goudkamp, *Winfield and Jolowicz on Tort*, 19th edn (London, Sweet & Maxwell, 2014).

[14] Lord Neuberger JSC, *Some Thoughts on Principles Governing the Law of Torts*, Singapore Conference on Protecting Business and Economic Interests: Contemporary Issues in Tort Law, 19 August 2016 [4] www.supremecourt.uk/docs/speech-160819-03.pdf accessed 17 October 2016.

decision-making. This is hardly a common law set in aspic. In both cases, the demands of human rights law have been the spur.

Chapter 2 has touched upon the role that considerations of 'policy' play in the development of tort law, especially the development of negligence. Two recent Supreme Court decisions must surely mean that those who deny the role of policy in legal decision making have lost this particular ideological battle. In *Willers v Joyce*,[15] by a narrow 3:2 majority, the Supreme Court has held that the tort of malicious prosecution of civil proceedings exists in English law. The claimant will have an action where he suffers 'injury' as a result of the malicious use of legal proceedings without a reasonable basis. Malice is signified by the deliberate misuse of the court's process. What is interesting for present purposes is the appeal by all their Lordships to 'policy' considerations. Lord Toulson who gives the leading speech for the majority examines the 'floodgates' and 'deterrence' arguments. Lord Mance, in dissent, states that the 'formulation of legal policy does not normally depend on statistics but rather on judges' collective experience of litigation and litigants and, more particularly here, their appreciation of the risks involved in litigation and … its misuse'.[16] Lord Sumption, also in dissent, urges that 'the proposed development of the law should be warranted by current values and current social conditions'[17]—all of which begs the obvious question, whose values shall prevail?

In *Patel v Mirza*,[18] the Supreme Court has departed from *Tinsley v Milligan*[19] and proposed a more flexible approach to the impact that illegality may have upon a claim. Lord Toulson gave the leading speech and said that consideration of whether the public interest would be harmed by enforcing a claim will be answered by asking: whether the underlying purpose of the prohibition which has been transgressed will be enhanced by denial of the claim; is there any other relevant public policy on which denial of the claim might have an impact; and finally whether denial of the claim would be a proportionate response to the illegality.

The most pervasive impact of the ECHR on the common law of tort has been in the fields of 'privacy' and defamation. Case law under the HRA itself has led to a deepening protection of positive obligations of the sort often claimed in failing tort actions. The remedial gaps in relation to ECHR rights arise where claims pre-date the HRA. As we have seen, incoherence may arise when claims are permitted under the HRA, but not under the common law. The rule of law requires that citizens should understand both their rights and their obligations too. Levels of professional responsibility and standards of care should not differ according to the pigeon-holing of a claim. There is much work to be done if the common law and the HRA are peacefully to co-exist as blueprints for conduct.

---

[15] [2016] UKSC 43, [2016] 3 WLR 477.
[16] Lord Mance, *ibid* [134].
[17] Lord Sumption, *ibid* [179].
[18] [2016] UKSC 42, 3 WLR 399.
[19] [1994] 1 AC 340.

INDEX